Joy of Nature

Reader's Digest

Joy of Nature

How to Observe and Appreciate the Great Outdoors

The Reader's Digest Association, Inc.

Pleasantville, New York / Montreal, Canada

Joy of Nature

Editor: Alma E. Guinness
Art Director: Gilbert L. Nielsen
Associate Editor: Susan J. Wernert
Assistant Editor: W. Clotilde Lanig
Associate Art Director: Dorothy R. Schmidt
Editorial Assistant: Josefina B. Grundtner

Picture Editor: Robert J. Woodward

Contributing Editor: Katharine R. O'Hare

General Consultant:

Durward L. Allen, *Professor of Wildlife Ecology, Purdue University*

Special Consultants:

William H. Amos, *St. Andrew's School, Delaware*
Mark R. Chartrand III, *American Museum-Hayden Planetarium*
Harold Gibson, *U.S. Weather Service*
Richard L. Lees, *Earth Science Consultant*

The Library of Congress has cataloged
   this work as follows:

Joy of nature : how to observe and
   appreciate the great outdoors /
   [editor, Alma E. Guinness]. —
   Pleasantville, N.Y. : Reader's
   Digest Association, c1977.

      352 p. : ill. ; 29 cm.

      At head of title: Reader's digest.
      Bibliography: p. 347-348.
      Includes index.
      ISBN 0-89577-036-9

      1. Natural history. 2. Nature study.
   I. Guinness, Alma E. II. Reader's digest.

QH45.5.J67   500.9   76-29320
                                    MARC

Printed in the United States of America
Third Printing, November 1983

Contents

CHAPTER ONE .... How to Look at Nature 10

CHAPTER TWO .... Trees and Forests 32

CHAPTER THREE .... Mountains and Highlands 70

CHAPTER EIGHT .... Weather and Astronomy 226

CHAPTER NINE .... Geology and Earth History 258

CHAPTER TEN .... Participation Is the Key to Enjoyment 288

Guide to Participation Features

This book is an invitation to become more aware of nature, more involved in the outdoors. The activities suggested here—called Participation Features—will help you put your knowledge to use. There are seven categories, each with a specific symbol—look for them as you read.

Judging a photographer to be no threat, this long-tailed jaeger (a tundra-nesting bird related to the gulls) perches defiantly on the intruder's hat. This amusing picture was the joint product of a mother-and-son team on a photographic trip to Mount McKinley National Park, Alaska.

CHAPTER ONE

How to Look at Nature

Allow the scene before you to take its effect—savor its special character. And put aside, for a while, whatever is on your mind.

We all know people who are very much at home with nature, who seem to fall in with its rhythms as soon as they set foot outdoors. All of us can be like this—capable of shedding the concerns of the workaday world. What it takes is concentration and practice. When a beautiful vista stretches before us, what is there to interfere with the pleasure of its color and contour? Nothing, really, except our own unfamiliarity. We may feel a sense of wonder tinged with awe, and perhaps a sense of regret at spending so little of our time doing this very thing.

Nature is not remote—limited to parks and wilderness areas. It is abundant and readily available, as close as your own back yard. Nature is a year-round source of inspiration. Think of the light that filters through the new leaves in spring, and the pungent scents of autumn. If you are dressed for it, a walk in the teeming rain can be strangely satisfying; perhaps it is a return to the feeling of joy you had as a child, splashing through puddles. A walk through a snow-covered woodland, where you are alone with the sound of the wind and the crunching of your own footsteps, may be a very personal pleasure. Such simple things extend your sense of the pervasiveness of nature.

Much of what you will find in this book may remind you of things your grandparents told you when you were young. Or perhaps you will recall the sayings of a friend who has spent a lifetime deep in the country. Whether your journey is one of discovery or rediscovery, there is infinite pleasure to be had in understanding the land and waters and the skies around you.

Suppose yourself to be here, at Lake Tear-of-the-Clouds, the source of the Hudson River. The scene is shrouded in morning mist, which gives a special clarity to the foliage in the foreground. The mist limits what you can see in the distance, creating an aura of mystery and enchantment.

Awaken to Nature's Sights and Sounds

One day in August, 1911, a Stone Age man wandered down from the mountains of northern California. His name was Ishi, and he was the last member of a tribe of Indians who had hidden in the mountains since he was a child. He had never used a metal tool or anything else not made from stone or wood. His arrival caused a sensation in scientific circles, but what is often overlooked is that Ishi knew how to look at nature. Within a few minutes after he went into the woods, Ishi would know where the animals were, where he could find fresh water and edible plants. His senses of sight, smell, and hearing were probably no more acute than yours—he simply knew how to use them.

Expert outdoorsmen like Ishi learn through experience. If there is one main lesson they can teach, it is that you do not have to know a lot about nature to be fully aware of it—you simply have to give your senses a chance. For example, sound is the key to seeing wild animals. If, on your next outing, you notice what attracted your attention to

Once you see the fine details of a blossom or bud through a hand lens, you'll want a lens along whenever you're on a nature walk.

For a Change in Perspective, Look Up, Down, and Through

A shift in your position can open your eyes to a whole new world. Look straight overhead through the transparent gold of aspen foliage to the blue autumn sky (above)—lie on your back for easier viewing or photographing. If it's spring, look at the fresh green of birches or the red of flowering swamp maples from the same angle. For another viewpoint, kneel or lie on the damp blanket of last year's oak leaves for a close-up of the fragile, fleeting beauty of hepatica blossoms (right) and the leathery texture of their leaves.

12

an animal, you'll be surprised how many times you heard it before you saw it.

Many animals rely on sound to communicate among themselves—and to alert them to danger. Therefore, you'll be able to observe even more wildlife by being careful about the sounds you make. If you are talking to companions, speak in low tones (oddly enough, whispers may carry farther—there is often a hissing sound to a whisper, which may frighten the very animals you are looking for). You can sometimes see the results of being quiet if you meet a noisy group of walkers clomping down a path. They will often be preceded by a "wall" of frightened animals, fleeing the noise.

For many people, one of the entertaining features of nature-watching is being observed by the animals themselves. After all, can you imagine how interesting a human being must appear to a tiny rodent or bird? Many wildlife photographers have had the experience of carefully setting up a camera at the entrance of an animal's den or a bird's nest, and waiting—only to discover that the occupant is off in the distance, much too busy observing the photographer to return home. Thus the secret of successful animal-watching is to become part of the natural scene.

The scents of the out-of-doors are nature's exquisite gifts to visitors. There is very little you can do to seek them out. But, when you encounter a noticeable fragrance, make the most of it. Many people forget how acute the human sense of smell really is. Ishi could track an animal by scent. (He refused to hunt with anyone who smoked.)

Occasionally, make a point of analyzing what it is you are smelling. You will undoubtedly be surprised not just by the variety of scents, but by your own ability to identify them. The aromatic odor of a spicebush (whether or not you know its name) undoubtedly enhances the day. It's a matter of allowing your sense of smell to be part of your "looking around."

Smell enables you to retain and savor experiences without collecting a thing. Curiously, odor seems to be connected with memory to an extraordinary extent. Probably the reason why so little is said about the human sense of smell is the difficulty of putting this particular perception into words. But if you are powerfully affected by a scent in a particular time and place, you can trust the scent to take you back again.

BIRDING TIPS
How to Listen to the Songs and Calls of Birds

When it comes to finding birds, your ears can often be more help than your eyes. The first step in sorting out the medley of bird sounds is to learn the difference between a call and a song. Almost all birds have a number of calls—usually very short bursts of sharp, high-pitched notes. Birds call to communicate with others of their species—to keep in touch, to signal the discovery of food, or to warn of danger. A song is longer, with a recognizable melody or rhythmic pattern. Only males of the songbird species sing. They do so to proclaim their identity and establish a territory.

• Birds of different species may heed each other's warning calls. When a hawk flies overhead, blue jays are quick to sound the alarm. Species may cooperate in calling and diving at a predator. This behavior, called mobbing, is a great help to birders in locating a hawk or an owl.

• Most birds are quiet at midday. You will hear the most songs just before or during the breeding season. In midsummer, most birds are silent. Warblers, finches, and sparrows often sing during migration.

• Many birds obligingly call out their names. Pewees, phoebes, and whip-poor-wills repeat their names over and over.

• To attract birds, make squeaking noises by kissing the back of your hand. Birds are curious, and will come out to locate the source of the strange sounds.

A male red-spotted bluethroat is a normally shy inhabitant of northern European swamps and thickets. But in the breeding season, he will—when he feels challenged—come forth boldly to defend his territory with song.

Inflating its bubble-like vocal sac, a male toad creates concentric ripples in the shallow water—sound literally made visible. The toad's sweet, musical trilling will echo through the spring evening, attracting female toads and enchanting the ears of human listeners.

Seeing Patterns in Nature

Shapes and patterns of living things are functional, helping the species to survive. Their intricacy—or simplicity—seems designed to please the human eye. The inanimate world, too, is full of intriguing shapes that range from canyons cut by swift-flowing rivers to the latticework of ice on a frozen pond. Developing an awareness of this aspect of nature will enhance your enjoyment of the outdoors.

At first glance, the twining tendrils on a vine may seem tangled and haphazard. But look more closely. How perfectly formed are the tiny spirals in the stems, and how well they do their work of carrying the leaves toward light. If you look for patterns and textures, you'll find them all around you, even in the most ordinary rocks and minerals. Split a specimen of slate, and you will see the characteristic layered pattern of this common rock.

Living things cannot be split like rocks or minerals, but you can divide them in your mind's eye. Most of the more complex animals, such as birds and human beings, can be divided down the middle into two matched halves. Leaves with a central vein share this kind of organization, called bilateral symmetry. Slit such a leaf along the vein, and you will have almost identical parts. The match is never absolutely perfect, for nature provides many variations within any "scheme of things." If you have a front-face photograph of yourself—say a passport picture—take a square or rectangular pocket mirror and place it at a right angle to the picture, in the center of your face. Hold the mirror so that it reflects one side of your face; then turn the mirror and look at the other side of the photo. You will see that your own face would look quite different if it really were perfectly symmetrical.

Another form of symmetry—often three-dimensional—is the spiral. Like the tendrils of a vine, the horns of mountain rams are three-dimensional spirals. So, too, are fiddleheads (the young leaves of ferns). However, once the frond is unfurled, its bilateral symmetry can easily be seen. Thus many organisms have more than one kind of symmetry.

Many flowers are radially symmetrical—that is, the pattern radiates outward from a central point like spokes in a wheel. Actually, the basis of radial symmetry is the circle, which is a common form in nature. (Think of mushroom caps and daisies.) When a third dimension is added, the circle becomes a sphere—for example, the seed head of a dandelion.

Some shapes in nature are symmetrical polygons. The combs built by honeybees are hexagons—six-sided units that lend themselves particularly well to tight packing. Curiously enough, the first cell that the bees make is circular; but as the chambers are packed together, they become compressed, forming hexagons.

Pentagons are five-sided forms, and are frequently found among sea animals. Every starfish begins life as a five-sided embryo, no matter how many arms it may develop later. Scientists believe that this particular symmetry is an advantage to such species because pentagons have no natural plane of cleavage; hence they are unusually strong and can withstand considerable buffeting by waves.

Quite often, patterns and forms are marvels of efficiency—as in the aerodynamics of a bird's wing or the shape of a fish that enables it to glide in water with the least resistance. But nature's wonders are not all explicable; its patterns need not be appreciated for utility alone.

A Gallery of Symmetries

1. Bilateral symmetry, where the right side matches the left (to a great extent), is so commonplace that we tend to overlook it. But it's worth a second glance, whether in the stern visage of an owl, or in the balance of its wings.

2. Radial symmetry is often complex. A dandelion's seed head is spherical; each feathery "parachute" is radial.

3. Pentagonal symmetry is common among plants, but rare among animals—except for sea creatures such as starfish.

4. The geometric perfection of the spiral in a nautilus shell, seen in this cutaway view, is unusual. Other shells grow in spiral form. But the spiral is more prevalent in plants, ranging from tendrils to the whorled arrangement of branches, like the steps on a winding staircase.

5. The hexagons in a honeycomb are the most economical use of space possible—a shape often found in crystals.

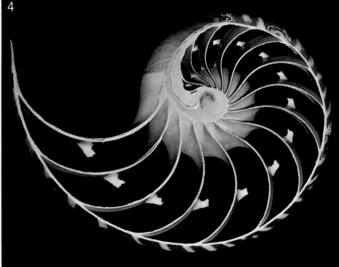

Colors That Communicate

Animals do not see colors as human beings can. To begin with, few species have eyes and brains similar enough to our own for them to see the same spectrum of colors. But an even greater difference lies in the interpretation of what is seen. The human response to colors in foliage and flowers, butterflies and birds, is aesthetic—we are struck by their beauty. But to many animals, colors are as utilitarian as traffic signals. They are frequently a means of communication—either advertisements or warnings.

Of course, animals do not make a judgment between colors that attract and those that repel. They simply see the message and react instinctively, almost like programmed robots. The colors displayed by a courting male bird cause the female's brain to secrete hormones that make her sexually receptive—no thought is involved. In some cases, however, the animal may be reacting to what it has learned from previous experiences. For example, animals that have been injured by the poisonous spines of a brightly colored fish may later avoid that species.

From blossom to child a message passes. That message is the compelling attraction of color. The flowers are sickle-leaved golden asters; the place is a July meadow on Nantucket Island.

A perfect bull's-eye, at the center of this peacock gazania (a shrubby South African perennial), is surrounded by a pattern of dots and spots. These direct insects to the flower's pollen-bearing parts.

The shiny red fruits of the winterberry holly attract a pine grosbeak, a large northern finch. Homeowners who appreciate berries on their holly plants may bemoan the depredations of fruit-eating birds. But by plucking the fruit, such birds help to disperse the seeds inside. The bright color of the berries is not mere decoration—it serves as an advertisement.

The distinctive colors of flowers advertise the pollen and nectar inside. Such colors attract birds, butterflies, bees, and other insects that feed on these substances. At the same time, the animals pollinate the plants (that is, they transfer genetic material from one plant to another). Many insects seem to prefer certain colors. For example, honeybees will usually visit a blue or yellow flower before they visit others. Hummingbirds and other nectar-eating species are attracted to red flowers.

Some animals change color just before the breeding season. This is true of certain species of fish. In temperate climates, numerous male birds take on bright plumage in the spring. Besides attracting a mate, the vivid colors make the male easily identifiable by other males. This is part of the process by which a male asserts his territorial rights. To a female rose-breasted grosbeak, for instance, the male's bright, heart-shaped patch is an attractant; to another male, it is a repellent. At times, conspicuous colors may be a disadvantage, because they make the animal more visible to potential predators. Thus many species display their colors only under certain circumstances. A red-winged blackbird flaunts his red and yellow epaulets (shoulder patches) when he spreads his wings; normally, the colors are almost hidden.

Many poisonous or noxious animals are vividly colored; tropical frogs and coral snakes are obvious examples. You might think that animals so well defended with poison would not need to warn away potential attackers. But even though a poisonous animal may emerge victorious in any battle, it is better not to be attacked in the first place.

Many harmless animals gain protection by mimicking the colors of dangerous species—the viceroy butterfly resembles the bad-tasting monarch. In other cases, one species of poisonous butterfly may mimic another poisonous one. By looking alike, the different butterflies increase the chances that predators will learn to leave them all alone.

Some scientists believe that almost every color found in nature has a function. The bright red of many berries is actually an advertisement to birds; the berries contain seeds, and if eaten by birds, the seeds will be carried to a new location. Such dispersal is an advantage to the plant species, because it lessens competition among plants.

Resembling a tiny, leotard-clad dancer, this arrow-poison frog warns predators, "Eat me at your peril!" Glands in the skins of Central and South American arrow-poison frogs secrete some of the deadliest venom known, long used by Indians to paralyze their prey.

Mimicry Is Borrowed Protection

The insect world has numerous examples of "sheep in wolves' clothing"—harmless creatures that resemble a more noxious species. Certain wasp-like insects are really flies; crickets mimic acid-spraying beetles. Birds, reptiles, and other predators are less likely to attack such mimics once they have eaten one bad-tasting species. Thus the survival of harmless species is enhanced. A model-and-mimic pair is shown below.

Monarch butterfly

The monarch is the model—a bad-tasting butterfly that predators learn not to eat. Its larvae feed on milkweed, which imparts an unpleasant taste.

Viceroy butterfly

The viceroy is the mimic—a palatable butterfly that evolved a pattern resembling the monarch's. Its larvae eat willow and poplar leaves.

Camouflaged by Color and Form

In all probability, most wild animals you see in their natural surroundings are moving when you catch sight of them—a deer bolting across a road, an eagle soaring overhead, a squirrel or rabbit scampering in the woodland. Many animals are so well camouflaged that you do not notice them unless they move and reveal their presence.

Many leafhoppers, caterpillars, beetles, and other insects are the same color as the leaves or stems where they

The least bittern often relies on its uncanny "reed posture"—neck extended, bill straight up, feathers flattened. Not even its eyes move. Thus it blends with its marshy habitat.

are usually found. Fish (such as flounder), crabs, snails, and other seashore creatures blend with the color of the sand or rocks. Many animals have less specific camouflage—they are darker on the back (or top) than on the underside. This is called countershading. At first glance, countershading may not seem to provide much protection. But most objects in the outdoors—animals included—are lighted from above, by the sun; the portions below are shadowed. Countershading compensates for the effect of light. In water, the dark back of a penguin minimizes reflection; the light-colored belly reduces the darkness of its shadow. Thanks to this countershading, a penguin is less visible to predatory seals than it might otherwise be.

Some animals actually wear their background. Caddisfly larvae, which live in streams, build cocoon-like protective cases with twigs and tiny pebbles from the stream bed. Decorator crabs are so named because they place bits of seaweed and sponges on their backs; these decorations continue to grow on the animal's shell.

Certain "masters of disguise" appear to be something they're not. A walking stick, for example, looks like part of a twig. Other animals adopt their disguises only when needed. When some birds are threatened, they assume a posture that helps them blend with the foliage (see the photo of a bittern at left). Certain caterpillars rear up when disturbed—a position in which they resemble parts of leaves or stems.

Many tropical fish are so brightly colored that one might suppose they could easily be seen. But when such a fish swims close to a coral reef, the color and pattern of the fish merge with the brilliantly colored background. Zebras are camouflaged in a similar way—when they are in a group, their stripes make it difficult to see where one zebra ends and another begins.

The effect of animal camouflage is often so dramatic, it seems as if the creature planned it that way. But the colors and patterns of a species are the result of millions of years of evolution. In many cases, animals that were not well camouflaged were preyed upon in large numbers, and thus left fewer offspring than their camouflaged relatives. Some present-day species are difficult to detect even among themselves; other signals—such as sounds and scents—

are the principal means by which they make their presence known to potential mates or competitors.

Some predators are blind to certain colors. What looks like a conspicuous pattern or color to a normal human eye may escape the notice of an owl. Like other nocturnal birds, owls are believed to be sensitive only to black, gray, and white. Of course, many predators are also camouflaged, thereby gaining an advantage when stalking prey. Witness the leopard. As Rudyard Kipling wrote of this magnificent cat, "You can lie out on the bare ground and look like a heap of pebbles. . . . you can lie right across the centre of a path and look like nothing in particular. Think of that and purr!"

Key to Camouflaged Insects

Few habitats in the world have the abundance of species to be found in a tropical rain forest. The painting at right illustrates a number of insects that flourish in a forest near Rio de Janeiro, Brazil. (Of course, you would never find them clustered this way.) It is a challenge to locate all of the 11 insects without referring to the key below—each one is so camouflaged. Not only do their colors blend into the background of bark and lichen; their shapes and postures help them hide.

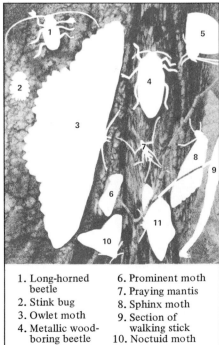

1. Long-horned beetle	6. Prominent moth
2. Stink bug	7. Praying mantis
3. Owlet moth	8. Sphinx moth
4. Metallic wood-boring beetle	9. Section of walking stick
5. Brush-footed butterfly	10. Noctuid moth
	11. Noctuid moth (different species)

Glowing Light, Shimmering Color

If you have ever caught a firefly, you know that the little insect's "fire" does not burn—in fact, it is one of the coldest lights on earth. Most man-made illumination gives off not just light, but a great deal of heat as well. In contrast, the firefly's tiny lantern is nearly 100 percent efficient; very little energy is wasted as heat.

Ancient writings from the orient abound with references to the "fitful light" of these and other light-producing insects. The firefly was once regarded as a patron of poor students, who were unable to afford oil for their lamps and supposedly used caged fireflies in order to read at night.

Firefly flashes are actually signals that enable males and females of the same species to get together. The female rarely flies (her body is heavier because she carries the eggs). In the evening, she takes a position on the ground where she can see and be seen —perhaps on a blade of grass. The males flash as they fly over the area. The female responds only to a particular pattern of flashes; she signals back. Different species have different patterns, and when a male sees the right pattern flashing below, he descends to the ground and the two mate.

Scientists have discovered that firefly signals aren't as simple as they seem.

Biologists lurking in the grass with tiny flashlights found that they could attract male fireflies by imitating the signals of females. They discovered that female fireflies of a certain species can mimic the patterns of other species. However, such behavior is not courtship. The female of this mimicking species is apparently predatory—when the males arrive, she devours them.

Surprisingly, bioluminescence (the ability of an organism to produce light) is not rare, although people seldom see it. Certain bacteria, toadstools, sponges, corals, marine worms, clams, snails, squid, and deep-sea fish can make their own light. In the darkness of the ocean depths, rows of luminescent organs on a fish's body may look like tiny portholes. These lights are believed to be useful in communication and in the search for food.

Some animals that seem to be bioluminescent are actually reflecting light, not producing it. The eyes of cats, deer, owls, and many other creatures do not really glow. A silvery reflective layer in the back of their eyes helps them to see at night by collecting weak light from the moon and stars. This layer, in effect, acts like a mirror, reflecting outward. Human beings have similar layers in their eyes, although the reflecting surface is not so large. One of the few times you can see "glowing" eyes in human beings is in the pink eyes that often show up in color photographs taken with a flashbulb.

Another distinctive phenomenon is iridescence—colors that seem to shimmer over the surface of birds' feathers, particularly those of hummingbirds and peacocks. Many insects—beetles, moths, and butterflies—are also iridescent. This kind of coloring differs from other colors in nature. For example, the green in plant leaves is caused by pigmentation, and the microscopic green cells appear green no matter what angle of light strikes them. By contrast, iridescent colors depend on the angle at which the light strikes—a feather may shimmer from blue to purple to green. Such colors are called structural. On close examination, there may be little or no pigment present.

Iridescence is an optical illusion. The colors are produced by tiny grooves and ridges on an animal's feathers or scales. These structures act somewhat like a prism, separating light into its component colors. A similar illusion is produced on phonograph records—if a record is deeply scratched, you can see it is black, not multi-colored. The same is true of the purple flashes on the throat of a starling—the color is in the eye of the beholder.

NATURE OBSERVER
Watching the Flashing Patterns of Fireflies

During summer in temperate regions, you may see fireflies for a period of about 2 weeks, especially on a warm, moist night. Most species in the eastern part of North America spend about 2 years as larvae, burrowing through the soil and feeding on slugs, snails, and worms. The larvae have a bite that anesthetizes their prey. Some look like short centipedes, and many have tiny spots of light on their abdomens. These lights may play a role in keeping the animals together. At a certain stage, the larva builds a little "igloo" of mud and spins a coat inside it. There, the larva changes into a winged adult. The adults live only long enough to mate and reproduce. In fact, some do not eat at all during their brief existence.

If you catch a firefly, do so carefully and release it after you have studied it. These insects are declining because of pollution, so every one should be handled with care.

Spectacularly colored plumage generally belongs to the male of the species, like this broad-billed hummingbird. The bright colors of male birds are thought to serve two important functions—attracting the females and warning off competing males.

The wings of a moth (or butterfly), such as the Urania below, are an iridescent mosaic. Millions of minute, tile-like scales form patterns on the wings. The name Urania means heavenly one.

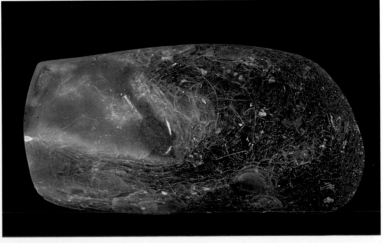

The sparks of color that seem to leap like flames from an opal (above) are caused mainly by impurities in this glass-like mineral. Yellows and reds are produced by iron oxides; trapped gas bubbles create a milky opalescence.

The silvery layer that causes the eyes of many animals to glow (such as the deer at left) helps the animals see in the dark. The "mirrors" are visible only in dim light, when the pupils are dilated—another aid to night vision.

What Is Ecology All About?

Ecology is the present-day name for what used to be called natural history. (The word ecology began to be used about a century ago, but did not come into common usage until the 1960's.) In their time, men like Charles Darwin, Alexander von Humboldt, John James Audubon, and Henry David Thoreau were known as naturalists; today, they would probably be called ecologists. These early ecologists studied plants and animals in their total environment, not as isolated organisms. The concept of evolution, which was explained by Darwin, had the unexpected effect of diverting many scientists from the study of natural history. Darwin's ideas on how species developed caused some scholars to concentrate on particular species, instead of observing them in relation to the environment as a whole. The biologist Charles Elton wrote that Darwin's discoveries sent "the whole zoological world flocking indoors."

Today, ecology has become something of a catchword. In almost any newspaper, you can find a story describing a controversy between "ecologists" and advocates of a new dam or power plant. Actually, this is a misuse of the word. Ecology is the study of the relationships of organisms to their environment (including all other organisms present).

The word environment should not be intimidating. It is a very flexible term—we often speak of the *total* environment (the earth) or the *home* environment (which is really a sociological idea). When ecologists use the word, they are generally describing a *particular* natural situation, and are including all the components of the place—the air, water, soil, and living things, both plants and animals. As a matter of fact, the living and non-living parts of an environment are so intertwined that it is almost impossible to separate them.

Of course, the total environment—the earth—is not the same throughout. The *biosphere,* the thin outer shell that supports life, is part sea, part land. The terrestrial environment is further divided into grassland, desert, deciduous forest, and so on. Each of these major divisions is called a *biome.* Specific biomes have many things in common. For example, deserts in Africa are much like those in Asia; rain forests in the Amazon region are similar to those along the Congo River.

The borders between biomes are called *ecotones.* These zones of transition, such as the seashore, harbor species from the biomes on either side. You may find a tiny crab that is temporarily living above the tide; many birds spend as much time on the water as on land.

In spite of the wide adaptability of most organisms, they usually inhabit specific neighborhoods, or *habitats.* In the sea, for example, there are numer-

Few biomes are as clearly defined as these tiny, forest-covered islands that dot a lagoon in the western Pacific. Here, through the nearly transparent water, you can see another biome —the coral reef that fringes the shoreline and encroaches on the shallow, sandy areas. There is a relatively sharp transition between these biomes; the ecotone, or zone of blending, is not extensive in this region because there is so little variation in the tides. Most biomes, such as grasslands, forests, and marshes, blend almost imperceptibly into neighboring zones.

ous habitats—the tidal zone, the shallow offshore regions, the ocean floor, and others. Habitats are often likened to the "addresses" of plants or animals. Unlike biomes, habitats are not restricted to physical surroundings. A dog may be the habitat of a flea; a flea's digestive tract may be the habitat of a microbe. These small habitats are often called *microhabitats*. For example, the underside of a fallen log is a microhabitat within a forest, as are the leaves of certain plants (see right).

Most of the organisms living in a specific habitat are affected in some way by the others. Together, these interrelated plants and animals are called a *community*. Each species uses the habitat differently, depending on such things as time of day. A hawk is a daytime hunter; a moth is a nocturnal nectar-eater. The role an organism plays in its habitat is called its *niche*. If you like, you can think of an animal's niche as its "profession."

The home range of these brilliant Anthias fish is the craggy, vertical wall of a coral reef in the Red Sea. Nearly every animal has a home range—a familiar area where it feeds and breeds.

Microhabitats Are Worlds Within Worlds

An entire community can live in the little pools of rainwater that collect in the hollows formed by the leathery leaves of bromeliads (a type of epiphyte, or air plant). These short-stemmed plants often retain water for long periods. A scientist who drained one of these miniature reservoirs found over a dozen kinds of insects in the water, even tiny crabs. Many creatures, such as tree frogs and mosquitoes, grow to adulthood in these pools, and others may remain all their lives. Not all microhabitats are as stable as the ones in bromeliads. Those that may develop in a snowbank adjacent to the shelter of a rock sometimes produce a small population and then die out.

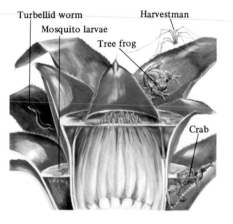

NATURE OBSERVER
A Niche Is More Than Just a Place

In architecture, a niche is a recessed place that contains a statue. In nature, a niche is more a role than a place. The niche of any species is its position in the community—what and where it eats, who its predators are, where it nests, and when it is active. The porcupine, for example, is a nocturnal forest-dweller that nests in hollow trees, eats twigs and bark, and is preyed upon by fishers (weasels).

• An animal's niche may change with time. A frog egg hatches into an aquatic plant-eating tadpole; later, it adopts a terrestrial, insect-eating way of life. Many ducks and geese hatch on the tundra (where they feed on insects); they fly south, feeding on freshwater weeds along the

way. They winter in saltwater bays.

• It is a basic assumption of ecology that no two species occupy the same niche in a community at any one time. So you can think of niches as a natural means of lessening competition. Consider two closely related water birds—the shag and the great cormorant. These birds are large, dark, and long-billed. In fact, they evolved from a common ancestor, but they have different niches. The shag fishes in shallow waters, the cormorant out at sea; the shag nests near the base of cliffs, the cormorant at higher locations. From their appearance, you might think that competition between these two species would be fierce. It isn't, because their ways of life are different.

Adaptation: Built-In Survival Mechanisms

An elephant's trunk, a giraffe's neck, a kangaroo's pouch, and a hummingbird's ability to hover have one thing in common—they are all adaptations. An adaptation is any characteristic of form or behavior that aids an animal's survival. Plants, too, are adapted to their environments. These adaptations took countless generations to develop, probably through many small changes. This is the essence of evolution.

The dynamics of adaptation can be demonstrated in a classic example of the way one kind of bird diversified into many species. When Charles Darwin studied the finch populations on the Galápagos archipelago, he found that these islands had a variety of habitats. Within the habitats, the niches (opportunities for making a living) were filled by finches that had evolved in different ways. They developed bills of different shapes, depending on the type of food available. Some retained the short, stubby, seed-cracking bill typical of finches. Others developed long, curved bills suitable for picking insects from crevices. One insect-eating species even took to using a "tool"—a long cactus spine for digging out insects.

All species of plants and animals are thought to have originated in much the same way, though not all continue to diversify. Gingko trees, ferns, dragonflies, opossums, and crocodiles have changed very little from their ancient forms (which we know from fossils). On the other hand, scientists believe that the perching birds (including finches) may still be evolving. The eastern and western meadowlarks of North America are examples of recently developed species. Their plumages and behavior patterns are almost identical, and their ranges overlap, but they have recognizably distinct songs and calls—and most important, they rarely interbreed.

Many vastly different groups have developed similar structures. For example, birds, bats, and insects all have wings. Conversely, similar life-forms often develop in different directions. The marsupials (pouched animals) of Australia are all closely related, but they are adapted to many different life-styles. Even their ways of locomotion vary—they run, hop, climb, burrow, or glide.

Populations are held in balance by natural factors. Among these are the food supply, predators, and disease. If a species is moved to a different environment, the natural checks may be absent. In that case, the introduced species may threaten to take over. Notorious examples are the starling of Europe and the walking catfish of Asia, both introduced to North America.

Sometimes plants and animals develop adaptations that prove to be a trap. For example, the Australian koala (a marsupial) is dependent solely on a few species of eucalypts for its food; it cannot live beyond the range of these trees. The distribution of many rare wildflowers also seems self-limiting. In other words, for some species a precarious existence is a result of evolution and not necessarily the fault of mankind.

Two Methods of Feeding

Two birds that feed in water are the brown pelican (left) and the American avocet (below). But the ways they have adapted to their aquatic environments are vastly different. The high-diving pelican, a ponderous, web-footed bird, uses a pouch of skin on its lower mandible to scoop fish from the sea. (True to the popular rhyme, the bill of the pelican indeed holds "more than its belly can"—up to 3 gallons.) The graceful, long-legged avocet feeds while wading through the shallow waters of tidal marshes and alkaline lakes. It moves its long, upturned bill from side to side, thereby dislodging small aquatic animals.

Seeds Give a Plant Mobility

One adaptation that enables plants to survive is their ability to travel. In the form of seeds, many are capable of extended journeys. Coconuts drifting on the waves have colonized remote oceanic islands. Dandelion and milkweed seeds are carried for miles by the wind. Winged fruits of maples twist through the air like miniature helicopters. Burs and tick-seeds hitchhike on the fur of animals and the clothes of people; small seeds cling to the feathers and feet of birds. Seeds are often carried thousands of miles by car, train, plane, and ship. These wanderers are tough. Some seeds that are centuries old have actually sprouted. Many can survive long exposure to extreme heat and cold. Some stay viable when immersed in salt water. Many withstand the digestive juices of animals that have swallowed fruits, which, of course, contain seeds.

Witch Hazel Has Ballistic Seeds

Witch-hazel seeds ripen for a year inside a tough case.

When the two smooth, tapering seeds are ripe, the case opens like a cannon's muzzle.

The case shrinks and expels the seeds with force, often for considerable distances.

Rough-surfaced, pointed pods of green milkweed open up when ripe and brown, launching wind-borne seeds into the air. The fluffy parachutes—modified parts of the seed coat—carry seeds for many miles. The silky fibers are so buoyant that they have sometimes been used to fill life preservers and safety vests.

The sacred lotus of Asia (left) is prized worldwide by owners of garden pools. Its blossoms rise a foot or more above the water. The center is the seed receptacle. As the seeds mature (above), this part grows heavier and changes color. The "seed carton" breaks off, turns over, and drifts—allowing the seeds to drop out and plant themselves in the shallow water.

The Varied Life-Styles of Animals

Most animal species live in comparative peace. Much of the noisy squabbling among birds and sparring among mammals is only ritual fighting—bluffing rather than the real thing. Such activities are signaling systems that enable the animals to assert their claims. It is only after the signals have failed that animals come to blows. This is especially true of fights between individuals of the same species.

Within any species, there is generally a definite social system. Some animals are solitary for most of the year. Others live in groups—wolves in packs, lions in prides, antelope in herds, and penguins in tremendous colonies. The most complex social systems are those of some insects, such as termites and honeybees. These social insects are so strictly organized that they almost seem to comprise a single identity.

Within each social system, "rules of conduct" give order to the group. For example, many gregarious animals will not allow another of their kind to come too close. When swallows perch together, they do not bunch up, but look as if they had precisely measured the spaces between themselves. Walruses, on the other hand, lie all over one another on an arctic beach, noisy but peaceful.

In the breeding season, many animals —especially birds and mammals—become feistier about space. Male songbirds proclaim ownership of a territory —a segment of field or wood. Colonial-nesting seabirds also claim a territory, but it is usually small and can often be measured by how far a sitting bird can jab with its beak. The chief purpose of a territory is to attract a mate and then to rear offspring. The animals don't "know" this, of course, but they act as if they do, and strongly defend their territories against intruders.

Solitary animals do not always have a territory. However, they may have what is known as a home range. Each animal hunts and pursues its other life habits in the area with which it has become familiar. A home range is like a home town, where you know all the important places. Tigers have enormous ranges. For many species, home ranges overlap, but there is no problem so long as two individuals don't meet.

Among most mammals, the females care for the young without help. Male elk, antelope, and elephant seals round up large temporary harems, but totally ignore their offspring. Only a few species —wolves and some monkeys, for example—share parental tasks. The duration of male-female relationships and the length of infancy vary with each species.

Most animals of different species are indifferent to one another. An elephant pays no attention to a zebra. Then there are animals that compete for the same food. Hyenas have first choice at a kill, while vultures wait. Actually, plant-eaters (herbivores) greatly outnumber meat-eaters (carnivores). Many animals live long, relatively peaceful lives.

Parasitism is a further interspecies relationship. A true parasite is an animal that lives at the expense of another species. Many kinds of worms are internal parasites, which damage their hosts but seldom kill them outright. In another form of relationship, the "guest" is aided, but the host is not seriously inconvenienced—for example, the barnacles that hitch a ride on a whale. In a different, more amiable relationship, each partner benefits. Small tropical fish remove and devour parasites from the skin of larger species, which hold still while the service is being performed.

Sometimes a solitary hunter, sometimes part of a pack, a coyote may hunt cooperatively with other species. Coyotes probably pair for life. A family stays together from spring into fall; in the middle of winter, the adults mate.

Penguins are colonial birds that spend most of their lives in close contact—millions may live in a single rookery. These are king penguins. Note the fuzzy youngsters, some with tufts still clinging to their emerging adult plumage.

A playful predator, the agile river otter may spend as much time cavorting as it does fishing. If you are lucky enough to catch a glimpse of an otter, you will probably find at least one other nearby. Otters sometimes team up to drive fish into shallow waters.

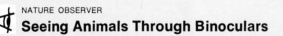
NATURE OBSERVER
Seeing Animals Through Binoculars

To get the most from your binoculars, you need to know how to use them. Practice with them on non-moving targets.
• Before you use your binoculars, find the quarry by watching for movement. Once you have spotted a bird or mammal, note a point of reference, such as a forked limb.

• Without taking your eyes from the spot, slowly lift the binoculars into position.
• To tell someone else where to look, describe your point of reference. *Don't lower your binoculars*. Identify the place using a clock system—"nine o'clock" if it's halfway up the left side, and so on.

To scan a large area quickly and systematically, sweep your binoculars from left to right and back again, as in the diagram at the right.

Special Relationships

When you think of interactions between species, the predator-prey relationship comes to mind first. But animals have evolved many other interdependencies, some beneficial, others detrimental.

This red-billed oxpecker appears to be whispering into the ear of an impala, but the bird is actually removing parasites, such as ticks and fleas, from the impala's skin. This type of relationship is called mutualism, and benefits both partners.

A European cuckoo dwarfs its "parent," a hedge sparrow. This cuckoo, like North American cowbirds, is a nest parasite; it lays eggs in nests of other species. The sparrow cannot distinguish an interloper, and instinctively feeds any gaping bill.

Cycles of Birth and Renewal

Nature is dynamic. The expression "balance of nature" is somewhat misleading—it suggests a stability that does not exist. True, much in nature *seems* the same and much can be predicted, but no two days and no two summers are alike. Though we are vaguely aware of certain patterns, only in comparatively recent times have scientists discovered fundamental cycles that affect our lives. The rhythms of day and night, the tides, the seasons are familiar to us all, but most other cycles escape notice because they are more subtle or occur over longer periods of time.

One man who noticed a recurrent cycle was Charles Greeley Abbot, an American astronomer. About 40 years ago, he predicted that a severe drought would hit the Great Plains "beginning about 1975." The drought arrived on schedule—crops were seriously affected, and topsoil was blown from thousands of acres. Farmers in the area were aware that droughts occurred every now and then, but had no idea when to expect them. From records of precipitation, Abbot realized that the dry spells had a cycle of about 20 years. He suspected that the earth's climate—especially the amount of rainfall—was greatly affected by the changing energy-output of the sun. Today, scientists believe that the solar output is cyclical, and that drought cycles have regularly afflicted the Great Plains and other parts of the world.

The longest cycle yet discovered (called an epochal cycle) is that of the earth's Ice Ages, which have occurred about every 250 million years. There are innumerable lesser cycles. The populations of many animals rise and fall every 8 to 10 years. Lemmings generally migrate every 3 or 4 years.

The land, too, has cycles, and perhaps these are the most important of all. The soil nourishes plants, which feed the plant-eaters, which in turn support the predators, including mankind. Thus, a decrease or increase in the productivity of the land is felt throughout nature. (Minerals washed from the soil by increased rainfall even influence similar cycles in the oceans.) Most plants sprout or resume growth in spring, when the soil is rich with accumulated nutrients and moisture. On the African plains, most grazing animals give birth to their young at this season, when the grasses are at their lushest.

In the course of a relatively long rainy cycle in temperate zones, grasslands may become moist enough to support trees. The first trees are likely to be conifers. The conifers will eventually be shaded out by broad-leaved trees, in a natural sequence called succession. In general, such forests can continue to grow for centuries, but if the weather cycle swings back toward less rainfall, the forest may dry out and perhaps be set afire by lightning, leaving the land open to become grassland again.

Because cycles of birth and renewal start with the land, it is the land that ultimately determines how much plant and animal life can be supported in any particular place. This is called the land's carrying capacity, and it is a basic concept that we are just now beginning to understand. Farmers, ranchers, and hunters have frequently attempted to increase the carrying capacity of land. But if the vegetation becomes overgrazed, erosion sets in, and the land can no longer support the herds and flocks that once thrived there. The carrying capacity of farmlands can be increased by fertilizers and irrigation, but these have limits because they, too, are affected by weather cycles. It is better to discover—and follow—nature's cycles than to fight them.

A venturesome fox kit, still wobbly on its legs, sets out to explore a buzzing, green summer world. The prosperity of any animal species ultimately depends on the fertility of the land and the abundance of vegetation. From year to year, all animal populations fluctuate.

PHOTO TIPS
From Bud to Flower

You can capture development from bud to flower by taking a sequence of pictures. Usually you will need close-up attachments —a bellows, extension rings, or a second lens. Almost any illumination will work—sunlight, flash bulbs, electronic flash. The light must be bright enough to let you stop down to about f/11 for sufficient depth of field. You can produce a sequence by shooting the same bud, such as this pussy willow, over a period of days. Or photograph different buds at different stages. Keep the composition consistent in each photo.

The Tenacity of Plants Serves Us All

Central Park in New York City was planned by a man of great foresight—Frederick Law Olmstead. In the 1850's, he won the land for a park in the face of bitter opposition.

Human beings depend on oxygen, and all of it comes from plants. Yet for decades, by some incredible lapse of reasoning, the builders of cities have regarded parks and plantings as impractical amenities. Many people are now insisting that urban trees be protected. "Pocket parks" are being established, making everyone aware of the renewal of spirit that is created by these green oases. Not only do trees constantly replenish the oxygen supply —they cleanse the air of dirt particles, cool it on hot days (they are tireless, absolutely free air-conditioners), and conserve heat at night. Trees are also excellent sound-absorbers, a boon to any city or town with heavy traffic. It is time to be vigilant on behalf of trees and other plants—even weeds.

A crack in the sidewalk is filled and enlarged by the exuberant growth of a young ailanthus (which will become a tree, if allowed). With it are a number of other city-adapted plants.

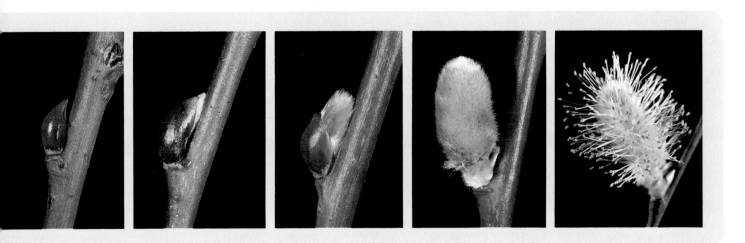

29

Your Awareness of Time

Clocks and calendars are ways mankind has invented to measure time, but nature goes by more intricate measures and rhythms. Time of day and season of the year come to mind first. But each of us is concerned with a larger time-scale as well—our own lifetime. Oddly enough, awareness of this unique, personal time-span seems to be the first casualty in the hurry of everyday living. On a grander scale, presiding majestically over all the others, is geologic time —the millions of years it takes for mountains to form and wear away.

There are other kinds of time, always present but often forgotten. Lunar time is one. The moon makes its rounds, pulling on the surface of the earth, and creating the powerful, rhythmic rise and fall of the tides. All living things—plants as well as animals—seem to follow inner timers. These so-called biological clocks govern periods as diverse as the customary time of day that a bird will begin to sing, a lion will nap, and a flower will open (four-o'clocks are named for the late-afternoon hour when the blossoms open). There are biological clocks that tell seventeen-year locusts (or insects on other schedules) that the time has come to emerge from underground burrows and whir about in the world above.

Human beings are strongly influenced by day-night rhythms. Everyone recognizes the "owls and fowls" among us— those who are most active at night, and those whose energies are stimulated by the rising of the sun. These are personal patterns that seem to be inborn. But regardless of this tendency, whenever a traveler flies over long distances to a different time zone, effectively turning night into day (or vice versa), the individual usually feels uncomfortable.

Time might be thought of as absolutely democratic because a day gives each of us exactly the same allotment of hours. But this isn't accurate. Time is subjective—a very personal perception. For example, a child and an adult together on a trip will experience time in vastly different ways. A very young child may barely understand what "again" means, or "tomorrow," or "when I was your age." As an individual matures, time becomes more structured. The snows of winter do not come as a surprise. In fact, unless there is a toddler around discovering what wonderful stuff snow is, an adult may think only about shoveling it.

A person's perception of time keeps shifting. As the very old can tell you, time goes more swiftly the longer you live. An old man may look at a forest and remember when, in his childhood, that land was a plowed field. Time becomes telescoped, not by failing faculties, but by overlapping images. Each age offers a different vision, which you can capture, borrow, and savor.

The point is this—somewhere along the way each individual needs to recognize that there is such a thing as personal time. Immediate events—ranging from toothaches to far-reaching political crises—cannot be set aside. But we really have a great deal of leeway in choosing what we do with our time. If you have been thinking about getting outdoors more often, have you set aside the time?

Seeing Time in Four Different Perspectives

Many ancient peoples attempted to develop calendars that included the major elements of time—length of day, phases of the moon, and return of the seasons. For the most part, the calendars were faulty because these three elements cannot be synchronized. The most accurate calendar was that of the Maya of Central America. They recorded each kind of time separately—although they often checked one against another. In a sense, the Maya recognized the true complexity of time. Their intricate calendar is a parable for us today —time has many faces. Subjectively, for any one individual, time can be recollections of important moments, best-loved seasons, the stages of a lifetime, and those memorable occasions when we suddenly become aware of the deeper etchings of geologic time.

Night gives way to day over Prince William Sound in Alaska. The morning light has penetrated the hovering bank of thick fog, and now glitters on the gently rippling waters.

A sparkling winter sun turns the graceful birch branches into a filigree of crystal-clear ice.

Reading Sundials—Ancient and Modern

Sundials are believed to be the oldest time-telling devices in the world. Some are known to be 4,000 years old. You can make one yourself by simply putting a stick into the ground at high noon. Fix it firmly in place, at an angle, so that you get a shadow. Tilt it northward in the northern hemisphere, southward in the southern hemisphere. Put a pebble at the tip of the shadow. An hour later, put another pebble at the tip, and so on during the afternoon. The next morning (if it's sunny), repeat the hourly placement of pebbles until you have reached high noon once again. Set an alarm clock at hourly intervals so you won't lose track of time.

• Thereafter, the pebbles will tell the time by themselves. You will see that the shadow moves faster in the morning and evening than around noon. This is why numbers on a sundial are unevenly spaced. On the type of sundial usually seen in gardens and parks, the stick is a stone or metal angle called a gnomon (NO-men). The study of sundials is called gnomonics, and the dial face is called the plane. Your advantage over all primitive sundial-makers is that you know the right time from the start; *they* had to arrive at it

by the painstaking method of trial and error.

• Of course, sundials can be constructed in many different forms—some are rings, spheres, curved bars, cylinders, or indented plates. All sundials function because, as the earth rotates, the sun seems to move across the heavens and cause shadows to shift precisely. Because of the change of the earth's orientation to the sun (which causes the seasons), a

sundial will be exactly on time only twice a year, when the sun lies directly over the equator. But they are generally accurate enough to give you pleasure from having or making one. While no sundial will ever "run down," sundials obviously are of no use on cloudy days or at night. Hence many of the inscriptions, which seem to be traditional on sundials, read, "I show only sunny hours."

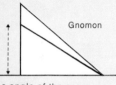

Sundials like the one at the left are so sturdy, they are almost part of the landscape. They will tell time for centuries, although every year their accuracy decreases a few seconds.

Gnomon

The angle of the gnomon depends on the location— the farther from the equator, the higher the gnomon.

A tree you plant in childhood will soon tower over you. Here, two pine seedlings begin life.

The span of geologic time is clearest at the Grand Canyon. The oldest known rocks are at the base; here, at the South Rim, are rocks that once were on the bottom of an inland sea.

CHAPTER TWO

Trees and Forests

What plants do—how they live and adjust—
is so ingenious, it's hard to believe they
can't think, plan, or cooperate consciously.

The plant kingdom comprises more than 95 percent of the living substance on earth. Trees—especially when massed in forests —are the most impressive members of the plant world. Because most species of trees live longer than human beings, they seem timeless to us. We assume a serenity in their lives that is far from the truth. As among animals, trees compete vigorously for the necessities of life—space, light, water. Their struggle for survival is beset by drought, fire, and various pests. But trees have many systems of defense. They are amazingly resilient (a chestnut tree with a dead trunk will send out shoots for decades); some exude a chemical repellent to discourage competitors (few plants can sprout beneath a eucalypt tree); one species even has insect guardians (the bull's horn acacia is host to fiercely biting ants that ward off all animal invaders, large and small).

Just what is a tree? or a forest? Dictionaries do not provide satisfying definitions. They say a tree is a "woody perennial"— which means a plant that develops woody tissues and that continues its growth year after year. But the same can be said of shrubs. Some definitions specify a height of 15 feet, but shrubs such as rhododendrons often exceed this height. A forest is called a dense concentration of trees, but how many is meant by "dense"?

It is tantalizing to know what a tree is, and what a forest is, yet to find their definitions so elusive. We know what trees do. They give off vital oxygen. They moderate temperatures, hold soil, and prevent erosion. They are beneficial to the animal world, including man. Not the least important thing about trees and forests is their power to influence the human spirit—somehow to soothe and inspire at the same time.

Standing within the ramparts of a forest, looking out at the
world, you are in a perfect place to contemplate trees. How strong
and beautiful they are! A choir of bird song fills the morning.
There is stillness at noon. Then, in the evening, the setting
sun turns the fringe of rustling leaves to bits of stained glass.

Every Woodland Is Unique

When you inhale the odors of a forest, the mixture of scents is dominated by its most numerous trees. Pine forests have an unmistakable, resinous aroma. Other woodland scents are harder to define, but no matter how subtle the fragrance, there is usually something distinctive about a particular woodland. Even years later, a single whiff is often all that's needed to recall the times spent there.

The seasons have scents of their own. There is the invigorating air of spring, tinctured by new growth and snow-melt pools; the mixture of midsummer smells, when the thatch of ground-cover and humus keeps the soil musty and damp; the hearty autumn odor of drying vegetation and fallen leaves.

Many parts of the world share the same types of trees, especially in the northern hemisphere where the continents are close together. Early immigrants from Scandinavia to the New World felt at home because the coniferous forests of the region around the Great Lakes were like those they had left behind. Perhaps this similarity encouraged them to settle there.

But more commonly, a traveler is struck by the vast differences among regional forests and woodlands. Tropical rain forests such as those near the Amazon River have such a diversity of species that they are difficult to classify. At far-flung sites, there are odd pockets of one particular species, such as the giant sequoia (a conifer native to small areas of California) and the coco-de-mer (a palm found only on a few islands in the Indian Ocean).

Australia furnishes a prime example of unique native forests—and many other unusual plants and animals as well. Isolated from other continents for millions of years, Australia is dominated by one group of trees, the eucalypts or gum trees. In response to local differences in soil and climate, these trees have diversified to such an extent that today there are some 600 different kinds.

So impressed were early European explorers by the vegetation of Australia—not just the eucalypts but such novel flowering shrubs as banksias—that an inlet was named Botany Bay to celebrate the variety of plants. This one area had some 1,000 unfamiliar species.

Some botanical expeditions were intended to enhance the beautiful gardens of wealthy Europeans. Other voyages were more commercial. When certain prized plants were lacking in newly colonized places because of geographical barriers such as oceans and mountains, people supplied the transportation. (The famous mutiny on the *Bounty,* which took place in 1789, interrupted the collecting of breadfruit plants. Not only was Captain Bligh set adrift by the mutineers, the plants were tossed overboard as well.)

In spite of the widespread introduction of alien species from one continent to another, native forests remain diverse, individual, and typical of their locales. The leaves of many temperate-zone trees change color before they drop in autumn. But in no part of the world is there so spectacular a show of autumn colors as in the eastern broadleaved forests of North America. This is because the climate there often provides perfect weather conditions for producing such effects: sunny autumn days, cool nights, and not much rain.

Some forests are marked by mankind. For centuries, the European attitude toward nature was that it was unruly and could be much improved by planning. Hence many magnificent old parks lend a special—if formal—grace to the world of woodlands. Strictly speaking, they may not seem natural because they have not been allowed to grow wild. But the workings of nature can readily be seen in such places—and enjoyed just as much.

PHOTO TIPS
Taking Silhouettes of Trees

What does silhouette photography show that ordinary pictures do not? For one thing, it gives a simplicity that sets off the line of the subject—in this case, a tree. Its symmetry tells you that this tree has grown alone during its formative years, unpruned, uncrowded by other trees. This is an easy clue to identifying a good subject for your photography—choose a tree that's free-standing, free-moving.

• Take photos at times of day when the background sky is most colorful. Sunset and sunrise can be equally dramatic.

• Try different exposures: one photo while standing in the shadow of the tree, then at the edge of the shadow, then in direct light (which may give you bright flares). There is no one "right" exposure, only an expression of mood.

• You don't need to know the species of tree. But chances are, if you have taken a real beauty, you'll want to know its name. Before long, you'll be on your way to learning much more about trees.

Slender mountain ashes, trailing long strips of shed bark, emerge like ghosts from the winter mist in an Australian eucalyptus forest. A dense undercover of tree ferns and antarctic beeches provides the damp, shady habitat favored by lyrebirds.

Orderly rows of trees are features of many European landscapes. They were planted to dignify the entrances to great estates and mark the highways of kings and noblemen. The inspiration for planting such groves has vanished, but their charming remnants delight the eye.

The fragile look of birches, with their chalk-white trunks and pale green leaves, stands in marked contrast to the environment that fosters them. It seems almost impossible that something so airy looking can dwell in a Finnish woodland, so near to the icy arctic region.

Brilliant autumn foliage is a special glory of North American forests. At a distance, it's possible to guess at the identity of trees, based on color. The scarlets are probably maples; the yellows are likely to be birches or poplars; the dark greens are almost certainly conifers.

Where the Trees Are

Most people know that climate determines where certain trees can grow. What is less apparent is that it also works the other way around: trees have a significant effect on climate. All stands of trees, even narrow hedgerows, have a part in the great water cycle on this planet. Trees collect water with their roots and give off water vapor from their leaves. A forest and the surrounding area are usually more moist than grasslands.

This map shows where different types of trees dominate the vegetation. Human beings have cleared off trees for farming, for living space, and for timber, so much of the land is no longer fully forested. Human activities, going back to prehistory, have progressively destroyed great stands of trees, thereby creating a climate drier than before.

The body plan of a tree is organized to gain maximum exposure to sunlight. Not only do the trees compete with one another for the light, but leaves on the same tree are in competition, too. This is apparent not just among broad-leaved trees such as oaks and maples, but among the species with needle-like leaves, such as pines.

Broad-leaved trees prosper in tropical and temperate regions. In the tropics, where maximum sunlight strikes the earth, leaves—which, by temperate-zone standards, are sometimes huge—can frequently be seen crowding one another in a dense canopy high above the ground. Although sunlight strikes less directly in temperate zones, a broad leaf is still advantageous.

Conifers dominate the high latitudes. Here, the light of the sun strikes the earth at an oblique angle (because of the tilt of the earth on its axis). In effect, the light has to take a longer path through the atmosphere, and the sunlight is diffused. Under these conditions, the narrow needles of a conifer come into their own, able to capture light from any angle. Needles also lose less water into the air than do wide, flat leaves. During winter, when the water supply is locked up in ice or snow and therefore unavailable, such water conservation is important.

Where winds are harsh and frequent, as at high altitudes, conifers usually do better than broad-leaved trees, regardless of latitude. The tough needles withstand gusts of wind that would tatter the leaves of such trees as maples. The wind's influence on trees is evident not only on wind-whipped coasts and mountains but also in your own back yard.

A wide belt of coniferous forest stretches across vast tracts of Canada.

Subarctic Alaska has spruces and aspens in the valleys.

Three super-trees grow in the mountains of western North America: bristlecone pines (the world's oldest); giant sequoias (the largest); redwoods (the tallest).

HAWAIIAN ISLANDS

Hawaiian rain forests are rich in tree ferns, which, like all Hawaii's native plants, are immigrants to these volcanic islands.

The humid, coastal rain forests of Colombia and Ecuador contrast with deserts to the south.

Relatives of Appalachian hickories and sassafras grow in China—the only other place where they survived the Ice Ages.

In the Amazon Basin, the world's largest and most varied rain forest is threatened by new highways.

Antarctic beeches, also found in New Zealand, grow to the continent's tip.

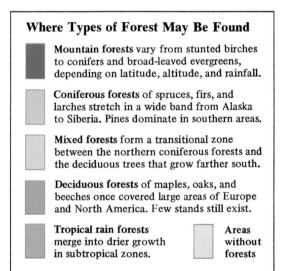

Where Types of Forest May Be Found

Mountain forests vary from stunted birches to conifers and broad-leaved evergreens, depending on latitude, altitude, and rainfall.

Coniferous forests of spruces, firs, and larches stretch in a wide band from Alaska to Siberia. Pines dominate in southern areas.

Mixed forests form a transitional zone between the northern coniferous forests and the deciduous trees that grow farther south.

Deciduous forests of maples, oaks, and beeches once covered large areas of Europe and North America. Few stands still exist.

Tropical rain forests merge into drier growth in subtropical zones.

Areas without forests

Curious Trees of the World

Most of us have a preconceived idea of the way a tree should look: a single, narrow trunk, a leafy crown, and spreading branches. But certain trees don't conform to this "lollipop" pattern. Scientists believe that shape helps the survival of a species—as, for example, when it aids in water conservation. The advantage is easy to see in some cases; at other times, the "value" to the tree is more of a puzzle.

Bristlecone pines of the high Rockies, twisted and half dead, outlive all other trees.

The Eurasian taiga of
firs, larches, and spruces
is the greatest expanse
of forest in the world.

Scandinavia has
large areas of birch
forests, high on the
mountain slopes.

Long ago, much of China
was forested. An intensive
reforestation campaign is
bringing back the trees.

Mediterranean lands,
once wooded, have
been eaten bare
by livestock.

With little space
for forests, Japan
has about 170
species of native
trees—twice as
many as Europe.

Located in the heart of the
tropics, the islands from the
Philippines to Indonesia have
incredibly varied rain forests.

New Guinea's humid
rain forests are home
to many species
that have colonized
nearby Australia.

North Africa has
patches of
mountain forests.

In the Himalayan
foothills, rain forests
shelter luxuriant
rhododendrons.

A wide band of
tropical rain forest,
second only to the
great Amazonian
forest in extent,
spans 3,000 miles
of equatorial Africa.

Remnant forests on
Madagascar shelter
lemurs—primitive
primates unique to
the tropical island.

In Burma and Thailand,
monsoon forests of
teak and other valuable
hardwoods are leafless
in the dry season.

South Africa has a few
forests of yew-like trees
called podocarps, which
are evergreen conifers.
But most of the region
is a dry, treeless plain.

The dominant trees of Australia,
eucalypts, have diversified
tremendously. They thrive on
windy mountains, in the tropics,
and in the arid interior regions.

Startlingly different
from Australian forests,
those of New Zealand
are dominated by tree
ferns and kauri pines.

Boojum trees of Mexico
develop leaves only after
rain; trunks store water.

Baobabs of Africa and
Australia store water
in fibrous tissues of
the bulbous trunks.

Banyan tree of Asia,
a strangler fig, sends
down aerial roots that
thicken into trunks.

Grass trees of Australia have
floral spikes that make them
look like large candelabra.

The Evolution of Trees

Forests seem to us to possess a timeless and enduring quality—yet they have not always been as we see them today. The evolution of trees has taken some hundreds of millions of years. And when forests first evolved, they were low-growing, swampy, silent places. It is strange to think that trees came before insects—and even before grasses.

The long drama of plant evolution began in the primeval seas, where the waters contained every element needed for growth and reproduction. Algae were probably the first plants to leave the water and colonize the barren land. Over the millennia, algae developed certain characteristics they had not needed in the sea—a tougher coat that retained water in the plant; pores that absorbed and gave off gases; and supporting tissues that helped them withstand the pull of gravity.

About 400 million years ago there appeared the rootless, leafless progenitor of all trees—a plant called Psilophyton (si-low-FI-ton), from Greek words meaning naked plant. Little more than a spiny stem with branches, Psilophyton had one remarkable characteristic: it stood erect, reaching a height of 1 to 3 feet. This isn't much by modern standards, but it meant that the Psilophyton was taller than its low-growing neighbors. The added height enabled it to capture sunlight—at the expense of any other plant in its vicinity.

Slowly, over countless generations, some plants grew still taller, evolving woody tissue that supported their height. One primitive kind of woody plant, called the Gilboa tree, grew as tall as 40 feet. Gilboa trees developed long, fern-like leaves and reproduced by means of spores.

Spores are produced by a single plant and can develop into new plants without having a second "parent." (Most spore-producing species have, at some point, a sexual stage, where male and female traits are mixed. But clusters of spores are what one can usually see on plants such as ferns.)

Many scientists object to mention of sex—male and female reproduction—in connection with plants. True, it is an oversimplification, but it is also a long-standing tradition, and a convenience as well. Essentially, what sexual reproduction accomplishes is the mixing of inherited traits. This means that each offspring has a different combination of traits from the others, and so there is greater variety. Such variety enables plants (and animals) to adapt to changing conditions over long periods.

When sexual reproduction takes place among the more advanced plants, a seed is eventually produced. The seed is a tiny plant embryo with a built-in food supply: this is an important advance over the microscopic spore because the food gives the young plant a head start. Among the first trees to produce seeds were the Cordaites, ancestors of the conifers.

Conifers have survived to our day, but they have lost ground, literally, to flowering trees. These trees, including the widespread family of maples, have taken over the temperate and tropical zones of the world.

Two adaptations of flowering trees seem to have been especially important in giving them the advantage over conifers: a more efficient water pump and a more advanced reproductive system. Rather than depending on wind pollination alone, some flowering trees attract insects and other animals by color or scent, enlisting their aid in pollination.

From Spiny Stems to Leafy Abundance

A comparison of living trees with some of their fossil ancestors reveals major changes. Most apparent is the tremendous increase in height and girth. Another significant change is in the method of reproduction—modern trees produce seeds, not spores. Diversity of shape seems to be greater now than in the past, but because the fossil record is incomplete, this is a matter of speculation.

Psilophyton was not a tree, but it did stand upright, higher than mosses nearby. This leafless, spiny plant produced drooping cases of spores after its branches had unfurled.

The Gilboa tree, named for the New York State site where its fossils were found, was one of the earliest plants that seems tree-like by modern standards: it reached a height of 40 feet.

The Cordaites are important to the story of tree evolution because they were some of the first trees to produce seeds instead of spores. The seeds developed in the leafy crown.

The heyday of the conifers, which bear their seeds in cones, ended millions of years ago. Once giant sequoias had an extensive range; today they grow wild only in California.

The Two Great Categories of Present-Day Trees

Though there are thousands of species, the living trees of the world can be divided into just two groups. A tree (like other plants) is classified by the way in which it reproduces—in this case, whether it has cones or flowers. Mature cone-bearing trees are easy to identify: look for their woody cones high in the branches or scattered on the ground. The identification of flowering trees is no problem for such species as magnolias, especially when they are in bloom. But there is greater variety among flowering trees than among conifers, and some tree flowers are so inconspicuous that they escape notice. Then, too, most flowering trees blossom only once a year (usually in spring), so this botanical habit cannot always be observed. If you see a tree that is not in flower, look around it for fruit, berries, or nuts. A tree that has any of these is undoubtedly a flowering species: these varied structures are the end-products of a flower's development.

Conifer Means Cone-Bearing

Young female cone

Pollen-bearing male cone

Old female cone (seeds have been released)

Near the tip of this pine bough is a male cone. It lasts only a short time and doesn't look at all like the more familiar female cones. (These become woody as the seeds develop.)

Most Trees Reproduce with Flowers

That most trees have blossoms may come as a surprise, for people often overlook the tiny flowers on many species (right). Tulip trees, which are close relatives of magnolias, have showier flowers (below).

Flower of a tulip tree

Curved "fingers" on a tulip-tree flower bear pollen; seeds develop in the center.

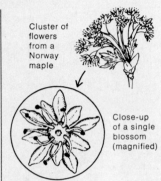

Cluster of flowers from a Norway maple

Close-up of a single blossom (magnified)

Look for the clusters of small flowers that hang from a maple in spring. (You can also find them beneath the tree.) Each maple flower is either male or female; the one above, with pollen, is male.

Flowering trees dominate the world's forests, except on mountain slopes and in the far north. Norway maples bloom in the spring, although their flowers are often overlooked.

Gingkos: "Living Fossils"

Noted for its exquisite fan-shaped leaves, the gingko stands by itself among living trees. Long before the evolution of modern conifers or broad-leafed trees, gingkos populated temperate forests all over the world; the fossil imprint of a leaf below reveals that gingkos once grew wild in Oregon. Gingkos survived the Ice Ages only in the Orient—but today the stately and pollution-resistant trees are planted in cities around the world.

What Is an Evergreen?

Evergreen is a gardener's term that is more descriptive than scientific: it means that a plant has leaves throughout the year. But the word evergreen causes confusion when it comes to learning about trees, because each of the basic types—conifers and flowering trees—has evergreen representatives.

To many people, the word evergreen means the same thing as coniferous, or cone-bearing. It is true that most conifers *are* evergreen. And because the leaves of conifers take the form of needles or scales, most conifers resemble one another. But some conifers, such as larches, are not evergreen: in autumn, they drop their needles.

Some broad-leaved trees, especially tropical species, *do not* drop their leaves seasonally. If an oak or maple is transplanted to the tropics, it may abandon its leaf-shedding habit and become an evergreen like its new neighbors.

Some of the most popular garden evergreens are broad-leaved plants, but many are shrubs, not trees. Certain hollies, laurels, and rhododendrons fall into this group. The leaves of these shrubs remain on the branches until the individual leaf dies, and the plant is never bare. So the word evergreen actually describes the habit of a plant, not the plant itself.

As botanists have discovered, the most reliable way of classifying plants is by their reproductive structures. Among trees, the critical question is: does the tree bear cones, or flowers?

Conifers have female cones and male cones, which are distinctively different but are usually present on the same tree. The female cone holds the ovules (egg cells), which must be pollinated in order to develop into seeds.

Pollen, produced by male cones in enormous quantities, is carried in the wind to the female cones. Most people recognize the female cones, but the male cones are there too. Often they are smaller, bright yellow or red, and borne on the lower branches of a mature conifer. Male cones have a short-term existence in spring and early summer and never become woody.

Before pollination, the egg-bearing scales on a female cone are open. After pollination, the scales swell up and the cone enlarges dramatically: witness the sugar pine of North America, which has a cone that reaches a length of some 2 feet. When the seeds are ripe—which in some species takes more than a year—the once-green and resinous cone becomes dry, brown, and woody. The scales separate and the seeds fall.

Coniferous trees are the earth's oldest and tallest inhabitants. Some bristlecone pines (mountain trees in the western United States) are more than 4,000 years old. Redwoods in California reach a height of more than 350 feet, rivaled only by the Australian mountain ash (which is not a conifer).

Some 500 kinds of conifers exist; nearly all are evergreen. Among the strangest conifers are the yew-like podocarps that grow mainly in the southern hemisphere. The pygmy pine, a New Zealand podocarp, is the tiniest of all conifers; it begins producing cones when only 3 inches tall.

Just three of these conifers—pine, spruce, and fir—make up about a third of the world's forests. Conifers furnish nearly three-quarters of all timber and nearly all our paper. In fact, the page you are now looking at almost certainly came from a coniferous tree.

Three Plants That Appear to Break the Rules

Larches are not typical conifers because they turn color in fall and lose their needles. This American larch, called a tamarack, has already turned gold and is shedding needles.

Juniper foliage is scaly and branching, not at all like needles—but the juniper is a true conifer. The fleshy, blue-gray structures look like berries but are really modified cones.

Most hollies are actually evergreens, for they retain their leaves year-round. But hollies have broad leaves, not needles, and their berries reveal that they are really flowering plants.

Different Ways of Identifying Conifers

Telling one conifer from another is simply a matter of narrowing down the many possibilities. First decide whether or not a particular tree is indeed a conifer. All conifers have needle-shaped or scale-like leaves. Look at the needles to discover the major group (such as pine). Tree shape may provide some clues. A cone by itself, away from the tree that produced it, is often difficult to identify as to species.

Guide to Needles or Scales

Needles are the easiest way to identify a conifer. Compare them with the ones shown here, which represent the major groups. A field guide will help you to determine the precise species. If the branches are too high off the ground, look at the fallen needles.

Larches
(Tamarack)

Clusters of many needles

Larches have bristling clusters of 12 to 20 short needles, which fall from the tree in autumn.

Pines
(Scotch pine)

Bundles of long needles

All pines grow needles in bundles, wrapped together at the base. Some kinds have two needles per group, other species have more.

Firs
(Balsam fir)

Blunt needle, round base

Fir needles have blunt tips and occur individually on a twig. Circular scars mark the points of attachment.

Spruces
(Norway spruce)

Sharp needle, woody peg

Spruce needles are stiff, pointed, and 4-sided. Each species has needles of a particular size and color.

Cedars and Junipers
(Northern white cedar)

Overlapping leaf-scales

Small, flat, and scale-like leaves (not the needles of other conifers) make cedars and junipers distinctive.

Hemlocks
(Eastern hemlock)

Flat needle, thin stalk

Soft, flattened needles give hemlocks a lacy look. Thin stems of needles (which aren't grouped) hug twig.

White spruce

Red spruce

Black spruce

The Shape of a Conifer

Experts can often identify conifers, such as spruces, by shape—the density and arrangement of branches. But individual trees vary greatly. For beginners, shape may be less helpful than needles in tree identification.

Cones Confirm a Tree's Identity

Each kind of conifer produces cones of a unique size and shape. The selection of cones below shows the tremendous diversity within one group—the pines. The cones have been drawn to scale, each at about half its natural size.

Jack pine

Eastern white pine

Piñon pine

Knobcone pine

Shortleaf pine

The "Family Tree" of a Flowering Tree

As a game, ask a friend or relative to name three flowering trees other than magnolias or fruit trees. Chances are, few people will mention oaks, maples, beeches, or elms. Such trees do have flowers, but their blossoms are often inconspicuous. For example, the tassel-shaped flowers of sugar maples are greenish-yellow and appear at the same time as the leaves.

The short-lived flowers of many kinds of trees may be overlooked entirely, not just because of their small size and camouflaged color, but because they may bloom only in the higher branches. You can get a better look at tree flowers from an upstairs window or by viewing them with binoculars.

Many trees bloom after the leaves have come out, so you don't notice the flowers. And sometimes, too, because of their shapes, you may not recognize a tree flower for what it is. The flowers of birches and willows are catkins, which are usually fuzzy, caterpillar-shaped clusters of flowers without petals.

Flowers are reproductive structures. Although they bloom only for a brief time, from generation to generation flowers are the most consistent part of a tree. Leaves may be large or small, even variable in shape—one sassafras, for example, may have leaves of several different shapes. Bark and branches help in identifying many trees. But only the flowers are always the same. Consequently, botanists rely on flowers as a means of classifying trees.

The magnolia family, generally believed to be the oldest of flowering trees, includes not only the various kinds of magnolias, but the stately tulip tree as well. The magnolia flower is complete, which means it has all four component flower parts: sepals, petals, and both stamens (male parts) and pistils (female).

Another group of plants with complete flowers is the pea family. The flower itself is shaped like a butterfly, with a large, showy, insect-attracting petal on top, two side "wings," and two fused petals at the base. The remarkable thing about the pea family (which includes many trees as well as trailing vines) is its great diversity. One member, the black locust (also called false acacia), is grown for its lovely drooping clusters of sweet-scented flowers. The golden-flowered broom and

Catkins Are Clusters of Incomplete Flowers

Most people have seen catkins (though they might not have been recognized as such). The furry, gray parts of a pussy willow are really catkins. A catkin is a dense cluster of tiny blossoms reduced to the essentials of reproduction. Unlike a complete flower, a catkin has no petals and sepals (modified leaves); a catkin is either male (pollen-bearing) or female (seed-producing), never both. The photo below shows male catkins from a poplar, one of the many plants that develop these clusters. In the close-up at right, note the purple structures; these produce pollen.

gorse shrubs that are native to European hillsides, the peanut plant, the Japanese wisteria, and the sweet pea itself all belong to the pea family.

Flowering trees have diversified over the long span of their development. There are many trees with incomplete flowers, simplified to petal-less, sepal-less, or single-sex flowers. In the main, these are pollinated by the wind, and it is to this large group that catkin-bearing birches and poplars belong. Male and female flowers may be on one tree (as in the case of beeches) or on separate trees (as among cottonwoods).

Learning about trees by their family relationships makes identification more entertaining. With the help of a field guide, survey local trees; then look to see if they have any relatives nearby.

PHOTO TIPS
Flower Close-Ups

Most simple pocket cameras are able to do justice to large flowers or clusters of small ones. However, to capture a delicate tree flower, you may need a special close-up lens. A telephoto lens can even take pictures of small flowers high up in the branches of a tree.

• The keys to success are steadiness and careful focusing. If you have a tripod, this is when to use it. Or brace the camera on a base—a fence, stone, or tree. Even when the camera is firmly anchored, there may still be a breeze to contend with. Either wait for the breeze to die down or shield the subject with cardboard or your camera bag.

• Some photographers carry reflectors; you can use ordinary white cardboard. Sunlight bounces off the white surface and helps to give more uniform light. An electronic flash will ensure good illumination, regardless of weather or time. A flash also enables you to shoot at a faster speed, which eliminates blurring. But take advantage of available light, too. Sunlight coming from one side may enhance the texture.

• You can experiment with different backgrounds. A blue sky makes a spectacular frame if the flowers are on the outer edge of a tree. But use a light meter to be sure the sky does not take over the picture. Put your meter near the flower first, then step backward; concentrate on the reading from the flower, not the sky.

• If the particular flower you want to photograph is crowded by other branches, you can tie them back temporarily, to avoid obstructions.

Roses and Fruit Trees Are Close Relatives

The rose family, with some 3,000 members, includes many more kinds of plants than just roses. Some of the best-known fruit and ornamental trees belong to this group. The flowering cherry shown above does not produce edible fruits—it is considered an ornamental. Other members include apple, plum, strawberry, and hawthorn. These seemingly diverse plants are classified into one family because of the similarity in the structure of the flower. Each blossom has five petals and five sepals; both stamens (the male components) and pistil (female) are present. The bulbous ovary, at the base of the flower, is where the seed grows. Many different types of fruits grow from this basic type of flower. Below are cross-sections of flowers and fruits from the rose family.

After a rose is pollinated, seeds develop inside the rose-hip—a bright structure slightly larger than the base of the flower. A rose-hip is really a group of fruits called achenes; each achene has a single seed. Cross-sections of both rose and rose-hip are shown at right.

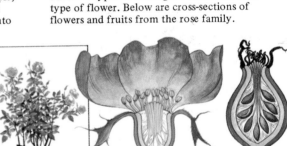

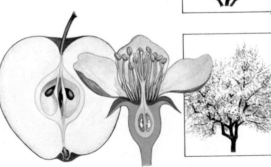

Botanically, an apple is known as a pome—a fruit that has a central core. Usually there are five seeds inside the core. If you compare an apple with an apple blossom, you can see that the base of the flower (surrounding the seeds) has enlarged greatly. Pears and quinces—both in the rose family—are pomes.

Though the plum's botanical name —a drupe—may be unfamiliar, drupes are easy to recognize. At the center of a drupe is a single seed, which is surrounded by a hard pit; this, in turn, is covered by a thick, juicy layer. Peaches, cherries, and apricots are drupes.

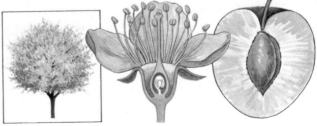

Two Oddities: Bamboo and Palm

A forest without trees sounds about as plausible as a city without buildings. Yet in warm, wet places, there are many treeless forests—populated by bamboo. These plants, with their hollow, jointed stems divided by watertight partitions, are more closely related to grasses than to trees.

Bamboo reproduces by means of sprouts sent up from underground stems called rhizomes (see below). Within months after new shoots appear, stands of bamboo reach their full height; in a single day, growth may be more than 3 feet! Unlike a tree, a bamboo grows only at the upper 2 feet of the vertical stem: from its sides, it produces a few small branchlets.

The flowering of a bamboo is amazing. Depending on species, the intervals may be 20 years or more. Madake, a common Japanese bamboo, is an extreme example—it blossoms only once every 120 years or so. Incredibly, all madake bamboo produce flowers at nearly the same time, no matter where in the world they may have been planted. The flowering is the "swan song" of the bamboo. After it blossoms, a bamboo stalk usually dies. Only the underground portion stays alive, capable of renewed growth.

Bamboo forests flourish not only in the tropics, but also in temperate zones. They spread rapidly and will quickly take over any available space. Such impassable thickets are natural sanctuaries for the giant panda of Asia.

Palms share some traits with bamboo. Although palms are classified as trees, they lack the branching habit and woody structure of ordinary trees. Like bamboo, a palm has only one growing point—a single bud at the center of the crown. This bud, which first appears at ground level, consists of tightly folded, cabbage-like leaves. Palm leaves unfurl close to the ground for several years. Then, as the plant develops, the bud is carried upward, concealed deep within the spiral of fronds. As long as the bud is intact, the palm tree will continue to grow. If it is removed or damaged, the whole tree dies.

The circulatory system of a palm is different from that of an ordinary tree. The transportation of water and nutrients is not confined to the outer part of the trunk, as in a pine or an oak; it takes place throughout its fibrous interior. When a palm is cut down, its stump shows none of the growth rings characteristic of other trees.

Palms have no bark. When fronds die and fall off, they leave successive scars, visible the full length of the trunk. These leaf scars protect the palm, just as bark does. But because a palm tree grows upward, rather than outward, this "skin" does not expand.

Palms yield two important foods: dates and coconuts. Date palms are remarkable for their capacity to prosper in dry regions where most other trees fail. In many parts of the world, date palms are grown near oases, and on land otherwise dependent on irrigation. By contrast, the coconut palm is almost the symbol of tropical coastlines (though it grows abundantly inland, as well). The world's largest fruit—the 40-pound coco-de-mer—is produced by a palm native to the Seychelles, islands in the Indian Ocean.

How Bamboo Shoots Develop

When a bamboo emerges, it reveals—right at the start—the full width that the adult plant will achieve. The shoot is the edible part of the plant. As the bamboo grows, the soft tissue of the shoot is replaced by a tough, jointed stem more suitable for furniture than for food.

Shoot

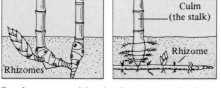

Rhizomes

Culm (the stalk)

Rhizome

Bamboo grows either in clumps or as single sprouts. The growth pattern shown at left results in clumps. The underground stem at right produces stalks that grow separately.

The quality of bamboo that makes it a useful and versatile building material—the extremely tough fibers in its stalks—creates hardships for anyone trying to cut a path through a bamboo thicket. Bamboo resists all but the strongest cutting tools. The floor of this Ugandan forest (right) is crisscrossed with fallen stalks, which create further problems for the hiker.

Coconut palms are great voyagers. These natives of the South Pacific have tough fruits that can float for as long as four months without damage. Thus currents explain their wide distribution—human beings have also provided transportation. Here, on a Polynesian beach, several young coconuts can be seen sprouting.

A single date palm bears thousands of dates (below). To begin with, there may be as many as 10,000 flowers in a single cluster. When a female tree flowers, it is pollinated by bees—and is often aided by date-growers, who place male flowers on the female tree to ensure productivity.

HIKING AND CAMPING
Palms Provide Food, Fluid, and Even Insect-Repellent

All palms (not just the coconut and date palms) are living storehouses for hikers and campers. The huge leaves provide material for both shelter and bedding. The hard mid-ribs of leaves make good kindling and also skewers for holding food over a fire. Many kinds of fiber-based products—from brooms to mats to ropes —can probably be made from some part of the leaves or the burlap-like fibers at the base of a leaf.
• Fluid and food can be had from most species. Palms are not only non-toxic to human beings, but nutritious as well. (Of course, some parts are too tough or dry to eat.) The soft, cabbage-like new leaves (when accessible) are the equivalent of a

salad—having both food and fluid value. If possible, take just the outer part of a bud, leaving the center intact. The sago palm of Africa and Asia has a soft, white pith that produces a flour after it has been pounded and kneaded with water.
• Coconuts, the most useful of all palms, sometimes present a difficulty: how to get through the tough husk? If you lack tools able to cut it, you can plant a sharp stake firmly in the ground. Then strike the nut against the stake, twisting it as you do so, to tear it into pieces.
• A mature coconut yields about a pint of clear, sweet, and sterile liquid; hence it is safe to drink without further ado. The nut-meat is jelly-like in its early development;

later the meat becomes firm and white. Either way, it is usually too rich for a steady diet. If beaten to a pulp, fluid can be extracted and mixed with other foods.
• Coconut oil is a good lotion to prevent sunburn, and an effective insect repellent. To extract it from the nut, boil small pieces in a container, then allow to cool. Skim the oil from the top and use as is. It is, of course, a staple cooking oil as well.
• Coconut shells can easily be made into utensils—pots, spoons, scrapers. To explore their uses, pick up nuts already on the ground; climbing a palm is much harder than it looks. Relaxing under a coconut palm can be hazardous—you can never tell when a nut or two will drop.

The Way a Tree Works

If you were to write a science fiction story, complete with incredible organisms, you would find it hard to invent anything more unlikely than a factual description of an ordinary tree. Trees can live for hundreds (sometimes thousands) of years—longer than any other living thing. They are able, annually, to launch millions of miniaturized offspring, each able to colonize a favorable location. Trees are able to live on nothing more than sunlight, air, and water (with a number of necessary minerals). But this hardly begins to tell how amazing trees are.

Trees have an elaborate body plan, adapted through eons of time. Only a small percentage of a mature trunk is actually alive. At its core is the heartwood, its cells filled with resin or similar materials. One might describe heartwood as dead, but inactive is a better word. Heartwood is often in a splendid state of preservation, and it performs a vital function: it provides a sturdy support that enables the tree to reach upward and catch the sunlight.

A tree is the most effective pump in the world. Silently and with no moving parts, it can transport an incredible amount of water. Even a sapling only a few feet high may move up to 10 gallons of water from the soil to its leaves in a day. A medium-size oak tree may pump 150 gallons a day to supply its needs—over half a ton of water.

How can trees raise water against the pull of gravity? Water tends to stick to most surfaces it touches. This characteristic causes it to "climb the walls" of hair-fine sapwood tubes in the trunk. Water molecules are also strongly attracted to one another. As a molecule of water evaporates from a leaf, another moves up the sapwood to take its place. It is followed by another, and so on. Thus the trunk acts as a natural pump, and its force is powerful enough to lift a column of water to the top of a 350-foot redwood.

Sapwood tubes eventually fill up. With use, they are plugged with resin and growth by-products, and become inactive heartwood. New tubes form in the thin growing layer, the cambium. Replacement occurs in the growing season (spring and summer in some regions, the rainy season in others). As long as a tree lives, it grows.

The growing layer also supplies cells to the outer layer, called the phloem. This layer carries sap throughout the

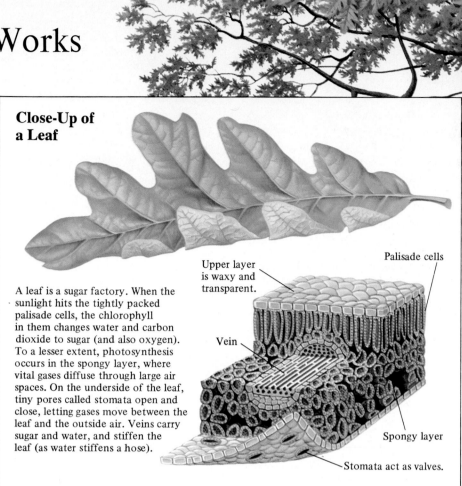

Close-Up of a Leaf

A leaf is a sugar factory. When the sunlight hits the tightly packed palisade cells, the chlorophyll in them changes water and carbon dioxide to sugar (and also oxygen). To a lesser extent, photosynthesis occurs in the spongy layer, where vital gases diffuse through large air spaces. On the underside of the leaf, tiny pores called stomata open and close, letting gases move between the leaf and the outside air. Veins carry sugar and water, and stiffen the leaf (as water stiffens a hose).

Upper layer is waxy and transparent.

Palisade cells

Vein

Spongy layer

Stomata act as valves.

tree, especially to the tips of branches (where new growth occurs) and to the roots. Sap is a sugary juice that supplies all living parts of the tree with food. Surplus food is usually stored in the roots. This reserve will carry the tree through its dormant period of winter or seasonal drought.

Tree roots are remarkable. Tiny root tips can penetrate soil so rocky and resistant it hardly seems possible. The ability of roots to detect and grow toward water is a recurrent feat we take for granted. But the mystery remains: how do roots know where to go? When they do find water, roots extract it through their delicate hairs and pump it up through the trunk to the leaves.

The word that describes the capture and use of the sun's energy by trees and other green plants is photosynthesis. The site of capture is the leaves, in cells with green chlorophyll. Here, with water and carbon dioxide, the plant produces energy-rich sugar, which fuels its life processes and growth. (Scientists know a great deal about this process but have never been able to duplicate it in the laboratory.) A by-product of photosynthesis is oxygen. It is upon this oxygen supply that life depends.

There are three kinds of roots: taproots, lateral roots, and feeder roots. The mighty taproot, which goes straight down, is an anchor for the tree. Not all trees have them. Trees in rain forests, which rise to heights of 120 feet or more, lack taproots; often these trees are supported by buttresses—thick structures above the ground. Lateral roots, which extend outward from the trunk and taproot, are usually close to the surface. They supply some or all of the bracing for the tree, and also absorb oxygen. Intricately branched feeder roots (at the ends of the laterals) take in water and dissolved minerals through microscopic hairs near their tips. Roots can function at a lower temperature than any other part of the tree. Thus it is in the roots that spring really begins.

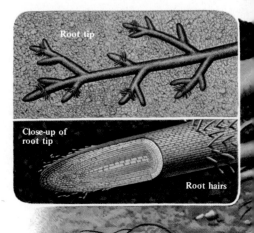

Root tip

Close-up of root tip

Root hairs

Make a Mental Map

You should carry a compass and know how to use it when hiking; but you can also sharpen your own perceptions:
• To avoid walking in circles (which we tend to do because most people take longer strides with one leg than the other), take a sighting. That is, visually line up three or more landmarks (conspicuous trees or rocks). As you reach one point, choose another.
• If you want to return the way you came, look back often; the same section of trail looks different when seen from the opposite direction. Afternoon shadows fall differently from those of morning. Mark turns in the trail with rocks.
• Listen for distinctive sounds—rushing water, noises from cattle, church bells, train whistles. Scents, too, can be a guide—pine forests, meadow flowers, ocean breezes.
• Trees sometimes tell direction. Trees growing in the open may have more leaves on the southern side in the northern hemisphere (the northern side in the southern hemisphere). Green "mosses" (which are really algae) tend to grow on the side of a tree away from the equator.

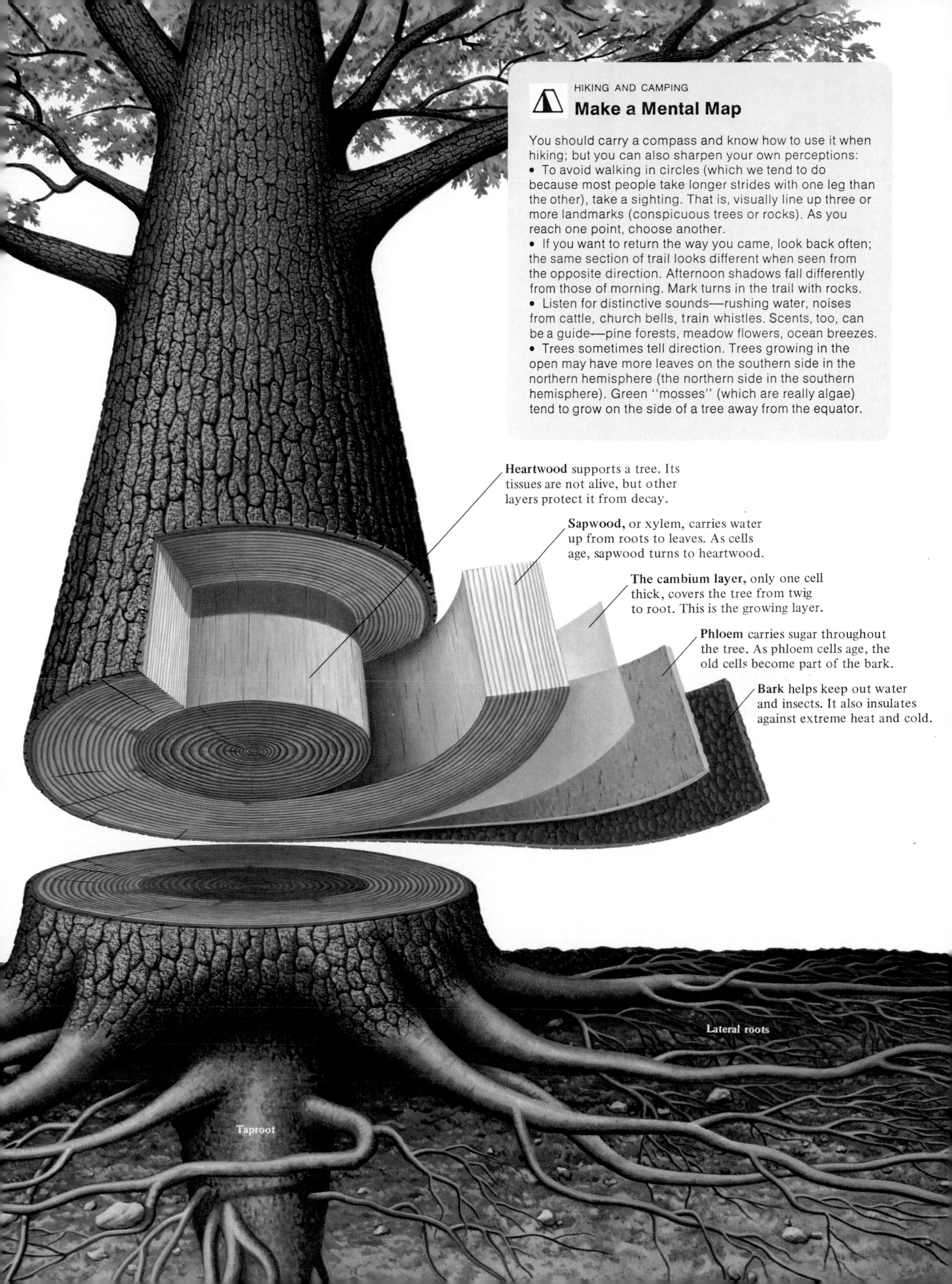

Heartwood supports a tree. Its tissues are not alive, but other layers protect it from decay.

Sapwood, or xylem, carries water up from roots to leaves. As cells age, sapwood turns to heartwood.

The cambium layer, only one cell thick, covers the tree from twig to root. This is the growing layer.

Phloem carries sugar throughout the tree. As phloem cells age, the old cells become part of the bark.

Bark helps keep out water and insects. It also insulates against extreme heat and cold.

Lateral roots

Taproot

Bark: A Tree's Protective Skin

Like human skin, the bark of a tree is a barrier that protects against any invading diseases. And like skin, bark breathes, regulates the escaping of moisture from within, and has the capacity to repair itself. However, while human skin constantly wears off and is replaced, the bark of a tree often accumulates to a great depth.

Growth in the trunk and twigs of a tree originates in a remarkable layer called the cambium. But unlike human skin, with which it is often compared, the cambium layer grows in two directions. The inner side of the cambium adds to the girth of the tree (woody tissue), and the outer side eventually adds to the bark (also called cork). This may be hard for us to grasp because our conception of skin is geared to the kind we have ourselves, which replaces itself (human skin has no part in the building of the inner tissues of the body such as muscles).

The cambium is only one cell thick —a fact that becomes amazing when you consider the cambium's many feats. Cells reproduce by splitting. In this growth process, a cambium cell will contribute a daughter cell to one side or the other (either to the inner part that will become heartwood, or to the outer part that will eventually become bark). But before they reach these stages, the daughter cells perform activities that are essential to the tree.

For a time, the cells developed by the cambium serve as the circulatory system for the whole plant. The inner layer (the sapwood or xylem) transports water from the roots to the leaves; the outer layer (the phloem) circulates the sap—the nutrient-rich products of photosynthesis that enable a tree to grow. It is this organization of layers that allows sap to be "harvested" without damaging the tree. The skillful tapping of a tree depends on carefully preserving the essential growing layer (the cambium). This is often done, and entire industries depend on it—the rubber industry, for one.

A homey example of the difference between human skin and bark is in the adolescent child who, while growing, may split a clothing seam. The gradual expansion of human skin can only be detected under a microscope. But trees do split their seams, quite literally. The ridges and striations on a tree are from the pressures of growth, which usually affect only the dead portions of the bark. The patterns of growth—stretch marks or furrows—are special characteristics of individual species, and are often used in identification.

Appreciating the Variety of Texture in Bark

Bark grows from the inside outward. What we see is the dead tissue that has been displaced by new growth underneath the bark. This growth process produces the different textures and patterns of bark—ridges, flat plates, and deep furrows—that characterize each kind of tree. Knowing the various types of bark helps in tree identification, especially in winter.

The satiny red-brown bark of the pin cherry is marked by long, horizontal pores (lenticels), through which the tree breathes in winter.

Peeling layers of chalky white bark split and curl on the trunk of a mature paper birch. The young tree (left) will turn white with age.

Deep furrows form ridges in the bark of some species of maple and oak. (Ash trees, too, are heavily ridged, in an unusual diamond pattern.)

Shagbark hickory is a perfect description for this member of the walnut family. The thin, splintery plates curl outward at the ends.

The Surprising Bounty from Bark and Sap

Trees have a remarkable ability to repair damage and compensate for losses. It is this characteristic that allows man to make use of trees on a continuing basis, tapping a variety of trees for their fluids and bark. Today, of course, man-made products have replaced many substances that were extracted from trees in times past.

One of the most delicious tree products is maple sugar, made from the sap of the sugar maple. This sap rises in the trees during late winter and early spring. The best "runs" take place when nights are cold and days warm: a tree may yield a hundred drops a minute under these conditions. Though this rate is impressive, it makes "maple-sugaring" sound easier than it really is—the liquid is so watery that some 40 gallons of sap must be boiled down to make one gallon of syrup.

Sap refers to a specific substance—the sugary liquid that flows through certain plant tissues (phloem). Not all liquids made by a tree are really sap. The latex that drips from cuts in rubber trees is believed to be a protective substance, similar to the milky fluid that oozes from other wounded plants. An individual rubber tree can be tapped for a period of more than 20 years. But between tappings, the tree requires a rest period; trees on some plantations are tapped every other day.

Cork comes from the cork oak, a tree native to the Mediterranean regions of Europe and Africa. The cells in its bark are filled with air, making it a good insulating material. In harvesting cork, the bark is carefully peeled off; to avoid permanent damage to the tree, this is done only about once every 10 years.

Cinnamon, the fragrant spice from India and Sri Lanka (Ceylon), is obtained from the bark of certain trees in the laurel family. Because the most productive bark grows on the twigs, trees are continuously pruned to stimulate twig growth. Quinine, used in treating malaria, is a bark product (from a South American tree); the active ingredient in aspirin formerly came from willow bark.

A worker harvests latex from a rubber tree in Liberia. This liquid oozes from a recent cut into a cup; as the cut heals, another diagonal slice is made near it.

Sharp, three-branched spines sprout on the trunk of a honey locust. They develop from deep buds; leaves may grow at their bases.

Spiraling scars left by the successive rows of leaves give the tropical pandanus its name of screw pine. Palm bark also shows leaf scars.

NATURE OBSERVER
Reading Bark Marks

Many wild mammals are secretive and elusive. So when you're walking in the woods, look for *signs* of the animals: some species leave characteristic marks in the bark of trees, usually while they are in the process of obtaining food.

When a beaver fells and carries off a tree, a pointed stump is left behind; this has wide grooves made by the animal's teeth.

Bears strip the bark from trees, then scrape off and eat the juicy pulp. They leave claw and tooth marks on the trees.

For winter food, porcupines gnaw large patches of bark. The resulting scars have smooth edges and many small tooth marks.

Deer use the bark of young trees as an emergency food supply, tearing it off with upward movements of their teeth.

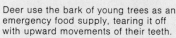

A cougar sharpens its claws by scratching on a tree. The scratches may signal the presence of one cougar to another.

The Autobiography of a Tree

Every tree keeps a permanent diary of its growth, recording the passage of the years, droughts, temperature changes, and even the death of neighboring plants. This history lies in the rings of wood added each year.

A ring of new wood is laid down just beneath the bark in the growing season. In temperate regions, there is only one period of growth (during the spring and summer months). Thus every ring represents one year in the life of the tree, and the total number of rings gives its age.

Normally, the annual rings are visible only after a tree has been cut down. Fortunately for trees, scientists have developed techniques for counting the rings while the trees are still alive and growing (see far right).

A tree may "lie" about its age. If cut near the top, it reveals only the number of years since it reached that particular height. To tell the true age of a tree, the annual rings must be counted on a section near the ground. Even then, the age may only be an approximation. A short period of drought during a growing season may create an extra, "false" ring that makes a tree look older than it really is.

Look at the rings on a tree stump, using a hand lens. Some kinds of trees, such as oaks and elms, actually have *two* distinct layers within each annual ring. The inner layer, known as early or spring wood, is laid down at the beginning of the growing season. Early wood is soft and light-colored; its cell walls—the microscopic structures that give wood its characteristic hardness—are very thin. Late (or summer) wood, which has thicker cell walls, is harder, darker, and more compact. Wood made at the very end of the season forms a narrow, dark band.

The more wood laid down in a year, the wider that particular annual ring. Thus a broad ring reflects favorable growing conditions, such as warm temperatures and adequate rainfall. A drought or insect infestation means narrow rings. Annual rings are rarely perfect circles, because different sides of a tree do not always grow at precisely the same rate.

The most interesting annual rings develop on trees in areas where growing conditions are most limiting. Bristlecone pines, for example, are found only in arid mountain regions where rainfall is never abundant; even minor fluctuations are reflected in their growth rings. These patterns offer scientists a precise measure of climatic conditions. (By contrast, trees in the tropics, where growing conditions are more stable, may show little variation from one year to the next.)

NATURE OBSERVER
What a Twig Reveals About a Tree

Only in winter, when trees are leafless, can the beauty and variety of their twigs be appreciated. Examining a twig will tell you something about a tree's history. Closely spaced rings mark the end of each year's growth; the farther apart they are, the more the twig grew that year. Twigs also help to identify a tree. Buds on the twig, which contain tiny leaves or flowers, are especially useful. Beech buds look like inch-long spears; flowering dogwood has onion-shaped buds. The labels below and at right point out other structures; the twig shown is from a Norway maple.

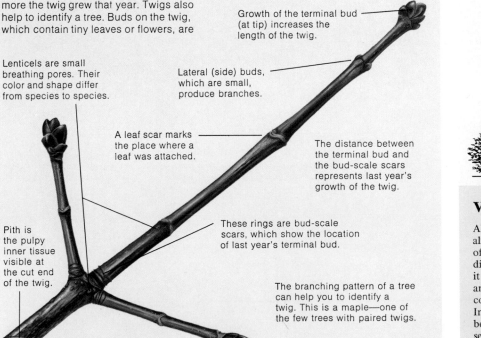

Growth of the terminal bud (at tip) increases the length of the twig.

Lenticels are small breathing pores. Their color and shape differ from species to species.

Lateral (side) buds, which are small, produce branches.

A leaf scar marks the place where a leaf was attached.

The distance between the terminal bud and the bud-scale scars represents last year's growth of the twig.

Pith is the pulpy inner tissue visible at the cut end of the twig.

These rings are bud-scale scars, which show the location of last year's terminal bud.

The branching pattern of a tree can help you to identify a twig. This is a maple—one of the few trees with paired twigs.

Characteristic Sizes and Shapes

Each kind of tree has a distinctive growth pattern, though no two trees of a species are ever identical. The ones shown here are classic examples of trees that have adhered to their inherent pattern of growth. Trees of the same type also have similar life-spans—yews are long-lived, poplars are not.

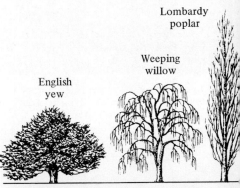

Lombardy poplar

Weeping willow

English yew

Variability Within a Species

Although the vigor of an individual plant is always a factor in its development, the quality of its growing conditions can make a great difference in how large and how quickly it grows. The influence of sunlight, moisture, and richness of soil can best be seen by comparing trees of the same age and species. In a study of 100-year-old redwoods, the best sites yielded trees about 240 feet tall; second-best sites had trees 220 feet tall; but the average height was 100 feet or less.

In the case of the bristlecone pines, which are the world's oldest trees, the history shown in their rings goes back more than 4,000 years. Trees alive today were saplings when Nero burned Rome (in A.D. 64) and in the year 800, when Charlemagne became emperor. The fascinating aspect of such records is the constant revision they must undergo as more tree-ring data comes to light. Comparison of irregular growth patterns in tree rings relates not just to human history but to the history of climatic conditions on earth. Fossil trees extend records even more.

Today, logs are occasionally taken into court, and their annual rings used as testimony. Because surveyors often mark trees with ax-cuts when land is purchased, such cuts can be used to establish the year that a survey was made. Such information may settle a dispute concerning the title transfer.

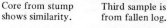

Core sample shows growth rings.

A Record of Growing Conditions in the Past

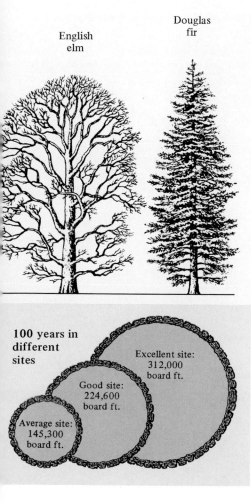

English elm

Douglas fir

100 years in different sites

Excellent site: 312,000 board ft.

Good site: 224,600 board ft.

Average site: 145,300 board ft.

A tree keeps a record of its growing conditions in annual rings, but the information is not only about the general environment. A tree also records incidents in its own life. In this cross-section, past weather conditions may be observed. So, too, can particular events that make this tree's life unique. Four major incidents are identified on the stump, and also in the story below. How is it possible to reconcile the two records—the general climatic conditions and the events that touched one tree? Samples taken from other trees in the same region help scientists draw conclusions.

Comparing Growth-Ring Patterns

Core is taken out with a boring tool.

Core from stump shows similarity.

Third sample is from fallen log.

Slim columns, called cores, are taken from several trees. When the cores are laid side by side, it is often possible to match patterns. One tree of known age leads to data on nearby trees.

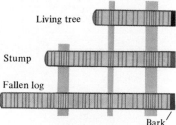

Living tree

Stump

Fallen log

Bark

1. In the cross-section (at top), a few major events in the life of a tree have been numbered. When this tree was a sapling, it was knocked to one side by another tree. The young tree bent, but it survived. It grew vigorously, and as the old tree decayed, the sapling resumed its upright growth.

2. Later, a forest fire damaged the bark and growing layer on one side of the tree; but years of growth healed the wound, eventually covering it.

3. The tree's growth-rate leaped when the forest was thinned out, and it was no longer deprived of sunlight.

4. Thin rings often indicate a long period of drought. But here, a road-cut damaged the root system on one side, and produced a similar effect. This shows how the "evidence" in rings can be interpreted in more than one way. A single tree reveals only part of the history of regional climate.

Where Forest Meets Meadow

The edge of a forest is a transition zone between two communities. On one side is the forest itself; on the other, a field, meadow, or marshy area. Each community has characteristic plants and animals, and the forest edge is the crossroads for wildlife from the two neighboring worlds. Forest-dwellers venture forth into sunnier regions to feed, and meadow animals seek food, shade, and hiding places. So a forest edge is richer in animal life than the areas on either side. It has not only its own residents, but also visitors.

A barrier to hikers, a forest edge is often a dense tangle of blackberry vines, hawthorn trees, hazel shrubs, and bracken ferns. The plants that grow here need more sunlight than those inside a forest, but less than meadow plants. Their water requirements are generally intermediate, too—less than a forest, more than a meadow.

Berry-laden brambles are a rich food source for fruit-loving animals. Such thorny plants also provide excellent cover—animals take refuge among the thorns. A nest in a thorny shrub is far safer than one in the open.

The cluttered look of a forest edge masks the structure of the forest interior. But if you know what to look for, you will be able to see—even at the forest edge—distinctive zones of life. Holes in the ground mark the entrances of nests and dens in the subterranean layer. The ground layer is covered with plant litter and populated with insects; ground-nesting birds and those that feed on the ground can be seen during the day. Because most small mammals such as mice are nocturnal, they are seldom seen.

The shrub layer, with its berry- and nut-bearing plants, often has the most animal traffic of any forest layer. Above the shrub layer, there is a region called the understory. It is relatively dark because it is shaded by the top layer, or canopy. More birds nest in the understory than in any other layer.

It is relatively easy to spot a chipmunk or a chickadee in a forest edge. However, if you want to see other, more timid animals, you will probably have to sit quietly for a while and wait.

The works of modern man have increased the areas covered by forest edges. Every clearing for a farm created four edges. Whenever a road penetrates a forest, each side of the road becomes a forest edge. Thus there is more space today for animals that flourish in such places. For example, the robin of North America is more numerous now than before European colonists arrived.

Hedgerows, which separate cultivated fields in many places in the world, have plants and animals similar to those of the forest edge. So hedgerows might be thought of as forest edges that do not have forests adjacent to them.

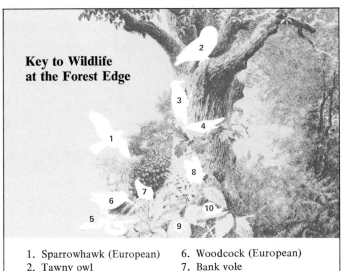

Key to Wildlife at the Forest Edge

1. Sparrowhawk (European)
2. Tawny owl
3. Green woodpecker
4. Wood warbler
5. Barred grass snake
6. Woodcock (European)
7. Bank vole
8. Red admiral butterfly
9. Seven-spot ladybird beetle
10. Banded snail

An old oak in a British woodland provides a home for a tawny owl, which drowses during the day in its branches. For other animals— passers-by or residents—the oak is part of the "edge" habitat. A green woodpecker drills for insects in the bark of the tree. A subtly colored wood warbler nests on the ground, but comes up to feed, while a red admiral butterfly pauses briefly on a blackberry. A banded snail, crawling slowly across a leaf, may fall prey to a bird or even a beetle. Grass snakes are common at the forest edge and often come out to bask in the sun. Russet feathers are an effective camouflage for a woodcock, as it hunts among the fallen leaves and grasses. A bank vole scurries under nearby bushes, hiding from a passing sparrowhawk.

Watching a Spider Build Its Web

Most spiders build webs of some type to catch prey (a few do not—they pounce on a victim, or build a trap). Of all spinners and weavers, the orb-web spider, shown below, is the easiest to watch at work. Its webs are often visible at a forest edge, where they may be backlit. Webs are made of a silk-like liquid substance, which the spider draws from its undersides, using its hind legs. The strands are pure protein, which the spider can recycle; when a line is no longer needed, the spider eats the silk. The strength of silk is shown by the drops it supports, as in the photo, right.

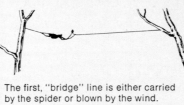

The first, "bridge" line is either carried by the spider or blown by the wind.

From the midpoint of the bridge, the spider establishes a third anchor.

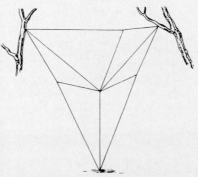

As the spider goes back and forth, it adds spokes and reinforces boundaries.

This close-up of the web shows two different spirals. The inner one, with widely spaced strands, is laid down first. The second, outer spiral has a special adhesive quality, and turns in the opposite direction. As the outer spiral is spun, the inner one is eaten.

From any point on the finished web the spider feels the slightest touch of an insect, and quickly pounces on it.

The Ever-Changing Forest

Suppose you were to plan a picnic in the country, choosing to go to a picturesque abandoned farm you remember from the recent past. On arrival, you will more than likely be startled by the tall weeds, sprawling shrubs, and even trees that have taken over the uncultivated fields.

What you are witnessing at such a moment is the phenomenon called succession—a predictable series of changes. Such changes occur in a forest that has been cut down or been ravaged by fire. There, the bare soil is an open invitation to new plant life.

From roots and seeds already in the ground, and from seeds carried by winds or wildlife, pioneer plants sprout, and soon occupy untended fields. Crabgrass and fireweed are often pioneers. Such plants have seeds that germinate quickly, and all of them can survive drying winds. Characteristically, these early plants thrive in strong sunlight.

By providing shade and protection, pioneer plants change the growing conditions near the ground. Their presence creates a more hospitable world for other kinds of plants that are not able to survive in bare, sun-baked soil. This is the ironic aspect in any story of plant succession: as pioneer plants grow, they make conditions worse for themselves, and better for other species that follow them. Newcomers such as asters and broomsedge shade out the pioneers. Later, young trees sprout. Fast-growing, sun-loving species appear first. Pines are early trees in the northeastern United States; birch, rowan, and hazel in Britain.

As the forest matures, some further changes take place. Pine seedlings do not grow well in dense shade beneath larger trees. Also, the older pines take up most of the water near the soil surface. The young trees that do best at this stage are shade-tolerant species, such as oaks and hickories. Their roots grow below the roots of the big pines and bring water from deep in the soil. When a pine dies, more sunlight reaches the saplings of oaks and hickories, and their growth rate speeds up. The pines, now at a disadvantage in the competition, do not reproduce as well and are gradually replaced. After about 150 years, an oak-hickory forest grows where pioneer plants once grew.

The final, climax stage of succession over much of the southeastern United States is an oak-hickory forest. Beech, maple, oak, hemlock, larch, and birch populate forests farther north. On other continents, in cold regions, and in the tropics, the species that make up a climax forest are different from those in the temperate zones of North America, but the principles are the same.

A climax stage lasts for centuries. Thus, in theory, there is no limit to the life-span of a climax forest, only the minor, constant replacement of dead trees. But such forests may be destroyed by a lightning-sparked fire, by flooding when a river changes course, or, more commonly, by the activities of man.

People affect succession in many ways. We keep millions of acres of land in the pioneer stage called a lawn. To grow desired species of trees quickly, foresters plant seedlings on open land. The resulting tree plantation is a crop, not a true forest. In both instances, human efforts prevent the natural succession to a climax forest.

How Tree Farms Differ from Wild Woodlands

Tree plantings can be considered crops in the same way as fields of wheat. But because trees grow slowly, compared with ordinary crops, people fail to see the essential similarity of these two forms of agriculture. Like a food crop, a tree farm is controlled throughout its life. Often, the land is prepared by clearing; then it is planted, tended, and eventually harvested. Fast-growing species such as pines and larches (above) are suitable for commercial use. A 30-year-old pine plantation (below) shows the orderly look of such a farm. Hikers are often welcome to visit, but there is less diversity of animal life than in a wild forest.

As Habitats Change, So Do the Bird Populations

The place to find birds is at natural feeding stations where they congregate. In the meadow stage of plant succession, seed- and insect-eating birds find plenty of food among the grasses and other flowering plants. As shrubs spring up, berry-eating birds such as thrashers take over. When pines succeed shrubs, nuthatches and brown creepers search the trunks for insects. In a climax forest, large, broad-leaved trees with dense foliage offer insect food and nesting sites for many species. There is a further change in bird populations with the coming of winter (insects die off, and the birds that depend on them migrate elsewhere).

Succession from Meadow to Forest in the Northeastern Part of North America

Meadow and Shrub

Most meadow birds nest on the ground or in low, tangled vegetation. Such birds are often protected from enemies by their plumage; mottled patterns and colors provide camouflage.

Pine Forest

Lacking dense undergrowth, stands of pines do not attract many birds. The crossbill is able to extract seeds from cones. Warblers may nest in pines, and owls may occupy old crows' nests.

Climax Forest

Among the many birds that nest in a deciduous forest are the scarlet tanager, the shy ovenbird (which is a ground-dwelling warbler), and the strikingly marked pileated woodpecker.

Meadowlark

Field sparrow

Brown thrasher

Red crossbill

Black-throated green warbler

Long-eared owl

Scarlet tanager

Ovenbird

Pileated woodpecker

A Closer Look at the Forest Floor

On your next walk through a forest, look down and give a thought to the living world at your feet. Although little sunlight filters down to this level, a carpet of small and exquisite plants covers the forest floor. A few, such as trilliums, trout lilies, wood anemones, may be wildflowers, but most of them have no flowers at all.

This is where mosses thrive—especially if the woodland is damp much of the year. Water is essential for the reproduction of mosses and many other non-flowering plants. As part of their life cycle, reproductive cells must "swim" to join other individuals of their species. The stems of mosses are sponge-like reservoirs that conserve water and foster reproduction. So mosses are hardy plants, able to withstand drought for considerable periods of time. When the rains come again, mosses resume growth and are once

A Patchwork of Plants

Mosses and lichens carpet the waterlogged soil of an evergreen forest. A decaying branch sprouts tiny umbrella-shaped fungi. Although flower-bearing plants are rare under conifers, the queen-cup, a low-growing lily, brightens this early summer scene.

1. Wintergreen	4. Lichen
2. Queen-cup	5. Gilled fungus
3. Cushion moss	6. Haircap moss

again springy under the visitor's feet.

Mingled with the mosses are ferns, fungi, and lichens. Ferns are a highly diversified group. Some climb like vines; others, such as staghorn ferns and polypody, grow perched on rock ledges, stumps, or tree trunks. Most ferns native to a temperate forest lose all their leaves in autumn—but polypody and Christmas ferns keep their shiny green fronds throughout the year.

The part of a fungus that you see above ground—which most people call mushrooms or toadstools—is always short-lived. By contrast, lichens endure for years. A lichen is actually an alliance between two different plants, an alga and a fungus. The forms that lichens take are as varied as any in the plant kingdom: in some instances, they look like smudges of paint on a rock; in other cases, they look rather like an olive-green salad.

The low-growing plants in one forest may be dramatically different from their counterparts nearby; it all depends on what trees shelter them. Coniferous forests have a sparse population of ground plants and shrubs because the cushion of fallen needles makes the soil acid. The crunchy litter in a broad-leaved forest is more hospitable to plants, and so this kind of forest is more likely to have thick undergrowth.

Litter is a forest's security blanket. It protects the soil from successive thawing and refreezing in winter, and acts as a mulch that prevents the ground from becoming parched by the sun. Eventually litter becomes part of the topsoil, which fosters plant growth.

No matter what the season for your forest walk, there's something to be seen. It's worth taking along a magnifying lens and exploring carefully, perhaps even on your hands and knees.

How to Look at a Fern

The "fruit dots" on the underside of this fern are clusters of spores.

Diminutive World of Moss and Lichen

Bristling like a miniature pine, a stalk of haircap moss is surrounded by pixie cups. These bluish-green lichens are often found in the company of another type of lichen, called British soldiers (in honor of the bright red reproductive caps on their inch-high stalks). When you find one of these lichens, look for the other. Such associations of plants are undoubtedly based on the growing conditions, but they seem mysterious nevertheless.

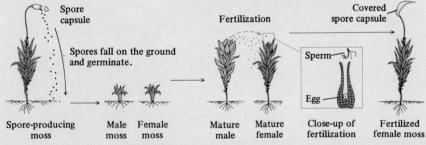

Spore capsule

Spores fall on the ground and germinate.

Fertilization

Covered spore capsule

Sperm

Egg

| Spore-producing moss | Male moss | Female moss | Mature male | Mature female | Close-up of fertilization | Fertilized female moss |

The spores from a haircap moss grow into separate male (sperm-producing) and female (egg-producing) plants. A sperm swims to a nearby egg (at the top of the female moss), and fertilization takes place. The fertilized female plant then grows a stalk, which is topped with a spore-bearing capsule. When the spores are released, a new cycle begins.

Ferns and mosses are often grouped together because they have much in common, including habitat and method of reproduction. But ferns have characteristics uniquely their own. New leaves of some types of ferns are called fiddleheads and uncurl from soft, downy protective scales in the spring. Ferns have leaf forms that range from very feathery to coarse and undivided; such patterns are an important means of identifying the different kinds. Although the leaves of ferns are usually green, those of certain species have a bluish tint, others are very dark, and some even turn a bronze color in the autumn. Another way of identifying ferns is by the location of their spores. The polypody above has spores on the undersides of its leaves; some other species have separate spore-bearing leaves.

Magical, Mythical Mushrooms

Awareness of the curious properties of mushrooms—the widely used name for the fungi—goes back to antiquity. There are Biblical references to these strange plants, and they were also known and eaten by ancient Greeks, Romans, and Chinese. Although many are edible and delicious, a fair number are poisonous.

Some species of mushrooms have a powerful effect on the human mind—they cause hallucinations. Small wonder, then, that superstitions have grown up around them, and not a little fear. Among some Indians of Mexico and Central America, hallucinogenic fungi are part of religious ritual.

In the English language, the word toadstool is often used to identify poisonous fungi. The name was apparently applied because toads were believed to be poisonous; and because fungi appeared in the same sort of damp, dark places, it was a case of guilt by association. However, the distinction between toadstools and mushrooms is not a scientific one, and more important, gives no assurance that the particular specimen will not cause illness or even death.

Fungi were thought to be magical because of their unusual, often bizarre shapes, and also the fact that they seemed to materialize out of nowhere. As you may have observed on your own lawn, mushrooms often pop up within hours after a rain. It is easy to see why primitive peoples believed mushrooms were a result of lightning.

The main part of the fungus lies under the ground. The mycelium, as this part is called, performs all the functions normally carried out by the roots, stem, and leaves of other plants. The white, web-like mycelium (which you occasionally see when you pick up a layer of decaying leaves or bark) has no chlorophyll, which means it cannot make its own food. As it grows through the soil, the mycelium absorbs water and nutrients present there. "Nutrients" in this case usually means material from dead plants and animals.

To bear fruit, a mycelium needs plenty of food and moisture. Typically, a button-like bud forms and pushes its way upward through the soil. Even though it is mostly water, the emerging mushroom is strong enough to break through the cracks in a sidewalk. As it quickly grows, the button rises on a stem and then unfolds like an umbrella.

On the underside of the umbrella are tissues, called gills, that release millions of microscopic spores. A tiny fraction of these spores will land where growing conditions are favorable, and a new fungus will become established. Often these plants will radiate in an ever-widening pattern, producing the circular "fairy ring" that figures in folklore. Some fairy rings have reached the amazing age of 600 years.

Mushrooms vary greatly in size, shape, color, and toxicity. Some are tiny, but one Australian specimen measured more than 5 feet in circumference and weighed 17 pounds. "Bird's-nest" fungi resemble their namesake, complete with egg-like spore sacs; puffballs are spherical, and give off a cloud of spores when tapped. Some are luminescent—the gills of the jack-o'-lantern glow greenish-white, and the honey mushroom gives off blue "fox fire."

Unfortunately, there are no clear signs to guide inexperienced mushroom hunters as to the safety of unfamiliar species. Some "edible" mushrooms become poisonous with age. Others are toxic only to certain people. Still others are harmful only if eaten day after day.

The only mushroom hunter that never seems to make a mistake in the quest for wild species is the pig that is trained by the French to root out truffles, a delicious mushroom that grows completely under the ground. A truffle-hunting pig may even be seen riding to "work," comfortably settled in its owner's wheelbarrow.

Oyster mushrooms, which may measure more than 5 inches across, grow in clusters on dead tree trunks and branches. Note the fluted gills.

A Mushroom Is the Fruiting Body of a Subterranean Plant

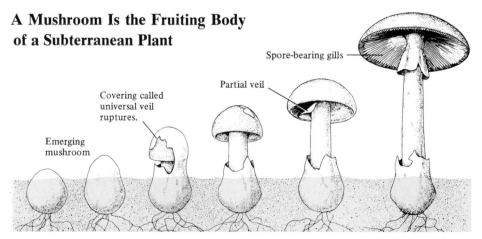

Spore-bearing gills

Partial veil

Covering called universal veil ruptures.

Emerging mushroom

The growth of the deadly amanita mushroom resembles the hatching of an egg. Initially, a membrane called the universal veil covers the mushroom. As the amanita increases in size and pushes its way up through the surface of the soil, the universal veil ruptures; the stalk and the cap are exposed. Another membrane, called the partial veil, gives extra protection to the gills on the underside of the cap. This veil also ruptures as the mushroom matures.

Both the toad and the toadstool shown above are toxic. Identifying poisonous mushrooms is difficult—this kind of amanita is yellow in Wisconsin but may be white or blood-red elsewhere.

A rainy-weather species that appears on lawns and pastures, these mushrooms belong to a group named Leucoagaricus (white agaric).

Scarlet cups are heralds of spring. These inch-wide mushrooms, which thrive on fallen logs, appear much earlier than most other species.

Two Flowering Plants That Live Like Fungi

Some flowering plants, such as Indian pipes and snow plants, are frequently mistaken for mushrooms. These curious species have no chlorophyll—the green substance necessary for photosynthesis. Recently, scientists have discovered evidence that certain of these plants actually obtain their nutrients from mushrooms nearby. The mushrooms, in turn, extract nutrients from decaying material or the roots of other plants.

Look for ghostly Indian pipes in North America throughout the summer. The "bowl" on each pipe is the flowering part of the plant; there are no leaves.

In the high Sierras, snow plants push up through a carpet of pine needles in early spring. The red scales are really modified leaves; the tiny blossoms are also red.

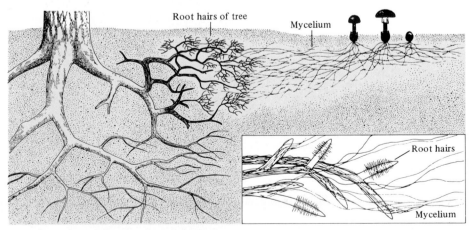

Root hairs of tree

Mycelium

Root hairs

Mycelium

A hidden but important part of any mushroom is its mycelium—the network of filaments that spreads through the soil, absorbing water and nutrients as it grows. Certain mycelia form a joint network with the root hairs of trees or other plants. This merger allows a mushroom to "tap" a tree for its nutrients, since the mushroom cannot make its own food. This does not seem to harm the tree—in fact, some trees do poorly if no mushrooms are present.

A Fallen Log Is Full of Life

The Townsend chipmunk is a ground squirrel.

A scarab beetle eats bits of fungi growing on a log.

The ceanothus silk-moth lives only on the Pacific coast.

The red-breasted nuthatch breeds in evergreen forests.

Sword fern

When an old tree falls, human beings are likely to see only the death of something beautiful, and not recognize that this event is part of a continuing cycle. During its lifetime, the tree collected and retained many materials from its environment. The energy from the sun, water, and minerals extracted from the soil were all converted into the substances that form wood, leaves, and sap. When the tree dies, all the nutrients that were locked in the tree become available again.

Bark kept out many insect invaders and disease organisms during the tree's lifetime. But now there are no more defenses; the hard, dry bark that protected the interior of the tree becomes loosened—perhaps by dampness, fire, or wind injury. Many animals and plants arrive, taking advantage of the opportunity. The succession of invaders is not haphazard. The first to arrive are pioneers such as fungi and wood-boring beetles and termites. The tunnels and egg-chambers made by insects serve as channels by which water, bacteria, and other species of insects may enter. Occasionally, the tunnels carved by young beetles can be seen as delicate "engravings" on the bare surface of the wood.

The log is gradually softened as the structure becomes a source of food and shelter for increasing numbers. Snails and insect larvae eat fungi and bits of log; each new wave of creatures attracts a new set of predators. With constant wear and tear, the entry points are expanded until the cavities are large enough to accommodate such animals as birds and snakes. Hollow logs are commonly used by raccoons for nests.

Even before a tree falls, shelf (or bracket) fungi may appear. Once the tree is down, it may support these and many other species of fungi. Mosses, too, flourish on and around a fallen log, especially in damp environments. In time, the edifice is so hollowed out and weakened that it collapses gently, merging with the soil around it. This rich mound of humus encourages growth of ferns and wildflowers.

The rate of decomposition of trees varies according to species—some have more porous fibers than others, and so are "dismantled" more quickly. And, of course, a big tree lasts longer than a small one. Temperature and moisture also play a role. Fallen trees in hot, wet places "disappear" more rapidly than their counterparts in cold regions.

The Oregon salamander hides in logs during cold or drought.

The large green slug lays its eggs under a damp log.

The western junco eats seeds, and nests on the ground.

The Elusive Animals That Visit or Colonize Logs

A fallen log is attractive to wildlife because it provides shelter (including nest sites) and food for a variety of species. In fact, as time passes, a food chain becomes established in and around the log. Insects that feed on the wood attract nuthatches and other insect eaters; these animals, in turn, encourage owls and other predators to visit the log. The illustration above depicts some of the wildlife that might be found near a decaying log in one particular region—a Douglas fir forest on the Pacific coast of North America. (Of course, all of these creatures would never be in the same place at the same time.) When you come upon a fallen log, don't be disappointed if it looks more like the one in the photo at right, which shows a decaying tree in an Australian rain forest. Logs and stumps only appear to be lifeless—most of their residents are insects or other small animals, visible only if you poke the log or remove bits of loose bark with a stick. If you sit motionless near a fallen log, larger animals may come to visit, especially if the tree has been on the ground for a long time.

Unlike most of its relatives, the 7-inch pygmy owl sometimes hunts during the day, sometimes at night.

False Solomon's seal

Oregon grape

Douglas fir seedling

The spotted skunk extracts insects from decaying logs; it also preys on rodents.

Queen-cup

The chickaree is a noisy, seed-eating squirrel.

Less than a quarter-inch long, an engraver beetle eats its way through the wood, hastening decay.

Although carpenter ants tunnel in logs, they do not eat wood; they feed on other insects.

Centipedes, which often live under loose bark, prey upon insects and other small animals.

Cave (or camel) crickets eat just about anything, including rotting wood. They prefer dark places.

HOW TO
Build and Use a Compost Heap

Nature constantly recycles material. In building a compost heap, you are simply putting nature to work on your own behalf.
• Choose a relatively sunlit place where the compost heap will be inconspicuous. A space about 4 feet square and 4 feet high will be ample; however, you can adjust the dimensions to fit your space.
• Set up the compost heap by fencing in the area; the fencing material should have holes for ventilation. Or you can dig a pit —although this arrangement does not bring about decay as quickly.
• The best compost has a variety of ingredients. Start with lawn debris—grass clippings, leaves, weeds. Add potato or carrot peelings, coffee grounds, and other kitchen wastes. The "fluff" from a vacuum cleaner can also be used. Newspapers, cartons, and other paper should be shredded before they are added. Don't include meat scraps, cans, or bottles.
• To speed the composting process, add

an activator. That's a somewhat formal name for the manure of horses and cattle —even dogs and cats. Or use fish meal.
• Build the compost heap in alternating layers of lawn debris, kitchen wastes, activator, and soil. Soak each layer well, and tamp it down firmly. Cover the compost heap with boards or cloth sacks; this will prevent odors from escaping.
• When the pile reaches a height of 4 feet, stop adding material. Let it sit for 6 months; if it dries out, spray it with a hose. If you have the space, you can start a second compost heap at this time.
• Bacteria will go to work on the material in the compost heap. When the heap is dark-colored and shows no traces of the materials that you put in, it is ready for use. If the outer portions haven't decayed, shovel them onto the second heap.
• Sprinkle your new humus in the garden. If you mix it with a few inches of topsoil, your garden will be greatly enriched.

Autumn Changes in the Woodland

Plants and animals *seem* to know that winter is coming because they do so many things that prepare them for the approaching rigors of that season—shortages of food and water, and exposure to cold. But animals do not "know" about the future; unlike human beings, they apparently do not even recognize the implications of cooler weather. They respond to something far more reliable than the chill of autumn. Their behavior is governed by the amount of sunlight present.

In temperate regions, the length of day decreases in late summer and fall; this occurs consistently every year, for it is a result of the earth's annual movement around the sun. Animals respond to the shorter days by a complex mechanism. Basically, what happens among the more advanced species (such as birds and mammals) is that the change in day-length registers in the "master-control" gland in the brain, the hypothalamus. The hypothalamus secretes hormones that trigger other systems throughout the animal's body.

The specific form of the adjustment varies widely. Some animals embark on breeding behavior. For example, autumn is the rutting season for many kinds of deer, the time when bucks lock antlers in competition for the does. Deer, like many other animals (such as porcupines and weasels), have about a 6-month interval between mating and giving birth. This pattern of behavior ensures that the young will be born in the spring, when food is abundant.

Another animal adjustment to waning day-length may be the urge to eat more, thus building up layers of fat that will tide the animal over the winter. In the fall, the most important source of food is seeds. Seed-eating animals are actually beneficial to a forest. Birds that digest only the coverings around seeds help plants to reproduce: they inadvertently disperse the seeds (in droppings) at places the seeds might not otherwise reach. Though squirrels eat nuts, their caches —buried and covered with leaves—are often abandoned. Instead of serving as food, the seeds grow into new plants.

Plants also respond to waning day-length—but without the help of a central controlling gland. Instead, the leaves of deciduous trees begin a transformation that eventually results in their falling. Color change is a dramatic sign of this transformation.

An autumnal display such as this scene (in Vermont) may last for weeks. The next time you have a chance to watch leaves turn color, notice which trees change first. Sourgums and swamp maples start their transformation relatively early; apple leaves turn much later.

Pressing, Preserving, and Printing with Leaves

Preserving leaves can be the basis of two hobbies—one, using leaves decoratively, the other, learning to identify different species. Autumn leaves make especially colorful collections; but in order to get good specimens, be sure to gather leaves while they are still supple. Collect as many types of leaves as possible (and their twigs). You may also want to photograph the trees and make note of names and locations.

How to Press Leaves

To preserve your collection, make a simple leaf-press. First, arrange leaves between thick layers of absorbent cardboard or blotters. Be sure layers do not overlap. Place entire stack between two flat, heavy boards or plywood, and bind tightly with straps or cords. Store in a warm, dry place for about 10 days, checking often and tightening straps.

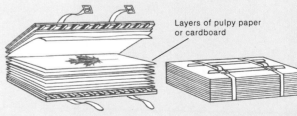

Layers of pulpy paper or cardboard

Note the arrangement of absorbent layers and how leaf is placed between them.

A tightly bound press ensures maximum release of moisture and flat leaves for display.

Why Leaves Turn Color and Drop with the Waning Year

Though leaves contain several substances that give them color, the influence of green chlorophyll in spring and summer is so great that other colors are obscured. But as the production of chlorophyll declines in autumn, the other colors begin to show up, and some new substances even develop. In the close-up of a pokeweed leaf (upper left), chlorophyll is still present along the veins, but a red hue predominates elsewhere; in the photo below it, the entire maple leaf has turned a brilliant gold. A leaf changes color because a layer of cells dries out at the base of the leaf stalk, where it attaches to the twig. Called the abscission layer, these cells seal the leaf from the circulatory system of the tree. Deprived of water, the leaf stops producing chlorophyll and dies. Autumn winds do not really tear a leaf from the twig—they snap it off at the abscission layer, leaving an abscission scar on the twig (see below). The leaf-shedding habit conserves water during the winter, when it may be frozen and unavailable to the tree.

Chlorophyll's green color predominates in spring and summer.

Other colors are revealed in autumn as production of chlorophyll stops.

Abscission scar, where leaf was attached

HORSE CHESTNUT
(*Aesculus hippocastanum*)

Old horse chestnut in full flower on Watson farm near Springfield. May 14, 1976.

A preserved leaf is shown with twig and a photograph of the tree; also its scientific name.

Display Leaves Under Plastic

Use two equal-size pieces of clear plastic—the type that is adhesive on one side. Choose leaves and plan their placement before peeling off backing. Handle adhesive only at edges; finger marks will show. Position leaves onto adhesive.

Remove backing from the second sheet. Smooth plastic sheets starting from one end, working air out as you go. Then trim edges.

Leaf Impressions in Ink

Put a dab of printer's ink or block-printing ink on a square of glass and spread with a small rubber roller. Place leaf on blotter (vein-side up) and ink with roller. Turn inked leaf down on page to be printed. Cover with paper; press firmly for imprint.

For very detailed prints, like the one at right, use plants with highly veined leaflets, such as honey locusts and ferns.

How Animals Adapt to Winter

The less you do, the less energy you need—that's the key to winter survival. Activity uses up energy, which comes from food; and food is in scant supply during a northern winter. Then, too, activity requires water, and near-drought conditions prevail when water is locked up in ice and snow.

Sleeping through the winter saves energy. Black bears and raccoons are winter-sleepers and conserve their body fuel by not moving about; they doze much of the time, but are easily awakened by intruders into their dens. Typically, mammals that adapt to winter by sleeping through most of it must keep their temperatures much higher than that of their surroundings. But it takes energy to do this.

Unlike winter-sleepers, true hibernators such as woodchucks have drastically lowered body temperatures. Reduced temperatures mean that everything happens at a slower speed, so pulse and breathing rate drop. (Hibernating woodchucks breathe only once every 6 minutes, which is about 200 times slower than their normal rate.) At this slow pace, life requires a minimum of energy, and a hibernating animal's fat layers can usually meet the slight demand.

Snow is a protective blanket for small mammals that neither hibernate nor winter-sleep. Snow is ten times lighter than liquid water and traps air; thus it is an ideal insulator (it also allows ventilation). Soil with a snow cover may be some 50 degrees warmer than the air above it. Under the blanket of snow, mice, voles, and other small mammals lose little body heat to their surroundings. They stay active and feed on plant food, including some they may have stored during the fall.

The chill of winter inactivates most "cold-blooded" animals. These creatures, whose body temperatures are invariably tied to that of the environment, don't move about when it is cold.

Reptiles and amphibians—such as turtles and the vociferous tree frogs known as spring peepers—remain covered and dormant during the coldest part of winter. So, too, do adult mourning-cloak butterflies, which stay immobile in attics, decaying logs, or hollow trees.

Another adaptation to winter is common among plants and insects. The adults reproduce and then die as winter sets in. All that remains of some species of insects are their offspring, which live out the winter as eggs or larvae. Similarly, plants known as annuals exist during winter only as frost-proof, drought-proof seeds.

Migration is yet another solution to survival in winter. Warblers, swallows, and other insect-eating birds fly to warmer climates, where insects thrive. Some of the large, hoofed mammals—moose and caribou—also migrate, but not to the south like the birds, and only to places where there is enough vegetation on which to feed.

Thick, downy feathers preserve the body heat of the ruffed grouse. On freezing nights they may dive into snow banks; at other times they simply fluff their feathers and sit in a tree.

Black bears awaken periodically in winter and leave their homes—usually a cave. Their normal temperature of 99°F. drops only a few degrees during periods of rest, which is why bears aren't considered true hibernators.

Although the winter forest may seem silent, life goes on above ground. Tracks reveal the comings and goings of grouse, bobcats, and snowshoe hares. But you can find more than tracks, if you know where such animals seek food, in thickets and similar places.

Winter is good for birding—the leafless trees allow for better visibility than in spring and summer. There are visiting birds—late migrants, perhaps. Waxwings and finches, jays and crossbills feast on seeds. If you carefully scan the branches of a conifer, you may discover a silent, motionless owl; other clues to the residence of an owl are small, oblong pellets of undigested food under a tree. Woodpeckers and nuthatches extract insects from trees, especially dying or injured ones. Ducks and eagles feed in open water, but a further clue is that they favor places where warm water is discharged. And, of course, a man-made feeding station is an ideal place for watching birds.

Active throughout winter, a bobcat pounces on small rodents, which live in tunnels and burrows under the blanket of snow.

Broad, heavily furred feet support a snowshoe hare as it hops across soft snow. Its fur—white only in winter—camouflages the hare in snow.

A Hibernating Ground Squirrel Awakens in Spring

Rising body temperatures trigger arousal in a hibernator, such as the golden-mantled ground squirrel (below). Hibernation is a physical state where all the animal's body functions slow down. For example, the temperature of this squirrel drops from an average of 90°F. to about 39°F. Its digestive and hormonal systems appear to stop; the heartbeat is too faint to be detected with an ordinary stethoscope. Essentially, hibernation is a means of conserving energy. While in this state, a squirrel can be picked up and brought into the light and still not be awakened. With the coming of spring and warm weather, the squirrel begins to stir; its breathing rate increases, as do its circulation and heartbeat, until it is completely awake.

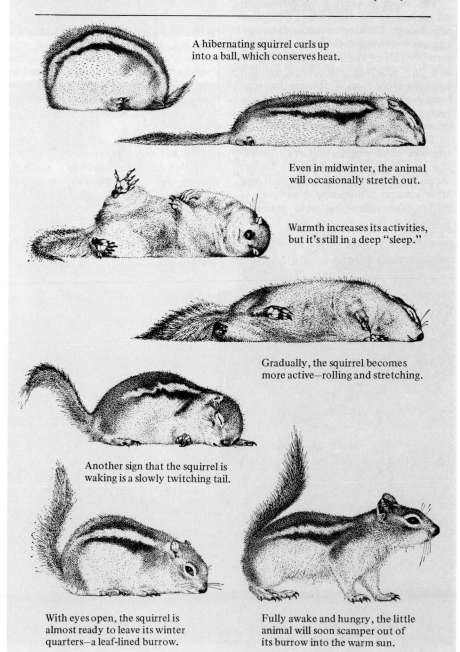

A hibernating squirrel curls up into a ball, which conserves heat.

Even in midwinter, the animal will occasionally stretch out.

Warmth increases its activities, but it's still in a deep "sleep."

Gradually, the squirrel becomes more active—rolling and stretching.

Another sign that the squirrel is waking is a slowly twitching tail.

With eyes open, the squirrel is almost ready to leave its winter quarters—a leaf-lined burrow.

Fully awake and hungry, the little animal will soon scamper out of its burrow into the warm sun.

Zones of Life in a Rain Forest

Walking in a tropical rain forest is surprisingly easy. The tall trees that make up most of the vegetation branch only at their tops, forming an umbrella-like canopy that may be 200 feet overhead. Thus the traveler encounters ranks of tall pillars in a dark, sheltered interior—a far cry from the tangled jungles of fiction.

Sounds in a tropical rain forest are tantalizing. They are loud and varied, but the creatures that scream and squawk are usually far above and can only be glimpsed through binoculars.

Unlike temperate forests, the floor of a rain forest has no thick carpeting of dead leaves and branches. When an organism dies, scavengers of all kinds convert the dead material (plant or animal) into nutrients for themselves. The result is that the rain forest soil receives little enriching humus from its own dead leaves. Thus, in spite of its luxuriant vegetation, the soil of a tropical rain forest is far less hospitable to plants than it seems. When cleared for farming, such land seldom produces abundant crops.

Tropical rain forests are usually divided into five distinct layers. Starting at ground level is the dark Herb Layer, which has tree trunks and a sprinkling of ferns and saplings. Only an estimated one percent of the sunlight that strikes a rain forest ever touches this layer, though you will occasionally see slender daggers of light stabbing the ground.

Next is the Shrub Layer, which extends from about 2 to 20 feet above the ground. Although this layer has relatively sparse growth, you may find cauliflorous trees and vines here. These plants have flowers that grow out directly from the bark and do, in fact, resemble cauliflowers.

The Understory—the layer you see when you look upward—is about 20 to 40 feet above the ground. The foliage here is thick enough to hinder movement, although some creatures do pass through on their way to and from the upper layers. Many small birds feed here and at lower levels.

The Canopy Layer is alive with birds —the boisterous macaws (whose cries can be heard for a mile), parakeets, parrots, and many others. Sloths (only in the New World), monkeys, and other climbing mammals are common here. This layer usually includes the intermeshing crowns of trees and numerous perching and climbing plants. Bromeliads and other epiphytes grow on trees and vines, getting their sustenance from dust and rain. A tree limb may hold several tons. Although epiphytes are not parasites (they take no nutrients from the trees), they sometimes strangle their hosts.

Unlike the other levels, the Emergent Layer is not continuous. "Emergent" refers to a scattering of trees that project far higher than the others. This "attic" has the most variable conditions of any place in the rain forest. It is more exposed to the elements and gets the full force of sun, wind, and rain. Many animals climb or fly between the Emergent and Canopy Layers.

Rivers are the main highways of the rain forest. Often changing course, they cut through the dense walls of vegetation that grow along their banks. In this Liberian forest (right), the trunks of emergent trees are visible above the canopy.

Buttress roots are a remarkable feature of this Venezuelan forest giant (below). These woody growths form between the trunks and roots near the surface of the ground, and may serve as supports for tall trees during heavy storms. The angles between these high roots make shelters and homes for many kinds of animals.

How Vines Reach for the Sunlight

1. Clinging vines are usually air plants with finger-like anchors that adhere to tree trunks, branches, and other vines.

2. Lianas, sometimes called monkey ropes, are fast-growing twiners. Their woody stems wrap tightly around trees as they push up toward the sunlight.

3. The lawyer vine is a scrambler. It puts out slender auxiliary vines with curving thorns that hook onto smooth tree bark or other neighboring plants.

4. Vines with tendrils possess multiple shoots so sensitive they can reach out and cling to the tiniest twig for support.

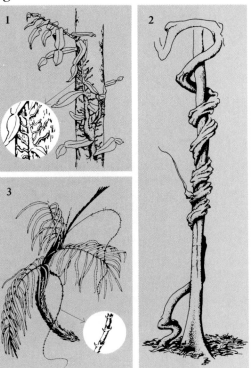

Parallel Lives Though Worlds Apart

Many animals of different species that live in similar environments have evolved along similar lines. These residents of tropical rain forests have strong resemblances and almost identical habits and life-styles.

EMERGENT LAYER

Living at the top of the tallest trees, the large birds of prey can scan lower treetops for potential quarry or take off in soaring flight.

Monkey-eating eagle
Asia

Harpy eagle
South America

CANOPY

The canopy is colorful with flowers and fruits, which are delicately plucked and eaten by these birds with enormous, light bills.

Great hornbill
Africa

Toco toucan
South America

UNDERSTORY

The bushbaby's suction-like grasp and the woolly opossum's prehensile tail are adaptations to life among slippery branches.

Bushbaby (galago)
Africa

Woolly opossum
South America

SHRUB LAYER

Tapirs and other large animals often race through the shrub layer at amazing speeds.

Malayan tapir
Asia

Brazilian tapir
South America

HERB LAYER

Pittas are among the elusive ground dwellers whose loud calls echo through the forest.

Fulvous pitta
Asia

Black-crowned antpitta
South America

CHAPTER THREE

Mountains and Highlands

*Though mountains are the largest landforms
that we are able to see, they conceal
far more about themselves than they reveal.*

Mountains were once believed to be eternal—mainly because their life-spans are so much longer than our own. Mountains rise, grow old, and wear away, but on a time-scale that is almost beyond human comprehension. Even when we see a mudslide or rock avalanche, it is hard to believe that such seemingly minor events can eventually bring down anything as massive as a mountain. Gravity is an unrelenting force, which affects everything. So, too, is the process of weathering that crumbles rocks.

The spectacular behavior of volcanoes was generally regarded as something apart. That many other mountains are still gradually rising was not even suspected until comparatively recent times. And the complex composition of mountains was not fully understood either, until engineers began tunneling through mountains. As the work progressed, there were often violent explosions as the pressures on particular segments of rock were relieved. Though explosions were common in mines, few people realized that tremendous pressures are present within mountains as well.

Nowadays, many people approach the airy heights with a new understanding. But one important fact is still not fully grasped—that mountains are fragile. The rocks themselves are vulnerable, and so are the pockets of soil lodged there, and the plants and animals dependent on the soil. The clearing and farming of steep slopes has imperiled many mountainsides. Even temporary loss of vegetative cover invites the disaster of a landslide—the soil accumulations of centuries can be lost in a matter of minutes. When this is widely understood, mountains will have a better chance of survival.

*To stand on mountaintops, as on this promontory in the
French Alps, climbers must take incredible risks. Yet the lure
of mountains is so great that even those of us who only
dream of such adventures can share the feeling of exhilaration.*

Mountains New and Old

When exploring a mountain, what you see depends on how good a detective you are. You might be able to discover evidence of major geological events. Many of the forces that shaped mountains have left clues behind. You don't even have to go to the mountains to get information. It is practical and very rewarding if you begin by consulting geology guidebooks.

If someone were to ask you about the mountains nearest your home, could you say how they were formed? You might be surprised to discover that you are living on land that was once under the sea, or that is covered by the remains of extinct volcanoes.

People sometimes learn about geology accidentally, as for example when drilling a well or excavating the foundations for a new home. If the bedrock of a worn-down mountain lies near the surface, the digging may be very expensive. The underlying geology of large cities influences the kinds of buildings that can be erected. Sometimes this, too, is discovered the hard way. For example, in Mexico City, high in the Sierra Madre mountains, many buildings are slowly sinking because part of the city rests on a former lake bed.

Like any good detective, you must be ready to look for clues in many ways. If you take photographs, you may be able to get an over-view of the mountain structure that would be hard to analyze by simply looking at it. Collecting rock samples from the actual site is extremely useful, too (of course, only in places where collecting is permitted). You can later compare the clues you pick up with geology books, or perhaps with someone else who is interested and informed about the geology of the region. This is the key to enjoying such a pursuit—concentrating on specific places and not trying to learn about the whole world all at once.

Mountains can be intriguing because their histories are complex. Few people will mistake the classic cone-shaped form of an active volcano. Extremely high mountains, such as the Himalayas, are clearly new formations. Old mountains, such as the Appalachians in the eastern U.S. and the Urals in the U.S.S.R., are likely to be lower and less imposing. This is the best clue to their antiquity. They were formed about 250 million years ago and have been greatly worn down in the intervening centuries.

But there is a further element that has to be taken into account in studying mountains—immense shifts in the earth's crust sometimes cause tilting of great layers of rock. You might expect that in a mountain range, the older rock would be at the bottom. But this is not a reliable assumption. As layers are pushed up like waves, the buckling layers may flop over on each other, burying newer layers under the old.

Exposure to the elements takes its toll. Weathering can cover the trails left by mountain-raising forces; but weathering leaves clues, too. In many places—in cities as well as on mountains—you may be able to discover the grooves scratched in rocks thousands of years ago by glaciers.

A good detective must expect the unexpected. Recent glaciations (that is, recent in geological terms) have chiseled portions of the northern Appalachian Mountains, with the result that peaks such as Mount Katahdin in Maine have acquired the sharp, jagged look of much younger mountains.

The jagged silhouette of the Cordillera Real, looming over the high plateau of Bolivia, is typical of the relatively young Andes system. Its beginnings go back 100 million years, when the earth's crust buckled and folded. Much later, only 2½ million years ago, intense volcanic activity thrust up the long chain of towering peaks that runs down South America's west coast.

The giant domes (some 30 in all) that make up Mount Olga rise 1,000 feet or more above Australia's central desert. These sandstone outcrops are composed of some of the world's oldest sedimentary rock—first deposited in an ancient sea, then tumbled into boulders, and ultimately compacted into solid masses.

The low contours of the Great Smokies (below), which are part of the Appalachian range of eastern North America, testify to their age. The upheaval that produced these mountains began some 200 million years ago. More millions of years went by as rains wore down the heights and filled valley floors with soil. The Smokies were never covered by glaciers; many rare plants have survived there.

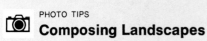 PHOTO TIPS
Composing Landscapes

When you photograph a mountain, your first impulse may be to move forward, freeing the subject from obstructions. Take this shot, but then, if there is foreground foliage, try using it as a frame or point of reference. Later, compare results.
• If the subject is near a body of water (as here, at Mt. Hood in Oregon), use the reflection as part of the composition.
• Because mountains often turn cold fast, camera and film need protection. Load the camera indoors. Freezing makes film brittle; to prevent cracking, be sure to advance the film slowly. Be careful not to breathe on the lens or view-finder; ice might form, obscuring your field.
• Before returning to warm conditions, put the camera into an airtight plastic bag. Any condensation will form outside, on the bag, and not inside the camera.

How Mountains Wear Down

When you look at a mountain, even a snow-capped peak, what you are seeing may be just a fraction of the original land mass. For example, an estimated 25,000 feet have been worn off parts of the Appalachian Mountains, and also from the once-great mountains in the Lake District of Britain. Some 50,000 to 60,000 feet are gone from an Alpine pass called the Simplon. All the mountains of the world are constantly being worn down —even those that are still being formed.

What whittled the mountains down? The answer is weathering—the process by which natural forces such as rain and wind wear down the surface of the earth. The process is slow; on the average, the height of a mountain is lowered less than one-thousandth of an inch a year. But because most mountains are millions of years old, the cumulative effect is impressive.

Running water has done more to change the face of the earth than has anything else in nature. Anyone who has ever aimed a garden hose at a patch of earth knows how quickly the force of the stream will dig a hole. Every time it rains, a similar thing happens; each raindrop is a tiny projectile striking the ground. The drops loosen and remove particles of rock. Rivers and streams, laden with particles, scour the land.

Water weathers rock in still another way. When water is in liquid form, it invades the cracks in a rock. Then, when the water freezes, its volume expands about 10 percent. Whenever freezing occurs, expansion exerts tremendous pressures—the ice may push with a force of 2,000 pounds per square inch.

Alternate freezing and thawing of water is only part of the crumbling process. Unlike water, other substances, such as rock, will contract when cold and expand when warm. Rocks have a tendency to crack when subjected to sudden changes in temperature (just as glass or china may do in the kitchen). Thus, when the sun heats a rocky surface, the rock expands slightly, and the exposed part may flake off.

Then, too, the sheer weight of accumulated ice and snow will wear a mountain down by abrasion. The ice in a glacier gouges the land over which it passes. This can be seen most readily at the bottom and edges of a glacier.

Wind plays a role in the wearing

Sheer on one side and rounded on the other, Half Dome (in California's Yosemite National Park) owes its helmet-like shape to glaciation and weathering of the granite. When the rocks above it eroded, the newly exposed surfaces peeled off on the rebound. The "missing" part, which weathered especially quickly, apparently collapsed; a cliff was left behind.

down of mountains, although it is a far less significant agent of change than water and ice. The wind carries away particles of rock that have been chipped off by other forces. A blast of mountain air carries a light but steady burden of pulverized rock.

Different kinds of rock weather at different rates. (If they didn't, mountains might "melt" away evenly, the way ice cream seems to subside in a bowl.) Some rocks weather quickly because their components are particularly susceptible to chemical attack: limestone, for example, is readily dissolved by the acids in rain or groundwater.

Sandstone and other porous rocks often contain a great deal of water and consequently weather at a faster rate than dense rocks. In dry climates, where water evaporates quickly after a rain, sandstone outcrops become immense "wicks" that soak up water. When temperatures drop enough to freeze the water, such rocks are especially vulnerable to weathering.

But all weathering is not done by inanimate forces. Mountain plants are slow, steady agents of weathering. The roots of trees pry cracks apart, and some plants—notably lichens—actually dissolve the rock.

Although mountains are created by mighty shifts in the earth's crust, it is weathering that gives most mountains their distinctive shapes. The wearing-away process often reveals the geological history of the mountain. Softer layers go first; pillars and caps of harder stone, laid down in other periods, often stand out, creating fanciful-looking natural sculpture.

Rocks expand when hot, contract when cold (the reverse of the way water behaves). Abrupt temperature changes caused these fractures.

Into every crack in the rock, a bit of soil will drift, bringing with it seeds and spores. At first, only plants with small root systems are able to grow there. But under steady assault by infiltrating ice, changes in temperature, and plant roots, the rocks split farther apart.

Weathering Reveals the Structure of Rocks

Exfoliation is the onion-like peeling of rock. It occurs after release of pressure or after changes in temperature.

Block separations, often found in limestone, reveal the tendency of rocks to break along weak seams.

Granular disintegration may occur when coarse-grained rock (such as sandstone) weathers; it simply crumbles.

The round, pitted look of this limestone rock is the result of chemical weathering: rainwater, which contains a mild acid, has gradually dissolved and washed away part of the stone.

HIKING AND CAMPING

Do's and Don't's on Rugged, High-Country Trails

A mile-long hike doesn't sound like much, unless the direction is up. Everything changes as you hike higher up a trail—the temperature is colder, the winds are stronger, the air is thinner, and you may discover that you tire more easily (the reason for this is a combination of extra exertion and lower concentrations of oxygen in the air; you have to work harder to get enough to breathe). You are more likely to get a sunburn in the high trails than on lower ground because ultraviolet (UV) light penetrates the thin air more readily, and it is UV that gives you the tan. It is fun and exhilarating to go hiking in the hills, but it takes preparation—and practice, too—if the trip is to end well.

• Never climb alone. Most accidents can be avoided by staying with a party—preferably with a knowledgeable leader. Even expert climbers notify others of their whereabouts. If you sign into an area, remember also to sign out.
• Wear the right clothes—ones that are comfortable. Boots are especially important; never wear new boots on a trek, only ones that you have tried out. Mountain weather changes rapidly, so carry rain gear, an extra sweater, socks, gloves, a hat, and sunglasses.
• Prepare for emergencies. Take along a first-aid kit. A compass is essential, and so is a whistle. The latter is an easy, effective device for locating a lost member

of your party. Carry a water canteen and a supply of quick-energy foods, such as candy bars. If you have a feeling of light-headedness, which is often caused by high altitude, lie down on a warm, sun-exposed rock and prop your feet up. If cold, pull your hat down firmly and wrap your midsection; your extremities will soon warm up.
• Study (and take along) a map before going into an unfamiliar area. Plan your route, avoiding smooth, steep slopes and any landslide areas.
• Don't go out in poor weather. Hazards increase with rain and fog. And never stand on ledges; they may just break off if the rocks supporting them crumble.

Mountains and Plateaus

Except for isolated volcanoes, such as Kilimanjaro in Africa, Fujiyama in Japan, or Etna and Vesuvius in Italy, mountains seldom stand alone. They are usually grouped in belts or ranges; and several connected ranges form a mountain system. The Himalayan Mountains are a system, with the Karakoram as one of its ranges; the Rocky Mountain system has, as two of its components, the Brooks and Wasatch Ranges.

Some great plateaus stand independent of mountain systems. Such regions may have been formed by the tilting and shifting of huge plates in the earth's crust millions of years ago. In northern Australia, the Barkly Tableland is an elevated sea bed, where some of the most ancient rock on earth lies exposed. The Deccan Plateau in India and vast regions of Mongolia and Siberia are highlands of volcanic origin.

Mountains have influenced history. They have caused the isolation of peoples, which has resulted in a greater divergence of cultures. The Andean Indians are an example of people who developed a unique language and culture. So, too, are the Basques, inhabitants of the foothills of the Pyrenees (which separate the Iberian Peninsula from France).

For most of recorded history, the power of mountains to block invaders was so great that military historians have made much of the few conquerors able to cross them. For example, Alexander the Great is noted for his invasion of India through the Hindu Kush; Hannibal is famous for having invaded Italy from Spain, first by crossing the Pyrenees, then the Alps, with elephants carrying his military stores. Conversely, the lack of mountains has converted many a region into a crossroads, a marketplace, and, unfortunately, a battleground.

In summer, many species of animals migrate to the Brooks Range to breed.

The name Rockies is sometimes used to refer to the entire North American mountain system, but at other times to specific sections of it, such as the Canadian Rockies.

HAWAIIAN ISLANDS

The Hawaiian Islands are tips of volcanic peaks in the middle of the ocean. Some volcanoes, such as Mauna Loa, are still active.

The metric equivalents of certain measurements in feet are given below. See entry under Measurement in the Glossary-Index for more on converting to the metric system.

Feet	Meters
5,000	1,524
10,000	3,048
15,000	4,572
20,000	6,096
25,000	7,620
30,000	9,144

The Appalachians are old, worn-away mountains. Long ago in earth's history, these mountains were entirely submerged by an inland sea.

Many rivers flow from Brazil's two highlands—the Mato Grosso and Brazilian Plateau.

The Central American land bridge, which links two great continents, is volcanic in origin. The chain extends from Mexico's Sierra Madres down to the Isthmus of Panama, then to the Andes.

The Andes Mountains have a characteristic volcanic rock (called andesite). The mineral composition of lava varies widely throughout the world.

Aconcagua is the highest peak in South America; off the coast is a deep oceanic trench. From mountaintop to ocean floor is the earth's greatest vertical distance—9 miles.

Famous Mountains Worldwide

Height alone is not the measure of a mountain's fame. Though Everest is the highest, the Matterhorn and McKinley attract more climbers. All by itself on a plain, Kilimanjaro commands notice. So do active volcanoes, such as Mount Etna. Religious significance gives an aura to many—Popocatepetl, Cotopaxi, Ararat, Sri Pada, Fujiyama.

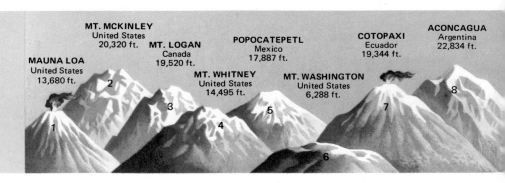

MAUNA LOA United States 13,680 ft.

MT. MCKINLEY United States 20,320 ft.

MT. LOGAN Canada 19,520 ft.

MT. WHITNEY United States 14,495 ft.

POPOCATEPETL Mexico 17,887 ft.

MT. WASHINGTON United States 6,288 ft.

COTOPAXI Ecuador 19,344 ft.

ACONCAGUA Argentina 22,834 ft.

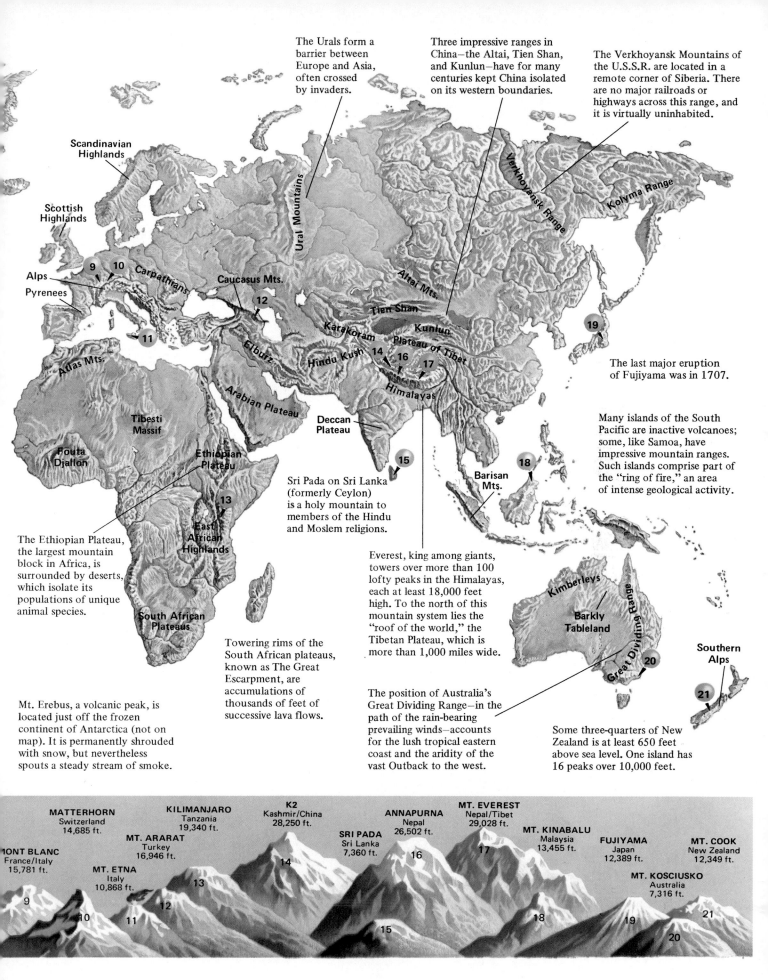

The Urals form a barrier between Europe and Asia, often crossed by invaders.

Three impressive ranges in China—the Altai, Tien Shan, and Kunlun—have for many centuries kept China isolated on its western boundaries.

The Verkhoyansk Mountains of the U.S.S.R. are located in a remote corner of Siberia. There are no major railroads or highways across this range, and it is virtually uninhabited.

Scandinavian Highlands

Scottish Highlands

Alps

Pyrenees

Carpathians

Ural Mountains

Verkhoyansk Range

Kolyma Range

Caucasus Mts.

Altai Mts.

Tien Shan

Karakoram

Kunlun

Plateau of Tibet

Elburz

Hindu Kush

Himalayas

Atlas Mts.

Arabian Plateau

Tibesti Massif

Fouta Djallon

Ethiopian Plateau

Deccan Plateau

East African Highlands

South African Plateaus

The last major eruption of Fujiyama was in 1707.

Many islands of the South Pacific are inactive volcanoes; some, like Samoa, have impressive mountain ranges. Such islands comprise part of the "ring of fire," an area of intense geological activity.

Barisan Mts.

Sri Pada on Sri Lanka (formerly Ceylon) is a holy mountain to members of the Hindu and Moslem religions.

The Ethiopian Plateau, the largest mountain block in Africa, is surrounded by deserts, which isolate its populations of unique animal species.

Kimberleys

Barkly Tableland

Great Dividing Range

Southern Alps

Everest, king among giants, towers over more than 100 lofty peaks in the Himalayas, each at least 18,000 feet high. To the north of this mountain system lies the "roof of the world," the Tibetan Plateau, which is more than 1,000 miles wide.

Mt. Erebus, a volcanic peak, is located just off the frozen continent of Antarctica (not on map). It is permanently shrouded with snow, but nevertheless spouts a steady stream of smoke.

Towering rims of the South African plateaus, known as The Great Escarpment, are accumulations of thousands of feet of successive lava flows.

The position of Australia's Great Dividing Range—in the path of the rain-bearing prevailing winds—accounts for the lush tropical eastern coast and the aridity of the vast Outback to the west.

Some three-quarters of New Zealand is at least 650 feet above sea level. One island has 16 peaks over 10,000 feet.

MATTERHORN
Switzerland
14,685 ft.

KILIMANJARO
Tanzania
19,340 ft.

K2
Kashmir/China
28,250 ft.

ANNAPURNA
Nepal
26,502 ft.

MT. EVEREST
Nepal/Tibet
29,028 ft.

MONT BLANC
France/Italy
15,781 ft.

MT. ARARAT
Turkey
16,946 ft.

SRI PADA
Sri Lanka
7,360 ft.

MT. KINABALU
Malaysia
13,455 ft.

FUJIYAMA
Japan
12,389 ft.

MT. COOK
New Zealand
12,349 ft.

MT. ETNA
Italy
10,868 ft.

MT. KOSCIUSKO
Australia
7,316 ft.

Volcanoes and Volcanic Clues

An erupting volcano is the only place in the world where you can watch a mountain under construction. In 1943 a Mexican farmer witnessed such an event—in his own cornfield. One evening there was a little smoke and an odor of sulfur coming from his field; next morning there was a hill some 30 feet high, spewing smoke and ashes. After a year, his cornfield had become a 1,000-foot-high volcano—Paricutín.

The famous "ring of fire," an area of intense volcanic activity that encircles the Pacific, runs along the western coast of the Americas, skirts the tip of Antarctica, and continues along the Pacific coast of Asia. Many relatively recent volcanoes are near coastlines or in the sea—as for example Krakatoa, which is an island in Indonesia.

Some geologists believe that the continents themselves began as groups of volcanic islands that had been built up from the bottom of the sea. The areas between these islands were later filled in, forming continental masses.

There are several thousand volcanic mountains around the world, some of them millions of years old and no longer active. Volcanic activity does not seem to be as great today as in times past. Nevertheless, there are about 500 still-active volcanoes. One of the youngest, Surtsey, was born off the coast of Iceland in 1963.

What forces create volcanoes? No

Hidden Layers of a Volcano

Sangay in Ecuador (left) is one of the few almost continuously active volcanoes in the world. Ecuador has at least 20 other active volcanoes within a 200-mile stretch, but none gives off smoke as frequently as Sangay. Intense volcanic activity along the Pacific coast of South America accounts for several chains of volcanoes. Such areas are constantly threatened by earthquakes. Some volcanoes have more violent eruptions than others—these are easily identified by the conical necks and relatively steep sides.

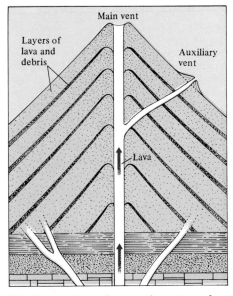

This diagram shows the general structure of a stratified volcano (such as Sangay). That is, its steep slopes were built up by alternating layers of lava and debris. This type of volcano is known as a composite or strato-volcano. In its center is a wide, cylindrical vent that extends down into the bedrock. Much of the material escapes through this main vent. With each eruption, lava flows out (settling mostly at the vent) and down the sides of the volcano. Rocks and other volcanic debris accumulate on top of the lava. Auxiliary vents, or fissures (also called parasitic or lateral cones), often break through the sides of the volcano.

one is certain, but most scientists believe that hot molten rock, known as magma, located some 20 to 40 miles beneath the surface of the earth, is pushed upward through cracks in the crust. The magma contains great amounts of steam and other gases. As the gases near the surface, they leave the magma like bubbles from an uncapped bottle of soda.

Gases escape with great force, breaking a hole in the earth's crust, which is called a crater. These gases carry huge quantities of dust and ashes. Molten magma also pours from the crater. Once magma reaches the surface, it is called lava. Tons of lava and other debris pile up, forming an unmistakable volcanic cone.

No two volcanoes are alike: shape is a clue to a volcano's past behavior. If a volcano has a steep cone, such as Ecuador's Sangay (see photograph at left), its eruptions were probably violent; but if it is low, with gentle slopes, its eruptions were probably more quiet. These gently sloping volcanoes are sometimes called shield volcanoes because of their low profile; the Hawaiian volcanoes are good examples. The main reason for the different kinds of volcanoes is the type and consistency of materials that erupt from them. Some release a lot of gases, thereby producing cinders and ashes; others are mainly lava and rocks. The viscosity (or fluidity) of the lava also varies.

Different volcanic mountains have different mineral content. The Andes Mountains, for example, consist mainly of andesite—a rock formed from very thick, slow-moving lava. Occasionally a volcano has accumulations of lava down at its base. This type usually stands alone or near larger volcanoes; examples of these are found in Mexico.

Sometimes an entire volcanic mountain blows up, leaving a large depression known as a caldera. The caldera may fill up with water. This is the way Crater Lake in Oregon was formed.

Volcanoes are feared by man. However, scientists believe that the steam and gases that escaped from volcanoes billions of years ago may have been the source of most of the earth's water. (Volcanoes are still making a minor contribution to the water supply today.) Another surprising "gift" from volcanoes is the millions of acres of farmland created and fertilized by tons of minerals from the earth's interior.

Unmistakable Evidence of Volcanic Activity

As inactive volcanoes erode, their remains often take on interesting patterns and shapes. Several factors contribute to the various forms of these remnants: the climate of the region, which influences the rate of erosion; their mineral content; and the rate of cooling and hardening of the different volcanic rocks. The examples shown here are three of many volcanic remnants that can be found.

Shiprock is a volcanic **remnant** standing some 1,400 feet high in New Mexico. All but the hardened core of lava has been worn away.

Swirling lava, from Hawaii's Mauna Loa, is called pahoehoe. The brownish color beneath is an indication of lava from a previous eruption.

The Giant's Causeway in Northern Ireland has famous polygonal columns; such columns are formed of basalt—one kind of volcanic rock.

Folded Mountains Large and Small

When Charles Darwin was mule-packing his way over the Andes Mountains in 1835, the great naturalist was impressed by a fossil sea shell he found embedded in a cliff. At the time, Darwin was about 13,000 feet above sea level. Yet here were the remains of shells like those he had found on beaches. This experience could happen to you, too, on many of the world's large mountain ranges—the Appalachians, Alps, or Himalayas.

This is evidence that not all mountains were made from the out-pourings of volcanoes, as had been thought previously. Scientists believe some mountains were formed of sediments laid down millions of years earlier, on the bottom of ancient seas.

According to this theory, the first act begins when sediments settle in the troughs of shallow seas. Much of the debris is washed from land and mixed with the limy skeletons of sea creatures. As the debris accumulates, it becomes heavier and sinks into the sea bed. Gradually the sediments are cemented together, forming layers of limestone, shale, or other sedimentary rock. These layers may contain fossils.

How do sediments change to mountains? Two tremendous forces are believed to be responsible for raising these flat-lying beds: pressure from the sides and pressure from below. This squeezing and lifting acts on the sedimentary layers the way ripples form on your skin if you squeeze a section between your thumb and forefinger. The size of the ripples in the earth's surface varies from microscopic folds to those that make up mountains, measuring miles from crest to crest and from top to bottom.

There are many theories to account for the squeezing, folding, and lifting. Change may have occurred when the crust of the earth cooled and shrank (the way the skin of a baked potato wrinkles as it cools). Another theory of mountain formation is that the folding resulted from the collision of huge, shifting plates in the earth's crust. Or the folds may be the result of the up-and-down movements of the fluid interior of the earth, which tugs and pushes on the surface. Whatever the causes, the bending and sinking of great masses of rock often created so much heat that segments of the rock melted. Many folded mountains are composed of granite and other types of rock, formed by melting.

Ripples in the Landscape

Ridges of limestone undulate across the face of Mt. Timpanogos in Utah's Wasatch Range. This rippling illustrates the way the forces of compression wrinkled the earth's rocky crust. In many places the folds were pushed so high they formed mountains such as this one. When you look at such folding, an obvious question may occur to you: how can solid rock be bent like taffy? When the folding took place millions of years ago, the layers of rock were under tremendous pressures, and were often heated to a point where the rock became relatively plastic. Not all rocks bend easily. At the base of many folded mountains, there are cracks where the rock broke instead of bending. The folding of rock layers is still going on in many regions of the world, but so gradually that the change can be measured only with sophisticated instruments.

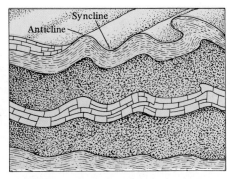

This diagram shows how folding in the layers of rock resembles waves in a body of water. The top (or crest) of a fold is called an anticline; the bottom (or trough) is called a syncline. Sometimes the anticline may rise so high it flops over, like a wave breaking on the beach, as shown at the right of the diagram.

You can often see the folds in rocks at highway excavations, and on cliffs where the formation is not yet covered with vegetation. But when you look at a mountain, you should bear in mind that you are not seeing the folds as they were originally formed. Thousands of feet may have been worn away.

Most mountains are a mixture of hard and soft rock. Whatever its structure, a mountain is most vulnerable to the forces of weathering at its summit (and also on its windward side). As ice and temperature changes wear away the mountain top, the rock formation is invaded—rather like the break in a sea wall. In fact, mountains generally erode faster than nearby valleys, especially if extensive deposits of soft rock are present. It is the nature of erosion that ice and water will take the easiest path downward, which generally means an ever-widening of already established gouges and cracks. Thus mountains keep losing ground; the mountain becomes a valley. This "role reversal" can most readily be seen in regions of folded mountains.

But even as the mountains are worn away, others are forming. Right now, the Mississippi River is depositing tons of sediments every day in the Gulf of Mexico. Quite possibly, these accumulations will be the raw materials for a new range of folded mountains.

What Is Now a Valley Was Once a Mountain Peak

Sometimes a mountain that was created by folding of the earth's crust is worn away and replaced by a valley. Peyto Lake (above), in Canada's Banff National Park, lies in a valley believed to have been the site of a mountain. Folded mountains are particularly susceptible to the forces of erosion because their folds may expose soft layers. Erosion wears away soft veins, like miners following a lode into the earth. This process can bring down an entire mountain. Rock at the side of the mountain may be relatively protected from erosion. Eventually, as the valley deepens, the sides may become separate mountains.

The valley in the photo at the top of the page may have been a mountain at one time; the dotted line shows its present contours.

Highways Are Prime Places to See Geological Formations

Roadcuts and other such excavations often reveal landforms that are otherwise hidden by vegetation or worn down by the forces of erosion. The way a road is designed must take into account the basic, underlying structure of the rock. As you drive along, you can often see—in miniature—such folded structures as the one at left. Two roads pass in opposite directions, with a remnant of the fold separating them—a small, perfectly matched continuation of the fold on the wall beyond. You will be able to see many such forms, different only in size and not in kind from the larger formation on the facing page. A road like this is relatively simple to design; engineers often have more serious construction problems—as when a road is literally blasted out of solid rock, with a jagged face on one side and a steep drop on the other. When you travel, examine the contours of roads, and you will gain insight into both geology and engineering.

Fault-Block Mountains

Some of the world's most spectacular mountains are not necessarily the highest. For sheer drama, few mountains can match those that rise abruptly from the surrounding plains: no foothills distract from their soaring grace.

These starkly beautiful mountains are often precisely what they appear to be—great blocks of rock pushed up from beneath the surface of the earth. Because they occur along fractures in the earth's crust, they are known as fault-block mountains.

The land bordering an active fault does not stay put. At intervals ranging from a few days to several hundred years, the ground moves. Each shift releases pressures from deep within the earth. Although each displacement usually amounts to no more than a few inches, over a long period of time the movements along a fault may cover great distances.

The San Andreas Fault in California is a famous example of a fracture where the land is slipping sideways, in a horizontal motion. Streams, roadways, and rows of trees that were once aligned are now displaced. If you look down on such a fault from an airplane, the landscape seems to zigzag.

But there are vertical shifts, too, and fault-block mountains may be the result. The land bordering these fractures has moved up or down, not sideways; sometimes both sides have slipped (one up, the other down). In any case, these movements may create a huge step—not immediately, of course, but probably over a long period of time.

Fault-blocks can be deceptive: they are readily identified only if you see them from certain directions. The classic fault-block has a distinctive profile. The side facing the fracture is steep (unless the forces of weathering have worn it down); the back of the mountain (the part away from the fault) usually slopes down to flat land. Thus unless a fault-block mountain is seen from the front or side, it might not be recognized as such.

Certain areas—including Utah, Montana, and Mongolia—have spectacular ranges of fault-block mountains. But you don't have to travel to any of these places to see this type of formation: look for small-scale displacements, produced by miniature faults, at road-cuts or on the face of a cliff.

Faults generally do not occur singly: movement along two nearby faults may leave characteristic marks on the surface of the earth. Sometimes the land in between is pushed up, forming mountains that resemble huge bricks lying on the ground. These "bricks," called horsts (from the German for aerie), are relatively uncommon. The

Vosges Mountains in France and the plateau of the Black Forest in Germany are extensive neighboring horsts, separated by the valley of the Rhine.

Land between two faults may sink. This creates a ditch-like depression—a graben, the German for grave. Large grabens are also called rift valleys. The Rhine Valley is a graben, where it is bordered by two horsts; so is Death Valley. A still deeper graben makes up part of the Jordan River Valley, near the Dead Sea. Here, the valley floor is about a mile below the land.

Although the depth of a fault is difficult to determine, some fractures are believed to extend downward for 30 miles or more. Faults act as channels that conduct heat, water, and molten rock from the earth's interior. Thus hot springs and geysers mark many faults; a line of volcanoes also indicates the presence of a large, deep fault.

When Fractures and Uplifts Make Mountains

A profile of Mt. Rundle (left) from across a lake in Banff National Park, Canada, is a classic example of a fault-block mountain, recognizable when seen from the proper angle. If seen from any other angle, it may look like another type of mountain. Distinguishing features of a fault-block mountain are a steep, jagged front-slope—the edge of a large fracture—and a more gradual down-slope, or back. Pressures within the earth fractured the even layers of rock, thrusting a section into the air. Many sections of the Rockies of North America were formed in this way.

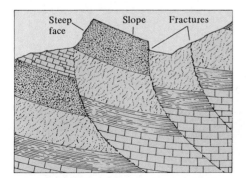

It is not possible to see the exact underlying structure of any given area, but the diagram (above) is a rough model of the bedrock layers found beneath a fault-block mountain. Note the order of the layers, and how they have slipped along the fractures and are now mismatched as a result of violent earth movements. The highest part, in the center of this drawing, represents Mt. Rundle.

Why Fault-Blocks Are Hard to Detect

Faults are something of a paradox—they are so clear in textbooks, but so difficult to identify out in the field. Mountains along faults are not made of any one particular kind of rock; it is the sharp fracturing of the land that gives them their identity. Soon the forces of erosion begin to wear them down. Why be concerned with faults at all? Partly because the wall of a fault may extend deep into the earth, and that wall sometimes influences the land around it. For example, if underground water collides with such a barrier, water may rise and form a spring (either cold or hot). Pressures within the crust of the earth are variable, and so are the substances that rise along faults—petroleum is another example. Beyond that, the structure of landforms has a fascination of its own, once you become interested in it.

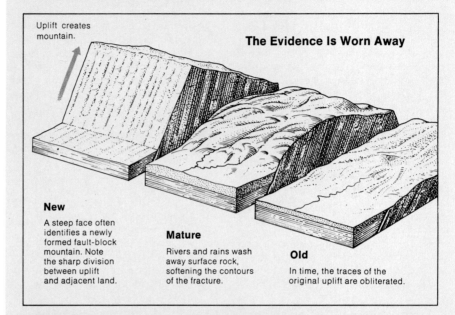

Uplift creates mountain.

The Evidence Is Worn Away

New
A steep face often identifies a newly formed fault-block mountain. Note the sharp division between uplift and adjacent land.

Mature
Rivers and rains wash away surface rock, softening the contours of the fracture.

Old
In time, the traces of the original uplift are obliterated.

If it weren't for the fact that these two sections of land (above and at right) were recently cut, there would be no way of knowing that they contain fault structures. The stepped formations probably made the ground above them uneven for a while, but now the fractures are best seen in cross-section. The leveling effect of erosion has prevailed.

Landscapes Carved by Glaciers

For centuries naturalists were baffled by curious landforms found in many parts of the world—huge boulders strewn across the countryside, deep grooves gouged in solid rock, strange hills and depressions in otherwise level plains. The prevailing explanation was that these curiosities were evidence of a worldwide, catastrophic flood. Yet this explanation had flaws.

It wasn't until the early 1800's that a Swiss-American naturalist, Louis Agassiz, found the answer in the mountains. By studying glaciers sliding slowly down mountain valleys, Agassiz learned that glaciers could produce the landforms that might be attributed to a flood. He was the first to suggest that long ago much of the earth was covered with glaciers during a great Ice Age.

The idea of an Ice Age was ridiculed at first. Who could believe that areas now occupied by Paris, London, Boston, and Moscow once lay beneath an ice sheet perhaps 5,000 to 10,000 feet thick? But by using the remaining glaciers as an outdoor laboratory, Agassiz and his followers were able to prove that ice had indeed carved the land.

For reasons no one knows, millions of years ago the climate turned cold for the first time in earth's history. There have been three, four, or perhaps more major Ice Ages. In these periods, more snow and ice accumulated during the winters than melted during the summers. The glaciers eventually spread over enormous portions of the globe. The immense ice sheets advanced and retreated several times, as the earth's climate fluctuated—possibly because of changes in the sun's output.

There are few great glaciers today (except in polar regions). Not all mountains form glaciers—some simply do not have a sufficient amount of snow. But there are a few mountaintop remnants of the Ice Ages. These mountains have natural catch-basins that trapped the snow. As the snow accumulated, it gradually compacted to form ice and eventually became heavy enough to begin a slow, long journey downhill, moving out through a low spot in the basin wall. As it slipped away, the glacier often enlarged the depression to form a cirque (French for circus, because it resembles an amphitheater). Sometimes three or more cirques were scooped out on the slopes of a rounded peak, transforming it into a jagged pyramid called a horn, like the famous Matterhorn in the Swiss Alps.

A river of ice is pushed from behind, as well as being pulled downward by gravity. It can move over level areas in the valleys and even up slight grades. It may create "stairsteps" in the valley. If the glacier eventually melts, these steps may fill with water, forming a chain of lakes called "paternoster" lakes. When a single lake forms in a cirque, it is called a tarn. Finger lakes may occupy depressions in the valley.

Glaciers do not follow fine contours in the land as rivers do, and so tend to straighten and widen valleys. Glaciated valleys are easy to recognize because they offer broad vistas—they are usually U-shaped, contrasting with the V-profile of most mountain river valleys.

The main valley is scooped out more quickly than the shallower tributaries that join it. If the glacier melts, the floors of the tributaries may be left "hanging" hundreds of feet above the main valley. Often streams of glacial meltwater flow down the hanging valleys, creating waterfalls, some of the most spectacular of all glacial scenery.

Immense Glaciers Grew During the Ice Ages

Melting glaciers were the mighty geological agents that sculptured the landscape during the Ice Ages. As massive sheets of ice shifted downward, they whittled mountains, scoured the lowlands, and scattered large rocks far and wide. Tributary glaciers sometimes joined the main glacier, forming a common bed of ice.

Small glaciers are tributaries of the main glacier.

The immense weight of the main glacier gouges deep valleys.

Ice cracks where depth of glacier changes.

Rubble beneath glacier dislodges rocks and also abrades bedrock as it moves.

The striations in a glacier —called medial moraines— are composed of debris.

Bedrock

Meltwater from glacier

Glacial till is unsorted debris deposited by melting waters.

This wide, **U-shaped valley** in the Pyrenees is characteristic of a glaciated landscape as it looks today. The icy stream, fed by meltwater from snow-capped peaks and nearby ice fields, meanders down a valley carved thousands of years ago by an advancing glacier.

Boulders known as erratics are also evidence of moving glaciers. As a glacier advanced, it plucked boulders from underlying rock and moved them far from their original sites. Such boulders usually have a different mineral composition from that of surrounding rocks.

When the Earth Warmed, the Glaciers Receded

Today, glaciers cover only about one-tenth of the earth's surface (mostly at the poles), but many rugged landscapes still reflect their work. Mountain lakes are filled by meltwater; beautiful waterfalls cascade from hanging valleys. Some of these glacial effects can be seen in areas such as the Alps and Rockies.

A cirque, which is a scooped-out basin, was the head of a glacier.

Snow-capped peak is all that remains of the glacier.

Bedrock

The hanging valley was left by tributary glacier, which did not cut as deeply as main glacier. Waterfall marks the base of hanging valley.

Erratics are large rocks moved great distances.

Crystal-clear glacial lake is fed by meltwater.

Outwash plain is a flat area below a glacier.

Drumlins are elongated hills of glacial deposits that block outflow from lake.

Glaciers: Slow-Moving Rivers of Ice

Deep crevasses on a glacier atop Mt. Hood (a dormant volcano in Oregon) present a special hazard to mountaineers. Some crevasses may be more than 40 feet wide and 100 feet deep. These cracks develop as the ice travels over an uneven surface. The masses of ice split—though not usually as far down as the floor of the glacier (where the ice flows like molasses).

Once a glacier forms, it tends to be self-perpetuating. As moist winds pass, the cold may cause condensation of vapor, adding new snow. Even if the air is not cold enough to produce precipitation, moist air commonly forms clouds, which shield the glacier from the sun. Cold mountain air also produces powerful downdrafts that drive away warmer air.

When snow reaches a depth of about 100 feet, its weight compresses the deeper layers into a granular snow called firn. If snow continues to pile up, the firn melts under the pressure and then refreezes into ice. This hard glacial ice may weigh nearly 20 times as much as newly fallen snow.

Something happens when snow and ice accumulate to a depth of about 200 feet. The seemingly solid mass starts to flow, spreading like a spoonful of batter dropped on a hot griddle. Steep slopes accelerate the movement of the ice, but the glacier can move on flat land, and even up slight inclines.

Tremendous pressures exist at the bottom of a glacier (28 tons or more per square foot), transforming ice from the brittle substance we know in everyday life to a substance that can flow like cold molasses. This is because ice melts under pressure. You can

How a Glacier Advances

The great weight of a glacier makes it move down a mountain. Because of the pressure on the lower part of a glacier, this portion may thaw (and then refreeze), causing the entire sheet of ice to slip downhill. Glaciers flow in crescent-like waves (see photo, at right, of a glacier in Washington's Olympic Mountains). Such waves develop because the center of a glacier moves more quickly than the sides. A measuring technique has been designed to plot the motion of a glacier: stakes are driven into the ice (see surface view diagram at right). As the ice moves, the stakes are carried along with it. The ones at the center move farther down the slope than the others, and the straight line becomes a curve. By using this method, scientists can determine the distance a particular glacier moves in a given period of time. They have discovered that the ice at the surface flows rather slowly—from a fraction of an inch to several feet a day (depending on temperature, steepness of the mountain, and width of the valley). But the ice at the bottom of a glacier moves even more slowly (see side view at right).

prove this by pressing a cold metal object into ice—a knife or the tines of a fork. The ice will melt gradually, and the metal will sink in. Similarly, the weight of an ice skater actually melts the ice, producing a thin layer of water that lubricates the passing of the blades over the ice. Much the same thing is believed to occur at the bottom of a glacier.

Glaciers may also "roll" on natural ball bearings. Tiny cracks occur between the individual ice crystals, crumbling the ice into pieces about half an inch in diameter. Thus the glacier may slip on crystals the way your foot might slide if you stepped on some marbles.

But while the bottom layers of a glacier may flow and slip, the upper layers, which are under less pressure, remain brittle. As the ice sheet moves, some areas crack, forming crevasses as much as 100 feet deep. Crevasses are normally bow-shaped, with the convex part facing downhill. This is because glaciers, like rivers, tend to move more quickly at their centers than along their margins, where they are in contact with the valley walls. As a result, the center of a crevasse, extending across a glacier, soon gets ahead of its edges. Some glaciers have so many crevasses that travel is impossible.

Crevasses make mountaineering especially treacherous, and sometimes skiing as well. A crust of recently fallen snow may bridge over a region that is pocked with crevasses. The crust may be thick and strong enough to support a person's weight; but then again, the crust could give way without warning.

The powdery snow that makes for good skiing often builds up on mountain slopes. This accumulation may move downhill, too—but far more rapidly than a glacier—in the form of an avalanche. Some of these snow slides have been clocked at speeds up to 200 miles per hour, sweeping almost everything in their path. When "powder" builds up on a slope steeper than about 45 degrees, it is often called an "avalanche waiting to happen." Almost anything can trigger an avalanche —a falling branch, a hopping animal, a skier, or even a passing airplane.

Tens of thousands of avalanches occur annually in the Alps, where the snow is sometimes brought down deliberately in small, harmless avalanches by the firing of shells or rockets. Occasionally, the sound alone is enough to trigger the cascade of snow, but contrary to popular legend, there is no documented evidence that a human voice can start a snow slide.

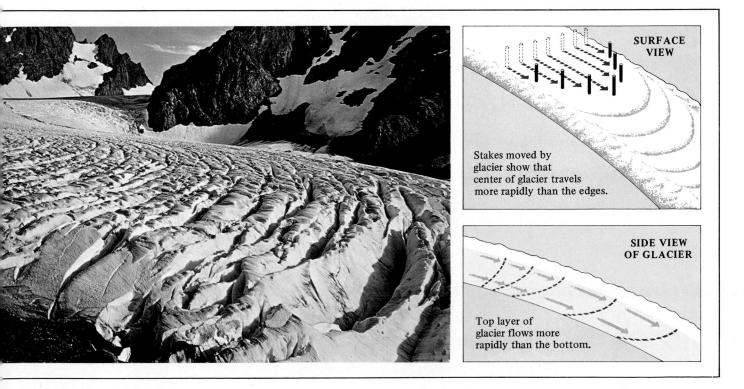

SURFACE VIEW

Stakes moved by glacier show that center of glacier travels more rapidly than the edges.

SIDE VIEW OF GLACIER

Top layer of glacier flows more rapidly than the bottom.

Zones of Life on a Mountainside

When you climb a mountain, you see and feel change—the most obvious is usually in temperature. For every 1,000 feet you go up, the temperature drops about 3.5°F. Thus the summit of a mountain 10,000 feet high, such as Mount Olympus in Greece, is about 35°F. colder than its base. This is because the gases that make up the atmosphere are denser at sea level and retain more heat. In effect, the earth's insulating blanket of air provides a mountain climber with less protection as he goes higher, even as a light blanket gives less warmth than a heavy one.

The physical conditions on a mountain—temperature, wind, exposure to sunlight, and amount of moisture—shape the environment for many plants and animals. There are distinct zones of life, which correspond roughly to the zones you would encounter if you were to travel thousands of miles from the temperate latitudes to the frozen poles. On a mountain, you can go from a temperate world to the arctic tundra by simply climbing upward.

Unlike these diagrams, real zones are not sharply delineated; the transition between two zones is gradual. Starting at the bottom of a pair of mountains in temperate latitudes, there's a Mixed Forest Zone—with coniferous and deciduous (leaf-shedding) trees. Next

comes the Coniferous Zone, where the environment is harsher. Above this is the Alpine Zone, where conditions are too cold and windy for any but dwarf varieties of willow and other low-growing plants. The line of demarcation between the Coniferous and Alpine Zones is frequently a ragged line of conifers trailing across a mountain—the timberline. Above the Alpine Zone lies a frozen, virtually lifeless region.

The types of vegetation anywhere on earth will determine to a great extent the kinds of animals that will be able to find food and shelter. Predatory animals go wherever their preferred prey may be. There are exceptions—animals

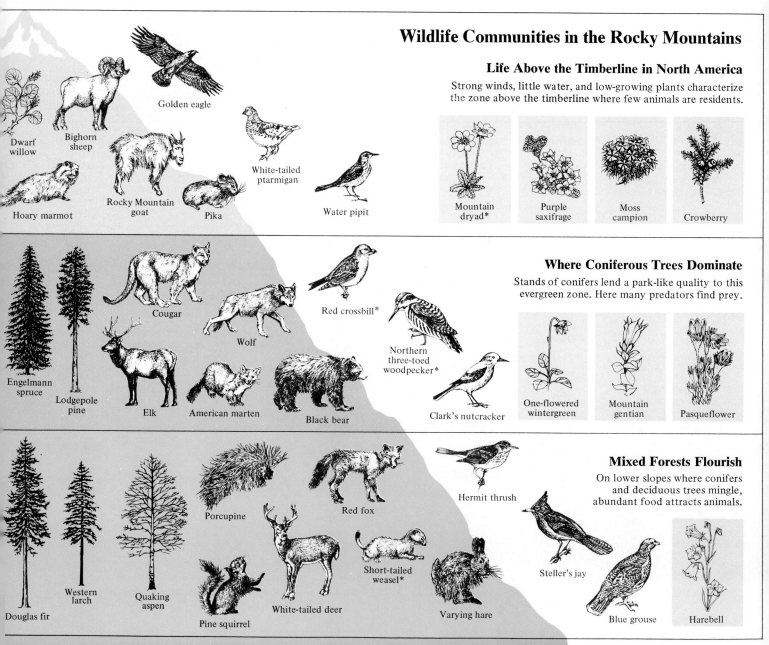

Wildlife Communities in the Rocky Mountains

Life Above the Timberline in North America
Strong winds, little water, and low-growing plants characterize the zone above the timberline where few animals are residents.

Dwarf willow · Bighorn sheep · Golden eagle · White-tailed ptarmigan · Water pipit · Hoary marmot · Rocky Mountain goat · Pika

Mountain dryad* · Purple saxifrage · Moss campion · Crowberry

Where Coniferous Trees Dominate
Stands of conifers lend a park-like quality to this evergreen zone. Here many predators find prey.

Engelmann spruce · Lodgepole pine · Cougar · Wolf · Red crossbill* · Northern three-toed woodpecker* · Elk · American marten · Black bear · Clark's nutcracker

One-flowered wintergreen · Mountain gentian · Pasqueflower

Mixed Forests Flourish
On lower slopes where conifers and deciduous trees mingle, abundant food attracts animals.

Douglas fir · Western larch · Quaking aspen · Porcupine · Red fox · Hermit thrush · Pine squirrel · White-tailed deer · Short-tailed weasel* · Varying hare · Steller's jay · Blue grouse · Harebell

* The same species has a different name in North America and Europe.

such as bears and deer, eagles and hawks, which move between zones.

The amazing thing to notice here is the similarity of life forms in each zone. Matching marmot for marmot, ptarmigan for ptarmigan, crowberry for crowberry, these two places, worlds apart—in North America and in Europe —are more alike than different.

Zonation is worldwide, but there are interesting variations. For example, the Alpine Zone may begin at about 7,000 feet in the Alps, but the comparable zone in the Himalayas occurs at 15,000 feet. What's worth considering is not the statistics, but the patterns of plant and animal adaptations.

As a family activity or a school project, you can work out a zonation chart for a nearby mountain or hillside. You can get started without knowing the specific altitude. However, in some instances, as a clue to vegetation, this information will help. You can consult road maps, or, if available, government geological survey maps.

• Begin with a narrow segment, going all the way to the top. Other segments may be different because of variations in winds and exposure to sun and rain. Establish a regular path, taking notes on each trip.

• As you get to know your own area, you can branch out, comparing one part of a hill or mountain with other segments, or with the adjacent hillsides.

• Regional field guides to trees, shrubs, and other plants are great time-savers; they eliminate all the species of plants that are unlikely to be in your study area.

• Animals are often easier to guess at than plants, but their mobility makes a positive identification harder. Many are shy, some are migrators that can be seen only occasionally, and others are mainly nocturnal. A field guide will describe the mammal, bird, or insect, and also its behavior and habitat. When and where can it usually be seen? What does it eat?

• As you collect data (perhaps on cards), plan your chart. You can pattern it on one of the mountains shown here (especially if you like to draw). Or use gummed labels with names of species written on them, ready for placement in a specific zone.

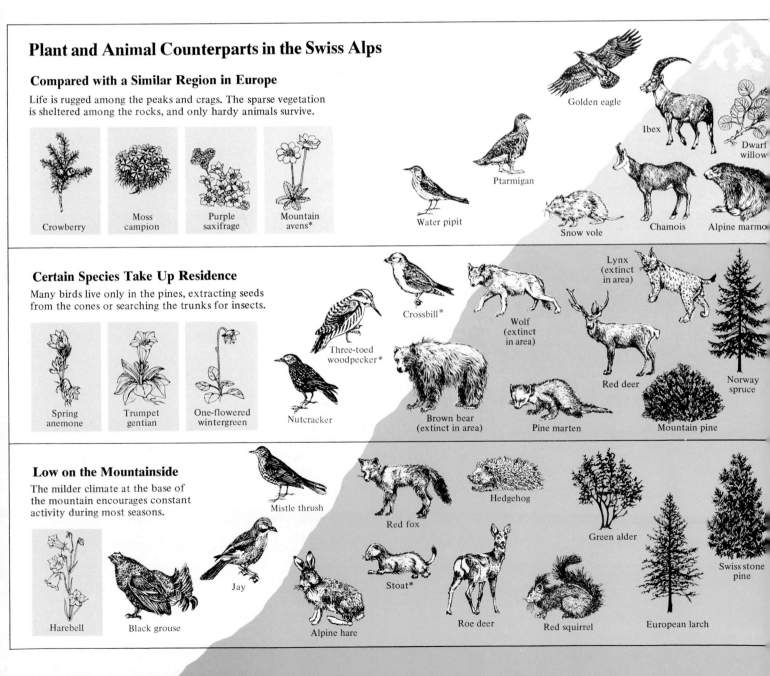

Plant and Animal Counterparts in the Swiss Alps

Compared with a Similar Region in Europe

Life is rugged among the peaks and crags. The sparse vegetation is sheltered among the rocks, and only hardy animals survive.

Crowberry

Moss campion

Purple saxifrage

Mountain avens*

Water pipit

Ptarmigan

Golden eagle

Ibex

Dwarf willow

Snow vole

Chamois

Alpine marmot

Certain Species Take Up Residence

Many birds live only in the pines, extracting seeds from the cones or searching the trunks for insects.

Spring anemone

Trumpet gentian

One-flowered wintergreen

Nutcracker

Three-toed woodpecker*

Crossbill*

Wolf (extinct in area)

Lynx (extinct in area)

Brown bear (extinct in area)

Pine marten

Red deer

Mountain pine

Norway spruce

Low on the Mountainside

The milder climate at the base of the mountain encourages constant activity during most seasons.

Harebell

Black grouse

Jay

Mistle thrush

Red fox

Hedgehog

Green alder

Alpine hare

Stoat*

Roe deer

Red squirrel

European larch

Swiss stone pine

Remote Gardens of Alpine Flowers

One of the most pleasant surprises in the mountains are the little verdant valleys, tucked away between the rugged mountain peaks like precious jewels. Travelers often hear the echoes from a valley before they reach it—the shrill whistle of a shepherd or the jingling bells of grazing animals. In the mountains of Greece, these bells, on sheep or goats, frequently sound like distant choirs, because the shepherds take pride in carefully tuning the bells. In the Alps, the sound is commonly a deep-throated gong from a cow-bell.

Grazing animals and mountain valleys go together because certain grasses with dense networks of roots are often the only crop that can be grown on slopes. It is impossible to use farm machinery there; the crop must be harvested by animal or by hand.

During spring and summer, many of these high pastures are dotted with colorful clumps of delicate-looking mountain (or alpine) flowers. The apparent fragility is deceptive, because flowering —as well as non-flowering—mountain plants are among the hardiest in the world. Many such plants grow in ground-hugging mats, or tussocks, thus keeping out of the wind and taking advantage of the warmth absorbed by the ground. The next time you see some of these flowers, such as cushion pinks, notice how their thin stems, leaves, and flowers intertwine. This intermeshing enables them to trap air near the ground, in much the same way that spun glass is used to insulate homes. The temperature inside such a cluster may be as much as 20° F. warmer than the air outside.

Fuzzy stems trap air, which is another insulating device of many alpine flowers—such as the red campion. On some flowers the bright fuzz is almost as colorful as the flower itself. The snow willow has two-toned fuzz on its buds—dark at the base and a light translucent color at the tips. Warm rays of the sun, passing through the window-like tips, are absorbed by the dark-colored base. The principle is basically the same as that used in solar-heated homes.

Many alpine flowers are insect-pollinated, as are those of the lowlands, but the cold mountain air often inactivates the insects. On a cloudy day you can see many bees lying numb on the ground, unable to move. When there is a break in the clouds, however, the pollinators revive with surprising speed, and are soon up and around.

Insects living in the mountains also take advantage of the warmer microclimates that exist near the ground, and in nooks and crannies. Many species of butterflies found in mountains fly close to the ground, thus avoiding being carried away by gusty winds.

Perhaps the most amazing adaptation of alpine flowers, however, is their ability to manufacture a kind of "antifreeze." The fluid content of such plants is often unusually high in salts and other chemicals. These high concentrations keep the fluids—and thus the plant—from freezing at temperatures that would kill other plants. Some mountain plants even generate small amounts of heat during their growth, melting their way through the snow to reach the sunlight of early spring. The growing season in the mountains is short, and plants set seeds quickly.

Certain alpine flowers, such as the edelweiss, sometimes develop unseen beneath a snowbank. On the first warm spring day, snow-clad mountain slopes may seem lifeless. Then, in a matter of a few hours, as if by magic, there is a carpet of bright blossoms.

Red campion flourishes both in the lowlands and on mountain heights up to 7,500 feet. This colorful, downy-stemmed plant is native to Europe and Asia. When brought to North America as a garden flower, the red campion "escaped" to the wild. No longer restricted to gardens, it now blooms along roadsides in the northeastern United States and Canada.

Fuzzy stems and leaves of pasqueflowers trap heat. This apparently enables them to open their delicate buds in early spring before other flowers—when snow still covers the ground.

High in the Himalayas, these gentian flowers look quite similar to related species. But these plants don't grow as tall as the typical gentian—an adaptation to alpine life.

Mountain Modifications

Many alpine flowers bear little resemblance to their lowland relatives. On the other hand, they often look like their neighbors on the mountainside—cushion pinks, rock jasmine, and dotted saxifrage have all adapted to harsh conditions by developing a rounded form. This shape is advantageous to plants in exposed locations—they are not so easily buffeted by the wind. The compact shape also retains heat. Deep roots provide anchoring.

This forget-me-not (left) is distributed worldwide. Usually, the flowers are borne on tall stems.

An alpine variety of forget-me-not (right) is most easily identified when in flower.

Wildflowers carpet an alpine hillside in the Olympic Mountains of Washington. Asters, lupines, and paintbrushes are just a few of the meadow flowers that seem to be present all summer long. In actuality, plants on the lower slopes blossom the earliest. Then, as the season advances and the snows retreat, the same species of flowers will bloom at a higher altitude.

91

The Beauty of Highlands

Highlands are, in actuality, a middle ground between the mountains and lowlands, whether they are the rolling, heather-clad Scottish Highlands, the arid South American altiplano (high plains), the picturesque western U.S. high country, or the teeming equatorial heights of East Africa. So, in a way, the term "highland" is a misnomer. The Andean altiplano, for example, is about 12,000 feet high, yet is surrounded by much higher peaks.

Most highland regions are damp, cool, and frequently foggy. They are sometimes dotted with moors, lakes, and streams. Even arid highlands such as those in South America are pitted with lakes because of saucer-like depressions that collect rainwater and melted snows. Lake Titicaca, one of the world's highest lakes, is a classic example—it fills a depression in the Bolivian altiplano, even though it occurs at an altitude of more than 11,000 feet.

For many people, the famous Scottish Highlands epitomize the austere beauty of these special regions, and localized terminologies for land formations enhance their charm. Rocky plateaus in northern Scotland are trenched by deep, narrow valleys—or glens—such as the Great Glen of Scotland, which splits the Highlands diagonally east to west. Deep firths, similar to fjords of neighboring Scandinavia, run many miles inland from the coast.

The Scottish moors are characteristically thick with low-growing vegetation. In late summer some sections are carpeted with the distinctive purple or white flowers of the evergreen heaths. These small, bell-shaped blossoms are so abundant that beekeepers often bring their hives onto the moors during this season for a special feast.

Wildlife abounds in the highlands, though the terrain is generally too rocky and infertile for farming. Some lightly forested areas of the Scottish Highlands are called "deer forests," because of the large numbers of red deer found there. Red grouse are also plentiful. However, small mammals such as meadow voles, lemmings and shrews, hares and rabbits make up most of the animal population.

In South America, the guinea pig—prized as a pet and laboratory animal the world over—is a native of the altiplano. Kruger National Park in the South African Highlands has representatives of most of the wild animals of Africa—from aardvarks to zebras.

Highlands have long been a preferred home for the human species. One of the earliest of European civilizations flourished in the mountainous highlands of Crete. Some of the oldest human fossils ever found—dating back several million years—were discovered in the Olduvai Gorge in the African highlands of Tanzania.

A feudal keep, Castle Varrich, stands guard over the Kyle of Tongue, a sea channel in the extreme north of the Scottish Highlands. This austerely beautiful land has deer and grouse.

The Comeback of the Deer

Once close to extinction, the deer of the Scottish Highlands—the large red deer and the smaller roe deer—have made a truly spectacular comeback. At one time, Scotland was covered with forests. But as the human population grew, and especially since sheep were introduced, most of the deer's habitat vanished. Red deer retreated to the moors and mountaintops; roe deer made a last stand in the remaining forests of the north. In the 19th century, however, enthusiasm for deer stalking led land-owners to establish huge deer forests. These reserves ensured the deer's survival. Without large predators, both species prospered so well that they were a threat to their environment. Today a successful management system controls their numbers. During the fall breeding season, stags are very jealous of their territories. At the right, two red stags fence with their antlers in threat display.

The Noisy Grouse Family Enlivens Highland Regions

Superbly adapted to the highlands of Europe and the colder mountains of North America, grouse and ptarmigans are protected by feathers on nostrils and feet. Most grouse are polygamous and compete for females with leaps and raucous calls. By contrast, ptarmigans are monogamous.

At a mating ground, male European black grouse engage in strenuous, ritual combat.

The mottled spring plumage of the female ptarmigan is excellent camouflage at the nest.

A strutting blue grouse of the American West emits loud booms from inflated throat sacs.

93

Wildlife at High Altitudes

The sure-footed chamois, which is the European equivalent of the Rocky Mountain goat, moves with care on narrow ledges, but its jumps seem audacious—it can leap across a chasm more than 20 feet wide.

Mountain sheep and goats are pioneers at the edge of the world, in regions where it is bitter cold and windy, where food and water are scarce and even the air is thin. One kind of Asiatic wild goat (an ancestor of domestic goats) lives up to 13,000 feet.

These mountaineers can survive on land that will support no other large mammals. Sheep and goats are ruminants, which means they have a four-chambered stomach. They can stuff themselves quickly, then bring the food up again and chew their cud like cows. Unlike most other ruminants, they can digest extremely low-grade plant materials—including lichens and twigs.

This capacity to eat every scrap of food has had an unfortunate effect on large areas of the earth. The indiscriminate appetites of domesticated sheep and goats have turned many places—especially the once-green Middle East—into deserts. They eat ground cover to the roots, killing the plants.

Archaeologists have found evidence that sheep and goats have been providing man with food and wool for six or seven thousand years. During the great Age of Exploration, these animals were carried aboard sailing ships to provide fresh milk and meat.

You are lucky if you chance to see wild sheep or goats in the mountains. It's almost impossible to get close to them; their vision is incredibly keen, and they avoid people. However, if you see one individual, keep watching: you may see others, for sheep and goats are social animals.

You may even be able to figure out their social relationships. Rams associate in all-male bands except during the mating season. If you see a group with large horns, and if no young are present, it's probably an all-male band. With the arrival of the mating season, male and female bands join. This period is easy to identify; there's lots of spirited chasing and fighting.

Can you tell sheep from goats? Roughly, yes. Usually, the horns of *goats,* both male and female, grow from near the top of the head and curve up and back; their foreheads are convex. The horns of *sheep,* generally prominent only in males, grow from the sides of the head; their foreheads are concave.

Horns are often used in battles between males during the mating season. Surprisingly, both horns and human fingernails are made of the same material—a substance called keratin. The horns of sheep and goats are permanent (unlike the bony antlers of deer, which are shed annually). The number of rings on a horn is sometimes a clue to an animal's age.

Visit your local zoo or game farm to get a really good look at these impressive animals. Usually you will find several representatives of this large sub-family, or tribe, of hoofed animals, the *Caprinae*. The roster includes not just domesticated varieties, but also ibexes, mouflons, and many others.

Notice the double hoofs. They are hard and sharp and grip rock almost like pincers. Between and behind the hoofs are padded soles that cushion the animal's leaps. Also notice their heavy, water-repellent coats. They are superbly suited to a life at high altitudes.

Rocky Mountain bighorn sheep winter below the timberline, where the climate is warmer and food more plentiful than at higher elevations. These hefty animals climb mountain slopes in spring, and descend from them in autumn. Such movement is called vertical migration.

BIRDING TIPS
The Great Gliders

Mountains are the only places you can get a really good look at the great birds of prey: hawks, eagles, falcons, and their kin. Instead of craning your neck and squinting into the sun, you can watch them from above, as they ride the updrafts with effortless grace.

• Notice that these birds seldom flap their wings, but take advantage of wind currents, banking and turning like gliders. These truly magnificent birds seem to cut the skies with their wings.

• Shape is the key to identifying birds of prey in flight. Buteos (a type of hawk) have broad tails and wings; accipiters (such as goshawks) have longer tails and rounded wings. Falcon wings are pointed.

• Fall migration is the best time for watching hawks and eagles. Large numbers go by in wave after wave. Choose a windy day, especially one that follows the passing of a cold front.

• The flight routes of these birds are well known. In the eastern U.S., visit Hawk Mountain in Pennsylvania. For flights from central Canada, visit the bluffs overlooking Lake Superior near Duluth, Minnesota.

• Bald eagles and ospreys are the first to migrate, starting in August; golden eagles are often last, departing for the south as late as November.

• Except during migration, you'll rarely see more than one or two birds of prey. As their name indicates, they are hunters and need a lot of space.

Small, Furry Mountain Mammals

There is an amazing similarity among the small mountain mammals on different continents. The ones shown here are all plant-eating animals that live in large groups; they have short legs and thick fur, which reduce heat loss. Unlike mountain sheep and goats, these little creatures remain at high altitudes throughout the year, hibernating in winter or sometimes moving about under the snow.

The North American pika has a variety of names, including whistling hare, rock rabbit, and coney. Other pikas live in Asia.

The rock hyrax of Africa, some 12 inches long, looks and behaves like a rodent—but it is really the elephant's closest living relative.

The chinchilla, long-whiskered and covered with extremely soft fur, occupies burrows and rock crevices in the Andes Mountains.

The alpine marmot, found near the timberline on many European slopes, has relatives all around the world.

95

Cold-Weather Vegetation

It seems hard to believe that anything could live on mountain peaks where the wind may howl at more than 200 miles an hour, and where temperatures often fall far below freezing. The little moisture present is usually frozen solid. Yet certain plants have developed amazing adaptations that allow them to survive under such extreme conditions.

Lichens, probably the hardiest of all plants, live where virtually nothing else can—not just on rugged mountain peaks but also on sun-baked desert rocks. They are usually the first life to appear on a mountainside that has been scraped bare by an avalanche.

Unlike other members of the plant kingdom, lichens are actually a partnership between two plants. The framework of a lichen is usually a network of minute hair-like fungus that anchors the plant (see below). The other component is an alga (similar to the green film of plant life that grows on stagnant pools), which is distributed throughout the fungus. Being green plants, algae are capable of photosynthesis—that is, using energy from the sun to manufacture their own food. The fungi are believed to supply water, minerals, and physical support to the partnership.

Lichens are famous for their ability to survive a water shortage. When water is scarce (as is often the case on a mountain), lichens may become dormant and remain in that condition for

Lichens Grow in a Variety of Shapes and Places

It may come as a surprise that lichens are so varied and numerous. There are some 16,000 species, which are classified into three types: crustose (crusty), fruticose (shrubby), and foliose (leafy). All three are common in mountain regions. Crustose lichens form patches on solid rock and are often the first plants to colonize barren, rocky soil; they actually help to make soil for other plants by secreting acids that eventually disintegrate the rock. Fruticose species such as beard lichen hang from branches or, like reindeer "moss" (the winter food of caribou), cover the ground. Foliose lichens grow on tree trunks, dead logs, and rocks. One species, a rock tripe, is shown below.

Foliose or leaf-like lichen (above) is the same type as the grayish lichens at the bottom of the adjacent photo.

Fine structure of the lichen shows that algae (green) are present only in a thin layer.

A lichen tapestry (left) of subtly interlocking forms enlivens the rocks of Utah's high country. In this community of several lichen species, each one has a characteristic color.

extended periods of time. Some lichens can even grow where there is no rain at all, surviving on only occasional dew. And unlike most other plants, lichens are little affected by the strong ultraviolet rays in the mountains.

Lichens use little energy, for they grow slowly. Some grow so slowly and are so old that they are called "time stains." You may find lichens that are centuries old; certain of these lichen colonies have been established for an estimated 2,000 years.

For decades, scientists wondered how the offspring of an alga and a fungus got together to form a new lichen. It seemed unlikely that they would just happen to encounter one another. It was finally discovered that in many cases the two partners have never been separated. Stalk-like "buds" that form on certain lichens are broken off by the wind, or by animals; these tiny offshoots roll or are blown to a new location.

Another long-standing puzzle was how the two components established their partnership in the first place. Under certain conditions, scientists were able to grow the alga and the fungus separately, but they could not combine the two to make a "test-tube" lichen. It is now believed that the two plants will form a partnership only if conditions are unfavorable. It is as if they agree to the partnership only when they can't make it on their own.

Most mountain plants—the lichens, wildflowers, grasses, and even trees—have a low profile that helps them take advantage of whatever protection rocks and ridges may provide. Near the timberline (the highest altitude at which trees can grow), woody plants become gnarled and twisted. These gnome-like plants are called krummholz, which means, appropriately, "crooked wood." Here, trees such as firs and pines are so contorted and dwarfed that they resemble an enchanted forest from a fairy tale. But the chilling, drying wind is the true architect of these shapes. The parts of the plants that would normally grow on the windward side have been frozen, dried, and even torn off by the wind.

At the upper edge of the timberline the krummholz-effect is even more extreme. Trees may be so dwarfed and intertwined that you can walk on top of them. A hiker in the mountains who says, "Today I walked over a forest," may be telling the absolute truth.

Veteran pines, growing near the timberline on the steep slopes of Idaho's Pioneer Mountains, still cling stubbornly to life. The fresh green of new growth contrasts with the silver-gray of weathered trunks and branches that have been damaged by the onslaught of wind and frost.

Stunted Trees of the Timberline Are Shaped by Winds

Severe spring ice-storms, blistering summer sun, and sub-zero winter temperatures combine with ever-present winds to prune timberline trees into bizarre shapes called krummholz. The timberline is not a rigid boundary that circles a peak at a certain altitude. It varies with local conditions, extending higher on the mountain in sheltered areas and on southern slopes.

A young pine grows on the protected side of a rock. Even there, some branches are bent down by the wind and will eventually take root.

In winter, a blanket of snow protects the tree from freezing, but new shoots that protrude are soon killed off by the dry, cold wind.

The tree has grown as tall as it can. Only the side branches, protected from the wind, continue to reach outward along the ground.

As the tree ages, older portions near the rock are the first to die. However, as the younger branches take root, the tree gradually creeps away from the protected site where it started. Strong prevailing winds create flag-like forms by shearing buds from the windward side.

97

Animal Life on the Arctic Tundra

Summer on the arctic tundra is brief; thawing begins about June, and freezing conditions return in August. It is the movement of the earth around the sun that brings the seasons. Because the earth turns on a tilted axis, light from the sun strikes the surface of the earth unequally. The greatest seasonal variation is apparent at the poles. Polar winters are dark even during the day; at midsummer, the sun does not set below the horizon.

The arctic tundra region, which is near the north pole, also experiences drastic seasonal changes. The temperatures, which may have been as cold as −70°F. in winter, rise to summertime peaks of 70°F. to 80°F., producing humid, balmy conditions. At night, temperatures seldom go below 40°F.

Even before the snows have melted, clumps of grass begin to grow, and dense, spongy carpets of moss and lichen come to life. Hordes of insects hatch in the meltwater pools that dot the landscape.

The stage is set for many animals—residents and transients alike—to breed, rear their young, and build up their physical strength for the hardships of winter. Some birds, such as ptarmigan, are year-round residents. In winter, these birds have white feathers, which provide camouflage against a snowy background. With the changing season, their plumage changes too, to a mottled pattern that blends perfectly with the summer tundra. Ptarmigan eggs are also mottled. When the tiny chicks hatch, they are so well camouflaged as to be almost invisible.

Like most of the larger tundra nesters—such as geese, swans, and ducks—young ptarmigan are capable of feeding themselves from the time they hatch. So are the chicks of nesting shorebirds, such as sandpipers and plovers. The young of these species are called precocial. The parents' role is to guard, guide, and brood them (providing warmth at night) until they achieve independence.

But there are other species of tundra-nesting birds with different patterns of infant development. Tree sparrows, for example, have altricial nestlings—helpless young that stay in the nest and must be fed by adults. The abundance of insects on the tundra allows parent birds to feed their offspring hundreds of times during a long arctic day. Meanwhile, hidden nests provide protection from foxes and other predators.

Hawks, eagles, and falcons soar overhead, searching for prey. Other birds account for much of their diet. But multitudes of small rodents are also available prey. Lemmings, voles, and marmots, which live in burrows and tunnel systems throughout the winter, come out to bask in the sun and feed on the new vegetation. These little animals respond to favorable conditions by increased breeding. Some are capable of producing four or five litters a year, with five or six offspring per litter. Their numbers climb for as long as the food supply holds out. This wealth of prey attracts snowy owls, arctic foxes, and other predators from outlying regions. The predators, in turn, successfully rear more offspring.

The end of a population explosion comes when the prey animals exhaust their food supply. High mortality follows—caused partly by starvation, partly by stress, which leaves the animals vulnerable to disease. Soon after, predators experience the same downward trend in population.

BIRDING TIPS
Tundra Nesters That Visit Us

Have you ever wondered why birds travel thousands of miles to nesting sites on the arctic tundra? Scientists believe they are attracted by the incredibly rich food supply —grasses, berries, aquatic plants, and myriads of insects, such as mosquitoes and blackflies. Long daylight hours allow young birds to feed and be fed almost around the clock. Thus the young birds fledge quickly. When the breeding season is over and the food supply dwindles, these tundra nesters head south. The map shows the approximate breeding range and migration routes for three species of birds.

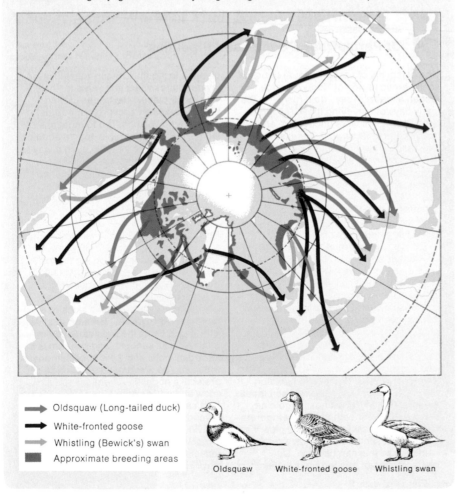

→ Oldsquaw (Long-tailed duck)
→ White-fronted goose
→ Whistling (Bewick's) swan
■ Approximate breeding areas

Oldsquaw   White-fronted goose   Whistling swan

Lemmings are extremely prolific rodents that literally eat themselves out of house and home. Periodically, the stress of crowding sends them swarming over the tundra.

Perched in a commanding position, the snowy owl is on the alert for lemmings—the main food of this powerful hunter.

Caribou are the nomads of North America. Following routes that are centuries old, these deer migrate from forested wintering areas to calving and feeding grounds on the tundra.

CHAPTER FOUR

Sea and Shore

*The ocean is a giant circulatory system
for the earth. And the motion of currents and
tides lends vitality to the waters.*

No part of the planet exerts a more powerful emotional pull than the sea. Poets and painters, writers and photographers, have sometimes captured a measure of the sea's mystical attraction, but none has explained it fully. Perhaps we feel the tug of the sea because of an ancient relationship—scientists believe that billions of years ago life originated in the sea.

The waters themselves are a source of wonder—far from being a uniform mixture of water and salts, the ocean environment has many different zones and provides varied habitats for plants and animals. The waters around a tropical reef have a wealth of local life forms. These influence both the water and one another. Transport a tropical fish to another environment—even to one at the same temperature—and chances are it will not live. Stranger still is the fact that the jostling of the waters seems to be essential to its vitality; if you take part of the sea home in a jar, it will soon become stale and lifeless.

The odors of the sea are infinitely varied. The basic scent comes from sodium chloride, which is ordinary table salt. But in some places its smell is medicinal (like iodine), in others, pungent with seaweed. The high amounts of dissolved salts make seawater sting when blown across our faces, and give it an astringent taste. The sea captures all our senses.

The movement of oceans over two-thirds of the globe acts like a huge heat engine, stirring the atmosphere and creating climate worldwide. Thus the influence of oceans, so apparent on the coasts, extends even to remote inland regions, where seas are the stuff of story and legend.

It is only at the shore that waves break in this way—dashing against an underwater slope, then erupting. The result is a magnificent spray that looks like a fan of etched glass. As a wave topples, sunlight on the shallow waters transforms the deep blue colors of the open ocean to pale, translucent tones.

Rocky, Sandy, and Marshy Shores

Seashores are narrow margins on the vast ocean world, but they are the only part of this realm that people can easily explore. At the shore, you can see the endless contest between land and sea. In some places, the sea is winning—dune fences and even buildings have toppled into the water as the surf cuts deeper into the land. In other places, the land seems to win. Sometimes, in just a matter of hours, a storm may pile up countless tons of mud, sand, and rock against the shore, creating land where there was none before.

For convenience, you can classify a particular shore into one of three types—rocky, sandy, or marshy. Rocky coasts are the most dramatic; jagged cliffs often rise sharply above the seas. The seething water seems to be ripped apart by sharp fingers of rock. But just the opposite is actually happening; the waves are slowly wearing away the rock, breaking it into fragments, sculpting it into arches, ledges, and caves.

The waves often cut the rocks like a huge horizontal saw, undermining the face of a cliff and causing it to collapse. Then the waves break down the rubble, grinding boulders into pebbles and pebbles into sand. Sometimes you can even hear a grinding sound as waves wash a rocky beach.

It has been estimated that the sea may take several hundred years to reduce a boulder a foot in diameter to sand. Ocean currents may carry this sand far from the site where it originated, or it may be caught and held nearby in cup-shaped depressions in the rocks. Sometimes the currents drop particles washed from cliffs at the end of a long, rocky shore, and a sandy beach develops at that point.

Though many times smaller than boulders, the tiny sand particles usually last much longer on a shore. You can discover why as you walk along a sandy beach. Your feet will sink in dry sand; damp sand supports your weight and provides a natural boardwalk between the shifting dry areas and the submerged beach. This is because a thin film of water envelops each grain in damp sand. The film acts like glue, holding the grains together and also insulating them from one another so that the waves do not grind them down.

This watery insulation protects many animals that live on sandy shores. These species are different from the inhabitants of a rocky coast, which tend to attach themselves to rocks. The more mobile creatures of the sandy beach—crabs and clams, for instance—occupy burrows. Some even live in the minute spaces between the grains of sand. This is a more cushioned world than a pebbly beach.

Rocky coasts are wonderful places for photographers, philosophers, and geologists (not to mention gulls and other birds). The pounding of waves steadily dissects the rock—water infiltrates along the seams, where it is weak. Here, slightly tilted horizontal layers of sandstone can be seen.

Eventually—probably after thousands of years—sand grains are broken down into smaller pieces and become mud. The pulverized material—silt and clay particles—is readily swept away by shore currents, but in a protected area (such as a bay or inlet), the material may accumulate and form a muddy shore. Mud flats also form where rivers flow into the sea.

Mud flats are quickly colonized by plants and animals. Eelgrass grows on the muddy sea floor just beyond the surf, and marsh grasses gain a foothold on the shore. The maze of roots and intertwining stems traps more mud and provides a sanctuary for creatures of sea and land. This relatively sheltered world retains plant debris, and gradually fills in with soil. Salt marshes, as environments, are relatively short-lived, but for as long as they exist, they are superb natural wildlife refuges.

PHOTO TIPS
Taking Pictures Where It's Salty and Sandy

The first rule of beach photography is to protect your camera and film. Carry them in a waterproof, insulated bag. Never put your camera on the sand—the lens may be scratched. People who wouldn't dream of going to the beach without hats or sunglasses often forget that their film also needs protection from both excessive light and heat. Sunshades and lens filters are important aids to seaside photography.
• For color photos, an ultraviolet (UV) haze filter will reduce the blue haze caused by dust particles and moisture.
• A polarizing filter will cut down unwanted reflections, and will darken skies and water. This applies to both color and black-and-white film. Film speeds are affected by such filters, so follow the instructions that come with the filter.
• Bright light can be turned to an advantage by using slow-speed films. These generally register details best.

A sandy shore may seem desolate, almost devoid of life, but beneath its wet and glistening surface is an incredible variety of tiny animals. The most important factor in their lives is the water that surrounds them: it brings them food, keeps them cool and moist, and may eventually wash them away.

Salt marshes are also shores, though their outlines are less defined than those of other coasts. Man has been slow to appreciate the importance of these productive regions. Some animals (including fish) use marshes as incubators for their young; other species (such as egrets) live here the year round.

Warm Currents, Cold Currents, and Climate

Currents are like rivers in the sea. Some of the currents that circulate in oceans are more than 50 miles wide and transport about 50 million tons of water a second. Ocean circulation has a profound effect on climate. Heat from a current is transmitted to the winds that pass over it; the net effect is that of a gigantic hot-water heating system for the whole globe.

Energy from the sun drives the currents—surface waters are heated, which causes them to expand, especially in the region around the equator. This increased volume of water flows outward, toward the poles, where it gradually cools and sinks. At the same time, cold water from the ocean depths comes up, replacing waters that have flowed away.

The motion of the earth stirs the seas. Many currents become part of immense, slow-motion whirlpools. For example, the Gulf Stream flows into the Canaries Current, which branches west into the North Equatorial Current and (to a lesser extent) south into the Guinean Current. The currents are mainly clockwise in the northern hemisphere, counterclockwise in the southern hemisphere. This general pattern is greatly influenced by the winds, and is modified by the contours of continents and the presence of islands. Many currents fluctuate in their range. The Humboldt Current, for example, sometimes turns toward the west before its cold, oxygen-rich waters reach the coast of Peru. This adversely affects fishing off the Peruvian coast.

Warm air holds more moisture than cold air. When two temperature systems collide, the result is usually precipitation. When warm winds from the Gulf Stream strike cooler air from the arctic in the vicinity of the British Isles, fog results. So, too, when the cold winds from the Labrador Current touch the Gulf Stream off Newfoundland—the seas are blanketed by mist.

Whale-Watching Close to Land

One of the joys of ocean-watching is the surprising frequency with which whales can be sighted, both from shore and (more often) from ship. Whales regularly visit waters off California, Bermuda, and eastern Canada for breeding, or during migration. They often reveal their presence by spouting–in fact, most species have an identifiable spouting pattern. If a whale is nearby, look at the curve of its back to identify the species, and also at the shape of its fins and flukes (tail). Widely distributed whales, from the largest (the blue) to the smallest (dolphin), are shown at right.

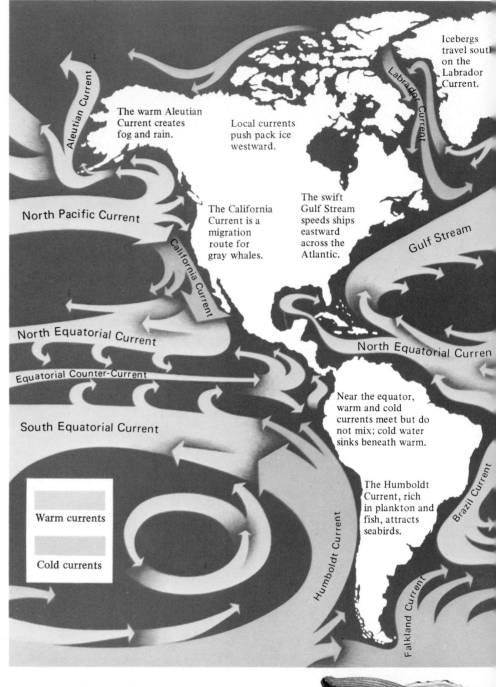

Icebergs travel south on the Labrador Current.

The warm Aleutian Current creates fog and rain.

Local currents push pack ice westward.

The swift Gulf Stream speeds ships eastward across the Atlantic.

The California Current is a migration route for gray whales.

Aleutian Current

North Pacific Current

California Current

Labrador Current

Gulf Stream

North Equatorial Current

North Equatorial Current

Equatorial Counter-Current

South Equatorial Current

Near the equator, warm and cold currents meet but do not mix; cold water sinks beneath warm.

The Humboldt Current, rich in plankton and fish, attracts seabirds.

Warm currents

Cold currents

Humboldt Current

Brazil Current

Falkland Current

The sperm whale, named for the oily wax that fills a reservoir in its enormous head, is a tropical species. The fictional Moby Dick was an albino sperm whale.

The beluga, or white whale, travels in large groups, usually in arctic waters.

The humpback whale, famous for its underwater singing, often leaps high, hitting the water with its flukes as it submerges.

Murmansk Current

E. Greenland Current

North Atlantic Current

In summer, fresh water from Siberian rivers influences local currents. Polar bears ride the drifting ice floes.

The cold Oyashio brings arctic waters to Japan.

Aleutian Current

Warm Atlantic waters keep Norwegian ports ice-free.

Western Europe gets its mild climate from the Gulf Stream.

High mountains cut off cold, arid grasslands and deserts of Central Asia from moisture-bearing oceanic winds.

The warm Kuroshio ("black stream") eventually reaches North America.

Oyashio

North Pacific Current

Kuroshio

Polynesians sailing Pacific currents in sea-going canoes settled the mid-ocean islands.

Columbus sailed south and west via two currents—the Canaries and the North Equatorial.

Arab sailing craft have used the seasonal monsoon drift for centuries.

Monsoon Drift

North Equatorial Current

South Equatorial Current

Equatorial Counter-Current

South Equatorial Current

South Equatorial Current

South Africa exports lobsters from tropical waters on the east; the west coast is cold.

Agulhas Current

Warm waters wash the Great Barrier Reef; a cold current lures whales to the southern coast.

Benguela Current

W. Australian Current

E. Australian Current

A stormy belt of frigid water circles Antarctica and pushes into the southern oceans.

Antarctic Circumpolar Current

Antarctic Circumpolar Current

The killer whale is the only species of whale that attacks large prey. In aquariums, these whales are surprisingly friendly.

The blue whale is the largest of all mammals—the record length is 108 feet. It is a filter-feeder, straining its food through baleen plates.

The right whale was named by whalers because it was so easily captured. Right whales live in northern and southern oceans.

The common dolphin (or porpoise) is a small, gregarious whale that often accompanies ships at sea.

The Open Ocean

On an ocean voyage, as land drops from sight, a sudden sense of isolation often overtakes a traveler—an awareness of the immensity of the sea. Washington Irving, the nineteenth-century American writer, experienced a "delicious sensation of mingled security and awe" when he climbed to the ship's maintop during his first transatlantic crossing. That was in 1804. Although ships have changed a great deal since that time, few modern travelers are immune to the experience described by Irving so long ago.

A sea voyage offers valuable insights into the marine world. For example, the coloration of the ocean varies widely. The reddish color sometimes seen in antarctic waters may reveal the presence of millions of krill, shrimp-like creatures on which many great whales feed. Vast numbers of tiny aquatic plants color many coastal seas green or blue-green. Such intensive plant growth occurs near the mouths of rivers, where the flowing waters deposit their load of nutrient-rich sediments.

In contrast, the typical color of the open ocean (the region beyond the coastal seas) is a deep blue. Too far from the land to receive much in the way of nutrients, the open ocean has relatively little microscopic life. Any sea (or deep lake) that is not colored by plants, animals, or dissolved materials looks blue. Although no one knows exactly why this is so, the reflection of the sky is believed to play a role.

Lights twinkle on and off beneath the surface of the nighttime sea. The English poet Coleridge, in "The Rime of the Ancient Mariner," called these ghost-like flashes witches' fire; today, the light is known as bioluminescence. Usually, the light comes from tiny animals that rise to the surface at night. Although some larger animals—certain fish and squid, for example—are also luminescent, this light is often produced not by the animals themselves but by bacteria living on or inside them.

During the daytime, you can see other, larger animals from the deck of a ship, especially near islands, shoals, or patches of seaweed. Flying fish leap in the path of a ship. Occasionally, sea turtles paddle by; these massive reptiles must come to the surface to breathe. Shearwaters (birds named for their habit of skimming low over the waves) fly across the ship's wake; birds known as storm-petrels patter on the water as they feed.

One curiosity of the ocean is that few insects have managed to colonize its vast surface. A few sea-going gnats are identified by scientists from time to time, but even though there is a steady stream of insects as the wind blows from the land, insects have never made a substantial contribution to the populations of the seas. Their absence may be one reason for the popularity of cruises, and of sailing generally.

The quintessential seabird is the albatross, a long-winged, stout-bodied bird famous for its habit of following ships. The word seabird usually refers to species that live far out to sea, returning to land only to breed. This species of albatross, called a light-mantled sooty albatross, roams southern seas and nests on islands near New Zealand and Antarctica. Other seabird species include fulmars, gannets, and puffins, but not gulls, which are birds of the shore.

A pod of dolphins leaps across a quiet sea. Though the names dolphin and porpoise are often used interchangeably, it is usually easy to tell one from the other: dolphins have beak-like snouts, porpoises have blunt ones.

NATURE OBSERVER
Reading the Waves

The surface of the sea responds to the movement of the wind—high winds transform a smooth, placid sea into a tumultuous swirl of whitecaps or driving spray. With the help of the Beaufort Wind Scale (right), you can gauge the approximate wind speed just by looking at the open ocean. Simply select the description that best suits the sea; the scale will give you the corresponding wind speed in knots. (A knot is one nautical mile per hour; a nautical mile is slightly longer than a standard mile.) The Beaufort scale was devised by an officer of the British Navy in the nineteenth century, when sailing ships battled one another on the open sea. Modern ships have anemometers, which measure wind speed with greater precision.

Beaufort number	Sea description	Wind speed (in knots)	Wind description
0	Sea like a mirror.	0-1	Calm
1*	Scale-like ripples; no foam crests.	1-3	Light air
2	Small wavelets; glassy crests, not breaking.	4-6	Light breeze
3	Large wavelets; crests break; few whitecaps.	7-10	Gentle breeze
4	Small waves; frequent whitecaps.	11-16	Moderate breeze
5*	Moderate waves; many whitecaps; some spray.	17-21	Fresh breeze
6*	Larger waves; whitecaps everywhere; more spray.	22-27	Strong breeze
7*	Sea heaps up; foam from breaking waves.	28-33	Near gale
8	Moderately high waves; crest edges break into spray; foam blown in streaks.	34-40	Gale
9*	High waves; sea begins to roll.	41-47	Strong gale
10*	Very high waves with overhanging crests.	48-55	Storm
11	Exceptionally high waves; sea covered with foam patches; reduced visibility.	56-63	Violent storm
12	Air filled with foam; sea completely white with driving spray; visibility very poor.	64-71	Hurricane

*Shown below

Edges of the Continents

Continents do not end at the seashore. They continue under the water, where, on gently sloping plains, there are hills, valleys, and other features much like those on land. This shallow underwater region is called the continental shelf, and it is considered to be the true edge of the continent. Beyond the shelf, the land drops steeply down to the deep, dark ocean floor.

On the average, the continental shelf is about 45 miles wide. But in some places, it stretches hundreds of miles out into the sea. The underwater descent from the shore to the edge of the shelf is gradual, dropping only about 10 feet for every mile. The outer edge of the shelf is usually covered by about 450 feet of water. Beyond that region, the sea floor plunges steeply (this incline is called the continental slope) and does not level off again until it reaches the bottom of the ocean basin.

Many of the continental shelves were formed millions of years ago, when forces deep within the earth pushed up underwater mountains near the coasts. In some places, the mountains rose above sea level, creating islands that have lasted to this day. Sediment washed from the land filled in behind these island dams, forming an undersea shoulder at the edge of the land mass.

During the Ice Ages, the oceans were lower because much of the earth's water was frozen. Glaciers gouged the exposed parts of the shelves. As the sea level gradually changed, the surf gnawed at the edges, creating terraces. Some parts of the shelves that were exposed during the Ice Ages were covered with forests. Fossils collected by research submarines and dredges indicate that mammoths, mastodons, and giant moose foraged in the vegetation there.

Today the continental shelves are once again covered with water. In some places, there are canyons that were cut by ancient rivers. For example, an underwater extension of the Hudson River valley forms a canyon nearly three-quarters of a mile deep and more than 5 miles wide. Occasionally, underwater avalanches race down the can-

---

SAFETY AND SURVIVAL
Beware of Sea Creatures That Sting and Pinch

When you set out to explore a beach or a tidepool, take some simple precautions to avoid a sting, pinch, bite, or jab:
- Wear sneakers when wading. Sharp edges of rock and coral, as well as broken clamshells, can inflict painful cuts. Sea urchins and stingrays have sharp spines.
- Don't pick up sea creatures with your bare hands. Some crabs may pinch severely if they are disturbed.
- Never stick your hands into a hole or crevice, especially on a coral reef where there may be scorpionfish bristling with poisonous spines, or moray eels that bite.
- If you see a jellyfish, get out of the water—these stinging animals usually swim in groups. Some species are harmless to humans, but others can cause reactions that vary from a rash or welt to a violent allergic attack. More dangerous still is the Portuguese man-of-war—its tentacles (as much as 50 feet long) can ensnare a swimmer. A dead jellyfish on a beach may still have active stinging capsules—don't touch it!

Buoyed by a gas-inflated "sail," a Portuguese man-of-war is not a jellyfish; it is actually a colony of many specialized animals. Here, its tentacles are wrapped around its prey.

Like a pulsating flower, the moon jelly swims by contracting its shallow bell. This species, common in shore waters of Europe and North America, is not as harmful as other jellyfish.

yons, scooping them out and making them deeper; river-borne sediments may fill in other depressions.

The shelves are rich regions of the ocean. Sunlight penetrates the shallow waters, stimulating photosynthesis—which is the basis of all life. Microscopic floating plants are the start of the food chain in the sea; they are eaten by microscopic animals and a host of larger creatures. Consequently, coastal seas are by far the most productive habitats—almost four-fifths of all plants and animals on earth live here. At first, this may seem surprising (if, for example, you had supposed tropical rain forests to have the largest populations of living things). But even on the relatively shallow shelves, the ocean is far deeper than a forest is high, so there is much more living space in the sea. Although the shelves underlie a relatively small percentage of the ocean's total area, the waters above them furnish nearly all the world's seafood.

Petroleum deposits are valuable resources of the shelves, especially in the northern Gulf of Mexico, the North Sea, the Persian Gulf, and Australia's Bass Strait. This substance is a by-product of the bountiful life in ancient coastal seas. Then, as now, minute plants and animals drifted in the water. After these organisms died and sank to the bottom, they were buried by sediment washed from the land. Over millions of years, these dead plants and animals were converted into petroleum and natural gas. Today the shelves yield more than a fifth of the world's total production of these fuels—a figure that is sure to increase in the future.

Afloat in its spiral shell, the chambered nautilus enlarges its home as it grows. The animal itself lives in the outer chamber; the inner segments provide buoyancy.(See cross-section, page 15.)

Where the Octopus and Its Relatives Live

The octopus and other cephalopods (meaning head-foot) are members of an ancient group. The ancestors of present-day nautiluses were larger in size and amazingly abundant. Now, however, cephalopods without shells are more numerous. These animals live at varying depths on the continental shelves. Octopuses occupy holes in the rocks, mostly in shallow water. Nautiluses are bottom-dwellers. Cuttlefish (with an internal, vestigial shell) inhabit warm, coastal waters. Many species of squid swim near the surface; others are deep-sea denizens.

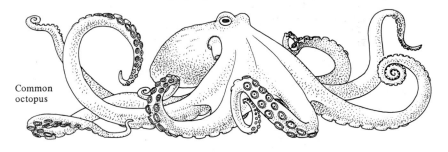

Common octopus

The Varying Profiles of the Continental Shelves

The shelves that edge the continents seldom show the same profile from one section of a coast to another. Coastal charts record great variations in width of shelf and depth of water. The surface of some shelves is irregular, with deep troughs and shallow banks. In the arctic, a smooth shelf slopes gently for hundreds of miles. Elsewhere, a narrow platform may end abruptly in rocky, underwater cliffs. An extreme example of such a drop occurs off the coast of South America (where there is a deep trench). The pitch-dark ocean floor, called the abyss, varies in depth throughout the world.

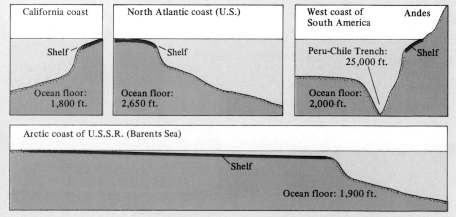

California coast

Shelf

Ocean floor: 1,800 ft.

North Atlantic coast (U.S.)

Shelf

Ocean floor: 2,650 ft.

West coast of South America   Andes

Peru-Chile Trench: 25,000 ft.   Shelf

Ocean floor: 2,000 ft.

Arctic coast of U.S.S.R. (Barents Sea)

Shelf

Ocean floor: 1,900 ft.

The Rhythm of the Tides

Day in, day out, the tides advance upon the shores, only to retreat again at predictable times. So regular are these rhythms that in ancient times some people believed them to be caused by the breath of a monster at the bottom of the sea. We now know that the tides are, in fact, governed by a huge object, but not one on this planet. The moon is the main cause of the tides. Its gravity tugs at the oceans and creates a bulge on the side of the earth nearest to itself. The sun also exerts an influence, but the moon is dominant.

In addition to daily tides, twice a month the tides are extremely high. They are called "spring" tides—but not because of season. They are higher because the moon and sun are jointly exerting a pull on the seas. (To jog your memory, think of high tides as "springing up.") The opposite condition, where there is little tidal variation, is called neap. Neap tides reflect the situation when the moon, earth, and sun are at right angles to one another, which also occurs twice a month.

The movement of the earth also contributes to tidal action. The rotation of the globe, with its irregular distribution of continents and islands, causes the water to "pile up" when the land masses collide with the tidal bulges. (Ocean waters do not race around the world, but instead rise and fall in a much more localized way.) In a sense, you can think of the waters as being under the ever-changing influence of the moon and sun, and of the continents as doing all the moving—into tides and out of them.

The different sizes and shapes of the ocean basins have a profound effect on tidal movements. Everyone who has walked across a room carrying a glass of water or cup of coffee knows that if you hold the container level, you can go fairly quickly without spilling. But if you were to carry a pan of water of equal depth but greater diameter, you would have to go much more slowly; the sloshing effect is magnified.

Similarly, oceans react differently to the tidal bulges. For example, the tides at the Pacific end of the Panama Canal are 12 to 16 feet, while at the Atlantic end, only 40 miles away, the tidal range is only 1 or 2 feet in height. In some oceans, such as the Atlantic, the tidal bulges produce two daily tides of about equal magnitude. In the Pacific, successive highs and lows are often unequal. In some areas, such as Southeast Asia, one of the tides is barely detectable.

Shorelines also affect tides. As tidal waters enter the relatively narrow mouth of the Gulf of Mexico, they spread out and are diminished. Just the opposite happens at the Bay of Fundy on Canada's Atlantic coast. As tidal waters move in the funnel-shaped bay, they are squeezed higher and higher. In part of the bay the water rises more than 50 feet—the world's highest tide.

A further complexity is the "tides" in smaller bodies of water. The Mediterranean Sea, for example, does not have tides in the ordinary sense. Evaporation lowers the water level, and the influx of water at the Strait of Gibraltar seems to be a tide.

What Causes the Tides?

Tides are the result of the moon's pull (and, to a lesser extent, that of the sun) on the oceans. Bulges form where the pull is greatest.

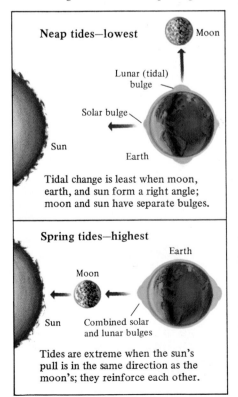

Neap tides—lowest

Moon

Lunar (tidal) bulge

Solar bulge

Sun

Earth

Tidal change is least when moon, earth, and sun form a right angle; moon and sun have separate bulges.

Spring tides—highest

Earth

Moon

Sun

Combined solar and lunar bulges

Tides are extreme when the sun's pull is in the same direction as the moon's; they reinforce each other.

Sea caves are formed by the pounding of waves. Starting as a crevice, a cave may grow so large that it undermines the rocky face of the cliff, causing it to collapse. Sea caves attract visitors; it's essential to know when the tides will be high, as the influx of water may cover the exit.

Tide flats are coastal regions where changes in water level are frequent. Like most such muddy regions, this broad expanse, located on an arm of Cook Inlet near Anchorage, Alaska, is protected from the pounding of the open ocean. Knowing when tides will go out is important for anyone boating near tide flats. If marooned by the dropping water level, a skipper may well have to wait for the next tide in order to float free.

NATURE OBSERVER
Taking Advantage of Tides for Boating and Fishing

Tides alter the seashores significantly for boaters and fishermen alike. (Even if you don't intend to boat or fish, you can observe the working of tides, starting with the high-tide marks on piers, rocks, and beaches. You can also follow human activities, which the tides alternately "encourage" and "prohibit.")

• At high tide, relatively large craft can cross shallows and negotiate channels that might otherwise be hazardous. On the other hand, low tide may enable a tall ship to pass under a stationary bridge where there is usually too little clearance.

• When anchoring, lines have to be adjusted to match the variation in tidal levels over the next few hours (or however long the vessel will be there).

• Many ships leave port on outgoing tides, taking advantage of the current. Low tide is also the time when boat and ship owners repair damages.

• For fishermen, the incoming tide is a boon because it stirs up sandbanks and mud flats, rousing many of the burrowing animals there. This attracts fish to feed. The presence of circling seabirds over a patch of water is often a clue to where

fish are feeding near the surface.

• As the tide goes out and shores are exposed, fishermen go after clams, crabs, and shrimp, and also dig for bait.

• Information on tides is usually given in local newspapers in seacoast towns and cities. The hours of low and high tide are also given on radio and TV. If you don't have access to these sources, don't hesitate to ask local boatmen or fishermen. Their knowledge of a particular area is often valuable because they know the idiosyncrasies of the underwater landscape, which affect the tides.

113

Living Conditions on a Rocky Coast

A receding tide on a rocky coast uncovers one surprise after another. As the water falls, previously hidden plants and animals come into view—crusty barnacles and limpets, filmy red algae, slippery rockweeds, and long strands of kelp. Unlike shifting sandy beaches, the more stable rocky coasts provide both plants and animals with many places to attach themselves. But when the tide goes out, they may be left stranded—to be heated by the sun, dried out and chilled by the wind, and washed in a freshwater bath if it rains.

As the tide ebbs, horizontal bands of differing colors appear on the rocks—as if a giant paintbrush had swept across the shore. These bands are most apparent on steep rocky coasts where the rise and fall of the tides is at least 3 or 4 feet.

Each band is a zone of life. It takes its characteristic color mainly from the dominant plants in that area. The upper zone often has two tones—grayish-green lichens at the top, black lichens and algae below. Yellow-brown bladder wrack enlivens the middle zone; strands of dark-brown kelp and other algae, commonly called seaweeds, hold fast to rocks in the lowest zone.

The zone in which a particular organism grows depends on how much wave action it can withstand and how long it can survive out of water. The extremely high tides that occur twice a month may be the only times when the top zone is covered with water. Lichens, for example, are rarely underwater, but sea urchins, crawling over the bottom, are seldom out of water.

Where crevices or tidepools disrupt the pattern, the bands may blend. These areas are usually cooler, darker, and wetter when the tide is out than the face of the rocks. Plants and animals that cannot survive much exposure to air, such as sea anemones, can sometimes live in these places.

Some residents seem permanent—almost as enduring as the rocks themselves. But many of them were once drifters in the sea. For example, mature barnacles, which cannot move to a new location, release milky clouds of larvae into the surf. The young barnacles spend weeks as floaters before settling down on rocks—or on the hull of a ship. Similarly, many mussels, limpets, and snails cast their eggs into the sea. Many algae, too, release tiny reproductive bodies, which drift in coastal waters, then attach themselves to rocks.

As you climb down a rocky shore, you are, in a way, traveling backward in time, for hundreds of millions of years ago the land was first populated by aquatic animals. Periwinkles (which are snails) illustrate the transition from sea to land. One species—the smooth periwinkle—lives near the bottom of the rocky shore and can survive only short exposures to air; it reproduces by shedding its eggs into the water. In contrast, the rough periwinkle, which lives at the top of the tidal region, will die if it is covered by water for too long a time. It can breathe oxygen from the air, and it bears live young on dry land. But apparently the rough periwinkle is not yet completely ready for a terrestrial life—it still requires periodic dousings of sea water. The ancestors of land snails made this transition ages ago.

Rocky shores in temperate regions have the greatest variety of life. The submerged portions of tropical coral reefs may have more species, but exposed areas are not as rich. Cold regions, too, have less variety. Under arctic conditions, the scouring action of ice denudes rocky surfaces, and what little life there is survives in crevices.

Limpets cling tenaciously to their places on a rocky shore. They are remarkable because they seem to remain in one place for weeks or even months. These mollusks move around at high tide, often at night (their locomotion is snail-like). They feed on algae, then go home.

Barnacles attach themselves to sea vessels by secreting a glue of amazing strength. As more barnacles accumulate, the ship is slowed—this is called fouling. On a rocky shore (right), examine these crusty little animals in their closed-up state, then try to dislodge one.

As the tide ebbs on a New England shore, this surf-washed rock reveals a layered community. The lowest layer here is fringed with bladder wrack, a yellow-brown alga. Next comes a band of black rock tripe (a lichen), then a wider, still-damp zone inhabited by grayish-white barnacles. At the top, dark patches of lichens and algae are browsed by tiny periwinkles.

HOW TO
Know Your Own Shore

Choose a relatively small, well-defined area for your survey—a large boulder or two at the edge of the water—not a whole stretch of shore. Eye-catching bands of color often mark a likely spot.

• See if you can sort out the major classifications of plants and animals—lichens, algae or seaweeds, barnacles, limpets, and snails. You might make a zonation chart like the one below.

• As an amateur naturalist, you may find a scarcity of information about common seaside animals and plants. There are several field guides to the shells that help in identifying the mollusks, but you will probably have difficulty with lichens and algae. Your public library may be able to suggest sources. You might chip off a hard-shelled specimen or collect empty shells and compare them with displays in a natural history museum.

• Color photographs of your chosen rocks are perhaps your best record. A sketchbook of the seaweeds and sea creatures is another worthwhile project. Or you could press and dry some of the delicate seaweeds as you would leaves.

Zones of Plants and Ranges of Animals on a Rocky Shore in Britain*

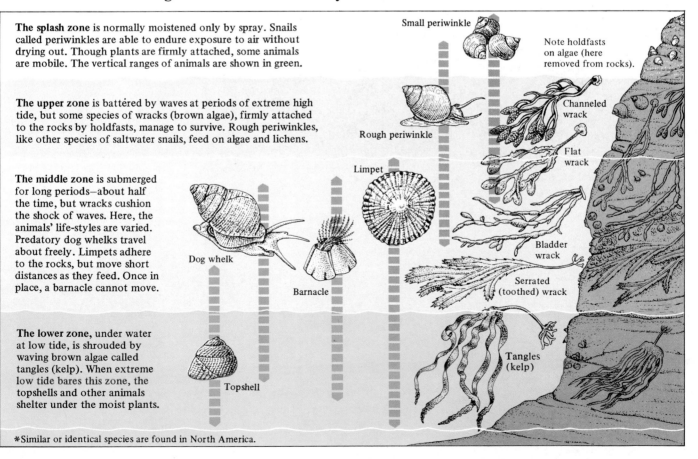

The splash zone is normally moistened only by spray. Snails called periwinkles are able to endure exposure to air without drying out. Though plants are firmly attached, some animals are mobile. The vertical ranges of animals are shown in green.

The upper zone is battered by waves at periods of extreme high tide, but some species of wracks (brown algae), firmly attached to the rocks by holdfasts, manage to survive. Rough periwinkles, like other species of saltwater snails, feed on algae and lichens.

The middle zone is submerged for long periods—about half the time, but wracks cushion the shock of waves. Here, the animals' life-styles are varied. Predatory dog whelks travel about freely. Limpets adhere to the rocks, but move short distances as they feed. Once in place, a barnacle cannot move.

The lower zone, under water at low tide, is shrouded by waving brown algae called tangles (kelp). When extreme low tide bares this zone, the topshells and other animals shelter under the moist plants.

Small periwinkle

Note holdfasts on algae (here removed from rocks).

Rough periwinkle

Channeled wrack

Flat wrack

Limpet

Bladder wrack

Serrated (toothed) wrack

Dog whelk

Barnacle

Tangles (kelp)

Topshell

*Similar or identical species are found in North America.

115

Life in a Tidepool

A tidepool is a fascinating pocket of life at the edge of the sea. Tucked into a rocky crevice, often camouflaged or rendered inaccessible by slippery algae, tidepools are the secret treasures of a rocky shore. Once you know about them, once you have seen beneath the deceptive reflections of the sky, it is almost guaranteed that you will become entranced by their inhabitants.

Some of the world's most adaptable creatures live in tidepools, where they are alternately drenched (and often pounded) by salty seas, then left land-locked by the outgoing tides.

This is an enormous adjustment for any plant or animal to make: to change environments daily, and so drastically! Despite this, some large tidepools have such a rich supply of plants and animals that they seem almost to be jungles. Plants predominate—filmy mats and miniature forests of algae. Animal inhabitants, which often lurk among the algae or in crevices, may include crabs; periwinkles; dog whelks or drills, which are predatory snails; small barnacle populations; shrimp-like animals of all sizes from the visible to the microscopic; and limpets.

No two tidepools are the same. The life forms that a pool supports depend on its size and location on the rocky sea wall. Tidepools high up on the wall are usually the least populated. Not only must they rely on high tides for their existence—supplemented by water that is splashed up by the waves—but they have the further problem of being vulnerable to excessive freshwater run-off from higher ground. If a pool receives too much fresh water, even the hardiest of tidepool animals will die.

Pools in the middle of a tidal zone are probably the best to explore. This is because they are likely to be rich in plant and animal inhabitants, and because they are relatively safe to visit. Tidepools located low on the rocks, which are thoroughly flushed by sea water and are exposed only for brief periods, are often difficult to explore. Surrounding rocks are likely to be extremely slippery. Such pools should be approached with caution (sometimes even on hands and knees). It is essential to know at what hour the tide will come in that day, as it is dangerous to get caught by an inrushing tide with no handholds to pull yourself out.

In middle-zone tidepools, it is easy to distinguish between permanent residents and visitors. Transients such as jellyfish may be trapped in a tidepool for a while, only to move out with the next tide. You can check on this by visiting the same pool several days running, seeing which animals have left, which have remained behind, and which are new to the pool.

The depth of a tidepool influences its inhabitants greatly. A deep pool is not likely to have good circulation; fresh water (from rain or runoff) lies on the surface, while the denser salt water accumulates in the deeper part of the basin. This layering limits the travels and interactions of tidepool organisms, but it may mean that the tidepool has a greater diversity of species.

Like a flat pan of water, a shallow tidepool heats up more rapidly than a deep one. Warm water holds less oxygen than cold water, but higher temperatures speed up the metabolism of plants and animals. Consequently, the little oxygen in a warm pool is used up rapidly. Such a pool may choke on its own productivity. Tides and storms, which fill pools, govern their lives. A pool that disappointed you on one visit may be full of life the next time.

Tidepools are transition zones between sea and shore. The land is alternately soaked in salt water, then left high and dry. Erratic rains and occasional flooding complicate the lives of all inhabitants. Scientists believe that this zone is where some marine forms invaded dry land.

At low tide on a Pacific shore, a turnstone (named for the way it finds food) pauses on a rubbery carpet of green sea anemones.

Flower-like anemones are actually animals. The white tentacles on this Pacific coast species retract during digestion, and only a smooth button is seen.

Which ones are plants, which ones are animals? Lavender coralline algae are slender, twig-like plants, named for their resemblance to coral (tiny animals with a brittle skeleton). Royal purple sea urchins, nearby, are animals with bristling spines. At lower left is a turquoise sea anemone. Its soft tentacles are actually armed with minute stinging structures that paralyze small prey; the bright greenish-gold center is the animal's mouth.

Explore a Tidepool with an Underwater Viewer

All bodies of water, large or small, have a "skin" on them. That is, the molecules of water at the surface adhere more firmly to one another than do molecules completely surrounded by water. From the standpoint of the shore explorer, the effect of this skin-like surface is that light bounces off and dazzles the eye. Even on a gray day, it is hard to see into a tidepool.

• The problem is solved if you put a viewer into the water, one with sides high enough to block out reflected light. A snorkeling mask is ideal for this. It's waterproof, has shielded sides, and may already be part of your beach equipment.

• But an ordinary clear plastic box or cylinder will do just as well—the bottom goes into the tidepool, and your face stays out of the water. You can also make a viewer by substituting clear plastic wrap for the bottom of a container and attaching the plastic to the sides. (The simplest viewer would be an ordinary soup can with both ends removed.) Attach the plastic wrap firmly to one end by means of a sturdy rubber band.

• Light travels at different speeds through air and water. So what you see in a tidepool will be distorted. For instance, when you reach into a pool, the water may turn out to be deeper than you guessed it to be. The snorkeling mask or plastic box will help counteract this distortion.

• Be careful not to damage any plant or animal you pick up. Replace it in the same position you found it.

The Amazing World of Sea Shells

We call them sea shells, but shells, and the living animals that produce them, are distributed worldwide on land and in water. The mollusk group ranges from common garden snails to giant clams on Australia's Great Barrier Reef. And though these huge clams (which may grow to 3 feet in length and weigh several hundred pounds) probably never trapped a diver, as popular legend insists, there are dangerous mollusks: a 2-inch-long cone shell of the Pacific has killed human beings with its venom.

There are five categories of shells, and it's easy to tell one from another. The *univalves* have a single shell that is usually coiled. *Bivalves* always have two sides, hinged together. Most shells you will find fall into these two categories. *Chitons* have eight overlapping plates and can curl into a ball like a frightened armadillo. *Tusk* or *tooth shells,* which are also few in number, look like conical tubes. The fifth category is *cephalopods;* though they are numerous, few people think of them as shells because most species (including squid and cuttlefish) grow their "shells" inside their bodies. The spiral-shaped chambered nautilus (shown on page 111) is the only cephalopod that has an external shell.

About 100,000 species of animals have shells. Each region has its characteristic populations. The cool regions produce shells of subdued color. The North American moon shell, bay scallop, and razor clam are examples of this. Warmer climates produce a greater variety of vividly colored species, including the great West African land snail, the fluted giant clam from the Philippines, and the deep-purple noble scallop from Japan. Color pigments are obtained by each animal from food and transported to the shell-forming layer.

Mollusks crawl and leap. Snails have given mollusks a reputation for slow movement, but there are many species, such as scallops, that are jet-propelled. When a starfish (which consumes a scallop meal as readily as any human being) approaches, the scallop spits a stream of water. This jet-action carries the scallop away in leaps.

Some mollusks have plagued man: burrowing shipworms have sunk many a wooden-hulled ship, and their close relatives can bore through solid concrete. But people have always treasured shells. Shells have often served as money, and they have been found in ancient tombs, often far from the sea.

A treasure of sea shells washes up with each tide on the wide beaches of Sanibel Island, off Florida's west coast. After a storm, lucky searchers may find rare tropical specimens.

Univalves Are Mollusks with One Shell

Most univalves have a spiral shell, though the spiral is not always obvious. A muscular foot enables the animal to move about.

Tentacles

Respiratory holes

Sand collar (egg mass)

Lewis' moon snail is common on the Pacific coast. Eggs are laid in a mucous collar that collects sand.

Foot

Cut-away view

The green abalone, one of eight Pacific coast species, is now rare. Sea otters dote on abalones; so do gourmets.

Inside of shell

Egg case

Alphabet cones, of varied colors and patterns, are favorites with collectors, but the living cones are poisonous.

The lightning whelk lays egg cases in long strings. Other whelks lay similar egg cases, which often wash up on shore.

Operculum (lid)

Cone with poisonous barb extended

Foot

The knobby keyhole limpet resembles a barnacle and clings just as tightly to a rock.

Inside of shell

The flame auger is rare and highly prized. Like many univalves, it seals its shell with a lid on its foot.

A shell collection is easy to start. You can find interesting shells in fresh water and even on land, but the seashore offers the greatest variety and largest number of specimens.

• Shells that wash up on beaches are usually empty and clean, though they may be damaged. With persistence and luck, you will be able to assemble a fine collection without disturbing any living mollusks or their environment. In many areas, local laws forbid collecting live shellfish, especially rare species.

• Bring a small rake or shovel to uncover shells. A kitchen strainer is useful for sifting small shells out of the sand. You will need some plastic bags to carry your treasures home. Wear sneakers if you are collecting on a rocky shore.

• The hours before and after low tide are the best for shell hunting. Tide schedules in local papers give the hour of low tide, which changes each day

and also varies from place to place.

• When you get home, scrub your shells in warm, soapy water. To remove algae and stains, soak in laundry bleach. Dry shells outdoors, out of direct sunlight so that the colors will not fade. Rub lightly with mineral oil to restore luster.

• Each shell should be identified by a number in india ink, protected by a coat of clear nail polish. Record this number, name of the species, date and location in a loose-leaf notebook or card file. You will need to consult a field guide to shells for help in identification.

• You can display your treasures by tying them on window screening, by cementing them to glass, or by arranging them in labeled cardboard trays or wooden drawers in a cabinet. Keep tiny shells in vials plugged with cotton or in small plastic boxes. If you have many large shells like conchs and whelks, display them prominently on coffee tables and bookcases.

Bivalves Have Two Hinged Shells

A bivalve's left and right halves may look alike, but are always different. A ligament connects the shells.

Scallop swims by clapping shells and ejecting water.

Mantle

The jackknife clam swims well and burrows quickly out of sight, using its extensible foot. Razor clams are related species with broader shells.

Jackknife clam burrowing

Extruded foot

Byssal threads

Inside

Eastern oysters usually grow in clusters, formed as swimming larvae cement themselves to old shells.

The Iceland scallop is a colorful Atlantic species. Scallops have up to 100 blue eyes set around the edge of the fleshy part (the mantle).

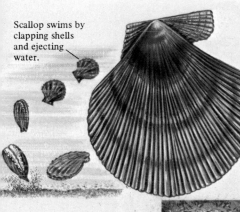

Mantle edge with eyes

Common blue mussels spin a tough thread (byssus) by which they attach themselves to rocks and piers. In Europe, mussels are prized as seafood.

Oyster clusters

Chitons Have Eight Plates

Covered with plates (valves) instead of a single shell, the primitive chiton clings to intertidal rocks with a suction foot.

The West Indian chiton is used locally for food. Most chitons are small, but one giant Pacific species may grow to a foot in length.

Side view

Underside shows oval foot.

Tusk Shells Have Open Ends

Water moves in and out of the tusk shell through the narrower opening; feeding threads extend through the wider end.

The Indian money tusk digs into the sea floor and feeds on minute animals. The shells were used as money by Pacific tribes.

Water intake

Feeding threads

Birds of the Rocky Shores

The world's great seabird colonies, which crowd the precipitous cliffs and boulder-strewn edges of rocky shores, are established there for two reasons. One is the availability of suitable nesting sites; the other is the abundant supply of fish in nearby waters.

Both sides of the North Atlantic—from Labrador to Maine, from Iceland and Spitsbergen south to the British Isles—have their famous seabird colonies, often many centuries old. For the most part, the North Atlantic seabirds are chunky, short-winged species called auks or alcids (members of the family *Alcidae*). In general, these birds correspond to the penguins of the southern hemisphere; and with their half-black, half-white plumage and upright stance, they certainly resemble penguins (though they are not related).

There are many kinds of auks, and you often see them together in one colony—razorbills, common murres (called guillemots in Europe), black guillemots, and the familiar, irresistible common puffins. The Pacific coast of North

Yellow-plumed rockhopper penguins breed on remote islands in the cold seas near Antarctica. More easily visited colonies, with other kinds of penguins, dot the coasts of South Africa, Australia, South America, and even the Galápagos Islands, which are near the equator.

Noisy northern gannets crowd cliffs on both sides of the Atlantic. Offshore, these strong fliers and spectacular divers are easy to spot.

America has tufted and horned puffins, auklets (small auks), and murrelets.

Whether or not you are a seasoned birder, a visit to one of the well-known bird cliffs—such as Bonaventure Island off Canada's Gaspé Peninsula, Skomer off the Welsh coast, and Noss in the Shetland Islands—is an experience to be treasured. When seen from a small boat (the best way to get the full effect of the teeming colony), layers upon layers of gleaming, white-breasted birds tower above you. Every ledge, every cranny, has its contingent of birds.

At the water's edge, boulders are animated by adult birds, relieved for the moment of the tasks of brooding eggs or young. The parents take turns bringing home quantities of small fish to feed their ravenous chicks. The swelling surf on which your boat bobs up and down is carpeted with swimming and diving auks; you can follow them underwater by the flash of their brightly colored feet and legs. Meanwhile, hundreds of others go whirring over your head on stubby, fast-beating wings. There may also be a mass flight of dove-like kittiwakes (a small species of gull), touched off by some sudden alarm.

The noise produced by a seabird colony is indescribable. Each species contributes its own raucous or piercing cry, caw, kik-kik-kik, growl, or snarl. And throughout the tumult, streamlined gannets, the largest birds in the colony, cut the air in their stupendous, straight-down dives.

Chaotic though a bird cliff may appear, it is really an organized, orderly community. Each species of bird has its own preference as to location on the cliff. For example, black guillemots lay their eggs in crevices among the boulders at the foot of the cliff; if cormorants are present, they build their untidy nests in this area. Narrow ledges along the steep face are crowded with row after row, by species, of razorbills and murres, which lay a single, large egg directly on bare rock. Gannets occupy wide ledges at the top of the cliff.

Harsh though the conditions of life on a rocky shore may seem to a human observer, the birds obviously thrive and multiply. Living in a crowd stimulates mating activities. Seabirds are very curious—watching the neighbors and following their example, whatever they may be doing. Within the huge colony, the birds of each neighborhood are thus stimulated to mate and lay their eggs in the space of a few days. The greater the number of breeders, the earlier they tend to mate. (Pairs on the outside of the colony tend to mate last.) This synchronized behavior makes for a coordinated defense against the inevitable egg-robbing and chick-snatching by predators such as herring gulls.

BIRDING TIPS
Seaside Techniques

The most important tip for birding at the shore is to make sure you'll be comfortable. Take along insect repellent, sun lotion, sunglasses, and a brimmed hat to shade your eyes (intense glare reflected off the water can be very tiring). A long-sleeved shirt and a sweater (or jacket) are advisable. Early morning is the best time to observe gulls, terns, and other shorebirds; late afternoon is also good.

• On cliffs and rocky shores, wear sturdy shoes with rock-gripping soles —a sprained ankle means trouble. The edges of a cliff may be undercut, and can crumble beneath you. A strong gust of wind may throw a child or lightweight adult off balance. So keep well back from the edge. A cliff is no place to go birding by yourself.

• You can usually get a good look at cliff-dwelling birds by approaching from below. Check for high tide if you go on foot. Viewing from a boat is even easier. At Bonaventure Island off eastern Canada and at some Pacific offshore islands, boat trips take you near the nesting sites of seabirds.

• On beaches and mud flats, plan your excursion during migration periods in spring or late summer (shorebirds start south early). Time the visit so you will arrive at low tide (local papers give tide tables). Low tide exposes small marine animals that attract numerous birds.

• The upper beach is the place to look for plovers and other small shorebirds. Dunes may shelter colonies of gulls and terns. Never walk through a breeding colony, and never let a dog run loose. The adult birds will inevitably leave in a panic, and eggs and chicks will be exposed to predatory gulls and hot sun. If a tern attacks you by diving at your head, you are too close!

• A beach trip in winter can be rewarding. A boardwalk makes a good place from which to sweep the ocean with telescope or binoculars for diving ducks, grebes, and loons. Pay attention to rock jetties and breakwaters for small flocks of birds—purple sandpipers on the east coast of North America, black turnstones and surfbirds on the west coast.

• At any time of year, a visit to the beach after a severe storm may turn up rare oceanic or tropical birds blown far from their usual range. Some bird clubs have a recorded rare-bird alert that you can telephone for information about any unusual species.

Clown-like common puffins burrow in turf or dig nests under rocks in Europe and eastern Canada. (Other puffin species live on Pacific shores. The southern hemisphere counterparts are penguins.) Once the breeding season is over, their gaudy beaks become paler in color.

Birds on the Beach

Twice a year, the beaches of the world are flooded with shorebirds —long-distance migrants from the tundra and uplands of the far north. In late July and early August, after a mere 6 weeks of hatching and brooding a family, tiny sandpipers, sturdy plovers, and long-legged waders begin their southward journeys. Some travel to the tip of South America or Africa, to Australia, or to islands in the Pacific.

Birds have impressive navigational skills. Often parent birds depart for the south earlier than their offspring. Young birds traveling in juvenile flocks find their own way to ancestral feeding grounds. Then, after having the benefit of a second summer of sunny days and abundant food in the southern hemisphere, many return to the north using a different route from their first journey. Nevertheless they arrive at the remote regions of their birth.

Traveling in either direction (north or south), shorebirds land frequently to feed and rest. Because they come in wave upon wave, with many leaving or arriving during the night, they seem to be full-time summer residents. For many North American birds, a stopover may be on a Florida or Gulf coast beach, a sand bar on Cape Cod or Cape Hatteras, or a pebbly shore in Nova Scotia. West coast migrants linger in the sheltered bays and coves of California.

The best place for beginning birders to sort out the baffling, look-alike shorebirds is a sandy shore where mud flats are exposed by retreating tides. The small birds, or "peeps," that busily scurry about or rest in compact flocks can be confusing. But a mixed flock can actually be of assistance in identification. Field guides often tell you which birds tend to associate with one another. When you have identified one species, you have a size comparison, and some hint as to the others in the flock.

The Differences Between a Gull and a Tern

Compare the herring gull at right with the common terns shown below it. Gulls and terns are close relatives— they make up the family of long-winged, web-footed birds called *Laridae.* Typical adult birds in this family are gray and white, accented with black. Gulls and terns nest in large colonies and are found all over the world, except in some deserts; they live on inland waters as well as near the sea. Here are some tips to help you tell one from the other:

• Although both gulls and terns vary in size, gulls are usually large, robust birds. Terns are smaller, more slender and streamlined.

• Gulls have long, stout legs and are good walkers. Terns have short legs and seldom walk about.

• Gulls are scavengers—they pick up scraps from the water or shore. Terns dive for living prey, often submerging completely when they dive.

• Gulls swim or float in the water. A tern's feet are not adapted for swimming; after capturing prey, terns fly upward immediately. They alight on water only to bathe.

• Gulls croak harshly or mew and scream at one another. Terns squawk raucously or utter rasping kee-ars or staccato kik-kik-kiks.

• Gulls build nests of dry grass or sticks. Terns simply scoop out shallow holes in the sand, or among pebbles and broken shells.

• Newly hatched gulls and terns are covered with down. Gulls take several years to develop adult plumage; during this time, they may be difficult to identify. In contrast, young terns (once they have shed their down) resemble the adults.

Identification can be aided, too, by the fact that some species do not form flocks, but are usually seen singly or in pairs—the avocet and the oyster-catcher are examples, as are many other long-legged, long-billed waders.

Behavior is also a help in identification. For example, the straight-billed dowitcher has a feeding action like a sewing machine. Sanderlings, as their name suggests, patter back and forth on sandy beaches, and neither enter the water nor venture into the dune grass higher up on the beach. On the other hand, the mixed flocks of small sand-pipers and plovers often rest on the sand, but they feed in muddy areas. Skimmers (black-and-white relatives of terns) feed by zipping along the water with their large red beaks open, scooping up prey with the lower mandible.

In spring, the presence of shorebirds in breeding plumage simplifies identification. Then, it is easy to spot the strikingly marked black-bellied plover, the much smaller dunlin with a black belly patch, the stocky little knot with its rusty breast.

Not all the birds of the beach can be seen only during migration—some species are also summer residents. Piping and snowy plovers, both as pale as the sand itself, breed above the high-tide line. Upper beaches and dunes are nesting areas for gulls and terns. Herring gulls and great black-backed gulls, fierce predators on tern colonies, often nest near their victims.

Gulls and terns deserve a second look. Many people think all gulls look alike ("It's just a sea gull"). Actually, there are obvious differences between species—comparative size, wing marks, banded or unbanded tail, dark or light mantle (plumage of back and upper wings)—that will be revealed by a study of your field guide. And the same holds true of the flashing, diving terns.

Herring gull

Gulls are strong fliers, with a slow, regular beat of their broad wings; their tails are square or rounded. They often soar on thermals (warm air), or ride air currents created by ships, or glide low over water.

Common tern

Terns are graceful fliers. Their wings are long and narrow, their tails more or less deeply forked. Terns often hover with rapidly beating wings and bills pointed down. They rarely soar or glide.

PHOTO TIPS
Capturing Bird Behavior on Film

If you approach slowly and quietly, birds of the shore will often go about their business—thus providing you with many opportunities to record their various life-styles. (Photography is often the way a birder gets started recognizing birds.)
• Shorebirds move quickly. You need a very fast lens or very good luck—or both. Come prepared to take many photographs (inevitably, some shots won't be in focus).
• A flock of shorebirds makes an excellent subject. The photograph below illustrates two aspects of sanderling behavior: they tend to keep by themselves, and often face in one direction—into the wind.
• Courtship behavior is a difficult but rewarding subject. You may be lucky enough, for example, to film a tern presenting its mate with a small fish.
• Be careful about intruding when shorebirds have eggs or very young chicks. If you must photograph, use a telephoto lens.
• Preening, feeding, and fighting are other photogenic activities to be seen at the shore.

Shadows and reflections of sanderlings at rest make a pleasing pattern of light and dark. A telephoto lens is necessary for capturing a flock of skittish shorebirds on film.

Inhabitants of the Sand

As waves wash the shore and then retreat back to the sea, the hard-packed beach resembles a freshly swept pavement—clean and flat, except for an occasional hole or bump in the sand. But if you know what to look for, the seemingly empty stretch of sand is crammed with life. And if you're fast enough, you may even be able to catch some of the residents.

As any child who has ever made sand castles can tell you, moist sand is an excellent building material—it holds its shape well. Most inhabitants of the sandy shore take advantage of this, and excavate homes for themselves.

Where are all the residents of the sand? The next time you watch a wave sweep over a beach, look for telltale signs. As the thin sheet of water goes back down the beach, tiny bumps appear in the sand. If, as soon as a bump appears, you quickly scoop out a double handful of sand, you may pick up the animal that is responsible for the bump. You can tell whether you have caught it if you feel a tickling on your hands as you hold the sand. Don't be afraid—this is just a little animal, perhaps a shy mole crab, trying to escape danger by digging deeper. If you carefully sift the sand between your hands, you may ac-tually see the crab, which is not much larger than a grasshopper. If you don't get the crab in the first scoop of sand, stop trying. No matter how fast you dig, it will always dig faster.

Mole crabs move up and down the beach with the tides, thus staying at the water's edge. They feed by digging just below the surface of the sand; their seine-like antennae project into the film of backwash and filter out minute marine plants and animals. Sometimes these exposed antennae reveal a crab's hiding place in the sand.

Most beaches have a line of rubble—pebbles, shells, and the like—that is tumbled up and down the beach with the waves. In this debris you may notice a shell that seems mysteriously to defy the rush of the water, often moving against the current. Take a closer look at such a shell; you may discover that, unlike the other shells, it has an occu-pant. Its inhabitant is a hermit crab, a "squatter" that moved in after the original owner vacated the shell. If you're patient, you may see two eye-stalks emerge as the crab peeks out. It is safe to pick up hermit crabs if they are relatively small.

Farther up the beach, just above the top range of the waves, you may notice holes that are about the size a mouse might make. The owners of these holes—fittingly named ghost crabs—scurry furtively near the mouths of their bur-rows. They are camouflaged by their sandy color to the point where they seem to vanish. And their holes also seem to disappear around midday, when the animals temporarily seal themselves in for a brief "siesta." The best time for ghost-crab watching is at night, when they emerge in large numbers to feed. You may even "catch" a platoon in the beam of a flashlight.

In addition to the many species of crabs on a beach, there are ghost shrimp, which construct complicated burrows there. Clams bury themselves in the sand, projecting their siphons into the waters of a rising tide. Lug-worms reveal their presence by castings left in the sand outside their burrows. Frequently, too, there are visitors from the sea—horseshoe crabs (which are not crabs but relatives of the scorpi-ons), sea turtles, and seals. These ani-mals, which breed on the shore, tend to arrive en masse—and the result is an impressive sight for any human visitors who are there at the right time.

With body raised high, a ghost crab surveys its sandy world, ready to take evasive action. Its bulbous eyes, which swivel around on stalks, enable it to spot an enemy approaching from any quarter. Scuttling sideways, the crab moves with amazing speed, vanishing into its burrow—it is seldom captured, even on film. Ghost crabs are bolder at night, when they emerge to feed.

The hermit crab borrows the armor of other animals—mainly empty shells. As it grows, the hermit crab must seek a larger home. When it finds a suitable shell, a quick transfer takes place. The crab is most vulnerable at this time because its own body defenses are weak. (Its soft abdominal membrane affords no protection from enemies.)

As waves ride up the beach, they form thin layers that retain a separate identity to a remarkable degree. The cross-hatched pattern on the sand is made by the backwash of the waves. If you look closely, you will see there are also small, rounded breathing holes made by sand-dwellers.

Burrowing Animals Hidden Beneath the Surface

   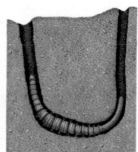 

Mole crabs move with the tide, and feed with their antennae above the sand.

Ghost shrimp constantly sift the sand for food with their flattened appendages.

Soft-shell clams draw in food and air through long, flexible tubes (siphons).

Lugworms, like earthworms, digest organic matter in the soft mud they excavate.

Ghost crabs dig deep holes in dry sand, but return to water to wet their gills.

125

The Shifting of Sandy Shores

Sandy beaches are constantly moving. The next time you're at a beach, simply stand at the water's edge and wait. Soon your toes—then perhaps both feet—will be covered by sand. The waves keep the sand in continual motion, with the result that some of it slips out from under your feet, starting at the edges, and you may sink slightly. At the same time, you'll find small deposits building up on the top of your feet. On most large beaches, countless tons of sand are moved along this way in a single day.

To discover which way the sand is moving, watch the waves as they wash up on the beach. Keep your eyes on some small object (perhaps a shell or bit of seaweed) to see in which direction it is being carried. The motion is not just upward; it is also sideways.

You will also probably notice that some of the water in each wave sinks into the sand rather than flowing back into the sea. As the water disappears, it deposits its floating cargo—bits of shells, grains of sand, pieces of seaweed and driftwood. Some water seeps out of the sand and runs back to the sea in tiny rivulets. But little sand is transported this way.

In addition to sand, the waves deposit pebbles and, if the waves are strong enough, even large rocks. Look at the slope of a beach on your next visit. Generally, the steeper the slope, the larger and more violent were the waves that brought the sand.

The force of waves is incredible. A gale striking the coast of Scotland once swept away a concrete breakwater weighing 2,600 tons. On the eastern coast of North America, storm-driven waves sent a 135-pound rock flying through the roof of a 91-foot-high lighthouse. Such tremendous forces are constantly pounding rocky coasts, converting rock into fragments, and eventually into sand.

Most sand originates inland, produced by the weathering and erosion of rocks. Pebbles and sand are transported by rivers and may be carried far out to sea by the current. But this sand may still find its way to a beach. Currents dredge up and can deposit sand from as deep as 50 feet beneath the surface. On many coasts, there are continental shelves (the submerged edges of continents) that are relatively shallow. In such places, river-borne sand may be dropped, only to be picked up again, and sometimes become part of a beach.

Most sandy beaches in the temperate zones are light brown or gray, shading into white. Generally, the coarse, light-colored sand is pulverized granite; fine gray sand is from basalt. In the tropics, the beaches are more varied. For example, on one side of Tahiti, the beaches are a brilliant white—the sand originated in the adjacent coral reefs. On the other side of the island, the beaches are jet black—the sand was derived from lava beds.

A beach may even be supplied with sand by wind blowing from a desert. For example, the prevailing winds over the Sahara carry sand to the Mediterranean region. Although the powerful wind carries the sand to the sea, it is the waves that do most of the work of gathering the sand into beaches.

Another beach phenomenon to look for is the way that waves pile up particles and sort them out. The larger pieces, such as pebbles, are not carried as far up the beach as the finer ones. On a California beach, thousands of tin cans were once washed ashore. The waves neatly sorted the cans, with the largest at the bottom of the beach and the smallest at the top.

On shores where a sandy beach exists at the edge of rocks, high storm waves may wash nearly all of the sand out beyond the surf. But during calm weather, smaller waves may re-deposit the sand, clean and fresh, as if it had just been laundered.

NATURE OBSERVER
Walking Dunes, Miniature Deltas, and Sand Close-Ups

A beach vacation is full of opportunities to try out sand experiments.

• Dunes are ideal places to observe the movement of sand, because dunes really do walk. A large dune may move forward by as much as 20 feet a year; small dunes move even faster. (The diagram below shows how you can gauge this movement.)

• Look for an area of walking dunes where sand is beginning to cover the bases of bushes and trees. Eventually, the sand will smother the plants. The dead trunks will later be uncovered, sand-polished by the wind. These relics make interesting photographs.

• Where grass grows over the dunes, look for circular marks etched in the sand as the wind swings the tough grass blades. This, too, is a good subject for photographs.

• Watch how the receding water cuts channels in the beach and deposits sand and gravel, forming miniature deltas. Here is a chance to play dam-builder. You can divert or stop the flow of water and alter the shape of a delta by moving several of the stones.

• Digging in moist sand is also appealing, especially to youngsters, but beach-goers of all ages can enjoy building elaborate sand castles. Sand sculpture has enjoyed a wide popularity in recent years. Marvelous dragons and innovative architectural forms have won prizes in a number of contests.

• When you dig on the lower beach, you reach water quickly; digging on the upper beach, you have to go far deeper. The depth of the hole will give an approximation of the height of the beach above water level.

• Pieces of "beach glass" are artificial sand treasures—actually, they are smooth fragments of bottles. Beach glass comes in different colors, with blue the most prized.

• A close-up study of sand will reveal many kinds of particles. Use a hand lens or magnifying glass and see if you can pick out individual grains of quartz or shell. Ruby-red specks may be bits of garnet. A magnet will allow you to collect particles with iron.

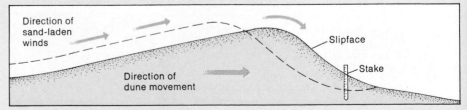

Direction of sand-laden winds

Direction of dune movement

Slipface

Stake

In a simple demonstration, you can see for yourself how fast sand travels—even how an entire dune moves along. Choose a moderately breezy day and a small dune. Place a stake on the sheltered side of the dune, a few inches from the crest. Soon you will notice that the grains of sand are moving up the windward side and accumulating at the crest. There, the wind combines with the weight of accumulated sand to push it down the steep front, or slipface, where it falls to the bottom. Thus the whole mass moves closer and closer to your stake.

An aerial view of the tip of Cape Cod gives a good idea of the structure of this unique Massachusetts peninsula. Before the Ice Ages, there was no Cape Cod. Outwash plains and rocky deposits laid down by glaciers some 30,000 years ago formed the basis of the Cape. The fragility of the land is clear. Vegetation holds the sand in some sections, but there are long stretches of bare sand, and many places where the sea can invade.

A miniature river system on a sandy, stone-dotted beach mimics the braided flow of some large rivers. (This could be an aerial view of a full-scale river.) The overlapping pattern develops only when water flows down a sloping bed, bearing a load of coarse sediment. In certain places, the water drops its load and the channels widen and grow shallow. Then they divide and join—over and over again.

Variegated grains of sand on a California beach include polished bits of white shell and many fragments of rosy quartz and other rocks, torn from the surf-battered cliffs of the Big Sur. This photograph was taken from a distance of about 2 inches, using a close-up lens attachment.

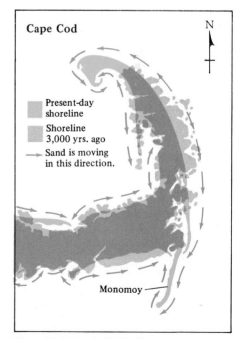

Cape Cod

N

▪ Present-day shoreline

▪ Shoreline 3,000 yrs. ago

→ Sand is moving in this direction.

Monomoy

The well-known crooked elbow of Cape Cod began to take shape many thousands of years ago, when increasing amounts of sand were deposited at the end of a curving spit. The ocean currents that carried this burden are still at work, constantly swinging around Monomoy, building up and washing away shoals, sand bars, and beaches as they go.

Dune Plants That Stabilize Beaches

To the casual eye, sand dunes behind a water-washed beach may seem somewhat untidy. But this back-of-the-beach, with its scattering of vegetation, is worth a second look.

Most dunes are born of small accumulations of debris, or perhaps a piece of driftwood. Blocked by this insignificant obstruction, the ocean winds that cross the beach lose much of their force and drop any sand they may have picked up. A little mound forms, enlarges into a hillock and eventually into a dune. Some dunes grow to a height of more than 100 feet.

Dunes are tough-going for would-be climbers, whose feet sink into the sand. They are also inhospitable to many plants and animals. Consider the deterrents—strong wind, salty spray, hot sun, and the probability of being overwhelmed by drifting sand. Many seeds wafted into the dunes by the wind manage to sprout, only to perish quickly.

But certain plants—beach grasses—are adapted to this difficult area. They sprout readily and send numerous runners into the sand. Though such plants may look fragile, they are durable and tenacious. They have an ability to grow back to the surface if their leaves are buried, to bend with the wind, and to survive drought, heat, and cold.

Beach grasses knit together a network of roots and stems, and the dune acquires a degree of permanence. (Beach grasses, especially a species known as marram grass, are often planted for the express purpose of stabilizing a dune area.) The sparse vegetation, serving as a windbreak, traps additional wind-blown sand, and the dune keeps growing. Though the grasses may look helter-skelter, these plants are the dune's defense against being blown away. This is why visitors to sand dunes are asked to keep off the grass—and off the dunes themselves.

Beach grasses are pioneer plants—they create an environment more attractive to other species of plants, and thus encourage colonization by animals. Slowly, the dune changes character. Beach peas trail along the sand, adding brilliant flecks of rose and purple when they flower. Dusty miller, an ashy gray plant native to Europe and now a common resident of North American dunes, also creeps along the sand. Shrubs take hold, including such species as bayberry or wax myrtle (evergreens with wax-covered fruits, which are used in making scented candles). Eventually, the dune may be transformed into a woodland of pine. If you walk away from the sea, cutting across ridges of dunes, you may traverse all these plant stages, until you finally reach the pines.

In some coastal areas, you may encounter another beach phenomenon—the development of a barrier beach. As waves re-locate sand in offshore shallows, a sand bar begins to rise. After many years, it may be high enough to show above the water. At first, the sand bar appears and disappears, as storm-driven waves wash over it and seasonal currents displace the accumulated sand. Eventually, these forces cut channels between segments of the bar, and water surges in and out of the protected area between the bar and the shore. In effect, the rise of the sand bar creates a lagoon between itself and the mainland. As the barrier beach becomes more stable, dunes form, plants become established, and the whole drama is repeated.

Densely matted roots of dune grass and beach plum help to stabilize the spreading dunes of Cape Cod. These pioneer plants are highly resistant to violent winds, strong sunlight, and salty spray, but despite this protection, dunes are still vulnerable. Vehicles should stay on established roads.

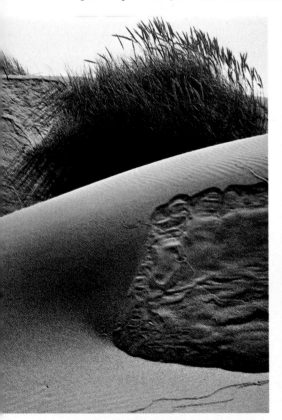

Sturdy clumps of beach grass struggle to hold down these Oregon dunes, where the constant wind cuts away at the surface of shifting sands.

Above high-tide line on a California beach, beach vetch hugs the ground and traps blown sand with its leaves and blossoms.

Five Stages in the Life History of a Sand Dune

This series of profiles shows the growth of a new dune and the role of plants in both the establishment and protection of a dune. At the start, winds and waves deposit sand on a mainland beach or on a newly emerged sand bar. Dunes follow a fairly predictable pattern of development. In time, there will be primary and secondary dunes (named not for their order of formation, but for their position relative to the ocean). They act as a defense against the assaults of wind and spray. Dunes are fragile and should be treated with care.

A dune begins when sand is blown inland by strong winds—and accumulates. Here, a sand-bar beach between the ocean and a bay is relatively barren at first.

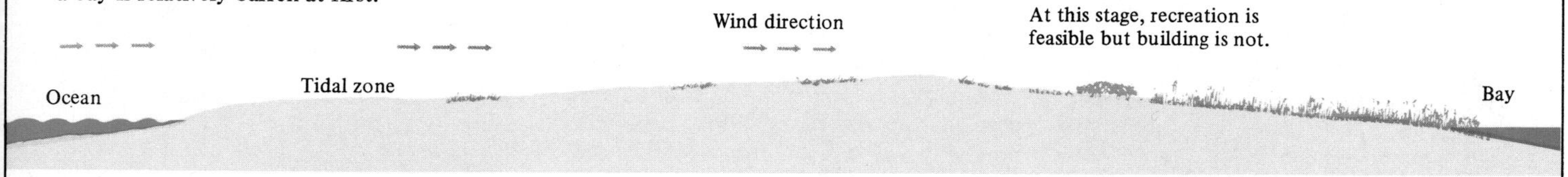

Wind direction

At this stage, recreation is feasible but building is not.

Ocean

Tidal zone

Bay

Dune build-up starts where small clumps of beach grass and other plants arrest the wind-blown sand. This eventually becomes the secondary dune. Shrubs grow behind it.

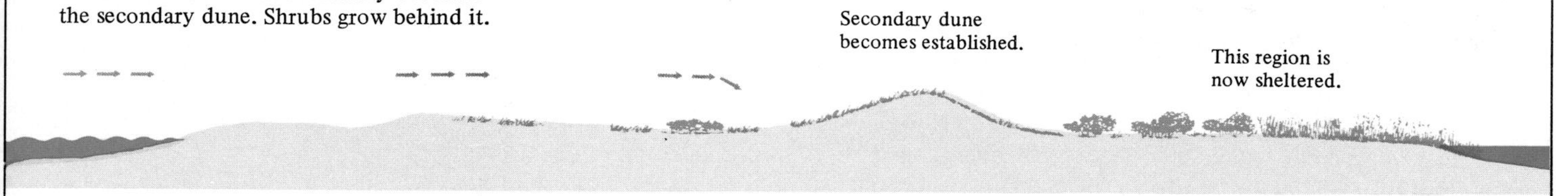

Secondary dune becomes established.

This region is now sheltered.

As beach grass grows seaward, a primary dune forms in front of the secondary dune. Behind the secondary dune, a thicket of bayberry and woodbine springs up.

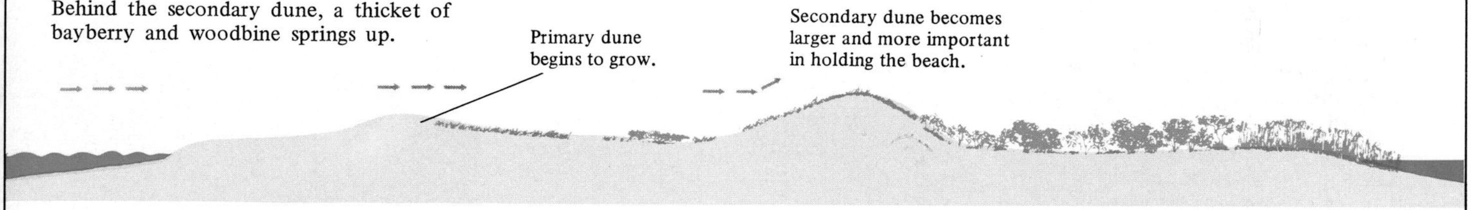

Primary dune begins to grow.

Secondary dune becomes larger and more important in holding the beach.

In the sheltered trough located between the dunes, shrubby growth joins the grasses. Cedars and pines climb the back slope of the secondary dune.

Vegetation on primary dune helps create a sheltered trough.

Secondary dune continues to grow.

The stabilized secondary dune now has tall trees and dense shrubs. The plant cover increases in the trough, and beach grass invades the tidal zone.

Trough is now suitable for picnicking and camping.

This region is eligible for some building.

Marshy region encourages wildlife.

129

Salt Marshes Are Valuable

Marshy shores look inviting from a distance, but they are best appreciated from a small boat or from higher, more solid ground. Close approach is deterred by tall, tough grasses. The muddy flats call for heavy rubber boots, and there is often a pungent odor that is less than inviting. Consequently, few people have first-hand knowledge of the rich life forms of a marsh—a region with more wild-life than any other type of coast.

Unlike the waters of other shores, those of a salt marsh are usually placid. The plants and animals do not have to withstand a pounding surf or surging sea for any length of time. In fact, a salt marsh will form only in a bay or quiet estuary where the shore is protected from coastal currents. Only there can silt, clay, and plant and animal debris collect and form a muddy bottom—the base of a salt marsh. Even the tides are relatively gentle, ebbing and flowing along meandering channels.

Occasionally, of course, storms do sweep a salt marsh. At such times, a marsh serves as a natural breakwater—the resilient plants bend and sway as they absorb the impact of high winds and crashing waves. The result is that areas inland from the marsh are buffered against the fury of stormy seas.

Grasses are the dominant plants in a salt marsh. Tall cordgrass and cattails grow along the edges of tidal channels. Characteristically, these sturdy plants are both salt-tolerant and adapted to occasional freshwater runoff from the land. Within the embankments of these tall plants, short grasses and other low-growing plants fill the flat stretches.

Where the marsh borders solid land, the ground usually rises gently, and the vegetation changes. Short grasses blend with the taller sedges—these are plants that thrive in salty mud but cannot tolerate immersion in sea water for any length of time. Still farther back, seaside goldenrod and rose mallow bloom in late summer.

The plant production of a typical salt marsh is enormous. It exceeds the plant material produced by a wheat field of equal area. It has been estimated that sugar cane is the only crop that can out-produce a salt marsh in sheer volume of plant material.

Marsh vegetation provides a food base for a large and diverse community of animals. The first to catch your eye —perhaps even before you see the marsh itself—may be gulls and terns flying over the marsh. You may also notice an osprey diving swiftly and silently to pluck a small fish from the muddy water. Numerous other birds stay concealed in the grasses, taking flight only when you venture too close.

But even the bare mud, exposed by low tide, contains a wealth of animal life. Marine biologists have estimated that one acre of marsh mud may contain as many as 82,000 individuals of a single species of worm. These and many other mud-dwellers live by filtering tiny plants and animals and bits of decaying matter from the water. These creatures, along with billions of bacteria, process immense quantities of food. What they consume ultimately fertilizes the mud, and gives the marsh its great vitality.

A frequently overlooked asset of a marsh is its capacity to produce oxygen, and to filter impurities from the air and water. This may seem like a paradox, if you consider the heavy odor usually associated with a marsh. Nevertheless, the presence of a salt marsh on the outskirts of a large city actually improves the air quality for all its neighbors.

Early on a summer morning, a salt marsh is full of activity. Its dense growth of salt-tolerant cordgrass provides a congenial environment for many creatures. Mollusks and crabs flourish in the brackish water and on the muddy shores. Marsh periwinkles cling to wet vegetation; ribbed mussels are firmly embedded in the mud;

Key to the Marsh Animals

1. Red-winged blackbird
2. Muskrat
3. Marsh hawk
4. Forster's terns
5. Clapper rail
6. Black-crowned night heron
7. Snowy egret
8. Long-billed marsh wren
9. Raccoon
10. Salt marsh periwinkles
11. Ribbed mussels
12. Diamondback terrapin
13. Marsh fiddler crabs

fiddler crabs leave their burrows in search of food. The diamondback terrapin, never found far from brackish water, feeds on these small crabs. Standing in the shallows, a snowy egret, in filmy breeding plumage, stirs the water with a golden foot, perhaps scaring up minnows. On the opposite bank, a black-crowned night heron stands poised to capture prey. The marsh's most elusive resident, a clapper rail, shows itself briefly. From a clump of cattails, a long-billed marsh wren exchanges a noisy challenge with a red-winged blackbird. A prowling raccoon, ending its nightly search for mussels and crabs, nears the water unobserved. In the middle distance, a muskrat swims toward its high-piled home. Watchful of the slightest motion by rodent or small bird, a marsh hawk hangs as if suspended in the air. And silhouetted against the morning sky, Forster's terns patrol the lush sea meadows bordering Chesapeake Bay, on the Middle Atlantic shore.

The Land-Building Mangroves

Some shores are built by trees. The unique mangroves grow in places where other trees and shrubs cannot survive—in the wet, salty world of tide-washed tropical and subtropical seas. Along such coasts, mangroves have created virtual jungles on stilts.

Most trees produce seeds that do not sprout immediately, even if they are planted. But one of several mangrove species, the red mangrove, produces exceptional seeds—they sprout while they are still attached to the branch. A root bursts through the fruit and forms a long, dagger-like point that may reach 9 inches in length. When the seed finally detaches from the branch, it falls, often planting itself upright in the soft, muddy bottom.

A mangrove seedling floats horizontally in the water, like a well-designed canoe. (You may see one drifting along a tropical beach.) The seedling can float for months, unaffected by salt water, scorching sun, and battering waves—and even continue to grow. Its sharp root tip turns downward; if the seedling strikes land, it quickly sends roots into the soil. New roots emerge in tiers that extend out and downward from the trunk, forming arches (called prop roots) that resemble umbrella stays. The prop roots may send up new trunks where they touch the ground. Red mangroves are so well braced that they can usually weather hurricanes that flatten other trees.

In 20 or 30 years, the red mangrove reaches its maximum height (about 30 feet). The profusion of prop roots and new tree trunks forms a dense, interlacing mesh that traps sediment, plants, and debris. Soon a swamp is formed at the edge of the sea. Gradually, as more mangroves sprout up, new land is created. Every year, the land advances a few inches into the sea.

Some kinds of mangroves, including the black mangrove, do not have prop roots, but send roots up from beneath the soggy ground. These "air roots," which may be a foot or more high, absorb oxygen from the air when the underground roots are covered.

There is a definite sequence to the seaward march of a mangrove swamp. In the Florida Keys, where mangroves have built vast areas of new land and new islands, you will see the youngest and smallest red mangroves growing next to the water. Their roots are usually submerged, except during the lowest tides. Behind them, washed only by high tide, are the taller black mangroves, which grow to 70 feet. Their thick branches and dark, dense foliage form a nearly solid canopy.

Trees and other plants more typical of the land grow behind the mangroves, but in the swamps, mangroves usually crowd out other vegetation. Numerous animals depend on mangroves for protection and support. Oysters attach themselves to the prop roots, where they are covered by high tides. At night these oyster beds are raided by raccoons. Fiddler crabs burrow in the mud between the roots; starfish move slowly over the muddy surface. High up in the dense canopy, large colonies of pelicans and herons may roost and nest. But even while one mangrove swamp, with its dependent animal life, pushes slowly out to sea, another one may be just beginning where a single seedling washes against a distant shore.

Where a Few Inches of Soil Make a World of Difference

Wherever mangroves grow, there are zones of plant life as the soil level changes. In time, soil accumulates around the roots and eventually builds a foundation for other mangrove species. At right is a diagram showing the zones of vegetation that occur in the Florida Everglades, starting with a red mangrove community at the edge of the sea. Such areas may extend inland for as many as 60 miles. The warm Atlantic shores have relatively narrow bands of mangroves. The tropical coastlines of Asia have much wider and denser mangrove "jungles."

Red mangroves are the first to colonize a narrow margin of shallow, relatively quiet waters. Their underwater roots trap sediments and debris, thus building up soil. Black mangroves grow farther up; their roots form a dense mat.

At a slightly higher elevation, white mangroves and gumbo-limbos thrive in brackish water (a mixture of sea water with fresh water from inland sources).

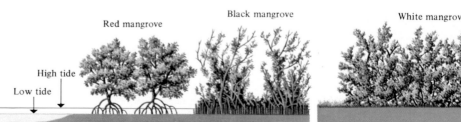

Red mangrove

Black mangrove

White mangrove

High tide

Low tide

A community of young roseate spoonbills (above) was probably born in this lush vegetation. They venture forth daily and return to roost here at night. Their plumage changes from white to pink as the birds mature. Notice the arching roots that are characteristic of red mangroves.

A coastal prairie (left) is named for its close resemblance to inland prairies. This panoramic view shows saw grass and mangroves in the foreground. As the land fills in, it takes on the appearance you can see in the background—a transition from low-growing shrubs to tall trees.

An underwater view of mangroves (right) shows how their prop roots jut downward. Some of these roots will penetrate the soil. A spiny sea urchin tumbles in the sun-dappled waters.

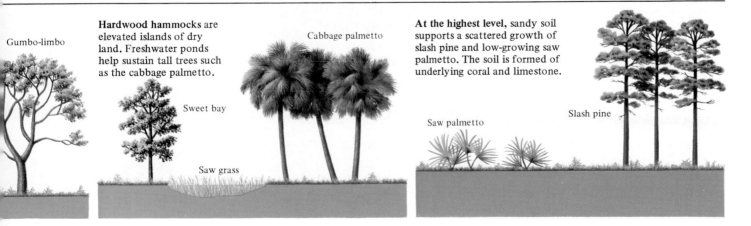

Gumbo-limbo

Hardwood hammocks are elevated islands of dry land. Freshwater ponds help sustain tall trees such as the cabbage palmetto.

Sweet bay

Saw grass

Cabbage palmetto

At the highest level, sandy soil supports a scattered growth of slash pine and low-growing saw palmetto. The soil is formed of underlying coral and limestone.

Saw palmetto

Slash pine

133

CHAPTER FIVE

Grasslands and Meadows

In ancient times, grasses fostered many civilizations, even giving rise to such inventions as calendars and currency.

Fields and pastures are often described as heartlands. This is no mere figure of speech; it is a reflection of the fact that our daily bread comes from grasses. Early civilizations developed where crops grew readily. The floods that made the Nile Valley fertile were predicted from one year to the next through the laborious recording of events (in the main, the stars provided guidance—and astronomy was born as a science). In time, calendars came into being. The surpluses of crops brought commerce to a higher level, beyond simple barter. Record-keeping, numbering systems, and currency all owe a debt to grasses.

How old are the grasses? No one knows for sure. The first fossils go back about 26 million years—which makes them far younger than mosses, ferns, and many species of trees. The fossil record shows that the grasses of antiquity were amazingly similar to present-day species. So, too, were the grasslands themselves—occupying broad, flat plains.

The fact that early grasses have endured to the present in relatively stable forms does not mean that grasses are simple. Rather, they have retained the early, successful forms, and have also diversified—spontaneously crossbreeding and forming new strains. Early forms of corn and wheat developed on their own, without the help of human beings.

Mankind has taken advantage of the remarkable flexibility of grasses and, by selective breeding, has produced "plants made to order." Dwarf wheat, which has dramatically increased food production in many parts of the world, is one example. Corn has even been grown with ears at uniform height, for easy harvesting.

Grassland scents are the pollen of countless, tiny grass flowers. The ribbed stems of grasses bend before the wind and rise again; their rubbing creates a rustling sound—an eerie music that, once heard, cannot be remembered without a pang of nostalgia.

Steppes, Prairies, and Pampas

No matter what grasslands are called —prairies, steppes, downs, savannas, velds, or pampas—they all have several things in common. They are usually situated on level or gently rolling plains, and are swept by nearly incessant winds. Grasslands are relatively dry, at least for part of the year. The similarities are reflected in the names: savanna is a Spanish word for plain; pampa, the Indian word for flat area.

The world's largest grasslands are the steppes of Europe and Asia. They once stretched in an unbroken expanse from the deep green meadows of the Danube Valley eastward nearly to the Pacific. Like most grasslands, the steppes have been largely converted to agriculture. It was on the steppes near the Caspian Sea that the horse was first domesticated. Livestock now graze where herds of wild animals once roamed. Domesticated grasses—wheat, barley, and the like—have replaced native species. But enough remnants of original grasslands are left to allow you to discover what these immense worlds were like before they were "tamed."

The prairies of North America were named by French explorers in the six-teenth century—the word prairie means meadow in French. Prairies receive more rain than many other grasslands, mostly in the spring and early summer. In fact, rainfall seems to determine where each type of grass grows on the prairie. Tall grasses, such as the 8-foot big bluestem, flourish in the east (near the Great Lakes), where rainfall is greatest. Farther west, the mid-grasses, such as little bluestem and western wheat grass, take over. Still farther west, in the arid region near the Rockies, the grasses are short—blue grama, buffalo grass, and others. The enormous herds of buffalo (actually bison) that once roamed North America were not restricted to the short-grass regions. These large, shaggy beasts grazed from the Rockies to the Atlantic seaboard.

The pampas of South America are among the flattest grasslands in the world. They are like a tabletop, perched between the foothills of the Andes on the west and the Atlantic Ocean on the east. Near the ocean, the pampas receive abundant rain, and make up the agricultural heartland of Argentina. But the western pampas, blocked from moisture-bearing winds by the Andes, are dry and mostly barren. Sometimes air masses from the two regions collide near Buenos Aires, producing violent rainstorms known as pamperos.

The word savanna is used to describe tropical grasslands on several continents, including South America (near the Amazon) and Australia (in the north). But to many people, East Africa is *the* savanna, a region famous for its spectacular herds of wild animals. There, a great variety of mammals shares a relatively restricted amount of vegetation. For example, zebras usually eat only the coarse tops of grasses; wildebeest and topi (two kinds of antelope) eat the leafy middle stems; gazelles eat the young shoots.

The grasslands of South Africa are usually called veld—also spelled veldt, but pronounced felt—a Dutch word for field. Although there is no clear distinction between the veld of southern Africa and the savanna farther north, the veld is usually drier and covered with various species of red grass. The animal inhabitants are similar—wildebeest, giraffes, elephants, lions, and cheetahs. In some cases, however, the individuals may be of a different species.

At the edge of the Argentine pampas, a stream from nearby hills waters the sparse growth. Elsewhere on the pampas, vast pastures, which stretch unbroken from horizon to horizon, sustain huge herds of beef cattle. Gradually, they are being fenced off for agriculture.

Meadow Patterns

To capture a field of flowers (as in the photograph below), use a tripod. Set your camera for a small lens opening, and check your light meter for an accurate reading. Your picture will be sharp from foreground to infinity.

• For a different effect, you can zero in on a few nearby blossoms and let the rest—in both the foreground and background—become fuzzy.

• Take one exposure in sunlight and one in the bright, shadowless light of a passing cloud. Try several angles to get side- and back-lighting. Grasses can also be photographed in this way.

The bison of North America (left) are ideal prairie-dwellers. Insulated by their shaggy coats, they can endure extremes of weather. These bulls are grazing in Yellowstone National Park; sagebrush covers the hills.

In the late afternoon, waterbuck leave their resting places in the shade to graze on the African savanna (above). These heavily built antelope have long, coarse hair; only the males bear the curved, ridged horns.

In amazing profusion, ox-eye daisies and hawkweeds bloom, framed by the deep green of a June meadow. To duplicate this photo, watch your focus and the wind.

137

How Grasses Compete with Trees

Rainfall is the most obvious factor in determining whether grasses or trees will dominate a particular area—most trees require more water than grasses. In some areas, there is about the right amount for either. Here competition is keen, but the advantages are usually with the grasses.

For a start, grasses are better equipped to withstand fire. Archaeologists have unearthed ancient charred plants that tell us there have been fires since vegetation first appeared on land. They were probably started by volcanoes or by lightning. Today, as you read this page, some 1,800 thunderstorms are sweeping across the land, and within the next 20 minutes, about 120,000 lightning bolts will strike.

Fires are most common in early spring, before plants turn green, and in fall, when much of the vegetation dies. After the flames pass, the soil is black with ash and charred stubble. The growing tissues of trees—especially saplings—are often destroyed, but the growing point of grasses, near or below ground level, is less affected by fire.

Soon after the burning, a rebirth occurs that is one of the most amazing in nature. The blackened earth absorbs the heat of the sun. In the African grasslands, temperatures on burned ground can be 30°F. to 40°F. hotter than on an unburned area. This encourages the germination of certain seeds. Grass seeds, borne on the wind, are universally present, and swift to sprout.

Burned over or not, grasses have the further advantage of an extremely well-established root system. The dense network of roots infiltrates the soil so thoroughly that you have to cut sod with a blade or tear it apart, if you wish to move it. (This tough binding is what made the sod-block houses of the early American prairie settlers so durable.) When, after a life of perhaps 20 years, a grass plant dies, the roots from surrounding plants quickly fill in the vacancies, sometimes following the pathways of the decaying roots.

Wind is also a decisive factor in the contest between trees and grasses. Grasses are able to bend in the wind, and their blades are slender and resilient. The branches of trees are more rigid and may break in the wind. The leaves of trees are often broad, and their attachment to the tree may be less flexible than the jointed stalks of grass.

But more important is the fact that all plants lose moisture through their

exposed surfaces, and a broad leaf results in greater evaporation. As the wind incessantly carries off water, the tree draws moisture up from its roots—roots that are nowhere near as extensive (in proportion to the size of the plant) as those of grasses. When the tree cannot replenish the water, the leaves wilt and become less capable of producing nutrients; a downward cycle begins, and the tree may die.

What kills trees actually aids grasses. They thrive in this windy world. Willa Cather, the American author, describing winds blowing over the grasses of Nebraska, wrote, "there was so much motion in it; the whole country seemed, somehow, to be running." The wind, which produced this romantic picture, also does much to shape the world through which it passes.

Many animals feast at fire fronts. The kori bustard above patrols an African savanna in the path of a blaze. Small animals that escape the fire may run into this predator.

A wall of flames sweeps across the grasslands in Zambia, forcing all the animals to flee for their lives. Most birds can fly away; some animals take refuge underground. Insects have the greatest losses, but their eggs survive.

Trees protect as well as beautify your property. A screen of trees breaks the force of the wind. This is beneficial in many ways—a windbreak can lessen fuel bills, improve the quality and quantity of crops, and create shelter for livestock. When you plan a windbreak, collect information about the kinds of trees that are recommended for the climate and soil in your area. Select slow-growing species with a maximum height that will not make your house look small. Perhaps you already have a row of shrubs on your boundary line, or on the windward side of your house. If you intersperse the shrubs with conifers and flowering trees, you will create an efficient windbreak. Include dogwood and cherries for spring bloom, oaks and maples for fall color, spruces and firs for winter greenery.

Thick shelterbelts of trees form wind barriers around this midwestern farm. Trees can protect adjacent areas for a distance roughly 20 times their height. For example, a row of trees approximately 75 feet high will protect a strip of land some 1,500 feet long. In cutting down the wind flow, two or three rows of trees are more effective than only a single row.

A solid barrier—a stockade fence or a tree with dense foliage—blocks wind flow and causes areas of turbulence on either side. This decreases a windbreak's efficiency.

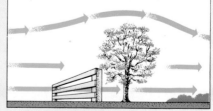

A rail fence or a widely branching tree with sparse foliage filters the wind. It reduces wind speed and force without creating turbulent eddies that may damage nearby vegetation.

Grazers Great and Small

The world's fastest animals live on grasslands, where hiding places are scarce and running is often the only way to elude enemies. In fact, speed is a requirement for predators, too, in their pursuit of prey. The holder of the animal land-speed record—the cheetah, which can run up to 70 miles an hour over a short distance—lives on the African grasslands. The runners-up, the gazelles, which are often the cheetah's prey, can reach 60 miles an hour. The third-place holder is the 50-mile-an-hour ostrich, which also lives on the African plains.

The red kangaroo of Australia's dry central grasslands is not exceptionally speedy (it goes all out at only 30 miles an hour or so), but its "strides" are actually giant hops on long, muscular back legs. An "old man" red bounds along in a series of 25-foot leaps that may be 6 feet off the ground, holding its small front legs as if in prayer and stretching out its strong, heavy tail for balance. These high leaps also enable the red and other 'roos to keep a lookout above the grass for considerable distances. The tail, which is a formidable club, serves as a rudder, enabling the 'roo to change direction quickly.

The fastest wild animal of the South American pampas is the ostrich-like rhea, a long-legged and flightless bird. Rheas usually form flocks of about 50 birds. During the breeding season, the male collects a harem. He prepares a nest by pulling up grass with his bill and creating an open zone around a shallow depression. All the females lay eggs in this nest, and the male incubates the eggs—sometimes as many as 50.

Like rheas and kangaroos, which gather in groups called mobs, many grassland animals form herds. On the grasslands, there is safety in numbers. The greater the number of sentries, the greater the chance of detecting an enemy. Herd members fleeing in all directions often distract a would-be predator.

Many grassland herds regularly migrate hundreds of miles to follow the food supply. As the rainy season in Africa's Serengeti Plain ends around March, immense herds of wildebeest form and move westward where the grass is greener, mating during their trek. The herds return east with the rains, in October, and calving begins on the lush, rainy-season grass.

Wildebeest are ruminants—animals with four-chambered stomachs—as are many large grazers such as gazelles, giraffes, and zebras (as well as domestic cattle). This complicated but efficient stomach allows ruminants to digest large quantities of tough, low-quality vegetation. It lets them eat and run.

As a ruminant eats, the food goes first to the rumen (the word for which these animals were named). There the food is fermented, as bacteria break down the tough parts of the plants. The food is later regurgitated and chewed as cud. Swallowed once more, the food then passes through the rest of the digestive system.

Grassland animals much smaller than ruminants also live in large groups. Burrowers such as North American prairie dogs and gophers, South American guinea pigs and cavies, Australian wombats and kangaroo rats, African hyraxes and meerkats, and Eurasian hamsters and susliks live in "towns" of 1,000 or more individuals.

If you have ever had a pet rodent (such as a gerbil), you know what vigorous diggers these animals are. Susliks, which resemble North American ground squirrels, riddle Eurasian grasslands with burrows up to 8 feet deep. In digging out their storerooms, sleeping chambers, passageways, and escape routes, the susliks bring up quantities of rich earth. Scientists believe that this continual tillage helps maintain soil fertility. Although the colonial diggers are small, without them the world's grasslands would be vastly different.

Flightless rheas (above), largest New World birds, travel in small flocks over the pampas. They feed on grass, grain, and insects, and are very fleet and wary. Once numerous, these ostrich-like birds are now becoming scarce.

Australia's grazing animals are the kangaroos (above, right). They thrive on the scanty, spiny grasses of the semi-arid plains and, when in need of water, dig holes in dry river beds. This benefits birds and other animals.

Ever on the alert for predators, the suslik—a ground squirrel of eastern Europe and Asia—basks in the sun (right). Susliks eat seeds, roots, bulbs, and insects, and seem to cover the dry grasslands with their many burrows.

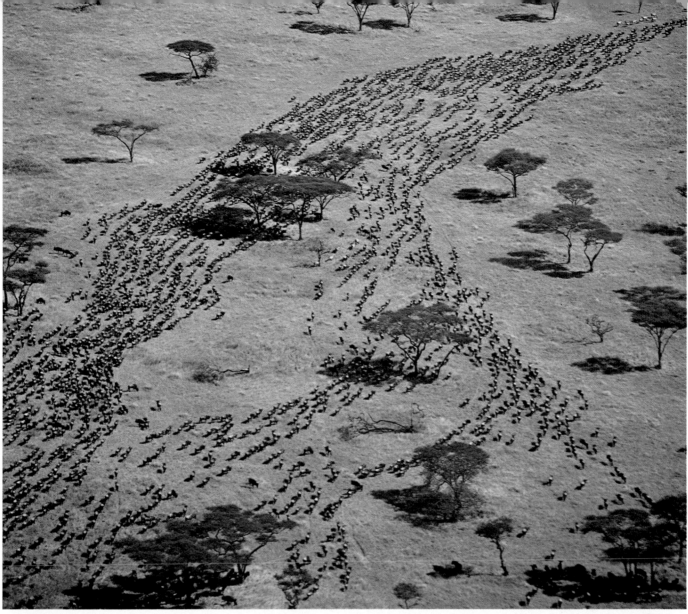

Multitudes of migrating wildebeest, up to 50,000 in a single herd, roam the East African plains seeking new growth of grass. These bulky antelope thrive on the sparse grasslands. As a large herd of wildebeest grazes, the grass is kept short, green, and succulent; with a small herd it becomes too tall and dry to serve as food. This may be the reason that wildebeest move across the plains in such vast numbers.

Pronghorn antelope are unique to the plains and scrublands of western North America. Not true antelope, they have horns that are shed every year, like the antlers of deer. Pronghorns are this continent's fastest mammals—they can reach 60 miles an hour in short bursts of speed. In summer, they travel in small groups, feeding on grasses, weeds, and shrubs, but in winter they converge into large herds.

147

What Is a Food Chain?

Every living thing depends on the sun. But only green plants, which make food by photosynthesis, can use the sun's energy directly. A plant-eater, such as a grasshopper on your lawn, gets a share of the sun by eating plants. Shrews and other insect-eaters obtain energy by eating grasshoppers. An owl may eat a shrew, thus acquiring the food originally produced by plants.

When a plant or animal dies, its tissues are still useful to the living world. Vultures and other scavengers eat some of the material; the rest is broken down by bacteria and fungi, and then re-turned to the soil, where plants take advantage of it in their growth. Decomposing tissue is called *organic* because it contains carbon compounds found only in living and once-living things.

The transfer of food from plants through a series of animals is known as a food chain. The various levels of consumption—the links in the chain—have been identified, but actually the word *chain* is something of an oversimplification. *Web* is really better, for it gets closer to a true picture—prey-predator relationships are neither limited nor predictable, but are often hap-hazard. For example, insects are usually eaten by small insectivores. But they are also consumed (sometimes accidentally) by everything from grazing animals to hefty carnivores such as bears. There is endless interlocking of consumption patterns in the natural world—thus the expression food web is often used, and sometimes network.

Regardless of the name used, the levels of consumption correspond to the transfer of energy. In each stage, there is loss of energy (usually in the form of heat). For example, the grasses and other plants on a North American

The Sun Powers the Energy Cycle for Plants and Animals

In this representation of an energy cycle (food chain) on an African savanna, energy from the sun is absorbed by the plants and then transferred to many plant-eating animals. The various animal participants —from ant to vulture—eat and, in turn, are food for others. In reality, a food chain is more complex than is shown here. For example, many carnivores are also part-time scavengers. And, of course, there are a number of species at any one particular level of the food chain.

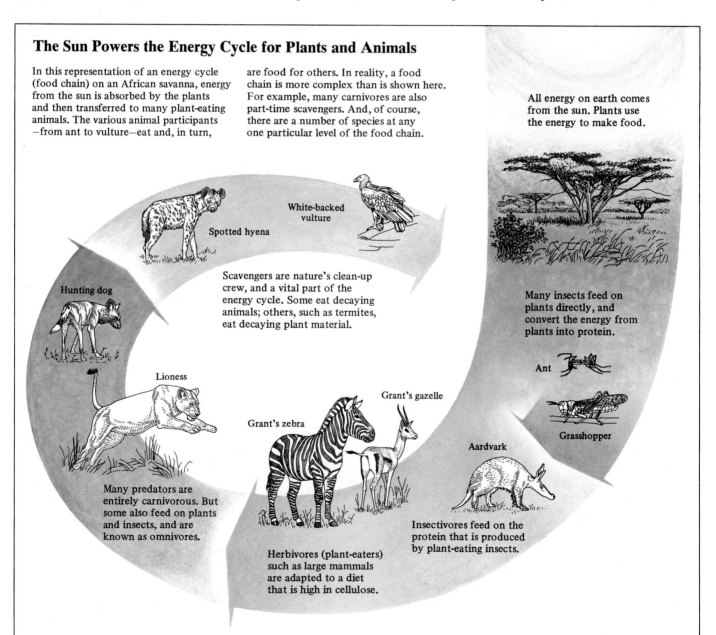

All energy on earth comes from the sun. Plants use the energy to make food.

Scavengers are nature's clean-up crew, and a vital part of the energy cycle. Some eat decaying animals; others, such as termites, eat decaying plant material.

Many insects feed on plants directly, and convert the energy from plants into protein.

White-backed vulture

Spotted hyena

Hunting dog

Lioness

Ant

Grasshopper

Grant's gazelle

Grant's zebra

Aardvark

Many predators are entirely carnivorous. But some also feed on plants and insects, and are known as omnivores.

Insectivores feed on the protein that is produced by plant-eating insects.

Herbivores (plant-eaters) such as large mammals are adapted to a diet that is high in cellulose.

prairie use only an estimated 10 percent of the solar energy that strikes their leaves. When plants (called producers) are eaten by certain insects, rodents, and grazing animals (all herbivores), they, too, acquire only a fraction of the energy that was lodged in the plant. Much of what they get is lost because it is not digestible, and what they do get is quickly used up in body processes—chewing, running from enemies, and so forth. Only a small amount of the original energy is stored in the tissues of the herbivores.

Consumers on the next level eat vegetarian animals. Hawks, owls, moles, weasels, skunks, and others are called secondary consumers. Animals that prey on secondary consumers are tertiary consumers, and these include coyotes, eagles, and bears. They, like all the others, use only a small amount of the energy stored in their prey.

This pattern produces a pyramidal picture. The greatest amount of energy and number of individuals occur at the first level—the plants, which comprise more than 95 percent of all living tissue. For example, on the South American pampas, it takes about 1,000 pounds of grass to feed 100 pounds of guinea pigs (which comes to about 100 animals). These will feed a 10-pound maned wolf, which, if eaten by a jaguar, would allow the jaguar to gain about a pound of body weight.

But again, food chains or webs are seldom simple, and a species does not always occupy the same feeding level. For example, sometimes a golden eagle is a secondary consumer (when it eats plant-eating mice and geese), and sometimes a third-order consumer (when it eats foxes and hawks). And it may be a scavenger (when it eats carrion).

Any description of food chains is complicated by the fact that although there is always a *loss of energy* when food is transferred from one level to another, there may also be a *concentration* of certain substances. This was dramatically brought to light when scientists discovered that pesticides build up in the tissues of animals far removed from the place where the chemicals were used. Nor is there anything simple about the ways this build-up occurs. An animal may produce tissue-building proteins that can be used by others, or cancel its role in the food chain by being inedible—possibly even toxic, like some tropical fishes.

Closing the gap, a cheetah is ready to attack a gazelle. Actually, prey and predator are more evenly matched than they seem to be. The cheetah is fast, but tires easily; the gazelle has stamina. To elude a predator, a gazelle must be able to recognize an enemy and to gauge how far away it is before beginning to flee.

Neither prey nor predator, a rhino is a plant-eater. The black rhino (left) is a browser, feeding on leaves and twigs; the white rhino—really gray— is a grazer, cropping grass with its wide muzzle. Rhinos are aggressive only if attacked or if defending their young.

NATURE OBSERVER
Rank Among Feeders—Who Eats First?

Animals do not waste energy in ceaseless warfare—many of their battles are settled in advance by the development of "rank." For example, in a study of five kinds of vultures in Africa, it was discovered that the different species approached the carcass in a definite order.
• Vultures are often the animals that lead other species to a kill. All eyes are upon them. A cheetah, which is a swift predator, may be driven from its kill by the arrival of more powerful predators, such as a pack of hunting dogs or even a few hyenas. These usually yield to a prowling lioness. In films and photos of the African plains,

you may notice that while one species feeds, others wait around the kill.
• You can observe rank among feeding animals right in your own home, if you feed more than one pet at the same time. Whether two dogs, two cats, a cat and a dog, or another combination, usually one gets first choice. And if you have a bird-feeder outside your window, you can observe rank among your local birds. For example, jays invariably assert their claims above those of sparrows. A squirrel is probably the only animal that will take on a jay—but even this feisty little mammal will avoid a pair of jays.

Predators: The Misunderstood Species

If you saw a hawk swooping down on a mouse or rabbit—an event that is particularly visible on a grassland—you might assume that the animal on the ground was living on borrowed time. Predators seem to have the upper hand. Some birds of prey can scan an entire valley in a matter of minutes, spot a mouse at incredible distances, and dive at speeds exceeding 100 miles an hour. Owls can even detect small, scurrying animals in the dark by the sounds they make.

What chance has a mouse, rabbit, or squirrel against such "super-hunters"? Surprisingly, the odds favor the meek.

Studies of hunting birds reveal that they generally miss their prey as often as they catch it. Birds that capture other birds on the wing have an even worse "batting average." For example, certain falcon species (such as merlins) are likely to fail 95 times out of 100.

Predators aren't always successful because prey species have evolved defenses against them. For example, many small mammals have acute hearing and can react swiftly to approaching predators. Some run a zigzag path and dodge their attackers or duck into a burrow.

With the resources of predator and prey so evenly matched, the question

changes: how do predators keep from starving? Like other animals, predators conserve their energy. Generally, they don't waste their time attacking healthy, mature animals. They look for easy kills—the sick, young, or old. One study of wolves on Alaska's Mount McKinley showed that full-grown wild sheep were almost immune to attack. A similar study of cougars in Idaho indicates that even these formidable predators usually attack the most vulnerable prey.

Predators that hunt strong animals run the risk of becoming victims themselves. A lion that attacks a zebra or giraffe may be killed by sharp, flailing hoofs. An osprey unable to withdraw its talons from too large a fish may be pulled underwater and drowned.

The diet of a predator is generally quite varied. Coyotes will attack deer, but in the absence of large prey, a coyote will hunt mice and other small animals. Small prey, in fact, makes up the bulk of a coyote's diet. If even these creatures prove elusive, a coyote will eat carrion. The line between predators and scavengers is not clearly drawn—some animals hunt for themselves, but also steal the kills of other predators.

Some predators resort to plants for food. Coyotes are known to eat a wide variety of plants. Bears consume large amounts of vegetation, as well as prey. Pioneering naturalist John Muir said of the grizzly bear, "To him almost everything is food, except granite."

For a long time, people have believed that predators controlled the numbers of prey animals. Thus many predators have been killed in the hope that this would mean more game for human hunters. But the facts do not give full support to the idea. For example, on the Serengeti Plain in Africa, the immense herds of wildebeest are preyed upon by lions, leopards, cheetahs, hyenas, and hunting dogs. But not even these many enemies have a significant effect on their numbers. The most important cause of death among wildebeest is the separation of calves from their mothers. The effect of a drought is much more deadly than the combined forces of the many predators.

In isolated situations, predators do play an extremely important role in regulating the prey population—as when wolves and moose are confined to a single, relatively small island. But in general, predators simply do not live up to their bad reputations.

What Future for the Restless, Far-Ranging Tiger?

The different life-styles of the two largest members of the cat family—tigers and lions—help to explain why lions are generally faring better than tigers. Tigers are solitary hunters that need about 10 square miles of living space to seek their natural prey—deer, antelope, buffaloes, and smaller mammals. Lions, on the other hand, need less room. They live in prides and hunt cooperatively. Unlike the restless, roaming tigers, lions are great sleepers. If well fed, they will sleep for 22 of the 24 hours in a day, and

so are less of a threat to man. A tiger has only itself to depend upon (except when a mother rears her cubs), and its habit is to wander ceaselessly. In recent years, human encroachment on tiger habitat has reduced its range and killed off its natural prey; the tiger has turned to domesticated animals for food. This brings retaliation from farmers, and the tiger is pressed even further. In general, tigers do well in zoos, which are becoming their last refuge. Their future is clearly in human hands.

The adaptable coyote of North America is the center of controversy. Sheep ranchers regard it as a killer that should be exterminated. Many conservation groups defend its right to live, and point out that it has a role in controlling rodent pests. Meanwhile, the coyote is not only surviving, it is actually extending its range. The coyote has taken up residence in the many steep, wooded areas in the city of Los Angeles. It has occasionally contributed its howls to the outdoor concerts at the Hollywood Bowl.

Young burrowing owls (above) cram the entrance to their den, awaiting the return of a parent with food. These owls are valued by farmers for their insect- and rodent-eating habits. The young may fall prey to skunks or snakes. Oddly enough, the owl's chief defense is a hissing sound—an almost perfect imitation of a rattlesnake's warning.

The meerkats of southern Africa (left) live in colonies on the grasslands. They are relatives of the Asian mongoose, and have a similar, almost domesticated status in many homes—they are excellent mousers. In the wild, meerkats eat mostly insects, spiders, and plant materials.

151

Birds of the Grasslands

The grasslands of the world are rich in flowering plants that produce seeds, and in insects that feed on them. One estimate puts the insect population on an acre of North American prairie in midsummer at 10 million. This abundance of insect and vegetable food attracts many kinds of birds to grassy pastures, meadows, and croplands.

Grassland birds are an asset to the farmer because they are voracious eaters of insect eggs and caterpillars, and innumerable beetles, grasshoppers, and other insects. European lapwings, for example, often follow a plow or tractor, snatching up grubs. Birds are not an unmixed blessing for agriculture—blackbirds and migrating geese are notorious crop raiders—but on balance, the many species of grassland birds are definitely an aid to farming.

Birds that breed in the grasslands share certain patterns of behavior. Almost all indulge in spectacular courtship rituals; these may be dances, fights, or song flights. Unlike forest birds, many grassland birds, such as bobolinks and meadowlarks, sing on the wing, or from roadside wires or fence posts. At least half of these birds build partially domed or concealed nests protected by arching grasses, which they enter by scurrying through the vegetation like little mice.

The champion dancers of the bird world are the 14 species of cranes. In North America, the sandhill and whooping cranes; in Asia, the common and sarus cranes; in Africa, the crowned cranes; and in Australia, the brolgas all perform their circling, bowing, and leaping routines on open plains.

A more aggressive kind of courtship ritual is that of the ruff (named for the male's extraordinary breeding adornment). These European sandpipers nest in damp meadows and display on grassy mounds. Such parade grounds are known as leks. Dominant males have small territories on the leks, which they defend pugnaciously. Fierce fights alternate with the raising of neck ruffs and ear tufts. No two males look alike; ruffs and body plumage may be black, white, brown, or reddish in any combination of colors. Females, called reeves, resemble the more typical sandpipers.

The sharp-tailed grouse and prairie chicken also stage fantastic shows on their dancing grounds. The males inflate brightly colored air sacs on their necks, patter their feet (a motion copied by plains Indians in their dances), and utter loud, booming sounds.

Even more spectacular is the courtship display of the great bustard, a rare resident of the central European plains. It is one of the heaviest land birds capable of flight. The male bustard turns himself into a snowy-white ball of feathers by exposing his fluffy undertail and wing coverts. Inflating his throat pouch to the size of a football, he utters deep, hollow, moaning sounds.

Celebrated in literature, the song flight of the Old World skylark is pure poetry. Spiraling up into the sky, the bird warbles continuously, then hovers and descends. Other larks on other continents make similar song flights.

Remnant of vanished prairies, this midwestern grassland is gay with wildflowers and lively with breeding birds. From hidden nests amid clumps of bluestem grass, a covey of sharp-tailed grouse takes flight. An upland sandpiper alights in a typical lifted-wing pose; it, too, nests in the grass. On a spray of sunflowers, a boldly marked male lark bunting, and a female (sparrow-like in appearance), ignore a foraging predator—the black-billed magpie. From an old fence post, a bobolink competes with the champion singer of the prairie, the western meadowlark. A western kingbird, bearing little likeness to its eastern cousin, awaits a meal of grasshoppers. Near last year's tumbleweed, a horned lark prospects for seeds. Later, when the thistles ripen, the goldfinch will weave the soft thistle-fluff into its nest.

Key to Birds of the Grasslands

1. Sharp-tailed grouse
2. Upland sandpiper
3. Black-billed magpie
4. Lark bunting (male)
5. Lark bunting (female)
6. Bobolink
7. Western kingbird
8. Western meadowlark
9. American goldfinch
10. Horned lark

Flowers in Abundance

Human beings are the main reason grassland flowers are so widespread. Land that has not been cultivated—prairies untouched by the plow—may have prairie clover, sunflowers, and others. But they never put on a show like the fields of Queen Anne's lace, daisies, black-eyed Susans, and such that bloom exuberantly in fields that were formerly tilled.

In agriculture, often the first thing a farmer does is clear off existing vegetation. This produces a highly artificial situation that is an open invitation to colonization by seeds in the vicinity. In a way, this sums up the farmer's prime concern—how to encourage one particular crop and exclude all other plants. With centuries of experience, farmers have learned to do just that—to grow plants selectively.

But throughout the history of agriculture, another recurring problem has been harder to solve—exhaustion of the soil. A field that will produce good crops for several years eventually uses up the nutrients in the soil, and crop yields drop. An ancient remedy still in use is crop rotation (where the type of crop is changed from year to year); another is allowing a field to lie unused.

A fallow field is inviting to the great opportunists of the plant world—the familiar roadside plants that spring up on cleared land. They produce a super-abundance of seeds that are spread worldwide by wind, animals, and man. For example, Queen Anne's lace (wild carrot) originated in the Middle East and traveled around the globe.

Such pioneer plants are tough competitors and grow well in dry, sunny, hot conditions typical of grasslands. The first species will grow rapidly—for example, crabgrass, ragweed, and sorrel. In quick succession, plantain, goldenrod, and other species appear. At this time, there is a great bustle in the fields, with insects and rodents tunneling in the soil, and incidentally aerating and bringing up nutrients. Eventually, the soil recovers its fertility, and the farmer may clear it again. Or, to accelerate and control the "recovery" of the land, he may plant red clover, which restores nitrogen to the soil and can be grazed while it is doing its work.

A flowering meadow is colorful with blossoms of red, pink, orange, yel-

Lacy discs of wild carrot and black-eyed Susan overshadow smaller blossoms in a Pennsylvania meadow (above). The carrots we eat are hybrids of several wild species.

The red clover in the field at right is not a weed; it has been planted in order to restore nitrogen to the soil. This will result in a more fertile field—and also a crop of honey.

154

low, blue, purple, and white. Despite the array of hues, nearly all the flowers belong to the same family of plants—the composites. To appreciate the intricate nature of a composite, first look at a flower that isn't one—say, a day lily. In its center is a single, protruding stigma, surrounded by pollen-bearing anthers, which are themselves surrounded by colorful petals.

Compare this pattern with that of a thistle flower. A thistle "blossom" is actually a dense cluster of tiny flowers—hence the term composite. In this type of composite, each unit looks like a miniature flower—a floret or disc flower. They have male and female reproductive parts, but no petals.

A typical composite flower, however, has a more elaborate pattern. Take the daisy, for example. The yellow center is a tight cluster of disc flowers, surrounded by white petals. The petals are actually ray flowers, but they function as ordinary petals do—as an attractant, bringing insects to the center where the disc flowers are located, and where seeds are produced.

There is yet another kind of composite, which is strange indeed. The dandelion is the most widespread example. It has no pollen-producing parts, but is composed solely of female ray flowers, and no pollen is required to fertilize the plants and produce seeds.

The Surprising Variety of Edible Weeds

Have you ever tried adding nutritious and tasty weeds to your camping menus? The leaves of violets have four times as much vitamin C as oranges; chicory leaves are an excellent source of calcium and vitamin A.
• Young dandelion leaves add zest to a salad of mixed greens. The mustard family provides a choice of greens for a mixed salad—watercress, winter cress, and garlic mustard, to name a few. Mustard greens are best in the spring when young and tender; later in the year, their seeds are excellent as seasonings.

• Weeds to use as steamed vegetables or in soups and stews include lamb's quarters, curled dock, sheep sorrel, and milkweed. Wild onion leaves and bulbs will add flavor.
• Delicious teas can be brewed from the leaves of sassafras and various wild mints; the twigs of black birch; and rose hips, which are especially rich in vitamin C.
• Wild plants should never be eaten unless you have positively identified them —there are many helpful guides to wild foods. And like all new foods, they should be tried in moderation at first.

Elderberry blossoms add flavor to fritters and pancakes. Fruits make good preserves.

Cleavers, a common plant in thickets, is excellent if it is cooked like spinach.

Oswego tea is a refreshing drink, if you steep its leaves in boiling water.

Day lily tubers make delicious steamed vegetables; they also thicken soups.

The Orderly Pattern of Sunflower Seeds

One of nature's most fascinating shapes is the spiral. The heads of composite flowers, such as the sunflower (right), are often spirals; note how the seeds at the center form two sets of spiral rows. Usually you can see one of these sets right away, but the other may require a closer look. If you count the spirals in each set (see diagram below), you will arrive at two special numbers—both part of the Fibonacci series, named after a thirteenth-century Italian mathematician. This series begins with the number 1; 1 plus 1 equals 2; 1 plus 2 equals 3; 2 plus 3 equals 5; 3 plus 5 equals 8; and so on. In other words, each number in this series is the sum of the two preceding numbers.

The diagram at right represents the arrangement of seeds in a ripened sunflower of average size. The two rows of spirals are indicated by the black and white lines; they spiral out in opposite directions from the center. The 34 black lines form a clockwise spiral; the 21 white lines, a counterclockwise spiral. Both are Fibonacci numbers.

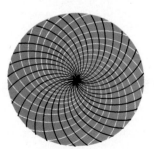

Goldenrod: A Golden Invitation

Every summer and fall, a temporary world comes into being in grasslands and meadows. Beginning as early as July in North America, a tide of golden flowers sweeps across the fields. To human observers, the change may seem no more than a pleasant indication of the changing seasons, but to countless animals, a billowing field of goldenrod represents a new environment in which to live and reproduce.

Though the appearance of golden-

Ragweed, not goldenrod, is the culprit when hay fever strikes in late summer. But because goldenrod grows near ragweed and has more conspicuous flowers, it usually gets the blame.

rod flowers is often quite sudden (they seem to come from nowhere), the plants have been there all along. Even in winter the brown stems are visible, sticking up through the snow. Goldenrod is a perennial—most of the plant dies during the winter; the roots survive and produce bright green shoots in the spring. During the summer, the new shoots grow tall alongside the old, dead stems, until the green prevails.

To truly see the flowers of goldenrod, look at them from three different viewpoints. From far away, the golden blossoms look like graceful plumes atop slender stems. If you approach more closely, you will see that each plume is made up of individual flower heads arranged along spike-like stems. If you look still more closely, perhaps with a hand lens, you will see that each flower head is made up of small, individual florets.

It is often difficult to tell just what kind of goldenrod you are looking at. There are more than 100 species in the United States alone (goldenrod grows across North America and in parts of South America, Europe, and Asia); the different species cross readily, forming new varieties. However, if you notice a delicious anise-like aroma wafting up as you walk through a field of goldenrod, you can be sure that you are among the species called sweet goldenrod. Its leaves make a savory tea.

But other eyes are on the goldenrod. As soon as the blossoms appear, so do hordes of insects that feed on their nectar and pollen. Monarchs and other butterflies flit from one plume to another, like children in a candy store.

Heavy-bodied soldier beetles fly clumsily to the flowers, giving the impression that they are bumping into the blossoms by accident. An abundance of bees and flies crawl among the florets.

Some predators use goldenrod as a hunting ground. One of the easiest to spot is the ambush bug, a small insect with irregular projections along its back and sides. It feeds on almost anything it can catch—it can even overpower an insect several times its size.

You will have to look very closely to see a certain inhabitant of goldenrod: the crab spider's yellow color blends perfectly with the flowers. This spider, which looks and moves sideways like a crab, does not spin a web. It catches prey by lurking on the flowers until a butterfly or other potential victim alights—then it pounces.

After their brief moment of glory, the goldenrod flowers begin to wither; their leaves turn brown. Most of the animals move to other areas. The crab spider may scuttle over to a purple loosestrife. Though at first the yellow spider looks out of place, gradually it changes color to match its new home. On a white flower, it turns white.

Many of the insects survive the winter in the same way as the roots of goldenrod—below the surface of the soil. Others die, but leave eggs that hatch in spring. Several insects leave offspring in the goldenrod itself. One of these is the goldenrod gall fly. Its larvae are lodged in ball-like lumps, called galls, that are visible on goldenrod stems. Like the brown goldenrod itself, the galls are a reminder that this world will reappear next year.

COLLECTOR'S TIPS
Common Flowers Versus Rarities

Some plants are as limited in their range and number as are rare animals. The rarity of a particular flower may be quite natural —in other words, lady's-slippers and similar species have probably never been common. It is interesting to discover (using a field guide) which of the common flowers that fill fields and line roads are native species, and which are aliens— that is, from another part of the world.
• Native flowers are more often protected by law than aliens. Obey signs that forbid picking flowers; many parks prohibit removal of even common plants. Be sure

to obtain permission before gathering from private property.
• Even when flowers are abundant, pick only a few of each kind, leaving some to reproduce. It may be time to restore the old custom of taking only one of each.
• Cut blossoms instead of breaking them off, and do not uproot the whole plant. The best way to collect flowers is on film.
• If an area is about to be cleared for roads, it's permissible—and desirable— to take and relocate any plants, common or rare. In this case, try to move them where the growing conditions are similar.

A waning summer's landscape is warmed by the glow of goldenrod, which towers over a sprinkling of small white asters. Some Indians and folk doctors used an infusion of goldenrod leaves and flowers as a pain-reliever; the plant also produces a yellow dye. Goldenrod nectar is a favorite food of bees, which often can be found buzzing about. Bees mix this nectar with that from nearby asters, and make a splendid honey.

Marching on long legs across golden florets, a soldier beetle seeks out the pollen-bearing parts of the blossoms. Though the adults eat pollen, the young prey on other larvae.

Gently poised with folded wings, a copper butterfly unfurls its long proboscis, which will be inserted in the flower tube to draw up nectar. Nearby, a bee collects pollen.

As yellow as the goldenrod, a flower spider lies in wait for its minute prey. When on blossoms of another color, this member of the crab-spider family may change its hue.

157

The Essential Work of Bees

The mining bee is a solitary insect—it does not live in colonies. Named for its digging habit, this bee deposits its eggs in underground tunnels, along with a food supply of nectar and pollen.

Dusted with pollen, a honeybee concentrates on gathering nectar, oblivious of its important role as a pollinator of vegetables and other food crops. Honeybees are social insects and live in colonies.

The busiest bee is the bumblebee, which visits twice as many flowers in the same time as other bees. Most bumblebees are larger and more colorful than honeybees.

Something for nothing is rare in this world, but every year we humans have a multibillion-dollar job performed for us virtually free of charge. The job is pollination, and it is done mostly by bees and a host of other insects. Without their tireless work, we would not have most fruits and many other foods —not to mention honey.

Before a plant can produce fruit or seeds, it has to produce flowers—and flowers must be pollinated. That is, pollen must be transferred from the male part to the female part, where fertilization takes place. Though many important plants, such as grasses, are pollinated by the wind, numerous others "enlist" the aid of insects.

One of the fascinating discoveries of botanists has been the way insects and flowering plants have evolved together, one influencing the other over millions of years. During this long evolutionary process, the partners have developed mutually beneficial working arrangements. In some cases, plant and pollinator are absolutely dependent on one another—if the plant dies out, so will the pollinator, and vice versa.

For most pollinators, the rewards are pollen and nectar, which is produced within the flower. Plants have evolved a variety of signals that help bees and other pollinators find their way to these desirable substances. Both attract insects by their sweet odor. Bright colors help to advertise the flowers. The petals of some blossoms are modified so they provide "landing fields" and guiding patterns, which lead insects to the right places.

Unlike pollen, nectar is purely an attractant and is not directly involved in reproduction. Most insect-pollinated flowers have special glands that secrete nectar. As a child, you may have sampled the nectar of honeysuckle by pinching off and sucking the lower part of the blossom. (You can make an artificial nectar by dissolving a small amount of sugar in a shallow dish of water. Put the dish outdoors in the sunshine, and see what insects will come.)

Bees, especially the species called honeybees, are important pollinators. Honeybees are social insects, highly organized into castes, which have specialized duties. Colonies of wild bees often live in hollow trees. Domesticated bee colonies are housed in a hive, usually a box-like structure.

All the work of the colony is done by female worker bees. Only one caste, the foragers, collects nectar; these bees carry it inside their bodies in a special crop, and feed it to other members of the colony. To obtain a full load of nectar, a forager may have to visit a thousand flowers.

Honey is derived from nectar. The nectar is aerated in the bees' mouths, a process that evaporates much of the water. The addition of digestive juices completes the transformation into honey. Worker bees seal the honey into the hexagonal cells of beeswax that make up the honeycomb. Stored honey will be used later as food for the bees—unless a human beekeeper removes the comb first. Solitary species, such as yellow-faced and carpenter bees, don't live in colonies, but nevertheless they gather nectar and make honey.

In collecting nectar, bees brush by the flower's pollen-producing parts. The golden powder is sticky and adheres to the bees' hairy bodies. Some of it is dislodged and pollinates the same or a different flower. The rest is carried back to the hive in the bees' pollen baskets—small depressions surrounded by bristles on their hind legs. If you watch a bee at work, you may be able to see such bee bread, as the pollen is called.

The pollen, an important food for bees, is stored in the hive. A typical bee colony may consume about 50 pounds of pollen a year; collecting this amount would require some 2 million trips.

White clover is a favorite with honeybees. This is because the bees can easily remove the nectar from its relatively small blossoms. Red clover, on the other hand, gives them more difficulty—occasionally the bees' tongues do not quite reach the nectar. Clover honey is one of the most subtle-tasting and popular varieties available.

Bees and Flowers Adapted to One Another

The construction of some flowers, such as certain orchids, determines the way a bee enters and departs. It is, in fact, a system that ensures pollination. Intent on gathering nectar, the bee follows lines and grooves, called honey guides, that lead to the nectar. The bee cannot extract nectar without being dusted with pollen. When it visits another flower, pollen is left behind, and cross-pollination results.

The lower lip of this flower is a landing platform for a bee that is seeking nectar.

The bee's weight depresses the lower petal, swinging the pollen-covered anther down.

As the bee leaves, it brushes against the anther, getting a liberal coating of pollen.

159

The Beauty of Butterflies and Moths

A flowering meadow is a splendid place to watch butterflies. Unconcealed by foliage, the butterflies flit about near the tops of plants, just at or below eye level. Here, in temperate latitudes in midsummer, you will see the greatest numbers of butterflies.

Settle down in the middle of a meadow. At first, let your eyes wander, taking in the blazing colors of blossom and butterfly, the scents of field and flower. Then select a particular nearby butterfly—just one, for a start. It takes some concentration to do this, for you'll see numerous other butterflies out of the corner of your eye. Note the size, shape, color, and any speckles or eyespots (large dots of color on the wings). These features can help you to identify the species. But whether you have a field guide along or not, watch how the butterfly alights on a flower, and how it sips nectar. It uses its long tongue (proboscis) as a straw.

When a butterfly lands, it usually folds its wings, concealing all but the relatively drab undersides. But if disturbed, a butterfly may suddenly spread its wings, revealing brilliantly colored patterns on the upper surface. A burst of bright color may startle a pursuer long enough for the butterfly to escape.

Butterflies and their close relatives, the moths, have other defenses. The eyespots may actually frighten a would-be predator. Other wing patterns may make the less-vulnerable tail look like the head. One of the most surprising defenses belongs to certain species of moths that are preyed upon by bats. Bats send out high-frequency squeaks, somewhat like sonar, that help them locate prey. But these particular moths take evasive action when they "hear" the high-frequency sounds. If the signal from the bat is strong (which means that the bat is near), the moth zigzags through the air; if the signal is weak, the moth dives and takes cover.

Butterflies and moths play a significant role in pollinating flowering plants (though they are not as important as bees). These insects obtain food—the sugar-rich nectar—and pick up pollen in the process.

There are butterfly flowers, and other flowers that attract moths. It is usually easy to distinguish between the two. Most moths are nocturnal. Moth flowers typically have a strong fragrance and are light in color; thus they are readily perceived in the dim evening

The American copper will drive off most other butterflies—regardless of size. It is not intimidated by larger animals, even humans. It sips nectar through its straw-like proboscis. The copper is identified by its bright color and dark spots (the color varies with the individual). Coppers are seen in open areas such as marshes, roadsides, and meadows.

A moth at rest is often very well camouflaged. The pattern of brown and green on the forewings of this small New Guinean species—an arctiid, or footman, moth—makes it resemble a bit of drying leaf. It might be overlooked by a lizard or a bird. There are more than 6,000 species of these arctiid moths, which are distributed worldwide from the Alps to the tropics.

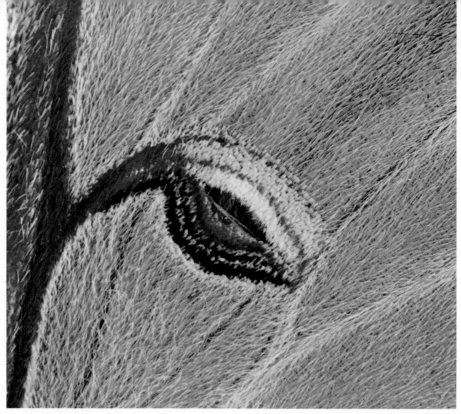

light. Another characteristic of moth flowers is that they often hang downward, easily reached by hovering moths.

When Charles Darwin, the famous British naturalist, visited Madagascar in 1862, he noticed a large orchid with the pollen- and nectar-producing parts recessed 10 inches in the impressive blossom. He knew that many orchids are pollinated by moths, and so he predicted that some day a moth would be discovered with a 10-inch proboscis. Eventually, such a moth was found.

Butterflies do not hover when they feed, but actually land on a blossom. Butterfly flowers are upright, which provides a stable landing platform. Butterflies, which are usually active during the day, are attracted to blossoms by both scent and color, and butterfly flowers tend to be orange or red. There is even an orange-flowered species of milkweed called butterfly weed—a veritable magnet for these beautiful insects.

Uncanny eye-like spots—one on each forewing (above) and also on the underside—are the luna moth's defense. A flash of these bold markings may confuse a predator and gain time for the moth to escape. The feathery texture on this moth's wing is typical of many moth species.

NATURE OBSERVER
Butterfly or Moth?

Here are some ways to separate moths from butterflies:
• Most butterflies love sunlight and are active during the day. (There are some tropical species that prefer the hours before dawn and the late evening.) Moths are generally night creatures, although there are some day-active species (especially in the tropics).
• The antennae are a good way of telling butterflies from moths. These "feelers" pick up the scents of flowers and other insects of the same species. Butterflies have long, slender wands with knobs on the ends. In contrast, the antennae of moths are feathery. Among some moth species, thicker "feathers" indicate a male, because it is the male that flies to find a female.
• The patterns of butterfly wings are generally bright and colorful, with almost transparent scales; some cold-climate species are dull-colored and have thicker scales. The wings of moths have more subtle coloration; they usually lack bright colors and blend with the surroundings—bark, leaves, and the like. Because of the moths' dull coloration and nocturnal habits, you are much more likely to notice a butterfly than a moth—even though there are about four times as many moth species as there are butterflies on a worldwide basis.

A Microscopic View of Delicate Wings

The colors on butterflies and moths are produced by overlapping scales, shown here through an electron microscope. The colors result from two types of scales. In one, the presence of pigments causes color. In the other case, a layered structure, without pigments, actually creates an illusion of color. Iridescence occurs when light hits the layered cells at different angles, transmitting now a shimmer of purple, now one of green.

The wing of a South American castniid moth shows finely structured, overlapping scales arranged in an irregular pattern.

Light bouncing off tiny ridges on the scales of an Asian swallowtail butterfly creates these beautifully blended colors.

Man Versus Insect

A twin-engine transport plane, roaring over a Texas grassland, is dropping a cargo to control screwworm cattle flies. The cargo is not insecticides; it is thousands of flies of the same species as the insect pests on the ground. All are male flies, raised in a laboratory and released to breed with the females that afflict the cattle (the larvae can kill).

This sounds like a perfect way to *increase* the fly population rather than decrease it. However, the laboratory flies have been sterilized by radiation. When they mate with the females, the eggs are infertile, and the females cannot mate again. The effectiveness of this strategy is demonstrated in the decline in infected cattle over one 8-year period, from 50,000 to 150 head of cattle.

This method of using one living thing to manage another is called biological control—biocontrol, for short. Animal populations in nature are balanced in this way, through predation, parasitism, and diseases, as well as food supply and climate. Biocontrol, as practiced by man, is not new. As far back as 1,000 years ago, the Chinese used ants to attack insect pests on fruit trees. One of the first applications in the United States was in 1888, when Australian ladybugs were imported to prey on scale insects infesting California fruit trees.

The Life History of an Industrious Pest

An iridescent Japanese beetle, seen here making lacework of an alder leaf, is an alien species. This beetle eats not just the leaves, but the flowers and fruit of some 300 kinds of trees and shrubs. It is especially fond of roses. Because it is an alien, it has few natural enemies —except the starling (which is itself an alien). Like many other insects, Japanese beetles pass through various stages of development (see below). Efforts to control Japanese beetles take advantage of the fact that they are most vulnerable at the larval stage. Spores of bacteria that feed on the larvae are injected into the ground, and kill the pests.

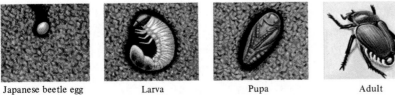

| Japanese beetle egg | Larva | Pupa | Adult |

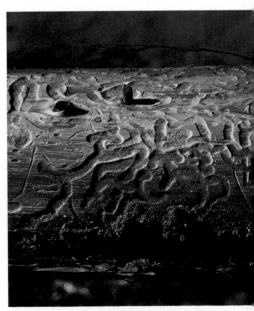

These etchings in wood were made by larvae of a metallic beetle while the tree was alive. Feeding on sapwood, the larvae gnawed broad channels and killed the tree. When the bark dropped off, the damage was revealed.

Biocontrols became more important after World War II, when the disadvantages of chemical pesticides such as DDT became obvious. Although they were often necessary to protect crops and to prevent outbreaks of disease, chemical pesticides build up dangerously in the environment and kill beneficial animals as well as pests.

One of the most successful biocontrols has been to "enlist" a pest's natural enemy as an ally. A good example is the mosquito fish, a North American species that feeds on mosquito larvae. In 1905, the fish were released into Hawaiian ponds and streams to help control mosquitoes. The results were so successful that the species has been introduced into South America, Europe, Asia, and New Zealand. In fact, the species may now be the most wide-ranging freshwater fish in the world.

The search for a natural adversary may lead around the world. After combing Europe and Asia, scientists found a wasp in Iran that served as a parasite of scale insects, which are notorious pests on California olive trees. However, the Iranian wasp did not do well in the new climate, and another search turned up a Pakistani wasp that was better suited to the New World.

The Japanese beetle has been suc-cessfully controlled in some places by spraying crops with bacteria that cause milky-spore disease. Though these bacteria are deadly to the beetles, they are harmless to other animals. Viruses can also be used to control insect pests.

One weapon was discovered when certain laboratory insects died before reaching maturity. Those that succumbed lived in cages that were lined with American newspapers, such as *The New York Times;* the survivors' cages were lined with copies of the London *Times.* The premature deaths were traced to chemicals found in American balsam fir trees used in the paper pulp, but not found in European trees. Similar chemicals are now used as sprays that prevent insects from developing normally, or cause them to emerge from cocoons at an unfavorable time.

But even the best biocontrols are not perfect. There have been renewed outbreaks of the screwworm cattle flies (biocontrols always leave a few remnants unharmed). Such controls also tend to work slowly. Scientists look on them as only one tool against harmful insects. Combined with carefully handled chemical insecticides, biocontrols offer a hope that we can protect ourselves and our crops without damaging our environment.

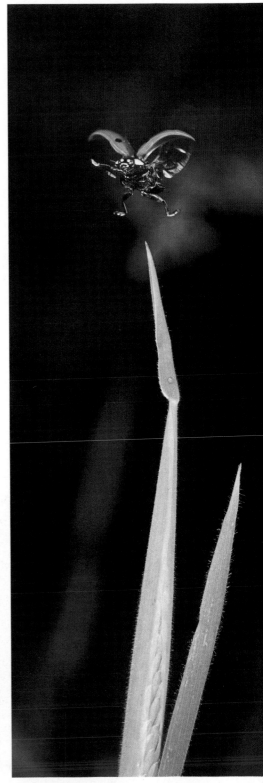

The praying mantis gets its name from its characteristic posture when at rest. Blending with the surrounding foliage, it waits with spiny forelegs raised; any unsuspecting insect is quickly captured and devoured. Because it feeds on beetles, caterpillars, and other insects, the mantis is considered beneficial. These predatory insects can be purchased by homeowners and released in the garden to help control harmful insects.

A ladybird beetle, with orange wing-covers raised, is about to alight. This insect, also called a ladybug, eats so many different destructive pests that it is introduced into orchards to help protect the trees.

How Farmers Manage Water and Soil

HOW TO
Stop Erosion

Topsoil is the layer essential for the growth of plants. Erosion of topsoil is a problem for farmers, and a concern for homeowners too. Loss of soil can be minimized by various techniques of water management (see below).

Small gullies and muddy streaks—which appear after rains—are warning signals of further erosion. Water will widen and deepen these channels.

Seeding the gully with ryegrass is good first aid. The roots will hold the soil even if the grass dies. Later on, plant a more permanent ground cover.

Water-carrying ditches, especially along roads, too often turn into ugly and dangerous pits. They may undermine paths and roads.

If you fill a ditch with small rocks, you will not impede drainage, but you will lessen erosion of the soil. Then too, the ditch will look better.

Animals such as otters sometimes make a slide in a grassy bank. Or damage may take place because of construction.

Stack flat rocks in the slideway. Start with larger rocks at the bottom of the bank, and build up toward the top. Check for stability as you proceed.

Human beings tend to think of soil and water as separate entities (and, of course they are); but all over the surface of the earth, the two are almost inseparable. Vapor in the air condenses around particles of dust; thus rain brings tiny bits of soil down to earth. Water dissolves many substances, and transports others. When rivers are dammed, to impound water or to generate hydroelectric power, the affinity of soil and water is sometimes overlooked. For example, the Aswan Dam in Egypt is silting up so quickly that it may soon become virtually useless. Meanwhile, the once-fertile Nile Valley is deprived of much of its annual renewal, which came in the form of silt-bearing flood waters.

The Aswan Dam example reveals the paradoxical nature of flooding—it is sometimes beneficial, sometimes catastrophic. In one instance, fertile soil may be deposited, but in other places, topsoil may be carried away, impoverishing the land. The loss of topsoil, which supports food crops, is regarded by some experts as the most serious of all depletions of our natural resources. As one scientist said, "If the soil disappears, so do we."

Usually, the longer water flows over the land, the more soil it picks up—and the harder it is to manage swelling streams. The water of a tiny rivulet on a high grassland generally carries very little soil, and it is readily controlled. But in the lowlands, where numerous streams may come together, the waters change character. There they may seem ruthless, like wild animals on a rampage.

Effective flood control and soil conservation must take place upstream. And in recent years progress has been made along these lines. Time was when farmers buried tiles in their fields to hasten the runoff of heavy rains. Nowadays, many farmers do all they can to detain water. If water soaks into subsoil, it becomes part of the water table, which is an underground reservoir.

Contour farming is an important form of soil conservation. That is, fields are plowed and planted following the natural contours of the ground. The furrows run across a slope rather than up and down. In effect, this forms a multitude of small dams.

Grasses have been enlisted in the work of slowing runoff and soaking up rain. Their extensive root systems capture tremendous amounts of water. On a hillside where drainage channels are planted with grasses, the grass is not cut. As water flows, the bending grasses form a blanket that prevents erosion.

Grasses are now used as a bed for other crops. Corn or some other grain is set into the grassy beds in narrow slits—in other words, the land is not cleared at all. Some grasses (chosen because they do not compete with the main crop) improve soil structure and help keep weeds out. Terracing, too, is an important means of controlling water. (See the facing page.)

Once a eucalyptus forest, this area in Victoria, Australia, was cleared for pastureland (most likely for sheep). The animals grazed the land to the point where its protective cover of grass was destroyed. The occasional heavy downpours of rain in this otherwise dry region washed away the topsoil. Deep gullies formed, and now the land is a desert.

Elevated rice terraces (above), characteristic of the Philippines and other parts of Asia, are an ancient form of farming. Terracing permits even steep hillsides to be utilized in regions where level land is scarce. The terraces are built so that water from a ridge above will spill onto those below. In some places, grapes are grown on terraces.

Using the Contours of the Land

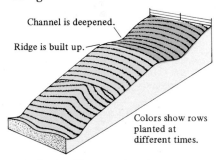

Channel is deepened.

Ridge is built up.

Colors show rows planted at different times.

This diagram illustrates how terraces are created on gently sloping terrain. Farmers make ditches (channels), and use the soil to create ridges. This artificial landscape functions to detain water and stem erosion.

Contouring and strip farming, combined in this Pennsylvania valley (left), are ideal conservation techniques. In contour farming, the crops are planted along lines that follow the curvature of the land; rain does not run off quickly, but remains in the ditches and is gradually absorbed. In strip farming, different kinds of crops are planted in alternating bands so that during plowing or harvesting, adjacent land has some plant cover.

Wonder Crops and Wild Plants

In guarded vaults at a federal installation in Colorado, there are treasures that are among the most valuable assets to life on this planet. The contents of these vaults (maintained at a constant temperature and humidity) are not precious metals or rare medicines. In fact, you could undoubtedly find some of these same treasures in your own yard. They are seeds.

Gradually, as more and more land has been taken over by agriculture, cities, and roads, countless wild plants have been displaced. Some species have died out entirely. The seed-storage system in Colorado is just one effort to keep alive as many genetic strains as possible. The vaults hold seeds from around the world, including the seeds not only of endangered species, but also of plants that are not in current use. For there are fashions in agriculture, as in every other human activity.

Most of our present-day food crops —such as rice and barley—came from wild ancestors, and apparently were easily cultivated by early farmers. Two of the world's most important plants, corn and wheat, are products of natural cross-breeding. Plant scientists have bred these and many other crops to achieve greater productivity. (The "miracle rice" of recent years is another example.) Two strains of any plant species are sometimes crossed to increase yield or nutrient content. Other crosses have given us crops that are particularly resistant to drought, or to insect pests.

So successful were these hybrids that they were planted on a continent-wide basis. Only after doing this a few times did scientists and farmers discover that there were hazards attending these successes. The corn blight of 1970 was just such a harsh lesson. This leaf virus reduced the U.S. corn crop by some 15 percent. The epidemic could not be halted because so many plants of the same strain had been planted on adjacent farms. Field after field was afflicted. Fortunately, plant breeders had many other types of corn available to replace the now imperiled strain. Present farming now encourages diversity.

Seeds are of great interest at present because agricultural specialists believe that technology—which has increased harvests in the past—cannot go much further in increasing production. For example, fertilizers are expensive, and farm machinery is already extremely efficient. The experts must look elsewhere. Up till now, farmers have had great success with relatively few species of plants. Some species have never been tested for their food potential.

There are interesting options available to plant breeders. For example, corn is now being bred to take greater advantage of the energy from the sun. Usually, the leaves of a corn plant grow opposite to one another. Now, a strain is being developed where the leaves grow all around—giving the plant more exposure to sunlight. Eventually, there should be more growth per plant.

The most amazing wonder crop may come from new "fused-plant" experiments, using genetic materials from two entirely different plant species. One proposed species may be "pomatoes," plants that would produce tomatoes above ground and potatoes below. Another visionary plant is called "soycorn," and would do much the same thing—grow more food in less space. Whatever the direction agriculture takes, the fundamental need is to preserve as many genetic strains of plants as possible. We never know when we'll need them.

Corn Began as an Ordinary Grass

Centuries before Columbus landed in the New World, Indians in the western hemisphere were growing primitive corn. Most likely, their corn resembled a grass called teosinte, which is shown at right. The natural cross-pollination among wild grasses, probably including teosinte, produced several varieties of corn. When European colonists arrived in the New World, Indians were growing all the major types of corn we have today—sweet, pop, flour, dent, and flint. The tremendous change in corn is shown in the photograph below. Teosinte (between the fingers at the left of the photo) has about nine kernels. Teosinte still grows wild, and is also cultivated for fodder in parts of the United States, Mexico, and Central America. An ancient type of South American popcorn (in the hand at right) has many more kernels. Multicolored Indian corn is next in size. The all-yellow modern hybrid in the background is the longest ear of corn that breeders have yet been able to develop. A single ear of this type may contain about 1,000 large kernels.

Techniques for Photographing Plants and Animals on a Farm

The grasslands, with their wide open vistas and grazing animals, are superb places for photography. But grazers—even some domesticated ones such as sheep—are noted for their keen eyesight and inclination to flee from intruders, whether predators or photographers. Fast shutter speeds and telephoto lenses should be used whenever possible. Long lenses allow a photographer to take the picture without getting close enough to scare the animals away.

• Even grasses swaying in the wind can be captured on film. Use a shutter speed of 1/125th or faster, to freeze the action.
• Try isolating a few grass stems by using a large aperture and letting the foreground or background go soft.

Strong backlighting from the mid-morning sun created the deep shadows and contours of this pastoral scene (above). Sheep are on a steep hillside above the photographer, and the sunlight is parallel to the slope. A polarizing filter was used to deepen the tones.

Clarity of texture is evident in this portrait of golden grain (upper right), photographed under the light of a noonday sun. To achieve this effect, use the smallest aperture and wait for a moment of stillness.

To get a silhouette, try for an uncluttered background. Early morning and late afternoon are favorable; the light is relatively horizontal. Photographed from a higher level, the horse (right) has been silhouetted against the grass. A slight underexposure increases density and contrast.

CHAPTER SIX

Lakes and Rivers

*The wonderful thing about water is
that it can be recycled endlessly. Most of the
present-day supply is billions of years old.*

There is probably no such thing as pure water. Even when water is created artificially in a laboratory from hydrogen and oxygen, it must be stored in something, and water will dissolve a slight amount of whatever holds it. Water is rightfully called the universal solvent. When you drink a glass of water, you are also drinking a few harmless molecules of dissolved glass.

Few physical facts have greater significance for all living things than this ability of water to dissolve and transport materials. Water is the main ingredient of life-supporting substances—in the blood-streams of animals and in the vascular systems of plants. It is indeed the medium of life.

Water begins picking up "passengers" when it falls as rain— it dissolves gases in the air and carries tiny particles too. As water flows over land on its way to the sea, it picks up a trace of almost everything it touches, particularly salts. Thus a river may already be somewhat salty by the time it reaches the sea.

But most freshwater on land is not in lakes and rivers; it is hidden underground in vast reservoirs collectively called the water table. It has always been clear that springs and wells were part of an underground water supply. But rivers and streams, too, are supplied by the water table, as are countless fertile fields, meadows, and forests. By its very nature, the water table is hard to survey. Over countless centuries, water has seeped where it could, some-times blocked, sometimes traveling along underground channels. Far more water is needed to replenish these reservoirs than is sup-plied by rainfall. Therefore, like so many other resources, water must be drawn upon carefully, that it may last.

*Zestful, noisy, and handsome, a flurry of ducks takes off from
a lake in Oregon. Green-headed male mallards stand out in
contrast with the less colorful females of the species. Mallards,
pintails, wigeons, and many other waterfowl stop off in
hundreds of waterways along their migration route. For them,
protection of every pond, lake, and marsh is of vital importance.*

Beautiful Freshwater Worlds

By far the most abundant substance on the surface of our planet is water. Surprisingly, only a tiny fraction—about one five-thousandth—of this water is fresh water that we can drink. Nevertheless, it is this "drop in the bucket" that keeps us—and all other land animals—alive.

It is hard for us to grasp just how small a share of the world's water is fresh. The supply seems unlimited. Yet, if all the water in all the rivers, lakes, ponds, swamps, and puddles were distributed evenly over the surface of the earth, it would reach a depth of little more than a foot. By contrast, the sea water contained in the oceans of the world measures more than a mile and a half.

There is one great difference between the water in most rivers and lakes and that in the oceans of the world—salt. Most fresh water contains only a slight amount of salt, which is mainly sodium chloride.

"Water is the driver of nature," Leonardo da Vinci once wrote. Without the evaporation of water from the sea, its fall as rain or snow, and its return to the sea via the world's network of rivers, there would be no weather. Without the water cycle, much of the world would become too hot, too dry, or too cold to support life.

Although the relative amount of water in the rivers of the world at any one time is minute, immense quantities pass through them annually. The Amazon, the world's largest river, discharges some 3,000 cubic miles of water a year—about a fifth of all the water that runs off the land. The flow is so great that it creates a freshwater "river" in the sea that stretches beyond the sight of land.

The water in lakes moves slowly or not at all. Filling in depressions in the land, they contain nearly all of the fresh water easily obtained by man. Most water in the United States is used to irrigate crops, but industry uses also consume large quantities—the manufacture of a ton of steel, paper, or woolen cloth requires from 250 to 600 tons of fresh water.

It is easy to appreciate the importance of a large lake as a freshwater reservoir, but another significant role is invisible. Lakes are some of the world's greatest evaporators. Only about a third of the water that falls on land flows back directly to the sea. Much of the remainder is evaporated from lakes back into the air, then carried by the wind to new sites where it falls as rain or snow. Marshes, swamps, and other wetlands perform yet another role in the world's water cycle: they are places where water readily soaks into the earth. This replenishes the store of underground water that supplies wells, springs, and contributes to many of our purest streams.

The many faces of water—rivers, marshes, swamps, bogs, lakes, and ponds—are all so different, they hardly seem to lead one into another. For example, marshes are usually well-lighted because trees do not grow within them. But bogs and swamps, which support trees, have a dark aspect—to some people, they are mysterious; to others, they seem forbidding, almost dismal.

For sheer picture-postcard beauty, few bodies of water can rival the sparkle of a mountain lake, or the quiet, silvery blue of such a lake as Geneva in Switzerland. Lakes are famous for their reflections—they are often large enough to mirror a whole mountain, but not so large that they are roiled by waves. This makes them probably the most changeable or "moody" of all inland bodies of water. If the sky is clear, their waters are brilliant. If thunderstorms gather overhead, the lakes take on the dark anger of the sky, or they may blaze with fire from the reflection of a spectacular sunset. Like all freshwater worlds, lakes expand our perception of nature, and put us in tune with the world around us.

PHOTO TIPS
Water in Action

Rushing water is a challenge: how can you catch its elusive, fluid quality on film? First, go where the action is, to a cascading falls or white-water rapids.

• When you have found water that is "alive," your choice of effects may be determined by what your camera can do; if it has adjustable shutter speeds, you can get a crisp, stop-action quality to the flowing water. Use a fast shutter speed, such as 1/250th of a second or faster, which will "freeze" the water, as in the photo at right. For an ethereal, veil-like effect, as in the waterfall on the facing page, use a shutter speed of 1/60th or slower—and a tripod or other support to prevent camera movement.

• Still waters, which are easier to photograph, can be enhanced by picking up sparkling highlights (as in the marsh photo, upper right). A lens shade should be used to prevent extraneous light from striking the lens and causing flares.

Marshes such as the Coto Doñana in Spain (above) shelter a wealth of wildlife—including animals as large as deer. Although marshes were once believed to give off noxious gases, we now know they produce tremendous quantities of oxygen.

The rushing waters of Eagle Creek (above) feed Lake Tahoe, high in the Sierra Nevadas. Tahoe is one of the few crystalline lakes in the world—which means that its waters are cold, clear, and relatively devoid of plant and animal life.

Visiting the Devil's Punchbowl in Oregon (left), it is hard to remember that this idyllic stream is part of a larger system. It is a tributary of the Columbia River. Collectively, many such streams add up to wide rivers that tumble into the ocean.

The Why's and Where's of Lakes

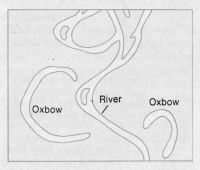

The looping pattern of a lowland river may create oxbows (crescent-shaped lakes) when the river changes course.

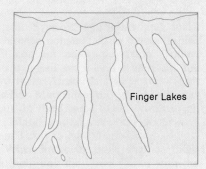

Long, slender lakes that run parallel to each other were once glacial valleys. These are the Finger Lakes of New York.

Lakes of irregular shape, such as these in Canada, were formed by the gouging action of glaciers that pitted the land.

A lake's shape often tells a great deal about its origins. If you see a narrow, comma-shaped lake in low country, near the bend in a river, chances are that the lake is an oxbow. This kind of lake is formed when a meandering river changes its course, and part of the river—a loop—is left behind. The oxbow becomes even more isolated from the river as evaporation lowers its level. But it may continue to exist for a long time.

Some lakes are souvenirs of immense glaciers from the Ice Ages. Where a glacier covered level land, it frequently scoured out shallow lake beds—in parts of the North American "canoe country" that extends from Minnesota through much of Canada, there are tens of thousands of such small glacial lakes.

Glaciers that were confined to valleys leave a different imprint. As they moved, they carried immense loads of rubble in the ice. When the ice melted, the rubble was left as a dam, and a lake formed behind it. The distinctive Finger Lakes of New York State are typical of such dammed valleys.

Some lakes develop rapidly. The round, high-walled lakes of many mountainous regions lie in a basin created when a volcano blew its top, or when the top of the volcano collapsed. Some of these lakes, such as Oregon's famous Crater Lake, are a result of both types of earth-shaking events.

The oldest and deepest lakes in the world were formed when huge blocks in the earth's crust sank. Lake Baikal in Asia and Lake Tanganyika in Africa were formed in this way some 25 million years ago, making them hundreds of times older than the majority of lakes. There are several lakes with a larger surface area than Baikal, but none holds more water. Baikal is more than a mile deep—by far the deepest lake in the world. Lake Tanganyika is the second deepest—4,700 feet.

Surprisingly, some lakes are no deeper than a mud puddle and no older than a few hours. These are the playa lakes, which form in flat areas in dry regions after a rare rainstorm. In Nevada's Black Rock Desert, a playa lake of some 400 to 500 square miles—but only a few inches deep—develops nearly every winter, then disappears.

Man-made lakes rival the largest natural ones, but perhaps the world's most devoted lake-builder is the beaver of North America and Eurasia. Some beaver dams may be 12 feet high and 1,800 feet long, containing hundreds of tons of logs, mud, and rocks. After population declines caused by trapping, these animals are being re-introduced into many areas as a conservation measure; they help control runoff and stem erosion. As one conservationist said, "Beavers will build you a $5,000 dam for nothing."

Crater Lake, in Oregon, was formed when a volcano exploded and collapsed. This lake, which has no inlet or outlet, is the deepest in the United States. Wizard Island is near its western edge.

Preparing for winter, a beaver carries an aspen branch back to the lodge—a prized addition to its underwater food cache.

A beaver dam requires constant repair. Dams are strengthened with mud and rocks; soil and leaves trapped by the dam reinforce the structure.

Engineering Feats of a Beaver Colony

A beaver colony has up to a dozen individuals, including the parents and offspring from two litters. (Each litter usually consists of four kits.) When the young are about 2 years old, they leave the colony and seek a mate. Beavers are renowned for their ability to build and maintain a dam; they also construct a well-engineered lodge, which has several underwater entrances. In addition, beavers build canals, which allow these aquatic animals to haul food (branches) from distant places. When the food supply is exhausted, the beavers will move elsewhere and establish a new colony.

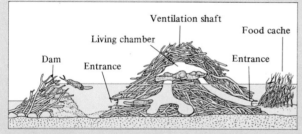
Dam, lodge, and food cache are close to one another. In fall, beavers may enlarge their living chamber—or even add a room.

This abandoned beaver dam in Alaska still shows its basic design—a graceful curve. The dam is widest at the bottom, where water pressure is greatest.

Insulated by snow and frozen mud, a beaver lodge keeps its inhabitants warm in winter. (Sometimes you can even detect steam rising through the ventilation shaft.) Beneath the ice at the surface of the pond, the beavers swim to and from their food cache. Air pockets under the ice provide oxygen. The beaver's warm, water-repellent coat can be seen at right.

Lakes Transformed by Time

As soon as a lake is created, natural forces begin to fill it in. Though the process may take only a few years, or as long as several centuries, every lake—no matter how deep or wide—is destined to become dry land.

A lake is born when water fills a depression in the land. Usually, the first community to thrive in the young lake is minute, drifting water plants and animals, called plankton. They do well because what they need is already present —sunlight, minerals, and other nutrients dissolved in the water. The plant plankton convert these ingredients into food, and are themselves "grazed" upon by animal plankton.

During its youth, the lake's waters are often a brilliant, transparent blue. This indicates that the water does not yet contain much life. However, the plankton usually increase their numbers and soon support many larger animals, including mussels, insects, fish, and birds. These attract other animals.

As generations of animals succeed one another, some plant and animal remains are recycled by scavengers, but inevitably, some debris accumulates on the bottom. Thus the bottom is built up, perhaps a foot or two a century; gradually, the lake becomes shallower.

The thick debris on the lake floor provides food and shelter for an increasing number of bottom-dwellers, including worms, snails, and turtles.

Many of the later settlers replace the original pioneers. Certain sunfish, for example, may be among the lake's first residents, but they require a clean lake floor for their eggs. As plants and debris accumulate, the sunfish give way to fish that are better adapted to the changing conditions. Generally, the older a lake is, the more diverse its plant and animal life.

Submerged water plants begin to take root in parts of the lake where the bottom is built up to within about 20 feet of the surface. They slow the currents and accelerate the accumulation of silt and detritus. Plants also encroach from the shore. Cattails, bulrushes, and burreeds thrive near the

The Inevitable Filling-In of Lakes and Ponds

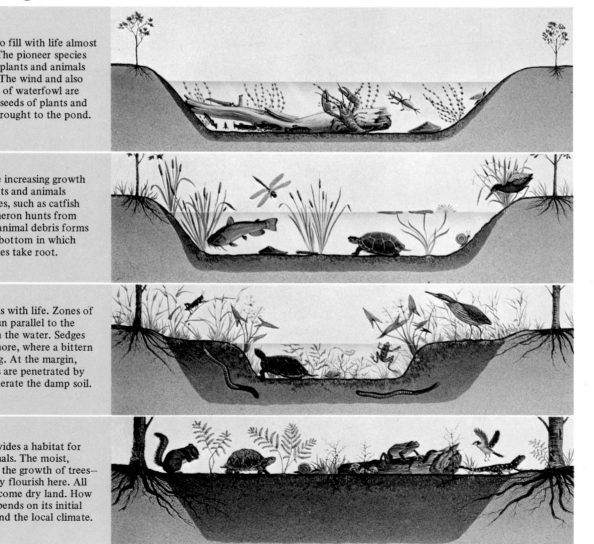

A new pond begins to fill with life almost as soon as it forms. The pioneer species include microscopic plants and animals known as plankton. The wind and also the feathers and feet of waterfowl are the means by which seeds of plants and eggs of animals are brought to the pond.

In a young pond, the increasing growth of small aquatic plants and animals supports larger species, such as catfish and turtles; a green heron hunts from the bank. Plant and animal debris forms a fertile layer at the bottom in which cattails and water lilies take root.

A mature pond teems with life. Zones of aquatic vegetation run parallel to the edge, encroaching on the water. Sedges invade the marshy shore, where a bittern eyes a swimming frog. At the margin, the thickening layers are penetrated by earthworms, which aerate the damp soil.

A filled-in pond provides a habitat for land plants and animals. The moist, fertile soil promotes the growth of trees— one day, a forest may flourish here. All ponds eventually become dry land. How long a pond lasts depends on its initial size, water supply, and the local climate.

water's edge. Farther from the land, smartweed, arrowhead, and water lilies reach the surface from depths up to about 5 feet. The roots trap sediment and decaying plant matter, gradually building new soil and making the lake smaller. Marshy shores and patches of floating algae are signs that the lake has reached old age.

The life-span of a lake depends upon its size and surroundings. Of course, the larger of two similar lakes will last the longest. Lakes in the tropics generally age more quickly because plants can grow year round.

Other local conditions may cancel the effect of climate. If the soil surrounding the lake is rich in plant nutrients, chances are they will be carried into the lake by streams. This speeds up the lake's plant growth and its aging. Some lakes seem to age more slowly because their surroundings are rich in salts that inhibit plant growth. As a rule, salt lakes are usually in dry climates, and will evaporate more quickly than their freshwater counterparts.

Cities and industries have had an impact on the life cycles of lakes. Materials dumped into lakes often accelerate the growth of plankton. The results are paradoxical—so much prosperity among species at the surface can (and often does) take up too much oxygen, suffocating species, such as game fish.

A spreading border of sedges and spatterdock will eventually transform this placid beaver pond into a marshy meadow. In places where the growing season is short (as here in Grand Teton National Park, Wyoming), the change occurs more slowly than in warmer climates.

When alkaline lakes dry up, they become deserts. Lake Elmenteita in Kenya has a high salt content, which promotes the growth of algae.

Vast flocks of greater flamingos gather in the shallow waters and feed on this rich nutrient "soup." Note barren land in the foreground.

177

Life on a Lily Pad

The **quiet beauty of a water lily** is appealing to the human eye. But to myriads of insects, the plant is a refuge and a source of food.

If you sit quietly at the edge of a pond in summer, you may occasionally hear a distinct popping sound. The noise comes from the water, but what's making it? No frogs, birds, muskrats, or other animals are to be seen—only water lilies on the pond surface. If you watch the water lilies closely, at the next pop you may see circles of waves spreading from one of the lily pads. Now perhaps the mystery can be solved. Get close to the lilies and look beneath the surface of the water. Chances are you will see a small, shallow-water fish, such as a sunfish or crappie, lurking under the lily pads. Suddenly, it may dart forward and take an audible nip at the leaf.

The fish may be eating the leaf, but more likely it is eating something attached to the leaf. Such floating green rafts provide a veritable feast for fish. Dozens of different kinds of creatures—including water mites, aphids, snails, caterpillars, worms, and even small freshwater clams—live on the undersides and stems of lily pads. These islands are also nurseries for various animals that lay their eggs there, such as beetles, caddisflies, and snails.

A lily pad offers several advantages to its residents. It provides them with a place of attachment so they do not drift at the mercy of the currents or sink to the bottom. The pads keep them at the surface of the pond, where there is plenty of sunlight and where the water is oxygenated by wave action. The air spaces in the stems of the plants enable animals to breathe, though a resident may be located several feet below the surface.

The long-horned leaf beetle is an example of a lily-pad dweller perfectly adapted to this small, special world. This rather large, metallic beetle, equipped with long antennae, feels its way as it marches across a pad. It spends some time in the water, but the underside of its body is covered with silky hairs that trap air and prevent the beetle from getting wet. It may be observed "shooting" a landing onto a pad.

You may also notice that many lily pads have holes in them, almost as if they were riddled with buckshot, particularly in late summer and early fall. The reason is that when the female long-horned leaf beetle is ready to lay eggs, she bites a small hole in the leaf and partially backs into the water, laying the eggs on the underside of the pad. If you carefully turn over one of the hole-riddled pads, you may see the white eggs, attached with a gelatinous glue. You are also likely to see many other small creatures scurrying and squirming to get back into the water.

In about 10 days, the beetle eggs hatch and the larvae drop through the water, beginning their search for water-lily stems. The larvae have special spines they use to rasp through the stem and get at the air channels inside, which they use as oxygen sources while eating plant material. (On the stem, the beetle larvae may have many neighbors—other aquatic beetles, caterpillars, and mosquito wigglers—which are also using the air supply.)

As you look at the bottom of a lily pad, notice the bubble-like air cells that help keep it afloat. The bottom surface clings to the water; the top is waxy and water-repellent. These textures on the top and bottom of the leaves aid in holding them upright, even when the water level changes. The pads of some tropical water lilies may grow to a diameter of 6 feet. On their undersides, these pads have large air cells that resemble an ice-cube tray; their edges are upturned—hence the common name, water platter.

The **purple gallinule,** a native of warm coastal waters in North America, has long toes that enable it to patter across mats of lily pads. It forages for snails and other small prey. Here, an adult (right) finds a bountiful supply of food for a young gallinule (in brown plumage).

Assembling and Caring for a Pond Aquarium

Here's how to establish your own indoor mini-pond, complete with native plants, insects, and even microscopic animals.
• A standard 5- or 10-gallon tank is ideal. To allow for air circulation, you will need a fine-mesh cover, or a piece of glass, raised at the corners with bits of cork.

• If possible, put the tank in a place with a constant temperature (60° to 70°F.). Avoid direct exposure to the sun.
• You can use pond water, but remember that a pint weighs a pound. An easier supply is tap water. Let it sit a few days to allow the chlorine to escape.

• Purchase sand in an aquarium shop. Rinse it thoroughly to remove dust. Spread the sand in a layer, graded from 1 to 2 inches. (Debris will collect at the lowest point. To remove wastes, use a dip tube.)
• To catch small creatures, you will need several pieces of equipment (see below).

Equipment for Collecting

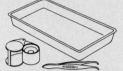

A white enamel pan, a hand lens, and forceps enable you to examine your catch.

Use small jars to carry your catch. Punch air holes in the lids.

A kitchen sieve can serve as a dip net. Attach a long handle if necessary.

One way to trap insects is to use a piece of screen attached to two sticks.

To dredge for tiny plants, make a net of fine-mesh cloth, wired to a hoop.

Supplying Your Aquarium

Your first trip to a local pond should be for plants. These can be supplemented by any pet store that carries aquarium supplies. Plants are important because they provide oxygen for a well-balanced tank.
• When adding water, pour it slowly to avoid dislodging the plants.
• Spring and summer are the best seasons for collecting small plants and animals. Fish usually do better if caught in autumn. Keep in mind that some fish eat others.
• Animals adapted to fast-moving water will not survive long in a pond aquarium.

Microscopic Life

A hydra looks like a plant and moves about by somersaulting—foot over tentacles.

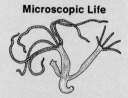

The cyclops is a tiny crustacean that often clings to plants. This female has egg sacs.

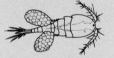

Daphnia, a transparent water flea, feeds on algae and pond debris.

Dragonfly nymphs do not resemble the adults (they live in water and do not fly). Nymphs must be fed insects or bits of meat.

Wild celery is a favorite food for aquatic life. Place such large plants against one wall of the aquarium; anchor them with stones.

Whirligig beetles skim the surface, making tiny ripples; their divided eyes let them see above and below the water at the same time.

Elodea (waterweed) does well in aquariums. Like other plants, it absorbs carbon dioxide and gives off much-needed oxygen.

Water striders "dimple" the surface of the water with their long spider-like legs. They feed on insects such as back swimmers.

Duckweed floating on the water can be decorative; but if it covers the surface, remove some, so that light reaches other plants.

Snails glide along on the inside of the glass, cleaning it as they go. You can watch their movement as they feed.

Clusters of snail eggs are sometimes seen on the wall of an aquarium.

A tadpole is a plant-eater. But when it develops into a frog, remove it from your aquarium—otherwise it will eat the smaller animals.

Water boatmen swim inside an air bubble, but must hold on to objects such as plants to remain submerged. They feed on waste matter.

Water milfoil, a fern-like plant, thrives in aquariums. Such plants provide food and a place for insects to lay eggs.

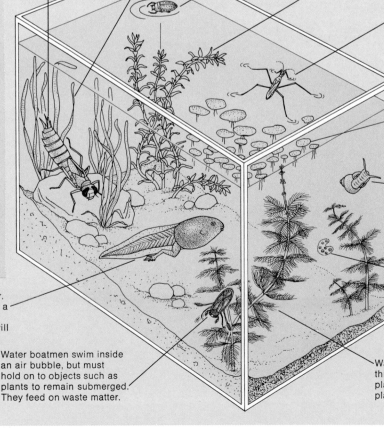

The Dynamic World of a Pond

There are millions of ponds throughout the world, and each one is unique. They share the common events of birth, growth, maturity, decline, and, ultimately, filling in. Nevertheless, their individual histories are so varied, and their numbers are so great, that pond study is one of the areas of nature begging hardest for amateur participation.

Pick a pond, any pond, preferably one near where you live that you can visit often. When and how was it formed? Sometimes the date and circumstances are known precisely. Local records may reveal the construction date of a dam that trapped water and created one or more ponds. In farm country, too, many ponds are created under conservation programs.

You can usually figure out a pond's general age. There is a variety of evidence—a newly formed pond will have certain pioneer species of plants and animals. Wind-borne seeds arrive at once and germinate around the edge of the pond. There's a fringe of plants, rather than a thicket. Flying insects such as water beetles take advantage of the opportunity and lay eggs. Water birds are quick to investigate a new pond. On their feet and feathers, they carry a cargo from ponds elsewhere—the eggs, spores, and seeds of numerous plants and animals. Colonizing a pond is not a miracle. It is only a matter of time before representative pond species arrive.

Then there is a period of adjustment. All the plants and animals settle down, influenced by one another and by the special conditions of the particular pond—its depth, exposure to sunlight (or shade from nearby trees), and whether its waters are replenished by springs, streams, or rain. General climate and the kind of basin—whether rocky or sandy—are also factors.

Gradually a pond matures. A pond's prime of life can be defined as that time when the greatest variety of species coexist. To the practiced eye, a pond is aswarm with life and activity. Distinct zones of vegetation can be seen. The cover provided by thick vegetation invites bigger animals—muskrats, water snakes, and turtles. Cattails and water lilies thrive, and vegetation begins to show in the middle of the pond.

Ponds start to die when the accumulation of sediment and debris fills the

bottom, and when plants encroach on the margins. As the pond becomes smaller, fewer aquatic species of animals can live there. Death or emigration of various species means less food for their predators. As its resources are depleted, the pond world narrows.

Next comes stagnation, with marshy conditions. New assemblages of animals and plants take over. The pleasure for the amateur naturalist is in knowing one pond well, watching the whole panorama take place, or in discovering that your pond is thousands of years old—a glacial holdover. It is probable that you know a pond, and it is also probable that it hasn't really been studied yet. This is to follow in the footsteps of the old-time naturalists, who knew their own world intimately.

Pond-Watching Throughout the Year

Whether you enjoy the diversity of pond life, or have a special interest in birds, plants, insects, amphibians, fish, or reptiles, the seasons will have a great influence on what you can see.

• The edges of ponds are richest in both plant and animal species; they can be most conveniently explored from shore. Wear rubber boots or old sneakers.

• Pond activity is greatest in spring. Large frogs and spring peepers are so noisy at this season—with their hooting and trilling—that you can even find an otherwise concealed pond by following their sounds. These amphibians are now mating and laying their eggs. Adult dragonflies and damselflies emerge from wingless aquatic larvae called nymphs. Ducks, coots, rails, and gallinules nest along the shores; herons and egrets roost in trees near the pond.

• In summer, turtles and water snakes hatch. Copepods and daphnia swarm in warm surface water, and water striders and water beetles are numerous. (You may find a male water beetle carrying the female's eggs on his back.) Herons and egrets are busily fishing to supply their young. Downy ducklings and coots swim among the lily pads. Turtles can be seen sunning themselves on logs and rocks.

• Fall is a less active season in the pond. Many amphibians and reptiles begin their long winter sleep. The pond may be visited by a migrating osprey in search of a fish, or a muskrat adding mussel shells to a growing pile near its lodge.

• In winter, a snow-covered pond is a good place to look for animal tracks, but be sure to stay off thin ice. At this time, some fish are active but comparatively sluggish under the ice.

The Intricate Relationships Among Pond Animals

Certain groupings, or communities, of animals appear again and again in nature. Ponds are prime examples of such communities. In each pond, the particular species may be different, but the "job openings"—the niches—will be filled by equivalent animals, which play the same role in the community. In the woodland pond shown at left, the species are North American. Given a similar climate and water, a pond of the same size and age on any other continent will support a community of animals that are remarkably similar.

Key to Pond Animals

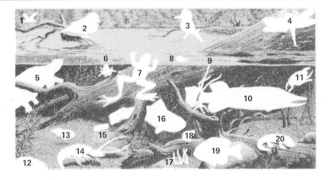

1. A great egret flies off to feast on a pond fish.

2. A male wood duck is an elaborately marked pond resident. The female is drab.

3. A belted kingfisher eyes the pond for a passing fish, which it will quickly catch with its large, strong bill.

4. Dragonflies always rest with wings outspread. Females lay their eggs on the leaves and stems of plants.

5. Snapping turtles are familiar creatures of most ponds; but be careful—they have a nasty bite.

6. Back swimmers are boat-shaped insects with long hind legs, which they use like oars.

7. The leopard frog—named for its spots—eats great quantities of aquatic insects.

8. The whirligig beetle is easy to identify because its name describes its motion.

9. Water scorpions often look like twigs as they hang upside down below the surface.

10. The chain pickerel is named for its markings. It is a swift, predatory fish.

11. A predaceous diving beetle traps air under its wings; this enables it to remain submerged.

12. Freshwater clams often live buried in the mud or sand.

13. Tadpoles grow from eggs to adult frogs at varying rates, depending on the species.

14. The crayfish is active mostly at night; it feeds on plants, fish, and aquatic insects.

15. Caddisfly larvae live in curious egg cases fashioned from twigs, leaves, or pebbles.

16. The black bullhead is a bottom-dweller. Like other catfish, it searches for food with its sensitive whiskers.

17. Tubifex (tube-building worms) look like waving fringes because of the motion of their bodies.

18. The pond snail glides about on a muscular foot.

19. Pumpkinseeds are brightly colored sunfish. The male builds a nest and guards the young. Pumpkinseeds are very popular as aquarium fish.

20. The red salamander is found underwater when it is in its larval stage.

The Still Waters of Marshes and Swamps

The difference between a marsh and a swamp eludes many people. Both may seem extremely humid and their waters stagnant. If a current is to be seen in either place, it is likely to be slow-moving. But the two habitats are as different as a prairie and a forest. In fact, a freshwater marsh resembles a wet prairie, while a swamp can be compared to a wet woodland; a marsh is dominated by grass, a swamp by trees.

Besides abundant grasses, typical marsh vegetation includes cattails and sedges. Cattails are unmistakable. But to distinguish between grasses and sedges, you may have to roll their stems between your fingers—grass stems are round, sedges triangular. One common marsh sedge, papyrus, has been used for centuries, and gave paper its name. The Egyptians used papyrus as early as 3,500 B.C.

Most marsh plants have extremely dense root systems, which trap silt and debris. (In fact, the word morass, which now usually means trap, originally referred to a marsh.) In some places, the interlacing roots form firm tussocks that rise above the water level and can be used as stepping stones. But take care: the roots also form false bottoms that only *look* like dry land.

If water currents are present and strong enough to keep a marsh swept clean, it may remain a marsh for centuries. Some marshes bordering the Nile are believed to have existed since the time of the pharaohs. But if the accumulation of debris continues, the marsh becomes progressively shallower, and shrubs and trees (cypresses, mangroves, red maples, and others) take root. Sometimes the marsh becomes a swamp. The surface of a swamp is much more uneven than that of a marsh—patches of relatively dry and solid land may be surrounded by small areas of open water.

Often linked by time, marshes and swamps are stages in the processes that slowly convert a body of water into dry land. You can see such a changing landscape at the edges of many lakes, ponds, or slow-moving rivers. The open water gives way to a marsh, which may become a wooded swamp bordered by forest. Often marshes and swamps are

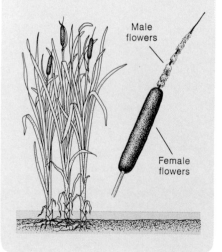

Male flowers

Female flowers

Notice the marked zonation of vegetation in this marsh at Point Reyes, California. In the foreground are brown-tipped sedges. Two mats of floating water pennywort are separated by a growth of rushes. Waving in the background, a lush forest of cattails indicates shallower water.

182

intermingled. Much of the Florida Everglades, for example, consists of extensive marshes surrounding swampy wooded "islands" called hammocks.

Although marshes and swamps seem uninviting to human visitors, they are havens for wildlife—especially snails, which feed on the plentiful supply of decaying plant material. Many species of reptiles—turtles, snakes, and alligators—seem to love these quiet wetlands, which also provide resting places for a wealth of waterfowl. Large land animals, such as deer and bears, venture into swamps on "bridges" of firm ground. Transitional zones between land and water, marshes and swamps are places where you can see aquatic and land animals living side by side.

Tall, feathery papyrus borders the extensive swamps along the upper Nile basin in Uganda. Wild date palms root in more solid soil.

Painted turtles, sunning themselves on a log, are extremely shy of human beings. A slight disturbance will send them diving out of sight.

Tall tupelos rise from the still, brown waters of a Mississippi deep-water swamp. Like the bald cypress, which also grows here, the swamp tupelo has a buttressed trunk, gnarled knees, and an extensive root system that effectively supports it in the soft, water-saturated mud.

183

Bogs: Where Plants Eat Animals

In a northern bog, a diminutive green tree frog perches on a cluster of blueberries and basks in the sun. Frogs are among the few permanent residents of this environment.

Occasionally, hikers walking on wet, spongy soil at the edge of a pond or forest are surprised when the ground quakes and trees as far as 25 feet away begin to sway with every step. Both these events are announcements that you have entered the special world of a bog. Like marshes and swamps, bogs are wetlands that often result from the natural filling-in of ponds and lakes.

Marshes and swamps grow from the bottom up as debris accumulates on the floor of a body of water. A bog grows in the opposite direction as well—from the top down. Several kinds of plants at the water's edge, particularly bog-bean, send out floating "runners" along the surface of the water. The water willow (which is not really a willow) makes a "pontoon bridge" out from shore. When the tips of this plant's arching branches touch the water, they form a spongy, air-filled pad from which new branches grow.

A floating network of plants forms a mat at the edge of the water. This mat is usually filled in and thickened by sphagnum moss, sedges, and grasses.

This floating "garden" may eventually cover the whole body of water. Many of these mats become sturdy enough to support a person or even several people. But anyone exploring a bog should proceed with caution. There is always the chance of breaking through a thin place.

The bright green carpet is sphagnum moss, the dominant plant in most bogs. Of course, bogs, marshes, and swamps often blend into one another so subtly it is hard to tell where one begins and another stops. Bog waters are low in minerals and extremely acidic. They also are low in dissolved oxygen because the mossy mat covers the water and prevents contact with the air. The high acidity and limited oxygen and minerals slow the rate of decay in a bog. Plants, animals, and even people that have fallen into bogs have been preserved like mummies for centuries.

The lack of certain kinds of nutrients in bog soils has caused some bog plants, such as the pitcher plants, sundews, Venus's-flytraps, and butterworts, to evolve a bizarre way of acquiring the missing substances. They trap insects.

Zones of Vegetation That Build a Boggy Shore

Bogs are widely distributed over cold, damp northern regions. Whether they occur in North America, Europe, or Asia, all bogs share certain characteristics. They occupy steep-sided, water-filled basins with poor drainage. They have cushion-like mounds of mosses and shrubby plants. They contain an accumulation of partially decayed plant material called peat. Like lakes and ponds, any open water in a bog is ringed by zones of vegetation.

These zones are not always clearly defined owing to the flourishing growth of sphagnum moss, which fills in the spaces between shrubs and other plants with a sponge-like, velvety carpet. The water-retaining sphagnum creeps into the more solid area surrounding the bog. The only trees that can establish themselves must be able to tolerate having their roots bathed with rainwater and seeping acidic water; black spruce is one example.

Scattered clumps of coniferous trees —larch and spruce—anchor the soil and add their debris of needles and cones to the accumulation of peat.

Yellow water lilies colonize the deep areas at the center of the bog.

A border of sedge floats on a water-saturated bed of peat, formed over the years from decaying roots, stems, and leaves.

Low evergreen shrubs, such as bog rosemary and Labrador tea, take root in soil that builds up on the peat. This peat formed from sphagnum moss.

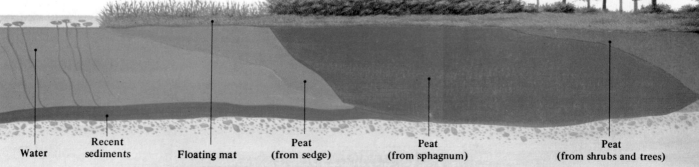

Water   Recent sediments   Floating mat   Peat (from sedge)   Peat (from sphagnum)   Peat (from shrubs and trees)

Many botanists believe that such carnivorous plants are acquiring nitrogen by this means.

Decay in a bog proceeds so slowly that there is usually a great deal of partially decayed plant material, called peat, which settles on the bottom. You may have used dried peat as potting material for house plants or in your garden—and therefore know that peat holds water extremely well. Sphagnum can hold 20 times its weight in water, but it is low in nutrients, and little will grow in it unless fertilizer is added.

When the peat and living moss around the edges of a bog dry out somewhat, certain species of plants become established (such as leatherleaf and Labrador tea). Eventually, trees take root. Thus, if you look at a mature bog from high ground, it has the appearance of a dartboard—a "bull's-eye" of open water, surrounded by concentric rings of moss, moss and sedges, shrubs, and finally trees. Gradually the bog becomes dry land, but because of the special conditions created by moss, bogs are longer-lived than most wetlands.

A climax forest of spruce and fir surrounds the bog. In some warmer areas, a climax forest may be made up of maple and birch trees.

Humus **Weathered rock** **Bedrock**

Sensitive hairs on the inner surface of each leaf-blade of the Venus's-flytrap operate like small triggers. When an insect, such as this fly, touches a hair, the halves close, trapping the victim. Exactly how the plant extracts nutrients from its prey is not yet understood.

Leathery leaves of a pitcher plant are lined with downward-pointing hairs. At the bottom of the leaf is a reservoir of water. If an insect enters the plant, it can't escape—and drowns.

Sticky, translucent beads "decorate" the long wands of the thread-leaved sundew. Here, a blue-winged damselfly and a cabbage butterfly have been fatally ensnared by the plant.

Birds of the Wetlands

Few habitats support more varied bird populations than the swamps, marshes, bogs, ponds, and sloughs of the wetlands. One reason is well known to anyone who has ever watched a birdbath. Water attracts birds. A majority of species—even those that do not live in wetlands—must travel to fresh water daily to drink.

But wetlands offer more than just a convenient water supply. They provide plentiful food, shelter, and protection from many predators. It is no accident that the world's major flyways (the traditional migration routes used by billions of birds every year) generally pass along large rivers and coastal regions, and over areas with shallow bodies of water. During the migration periods, it is not unusual to see patches of water nearly covered with birds.

Pond ducks, such as mallards and teal, usually feed at the surface of the water by snapping at floating food, meanwhile gabbling noisily. This raucous dabbling, which sends the water flying, looks comical to a human spectator, but it is actually very efficient—fine tooth-like projections around the rim of the ducks' bills sieve out tiny water plants and animals. Pond ducks also feed from the bottom in shallow water by tipping beak-down and paddling vigorously, with only their wriggling rumps showing.

A duck's short, widely spaced legs are fine for swimming and "tipping-up," but this arrangement is responsible for its typically awkward walk. The legs of stiff-tailed ducks, such as the North American ruddy ducks and Australian musk ducks, are placed so far back that they can walk only for short distances and rarely leave the water except to fly.

Diving ducks, such as goldeneyes and mergansers, often feed in deeper waters. They can dive as deep as 25 feet after their prey. The bills of the "mergs," as they are nicknamed, are pointed, with a hook-shaped tip and backward-pointing "teeth" that hold captured fish.

Perhaps the oddest method of feeding is that used by the small shorebirds called phalaropes. They stir up food in shallow water by spinning rapidly or swimming in close circles. Swans and ducks achieve the same effect by turning rapidly and paddling with their broad feet. Often food turned up by a stirrer attracts other birds, and a water

"parade" begins—a crazily spinning bird followed by dabblers and tip-ups.

Long-legged wading birds use other methods to capture their prey. Snowy egrets stir up food with their feet. Cranes, storks, and herons often "still-hunt"—they simply wait in the cover of abundant water plants for a small fish or frog to come within range of their lightning-quick, pointed beaks.

You can tell where a wading bird hunts by the length of its legs. Predictably, small, short-legged sandpipers hunt at the water's edge; other species, such as green and great blue herons, hunt in successively deeper water.

If you frighten the birds as you approach a marsh or pond, you will undoubtedly notice striking differences in the way they take flight. Pond ducks, sometimes called puddle-jumpers, can leap into the air from land or water. Many diving ducks and other wetland birds require a long "runway"—up to 650 feet—and a few cannot take off from land at all. Some of these birds, including grebes and loons, dive when startled, rather than trying to fly.

Some wetland birds with young that cannot yet fly or dive will take their offspring to hiding places before fleeing. But grebes have what may be an even better method. Like swans, these small, duck-like birds often carry their young on their backs. Young grebes hold on tight to the parents' feathers with their bills. The adult birds can dive with their young safely aboard.

A black-necked stilt, a bird of wet meadows and shallow waters, prepares to fold its long legs and brood its four camouflaged eggs.

Ready to strike at prey, a young green heron displays its hunting instinct. Later, its striped plumage will give way to rich cinnamon around the crested head and short neck. In some regions, almost every pond and wooded stream will have resident green herons.

Largest of the swan species, a trumpeter convoys her flotilla of downy 2-week-old cygnets through a floating sea of duckweed. Once nearly extinct, trumpeter swans are breeding in increasing numbers on the marsh-bordered lakes of the western United States and Canada.

BIRDING TIPS
How to Tell the Difference Between Geese and Ducks

Ducks and geese, together with swans, belong to an order of birds known as waterfowl. There are about 150 species in this order—most of them ducks. Both ducks and geese usually have short tails and legs; their feet are webbed. Bills tend to be flattened, with edges that help strain food. The young can swim and walk within a few hours after hatching. Gregarious in nature, ducks and geese form large flocks, especially during migration. Here's how to tell the geese from the ducks:

Male and Female Geese Have Identical Plumage

• Large birds with long necks, geese are good walkers.
• Geese, which molt only once a year, look the same at all times of the year.
• Nests are placed in hollows on grassy or marshy ground.
• Geese usually feed on land, grazing on grass and grain; brant, a sea-going species, feed on eelgrass. Though geese are powerful swimmers, they do not dive.
• Geese are strong fliers. They often form precise V's or long, irregular lines. They are quite noisy in flight.

Canada goose

Male Ducks Are More Colorful Than Females of the Species

• Small, plump birds with short necks, ducks have stubby legs and walk clumsily.
• Ducks molt body feathers twice a year. Most kinds have two plumages—breeding and non-breeding. Males in eclipse (non-breeding) plumage look like females.
• Ducks nest in various sites —some even in tree holes.
• All ducks can dive. Some species dive to obtain fish; others eat mollusks or aquatic plants.
• In flight, most ducks form loose flocks.

Female mallard

Male mallard

Where the Fish Are

We humans, as land-dwellers, tend to think of what lies beneath the surface of lakes and rivers as one big, wet, homogeneous world. But to freshwater fish, that watery world is as diverse as our own.

Some species of fish live only in clear, leaping mountain streams; others inhabit only slow, muddy, lowland rivers. Some fish patrol the wind-tossed surface of lakes; others prowl the less-disturbed bottom. Certain species can live in one particular lake or river and nowhere else on earth. And—as any successful fisherman can tell you—many fish move back and forth between "neighborhoods," depending on season and time of day.

Most freshwater fish are border-dwellers. They prefer to live and feed where one type of environment borders another. Thus, many fish may be found at the edge of a weed bed, near a drop-off on the bottom, where a stream enters a lake, or where fast- and slow-moving waters meet in a river.

Why are fish so choosy? Biologists believe it is mainly because the life processes of each species of freshwater fish function best at a particular temperature and salinity. Fish seek out areas where the most favorable conditions prevail. Temperature is also an important reason why fish are found at

different levels as the seasons change. The cool temperature many species prefer exists as far up as the surface in spring and autumn. In summer, the sun warms the surface, and fish go deeper. In winter, if surface temperatures drop below freezing, the fish move down.

The water-quality requirements of some species confine them to specific areas. Trout, darters, and sculpins are characteristic of swift upland streams. Warmer, muddier, and saltier lowland rivers and lakes usually contain carp, catfish, sunfish, bass, and crappies. Killifish and some kinds of flounder prefer estuarine rivers, where salt water mixes with fresh. The only sizable bodies of water without fish are those where temperature and salinity reach their extremes—in hot springs and salt lakes. An exception to this is the small pupfish of the American desert.

Sometimes you can tell where a fish lives just by looking at it. Streamlined, torpedo-shaped fish, such as trout, are usually from fast-moving streams. A flattened fish like a sunfish could not live there; it would be swept away the first time it turned sideways to the current. But in its customary pools, lakes, or sluggish streams, the sunfish can slip freely through the vegetation. A fish with "feelers," or barbels, around its mouth (such as a catfish) is usually

from a muddy river or lake; the barbels help it locate food in murky water.

By far the greatest variety of fresh-water fish live in tropical rivers and lakes. The Amazon River system alone contains about 2,000 species—from miniature catfish to giant arapaimas weighing several hundred pounds. Some of the most notorious residents of the Amazon are the piranhas. These ferocious fish rarely grow longer than 2 feet and usually feed on smaller fish, but they go into a frenzy at the taste of blood. A school of piranhas can consume an animal as large as a cow in a few minutes.

One tropical fish—an African species of lungfish—holds the record for staying alive without food or water longer than any other vertebrate. When rivers dry up, lungfish form cases of mucus and mud around their bodies; these balls dry as hard as bricks. Experimental specimens have lived in this condition for more than 7 years.

Life in Slow-Moving Waters

Most fish of lakes and slow-moving lowland rivers spend their entire lives in the quiet waters of their surroundings. Unlike fish of fast-flowing rivers, they are seldom strong swimmers. They range from lethargic carp to lightning-swift northern pike.

Yellow perch spawn at night in spring, laying jelly-like ropes of eggs as long as 7 feet. The young hatch a week later.

Fish of Brackish Waters

The brackish waters of bays, estuaries, and marshes are transition zones for migratory fish. Here they adjust to the change from salt water to fresh. However, some species live their entire lives within this environment.

Newly hatched sockeye salmon subsist on the yolk sacs attached to their bodies. (Notice the empty "cases," and the eggs ready to hatch.) Pacific coast species are notable because the adults die after spawning; Atlantic coast salmon recover from the journey and spawn again.

Fish of Cold, Swift Streams

The cold, rushing waters of mountain streams are the preferred habitat for some species of fish. These fish are usually muscular, adapted to swimming in—and against—swift currents.

Salmon migrate from the ocean to the freshwater streams of their birth when the time comes to spawn. Young salmon find their own way from the stream to the sea.

Brook trout, a favorite of fishermen, thrive in cold mountain streams. They are often grown in hatcheries.

Smallmouth bass breed in rocky shallows or near sunken logs. They are mainly predatory, feeding on other fish and on amphibians.

The **burbot** is a cod, a freshwater member of its family. This fish is active only at dawn and dusk.

Carp are found mostly in warm, weedy backwaters. They feed on insect larvae, crustaceans, and aquatic vegetation.

The **northern pike** is a large predatory fish that lurks along shores of quiet waters, particularly in oxbow lakes.

American eels range widely along the Atlantic shore. These eels spend most of their lives upstream or in brackish waters, but spawn in the sea.

Atlantic sturgeon, now uncommon, have been sought for centuries for both their flesh and unshed eggs—used for caviar. Like salmon, sturgeon are sea-dwellers that spawn in the freshwater of rivers.

Fishing Through Ice

In northern regions where lakes and ponds freeze in winter, ice fishing is popular. Many fish survive the winter by living at the bottom of these lakes —sunfish, yellow perch, walleyes, crappies, and bluegills, to name a few.

In summer, a lake or pond is warmest at the top, coolest at the bottom. Fish seek the temperature and feeding conditions that suit them best.

In winter, the surface may be iced-over. Temperature stratification disappears, and the location of fish is less predictable. Cold makes fish less active.

For pointers on ice fishing, you can talk to fishermen locally. They are usually friendly and well-informed about the best places. They may also be able to tell you where ice fishing is hazardous. You, yourself, must be on the lookout for thin spots in the ice.

• Equipment for ice fishing can be simple and inexpensive. You'll need a chisel to cut holes in the ice (you should make several holes). To extend the length of your chisel, use a "spud," which is a pole with a chisel attached firmly to one end. You will require a skimmer to scoop out bits of floating ice; a kitchen strainer will serve the purpose. You will need both bait and a pail to carry it. The strainer can double as a dip net for the bait. A sled is recommended for carting your gear, including several fishing lines and a thermos of something hot. The sled will also serve as a place to sit and to attach a windbreak.

• To find a likely fishing location, use a hole left by someone else, even if it is slightly blocked. It is easier to clean out ice than to open a new hole.

• Change bait often. Fish may become suspicious or bored by looking at the same bait. Mealworms, woodgrubs, and minnows are good bait. Where the water is deep, a weighted lure (called a "dipsey") such as a small, shiny spoon is often effective.

189

The Wonder of Waterfalls

Many of the world's waterfalls are so large that it is nearly impossible to see them at one glance. The highest one on earth, for example—Angel Falls in Venezuela—is best seen from the air. Here you can see the Rio Churún leap from Devil's Mountain and plummet 3,212 feet, barely making contact with the sheer face of the mountain. The existence of the waterfall was unknown to the outside world until it was observed by an American aviator-adventurer, James Angel, who first saw it in 1935.

The poet Ralph Waldo Emerson wrote that "frugal nature" gave waterfalls only one sound, and anyone venturing near a great waterfall will learn what that sound is—thunder! The noise seems to wrap itself around you like a heavy blanket. It is no wonder sound is often reflected in the names of waterfalls. Niagara Falls derives its name from an Indian word meaning "thundering waters." The original name for Victoria Falls in Africa was Mosi-oa-tunya—"the smoke that thunders." At Victoria Falls, during the rainy season, hundreds of thousands of tons of water crash to the bottom each minute. When the water hits the floor of the chasm, it is estimated to be moving in excess of 100 miles an hour. Here, after its plunge, the foaming water flows into a large canyon (in this case 45 miles long and hundreds of feet deep), which creates an impressive "echo chamber" for the waterfall.

The spray and fog produced by the rampaging waters are so dense that David Livingstone, the first European to discover Victoria Falls, wrote, "These columns of watery smoke . . . give the impression that the yawning gulf might resemble a bottomless pit."

Yet one of the pleasures of waterfall-viewing is that even a small cascade can be beautiful or inspiring. Some of the most famous and best-loved falls are rather small ones, located in all parts of the world—the glens of the

The wild waters of Virginia Falls in Canada's Northwest Territories are parted by an immense limestone spire. The pillar towers above a 300-foot drop in the South Nahanni River. Notice the layering of the rock, which reveals that this outcrop was once part of the canyon wall.

Scottish Highlands, the many charming sprays of the Appalachian Mountains.

Although human beings are drawn to waterfalls as by a magnet, the appeal is aesthetic, even spiritual. For animals, waterfalls are inhospitable. But there are a few species that manage to live with the tremendous pressures. Some kinds of insect hang onto the rocks, and small birds called dippers choose waterfalls for their home base.

Fish generally avoid waterfalls. But the salmon, which descend streams on both coasts of North America (and from parts of some other continents) when they are young to live in the ocean, return by the same routes when they are adults, ready to reproduce. Often a salmon will travel hundreds of miles upstream, leaping over countless waterfalls and rapids. These powerful fish are capable of jumping 8 to 10 feet in the air. The damming of rivers has interfered with the life cycle of these animals, but nowadays, fish ladders—a series of stepped waterfalls—have been constructed alongside dams, enabling the fish to return home.

This silky, shimmering veil of water is one of many such falls in the Cascade Range of Oregon. The water drops in a slender stream, providing a gentle spray that encourages plant growth.

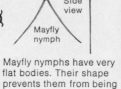

NATURE OBSERVER
Specialized Lives in Streams and Torrents

If hikers are lucky enough to see a dipper beside a rushing stream, they may not believe their eyes when it flies directly into a waterfall. The bird frequently nests behind such a falling curtain of water, rearing its young in this unlikely location. The dipper can search for food in the water, swimming with its stubby wings or "walking" along the bottom of a stream. It searches for caddisfly larvae and other insects, which attach themselves to rocks.

Insects Adapted to Rushing Water

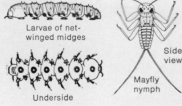

Larvae of net-winged midges

Underside

Side view

Mayfly nymph

Young net-winged midges (flies) have suction pads that grasp rocks firmly.

Mayfly nymphs have very flat bodies. Their shape prevents them from being swept away by currents.

The Cutting Power of Water

One of the best ways to appreciate the incredible power of water is to stand at the edge of a canyon that was cut by water. How can anything as seemingly pliant as water have such an impact on solid rock? Actually, it is not water alone that does the cutting. Water in rivers and streams is often somewhat acid in content (picked up from the ground over which it travels). This acid eats away at rock—particularly limestone. And, as water flows over the land, fine particles of clay, sand, and rock are picked up and carried along. Each part of this burden, no matter how small, is capable of scratching, scraping, and grinding off bits and pieces of rock.

The faster water moves, the more it can carry and the faster it cuts. According to the laws of physics, when a stream doubles its speed, the size of particles it can carry increases 64 times. During a torrential rainstorm in California, a train jumped the track in the Tehachapi Mountains and plunged into a flooded stream. The locomotive and tender were carried a half-mile downstream and buried under a deep layer of dirt and debris.

The heaviest loads of streams are rolled and skipped along the bottom of the stream bed, and this is where most cutting takes place. Fast-moving waters usually cut steep-walled canyons, rather than wide valleys.

The speed of a river is usually determined by its slope. Thus, mountain streams, where the slopes are steep, are usually faster and cut deeper than streams in the flatlands. The Mississippi, for example, cuts its broad valley in the gently rolling Midwest. Near St. Louis, the river drops only about 6 inches for every mile it flows. On the other hand, part of the Platte River, in the mountainous regions of Colorado and Wyoming, drops ten times faster, flows more swiftly, and is cutting a narrow V-shaped valley.

Throughout the world, there are zones where the underlying rock structure creates a row of waterfalls, called a fall line. If a river flows from hard to soft rock, the soft rock will be worn down more quickly. A step may be cut and a waterfall created.

One of the most distinctive fall lines runs near the eastern coast of the United States, where the hard crystalline rocks of the Appalachians meet the softer sedimentary rocks of the coastal plain. The line is marked by important cities including Philadelphia, Baltimore, and Washington, D.C. A similar fall line runs across England through Cambridge and several other cities. The cities were located here because the fall lines were barriers to settlers attempting to move up the rivers. Another reason for city growth was that falling water could generate power for industries.

The hard rock of many fall-line waterfalls lies over softer rock. Eventually, the turbulent water at the base of the waterfalls undercuts the overhanging hard rock, which breaks off. This process is causing Niagara's Horseshoe Falls to retreat upstream at the rate of about 4 feet a year.

Rivers have traditionally attracted people, tending to bring them together rather than separating them, in spite of waterfalls (an easy human solution was the building of bridges). However, very deep canyons cut by rivers have been effective barriers to many kinds of wildlife. For example, the Grand Canyon is a boundary between two distinct biological provinces, each with many different species. Certain snakes and squirrels on the north side differ markedly from close relatives to the south.

When a waterfall flows over extremely hard rock, as does Cloudland Falls in New Hampshire, erosion will occur very slowly and the falls may remain a step-like cascade for centuries.

Deer Creek is a small, spring-fed tributary that flows into the Colorado River, upstream of the Grand Canyon. This part of the gorge drops into a plunge basin, then glides along for a short stretch before dropping again. Notice the rocky debris caused by the cutting action of the water.

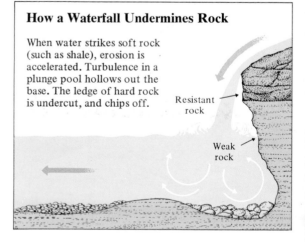

How a Waterfall Undermines Rock

When water strikes soft rock (such as shale), erosion is accelerated. Turbulence in a plunge pool hollows out the base. The ledge of hard rock is undercut, and chips off.

Resistant rock

Weak rock

Pierced by shafts of sunlight, this cathedral-like gorge (right) in Oregon invites exploration of its depths. Powerful forces formed the channel, but now this section of Oneonta Creek is level and relatively placid. Alder and maple, moss and sword fern, cling tenaciously to the steep walls.

Lowland Rivers and Deltas

Meandering rivers and oxbow lakes characterize this floodplain in central Alaska. Notice the deposits of sand and other sediments on some curves. These deposits indicate an uneven flow —slower and shallower on the sandy stretches, faster and deeper on the opposite shores.

Sprawling over a vast area, the Waitaki River in New Zealand seems to lose its identity in the maze of sand bars, spits, and islands that divert its waters. This random appearance of streams and sediments, here close to the sea, is an indication of extremely flat terrain.

In *Life on The Mississippi*, Mark Twain, a one-time river pilot, tells about a group of fellow pilots who organized a system for reporting the daily changes in the river's channel. Today, a century later, rivermen use radio, radar, and depth finders for the same purpose. Although it has been dredged and dammed, the "fickle" Mississippi is still changing.

The Mississippi is wide and sluggish in its lower reaches because it flows through a broad, flat valley. At some points, this river drops only about an inch per mile. The lowlands that border many large rivers (the Nile, Niger, or Yangtze, for example) are often only a few feet higher than the river itself. These valley floors, or floodplains, are a part of the river channel and are subject to frequent inundations.

For much of their length, these slow-moving rivers deposit more material than they pick up. These deposits may develop into sand bars, shoals, and banks, but such shallows can be washed away almost overnight. Sand bars may divert the current to the opposite bank, where erosion is then increased. This process causes the river bed to migrate slowly over the floodplain. If the river is navigable, its channel must not only be monitored, but also dredged from time to time. In any case, the channels are frequently marked with lights and buoys, and river charts are revised regularly.

Most of the sediment and other material dropped by a river falls out along its banks where the current is slowest. These deposits frequently build natural levees, sometimes 10 to 20 feet higher than the floodplain. Many lowland rivers—ranging from the Mississippi to the Hwang Ho in China—have such natural levees. Eventually, these deposits prevent tributary streams from entering the river. The blocked streams may form lakes, or run parallel to the main stream for great distances. Such accompanying rivers are called yazoo streams, after the Yazoo River, which meanders next to the Mississippi for about 100 miles before joining it.

Although serene and scenic most of the time, lowland rivers change drastically after spring thaws and thunderstorms. A swollen river may flood an entire valley from wall to wall with a sheet of water. For example, a section of Cincinnati, on the Ohio River, was once covered by flood waters to a depth of 80 feet. In more recent times, floods in Italy have jeopardized art treasures of incalculable value, notably in the city of Florence.

At the mouth of a river, soil that is not carried away by ocean currents may be dropped, creating a new platform of land. In the fifth century B.C., the Greek historian Herodotus named such formations deltas, after the triangular capital letter of the Greek alphabet. But few deltas are actually triangular. They may resemble open fans or hands with spread fingers, forming branching rivers.

The volume of soil dropped in a lowland delta is demonstrated by the speed with which a delta may grow. For 800 years, the Po Valley delta in Italy advanced seaward at a rate of from 80 to 200 feet a year. The town of Adria, a seaport during Roman times, now lies approximately 14 miles inland.

Deltas are not always solid accumulations of sediment. Instead, lakes may develop within their arms. An example is the famous Zuider Zee, near the mouth of the Rhine. This delta lake has been transformed by the Dutch; cut off from the sea, several regions have been enclosed by dikes, and the excess water has been pumped out. Because of the deposits of rich soil, such reclaimed areas become fertile farmland. The most extensive reclamation in the world is in The Netherlands.

The Netherlands: A Nation That Triumphed Over Powerful Seas

Several rivers empty into the North Sea in The Netherlands—including the Rhine, the Meuse, and the Scheldt. The resulting deltas have become more extensive with the years, as the silt carried by the rivers accumulated in the shallows of the North Sea. Delta regions are generally ideal for farming because they are fed by freshwater from inland, and because the land there is frequently enriched by deposits of topsoil. No other nation in the world has made more extensive use of deltas. The massive engineering feat that closed off the Zuider Zee resulted in a great gain of farmland, and later, in space for both residential and industrial development. There are many smaller projects throughout the country. But the current one, the Delta Project in the southwestern part, is intended more for flood control than for land reclamation. Flooding is a danger both from the rivers and the sea. Many islands and peninsulas have also been linked by bridges and roads.

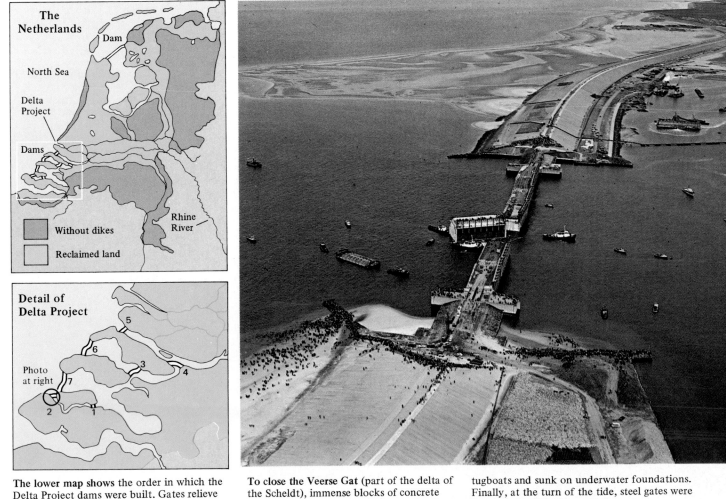

The lower map shows the order in which the Delta Project dams were built. Gates relieve the pressures of river currents and ocean tides.

To close the Veerse Gat (part of the delta of the Scheldt), immense blocks of concrete —called caissons—were pulled into place by tugboats and sunk on underwater foundations. Finally, at the turn of the tide, steel gates were lowered, thus blocking out the sea.

199

CHAPTER SEVEN

Deserts and Arid Lands

*Like oceans, deserts become more perilous
as you cross them. Those not born to
the rigors of deserts are safest at the edges.*

The deserts, like the continental shelves, are rich sources of oil. They also have extensive deposits of phosphates and other minerals. Consequently, deserts throughout the world attract prospectors. These modern explorers venture into the "forbidding" desert environment by truck or aircraft—usually loaded with supplies in case they get lost, and, in any event, capable of radio contact with the "outside" world. Occasionally they are confronted by the sight of native children, nonchalantly leading a goat or camel across the trackless waste with their meager (but adequate) supplies tied in a small bundle. Of all human beings, only a few hardy peoples have been able to survive in the desert—nomadic Bedouins, Mongol herdsmen, American Indians, and Australian Aborigines are among the few peoples whose social customs, and even physical attributes, have enabled them to live well there. These desert peoples—as much as the plant and animal inhabitants— throw light on just what the word *adaptation* really means. They are all truly at home on arid lands. They do not find deserts "hostile" or "searing," for such descriptions are an outsider's way of looking at this world. In fact, a cactus or a pack rat would find life nearly impossible in a well-watered, shaded woodland or meadow.

The reason a desert is *not* deserted is that many forms of life have adapted to the extreme conditions. You might even find the desert bursting with life—a procession of animals at a waterhole, or a profusion of wildflowers budding after a rare shower.

*In the aftermath of heavy rains, brilliant poppies and lupines
spring from the ground in astonishing abundance. In a
matter of days, they prosper, set seed, then vanish. When
drought returns to this Arizona desert, only a few sturdy plants
will remain, with the tall cactus standing like a sentinel.*

The Many Faces of Deserts

Shimmering mountains of sand rolling on endlessly for as far as the eye can see—this is the picture most people have of the world's deserts. Yet the Sahara, which contains more sand than any other desert, is sandy over only about 10 percent of its total surface. Like most deserts, the Sahara has hard, flat "desert pavement" cut by twisting chasms, stark mountains, and boulder-strewn badlands, with their pinnacles of weirdly sculptured rock.

The Sahara is the largest desert in the world, covering an area almost the size of the United States. It is mostly a barren plain covered with rocks and gravel, and crossed by dry stream beds. Such deserts are usually called hamada types, after the Arabic word for rocky desert. Another African desert, the Kalahari, and the immense Australian deserts are almost entirely hamada. By contrast, deserts in North and South America contain small hamada areas.

Perhaps the oddest features of the Sahara, and of many other hamada deserts, are sections of flat pavement, called billiard-table deserts. Some of these are actually bedrock that has been swept bare by driving winds. More often, the pavement is a crust of minerals; these accumulated on the soil surface whenever rainwater evaporated, the way a hard scale may form on the inside of a tea kettle. Some of these pavements are up to 40 feet thick, and those of the Australian deserts are believed to be several million years old.

Rocky deserts are raw material for sandy deserts. Particles are chipped from the rocks by strong winds and infrequent rains, and these may collect in dunes. This is why rocky and sandy deserts are often found next to another. Frequently, windstorms carry the sand far beyond the borders of the desert where it originated. Winds from the Sahara, for example, may carry dust and sand across the Mediterranean Sea.

Most of the deserts in the Americas differ markedly from those in the eastern hemisphere. The Great American Desert in Utah and Nevada, for example, is a series of gaunt mountains and hills separated by wide, level basins called bolsons. At the edge of a bolson, where deep mountain canyons stop abruptly, immense fans of rocky material often form. These distinctive fans are debris brought by occasional rains.

However, many desert formations have sharp edges. You may have noticed this in photographs of deserts, or seen it yourself when you traveled. In such places, the desert features have not been smoothed down by the steady workings of running water. Also, the angularity of a desert is exposed to view by the absence of vegetation.

You may have noticed desert rocks resemble one another in their reddish or grayish "paint." This hue is called desert patina, or varnish. The paint-like effect is a coating of metal oxides that have accumulated on desert surfaces. The varnish is believed to be the result of light desert dew that dissolves substances from the soil surface, and then evaporates. It is thought that at least 2,000 years are required for the thin coating to accumulate because it is found only on desert ruins known to be this old or older. Thus, on some deserts, you are seeing the color of time.

Clusters of cacti typify many North American deserts. This dense concentration (above) is cholla, perhaps the prickliest of all cacti.

These bleak, ancient slabs of rock (right) are in Argentina's Monte. Parts of this desert contain rocks that are believed to be more than 150 million years old—older than the Andes.

The golden dunes of the Sahara are among the most spectacular in the world. Here, the wind creates sculptures that are both softly contoured and razor-sharp. The enormous dunes in the distance provide a dramatic contrast with the delicately etched ripples in the foreground.

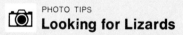
Sun-loving lizards, such as skinks (right), iguanas, and horned lizards, are among the few desert creatures that you are likely to discover out and about during the day. Though often well camouflaged, they are worth searching for; many of the species are sluggish and remain in one place long enough for you to take their portraits. More skittish lizards can be approached if you move toward them slowly and quietly. Have your camera ready in advance; check your light meter and use a filter to minimize glare.

The threat display of the Australian blue-tongued skink is an open mouth and an extended tongue. Skinks are short-legged (or legless) lizards with smooth scales.

From Desert Lake to Salt Flat

In 1933, in one of the most desolate mountainous reaches of the Sahara, a French officer, Lieutenant Brenans, clambered into the cool shade of a cavernous gorge. As his eyes became adjusted to the dim light, the young officer was astonished by paintings on the walls. In one of the driest places on earth, the rocks were covered with pictures of creatures from rainy tropical regions—rhinos, hippos, and elephants, some of them even spouting water.

For years, scientists believed that the world's large deserts had always been dry. Yet prehistoric paintings, such as those discovered by Brenans, argued against this idea. Gradually—sometimes in the most unexpected ways—new evidence has given us a different view. Geologists know that sand is made mainly by water, not by wind. For example, the expansion and contraction of water during temperature changes crack rock; it is crumbled further as water carries off small pieces. Sand is the end product of centuries of abrasion. So the most obvious clue to the onetime presence of water on or near deserts is the sand itself.

Grooves in exposed bedrock in the Sahara have been identified as glacial in origin. This is clear evidence that water must have been present in abundance. A further curious fact is that the distinctive red soils of the Australian deserts were probably the products of humid tropical conditions in the past.

When deserts were opened up for commercial exploitation, they provided even more conclusive evidence of the fact that deserts have changed. Vast oil and natural gas supplies lie beneath many deserts—and these come only from ancient sea deposits and, to a lesser extent, swamp vegetation.

The story of these epochal transitions has meaning today because we are able to see the continuing process in various parts of the world. The case history of the Great Salt Lake has been well documented. Some million years ago, the region was covered with a freshwater lake of nearly 20,000 square miles—about 20 times the size of the present Great Salt Lake. Many rivers flowed into it, and the lake itself drained into the ocean through the Snake and Columbia Rivers.

As the world's climate warmed, evaporation reduced the supply of water to the lake. (Former shorelines can be seen on neighboring mountainsides, where the surf cut beaches and terraces.) When the water dropped below the drainage outlets, the only way it could leave the great basin was through evaporation. As the water continued to evaporate, the lake shrank, and the original, relatively small amounts of salt carried down from mountains and uplands became increasingly concentrated. The salt flats that border the present shoreline were once deposits at the bottom of the lake.

Such deposits of minerals are widespread throughout the world. White Sands, New Mexico, is the largest area of gypsum in the world. The gleaming sands are piled up in dunes that reflect the desert sun with almost unbearable intensity. Many areas that were once regarded as wastelands are now understood to be treasure troves of minerals, some used in industries such as construction. Regardless of its modern uses, salt is important to mankind.

Although lakes and flatlands with high salt concentrations are inhospitable to life, salt is absolutely essential to the human body. Thus, from time immemorial, expeditions have traveled long distances to obtain salt. Until a few years ago, salt was transported by caravans of up to 2,000 camels from salt swamps in North Africa 450 miles to Timbuktu.

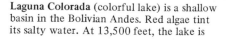

Laguna Colorada (colorful lake) is a shallow basin in the Bolivian Andes. Red algae tint its salty water. At 13,500 feet, the lake is the home of a rare species of flamingo. It is just a matter of time before the lake dries up and becomes a desolate, salt-rich plain.

This region of Death Valley in California is called Dante's View. From here you can see the lowest point on the continent of North America.

The name was derived from the dire experiences of gold prospectors, who searched for treasure, but found an inferno instead.

Drastic Changes in a Salt Lake

The Great Salt Lake in Utah (below) receives 90 percent of its water from rivers that feed into the southern part. When an old railway crossing was replaced by a new, nearly solid trestle, the lake was effectively dammed. The northern arm became saltier as its water evaporated and was not replaced; the southern arm became more and more diluted by river water. Rich salt deposits can be extracted from the north more readily, but this region is likely to dry up faster, and become a salt flat.

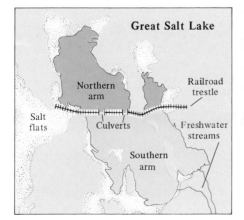

Great Salt Lake

Northern arm

Railroad trestle

Salt flats

Culverts

Freshwater streams

Southern arm

The Devil's Golf Course is the lowest part of Death Valley. Water with a high salt content flows down to this area, then evaporates. The jagged forms are salt, deposited over centuries.

205

Where Water Is Scarce

In many people's minds, deserts and the equator seem to go together. But if you look at the map, you will see that only a relatively small desert region—the Somali-Chalbi, in eastern Africa—actually touches the equator. Here, in the equatorial region, the sun strikes the earth most directly, and the heat is greatest. Water vaporizes at the surface of the sea. When this warm, moist air rises and strikes the cold upper atmosphere, the vapor condenses and drops to earth in the form of torrential tropical rains.

Winds from the equatorial region continue their travels, but they are now almost completely devoid of moisture. As they sweep over the land, they pick up any available surface water. It is this wind pattern that maintains arid conditions in deserts such as the Sahara.

Some deserts, such as the Gobi and Takla-Makan in central Asia, are dry simply because they are so far from any large body of water. In other places, moisture-bearing winds are blocked by mountains. For example, the western coast of North America is swept by damp winds from the Pacific. But as the air strikes the coastal mountains, it rises to higher, cooler altitudes, and the moisture condenses as rain or snow. By the time the winds reach the opposite (eastern) side of the mountains, the air contains little vapor. Thus, the deserts and scrublands of North America that are blocked from moisture by mountains are called rain-shadow deserts.

Swift evaporation accounts for some desert areas. They may receive as much rain as a grassland, but the moisture evaporates too quickly to support grassland vegetation. Sometimes the total annual amount of precipitation may be high, but if it comes in only one or two big storms a year, the area is dry the rest of the time. Many marginal regions are deserts for a few years, and then become grasslands—only to revert to desert conditions as the climate fluctuates. Eventually, this seesawing may stop—usually at the desert stage. That is, the area becomes a permanent desert.

North America has an interlocking maze of deserts. Many, like the Sonoran and the Mojave, have unique plants.

Death Valley is the hottest and lowest point in North America. The record temperature is 134° F., and it is 282 feet below sea level.

The extensive lava flows and cinder cones of Baja California create desert areas that look like eerie lunar landscapes.

Drying, erratic winds make the Brazilian Highlands a semi-desert. The Catinga, a thorny forest, has many species of cactus.

Different Degrees of Aridity

Rainfall, winds, soil quality, and temperatures all have an impact.

Barren deserts, such as the Sahara, receive less than 6 inches of rainfall a year.

Arid regions like Patagonia have slightly more rainfall and thus more plants.

Semi-arid regions support scrubby vegetation. Some are becoming more arid.

Non-desert regions include forested areas, farmlands, mountains, and tundra.

The Atacama is the world's driest desert. In some parts, rain has never been recorded.

East of the Andes is the arid Monte—a region with many salt flats and mud-filled hollows. Remarkably, some of its plants occur also in the Sonoran Desert 4,000 miles to the north.

The Patagonian Desert lies in the rain shadow of the Andes. It is an arid steppe with clumps of shrubs and grasses.

Small, Nocturnal Desert Animals

Almost every desert has its native species of rodents. In spite of their fragile appearance, they are well-adapted to a hot, dry habitat. Most are nocturnal, escaping the heat of day in deep burrows. One surprising adaptation is an ability to get along without drinking water. The marsupial mouse, which resembles a rodent, but isn't one, has a similar life style.

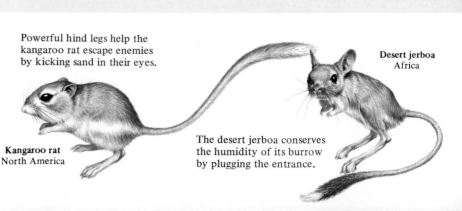

Powerful hind legs help the kangaroo rat escape enemies by kicking sand in their eyes.

Desert jerboa
Africa

Kangaroo rat
North America

The desert jerboa conserves the humidity of its burrow by plugging the entrance.

Fossilized eggs of dinosaurs, found in the Gobi Desert, reveal that these huge reptiles once lived here.

The Takla-Makan of Central Asia is one of the sandiest deserts in the world. It is drier than the Gobi; tremendous dust storms often rise to heights greater than 10,000 feet.

Dasht-e-Kavir, a dry, salty hollow in Iran, is often shaken by earthquakes.

Equator

The Sahara, largest desert in the world, covers a third of Africa. Despite its inhospitable climate, more than three million people live in areas surrounding the driest parts.

The discovery of oil under the Arabian Desert has brought wealth and a new way of life to its sheikdoms.

The Somali-Chalbi Desert is inhabited by nomadic tribes that have maintained much of their traditional way of life.

The almost uninhabited coastal desert of the Namib has rich deposits of diamonds and other minerals. Like other coastal deserts, such as the Atacama in South America, the Namib is a cool, dry area, influenced by cold ocean currents.

A "land of thirst" rather than a desert, the Kalahari lacks water only on the surface. Underground moisture supports plants and animals that keep the hardy Bushmen alive.

The interior of Australia is mostly a high, arid plateau, with three large deserts—the Simpson, the Great Sandy, and the Great Victoria. The Simpson is notable for its parallel ridges of red sand, some as long as 100 miles. Following seasonal rains, temporary lakes and rivers sometimes appear over much of the country.

Wide, furry feet enable the Namib gerbil to scurry across dry sand at amazing speeds.

Long-eared jerboa
Asia

The marsupial mouse is carnivorous. It stores fat reserves in its tail.

Namib gerbil
South Africa

Fat-tailed marsupial mouse
Australia

The large ears of this jerboa help alert it to the faintest sound of danger.

Vast Desert Lands of Africa

If you ever visit the Sahara, listen for Raoul, the invisible drummer. Winds sweeping across the desert create an eerie, rumbling sound. It may be caused by strong winds buffeting the eardrum. But many natives believe it is caused by Raoul, a drummer that no one has ever seen.

A sandstorm on the Sahara is an awe-inspiring sight. As the wind picks up speed, a dark wall of sand approaches with alarming rapidity. In a few minutes, the blazing desert sky may become as black as the darkest night—a particular danger to travelers who happen to be there at the time. Fliers have reported that the darkness may extend upward for several thousand feet.

Travelers familiar with the desert usually wait out a severe sandstorm, even if it lasts several days. Those caught far from shelter lie down on the ground, in a depression or behind a rock or other obstruction that blocks the stinging sands. Search parties cannot be sent out until the storm is over.

Tales of sandstorms burying people are mainly fictional, but the wind-borne sand can blast the paint off an automobile or airplane, and turn a windshield into a piece of frosted glass. The sandblasting effect is most pronounced near the ground, where the heaviest particles strike. Centuries of such abrasion have eroded desert rocks into mushroom-shaped pedestals and other bizarre forms. Sometimes the sand bores completely through the rock, creating uneven windows.

In some parts of the Sahara and the Kalahari (an arid region in southern Africa), the wind has excavated so much soil over the years that immense depressions, called blowouts or pans, have formed. On the Kalahari, the pans may be miles long and 50 feet below the level of the surrounding plain. Sometimes the wind is a boon to archaeologists; it unearths long-forgotten ruins.

Part of the Kalahari is a wildlife reserve called the Kalahari-Gemsbok National Park. This is a good place to see animals during the southern winter. Certain areas of the Kalahari have acacia trees, shrubs, and grasses, which support plant-eaters, including gemsbok, springbok, hartebeest, and other antelopes. Park roads follow the two watercourses, which have been filled with water only once or twice in a century.

Though the Namib borders the Kalahari, it bears little resemblance to its neighbor. The Namib is a narrow desert, stretching some 1,200 miles along Africa's southwestern coast. The western edge of the Namib (the part next to the sea) is cool—temperatures are usually about 50° F. to 60° F. Coastal breezes create a blanket of cool, moist air, and skies are often foggy.

The Namib is an extreme desert. Though it has large areas covered by slowly moving dunes, a large part of this desert is completely without soil or sand; the surface is solid bedrock, swept clean of any particles by the winds. Like other coastal deserts (such as the Atacama, in South America), it is almost

Man-made craters called soufs are a unique system of irrigation that has been constructed on the deserts of Algeria. These pockets allow palms to reach water that flows underground. To prevent the craters from refilling with sand, the banks are packed with fallen palm leaves.

rainless, despite the presence of heavy fog. The sporadic rains are usually brief showers, dropping only about half an inch of moisture each year in the driest parts. A few small, succulent plants manage to survive on the moisture furnished by the fog. But the Namib is mainly devoid of vegetation, a quality reflected in its name, which means "place where there is nothing." The word "nothing" refers only to plants; there are diamonds in this land.

NATURE OBSERVER
Reading Sand Dunes

Dunes have very definite shapes and patterns, which generally indicate the direction of the wind. Below are three common types of dune formations.

Transverse dunes are marked by ridges that form at right angles to the direction of wind. They are found mostly in areas of moderate breezes where tiny sand particles are blown about.

Crescent-shaped dunes, called barchans, are formed by strong winds. Sand builds up around obstacles, with the tips pointing in the direction of the wind.

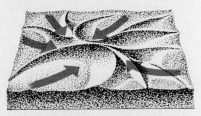

Star-shaped dunes are variations on the barchan type. Such shapes build where the wind comes from various directions. The net result is a stable formation.

A family of hartebeest (top) plods across the plains of the Kalahari. These normally friendly antelope seldom use their horns in combat.

Smallest of foxes, the fennec (center) is an inhabitant of Africa's most arid regions. Its large ears enable it to locate insects moving underground; the ears are also a means of radiating excess heat.

The ostrich (right) can outrun most predators. Its height enables it to spot an enemy when at a great distance. The ostrich is a "sentinel" for many other species —when it runs, others do too.

The Amazing Australian Outback

Imagine that you are standing a thousand feet above the desert floor, on the summit of one of the most unusual geological formations in the world—Ayers Rock, in central Australia. Shaped like a giant prehistoric creature, the Rock measures more than 5 miles around at its base. Yet this great outcrop is just the tip of a larger sandstone hill, even as the greater part of an iceberg lies below sea level.

Stretching in every direction as far as the eye can see, endless plains of red sand are interrupted only by other sandstone outcrops. This is the Australian Outback—the largest desert area outside of the Sahara. There is great variety in Outback deserts. One kind is the gibber desert. Gibbers (an Aboriginal word) are flat, red stones, frequently composed of an iron-rich substance called laterite and polished by the sand-bearing winds. Where gibbers cover the soil, they deter many a plant from sprouting.

A map of this continent can be misleading. More than 200 lakes and rivers dot the Outback; the largest of these, Lake Eyre, covers some 3,600 square miles and measures about 90 miles long. But these "bodies of water" are rarely filled. Some are remnants from the wetter climatic conditions that prevailed thousands of years ago. Others require a "gulley washer"—the desert receives a soaking rain, the rivers go on a rampage, and muddy waters flow onto the sun-baked land. Floodwaters fill Lake Eyre about twice a century.

When the infrequent and unpredictable rains do occur, the results are dramatic and colorful: the vegetation turns a luxuriant green, and new plants sprout in places where there were none. The Outback is vibrant with life—but within a matter of days, unless there is more rain, the grass turns brown and the flowers disappear.

Some water-filled basins, however, are less transitory (Nelly's Hole, near Ayers Rock, is an example). These waterholes are perhaps the best places to look for animals of the Outback. A patient visitor may see kangaroos (of which Australia has about 50 species), marsupial mice, lizards, and snakes. Australia has a higher proportion of venomous snakes than any other country, and many of these are found in the Outback. But the majority of poisonous species are small and not dangerous to man; their venom affects only prey.

Birds are present in abundance in the Outback, most of them adjusting their life cycle to the timing of the rains. Some 60 species, including the large and flightless emu, have been observed near Ayers Rock. Visitors may see large flocks of zebra finches—the zebra part of the name deriving from the banded, black-and-white tail. Pigeons (the wild kinds, such as the plumed pigeon) are common in some places, as are parrots—though the rarest and most mysterious Outback bird

Ayers Rock in the Outback is ancient sandstone, far older than the landscape over which it looms. Marked vertical grooves—a result of erosion—reveal that Ayers Rock was tipped sideways when the upthrust occurred. You can get an idea of the overwhelming effect of this monolith in the photo at right, where a man is dwarfed by the huge entrance to one of the many caves. In different lights, the rock changes color—from rich brown to dark red to steel gray.

is the species known as the night parrot (few other parrots are nocturnal, and this one may even be extinct).

According to the legends of the Aborigines (the first people to inhabit Australia), the deserts of the Outback were created by their ancestors during "dream time." Ayers Rock is especially significant to the Aborigines. Its caves are decorated with paintings that depict great events and ceremonies in the lives of ancient Aborigines. Paintings and names of places at Ayers Rock also immortalize the animal inhabitants—the rock python, marsupial mole (a subterranean animal that emerges only during rain or overcast weather), and the spiny-cheeked honeyeater (a bird associated with the gathering of fruit).

Many-trunked mulga trees (right), a species of acacia, cover large areas of Australia's arid interior. Mulgas do not have true leaves. Their scanty foliage, which is an adaptation to a dry habitat, consists of expanded leaf stalks.

A dingo trots across a sun-cracked stretch of the Outback, searching for rodents and other small prey. The dingo was probably brought to Australia by early Aborigines.

The swift-running sand goanna is found throughout Australia. This insect-eating lizard may grow up to 4 feet. It is not only able to swim but to climb trees as well.

Galahs are on the increase in Australia. These birds, also called rose-breasted cockatoos, devour huge amounts of seed.

North American Deserts and Canyons

Spectacular canyons are distinctive features of North American deserts. Some of these great geological formations—for example, the Grand Canyon and the knife-sharp chasms and pinnacles of Bryce Canyon—are world famous. But if you travel anywhere in the region generally referred to as the Great American Desert, you are likely to come upon smaller, no less intriguing formations. The reason that such canyons exist is that this region of North America has been moving upward for millions of years. Rivers, such as the Colorado, continue to cut the land as it is uplifted, creating narrow, steep-walled canyons that snake through much of this desert country.

The Great American Desert sweeps thousands of miles from deep in Oregon, across most of Nevada and Utah, through Arizona, and far below the Mexican border. "Tongues" of desert extend northward again into New Mexico and Texas. This vast arid zone, about twice the combined size of France and Spain, is actually many deserts in one, though some are only small pockets of sand or lava wedged between mountain ranges. Compared to deserts elsewhere, the North American desert has relatively plentiful vegetation.

By far the largest desert in North America is the Great Basin, which nearly fills the gap between the Sierra Nevadas and the Rocky Mountains (and contains the Great Salt Lake). This high plateau is sparsely covered with desert vegetation, mainly sagebrush. In places, the monotonous landscape is broken by huge sand dunes, some almost golden and others brilliant coral-red. If you think you've been here before, it's not your imagination. These areas have been used repeatedly as locations for western movies.

Nowhere is the Great Basin more colorful than in the region called Four Corners, where the states of Utah, Colorado, New Mexico, and Arizona meet. Vivid purples, reds, and yellows tint the Painted Desert (the colors result mainly from deposits of iron-bearing minerals). In the Four Corners area, monumental mesas and buttes—high, isolated, flat-topped remnants of rock layers from the past—project above the lowlands. Petrified Forest National Park is here, strewn with fossil logs that gleam with the hues of onyx, agate, jasper, and other minerals.

Near Death Valley—the lowest, driest, and hottest spot in North America—sagebrush gives way to one of the most startling plants on any desert. This is the Joshua tree, which produces leaves only at the tips of its branches. These odd-looking trees signal the approach to the Mojave Desert. More than a century ago, similar trees seemed to motion with outstretched arms, reminding Mormon settlers of a prophet beckoning them across the desert, and they named the plant after the Old Testament leader.

As you travel south, the vegetation becomes stranger still. You know you are in the Arizona Desert when you see saguaro, a tall, branching cactus. The Chihuahan Desert, which is nearly as large as the Great Basin Desert, extends from Mexico into the neighboring parts of the United States. Its eastern regions are desolate lands mostly covered with mesquite and yucca, but to the west, prickly pear and other cacti appear. The Sonoran Desert, which lies mostly south of the Mexican border, has many giant saguaros and other tree-like cacti, as well as a great variety of other succulent plants. Few experts agree entirely on the names and boundaries of these various deserts. When and if you visit, you'll see why.

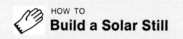

HOW TO
Build a Solar Still

In an emergency you can extract drinking water from desert plants and seemingly dry soil by using a solar still. The only equipment you need is a waterproof sheet and a container to catch the water.

• Dig a hole 3 feet across and 2 feet deep. Put the container in the center.

• If desert plants are available, put some pieces in the hole and mash them flat against the ground.

• Put the sheet over the hole and anchor its edges with sand or rocks. Place a fist-sized rock in the center of the sheet. The sheet should sag toward the center, but not touch either the ground or the plants.

• If possible, get out of the sun and wait for the water to collect.

The sun heats the soil and the vegetation beneath a sheet in this solar still. Moisture condenses on the underside of the sheet, which is cooled by the outside air. The water drips downward into the container.

Snow on the desert is not unusual. An inch or two falls every year on most North American deserts. Snow is more beneficial than rain because it melts slowly and sinks into the ground.

These shifting sands in New Mexico are composed of pure gypsum, which accounts for their startling whiteness. The sand is washed down from surrounding mountains into this basin. Notice the sharp borderline where the scrubby vegetation is losing ground to the advancing dunes.

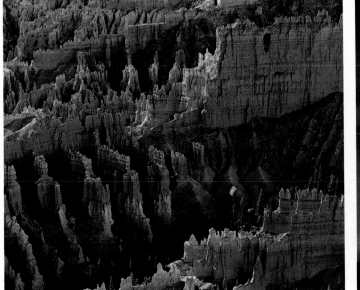

The brilliant russet spires of Bryce Canyon, Utah, were stained by iron deposits, as the forces of erosion whittled away at the land.

Sunset at Joshua Tree National Monument in California silhouettes these curious plants. They are not really trees, but a giant species of yucca.

Desert Contrasts: Day to Night

If you visited the same area of a desert at 3 P.M. and again at 3 A.M., you might not believe you were in the same place. Few regions on earth vary as much from day to night. In the afternoon, you need sunglasses and a broad-brimmed hat—the temperatures may soar to above 100°F. under a blazing-hot sun. At night, when temperatures often drop below the freezing mark, you would do well to have a winter jacket with you. The reason for the drop in temperature is that desert air contains little heat-retaining moisture. Thus, the heat of the day is not held over at night.

As you might expect, these dramatic variations in the environment cause great changes in animal behavior. Birds are the only conspicuous animals seen in the early morning. As the heat of the day intensifies, most animals take cover—even lizards, which are perhaps the hardiest of all desert-dwellers. They wait out the hottest hours, hiding in the shade of plants or in burrows.

The first time you visit a desert at night, you will probably be impressed by the darkness of its cloudless skies. (You may become aware—possibly for the first time—of the role clouds often play in providing some night-time illumination. Frequently, in other regions, light from below the horizon is reflected

Daily Parade on the Desert

During the day, at all different times, birds are the most easily seen of desert animals. In this Arizona desert scene, a Gila woodpecker pauses at its nest hole in a giant saguaro. Another nest hole houses a dozing elf owl. The Harris' hawk, carrying a lizard in its talons, heads for an untidy stick nest. Also carrying a lizard is a roadrunner—an odd-looking member of the cuckoo family. The cactus wren, perched on a bristling cholla, is impervious to spines. Plumed Gambel's quail share the waterhole with peccaries. Lizards bask, but the jackrabbit seeks shade.

Animals Seen by Day

1. Cactus wren
2. Harris' hawk
3. Elf owl
4. Gila woodpecker
5. Collared peccaries
6. Gambel's quail
7. Antelope jackrabbit
8. Tarantula
9. Roadrunner
10. Desert horned lizards

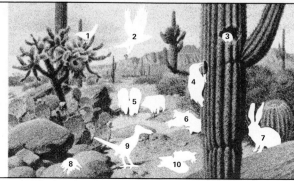

by clouds and produces a soft, diffused glow.) If the moon is visible, or if the stars are particularly bright, you may catch a glimpse of animal activity.

The night-time is well supplied with small, furry mammals—mostly rodents, such as mice, rats, and gerbils. As night falls, they emerge from their burrows, where the insulating soil protects them from the heat of the day. It is not surprising that these animals are active at night in deserts—that is their habit in other environments, too. What is notable is that many larger desert animals are more nocturnal than they are in other places such as forest and field. As the sun sinks below the horizon, foxes, badgers, and deer come out, searching for food and water.

Most desert snakes and predatory birds, such as owls, also take advantage of the cool darkness. They often hunt by waiting for prey to come within striking distance, and many nights they wait in vain. Compared with other natural regions, deserts are sparsely populated, except around waterholes. But if you visit such a place at night, do so only if you are wearing thick-soled, high boots that will protect you if you come upon a poisonous snake or scorpion. A waterhole is a "magnet" for animals as well as people.

The Night Guard Takes Over

In the cool of evening, mammals and some reptiles take over the desert. The pool attracts mule deer, a hog-nosed skunk, and a Gila monster (one of the world's two species of poisonous lizards). A desert tortoise has ambled out of its underground burrow for water. Poised to strike, a diamondback rattlesnake eyes a desert wood rat nibbling on a juicy prickly pear. The ringtail preys on small rodents, such as the pocket mouse hiding behind the saguaro. A long-nosed bat seeks nectar in a night-blooming cactus. Only now does the sparrow-size elf owl come out to feed.

Animals Seen by Night

11. Long-nosed bat
12. Elf owl
13. Mule deer
14. Ringtail
15. Desert wood rat
16. Gila monster
17. Hog-nosed skunk
18. Diamondback rattlesnake
19. Desert tortoise
20. Desert pocket mouse

Waterholes and Oases

On some deserts, regulations require travelers to equip themselves with a rope of a specified length before setting out. This is because a rope of the right length can make the difference between survival and disaster. Sometimes thirsty travelers have come upon a well, but were unable to reach the water. Another regulation requires travelers to report at each source of water (in the Sahara, these may be about 100 miles apart). If travelers are not heard from in 24 hours, a search party is sent out. The reason is simple: under extreme desert conditions, a human being dehydrates rapidly.

In addition to isolated wells, many deserts have natural waterholes and oases. An oasis is a moist, fertile region. The word oasis was applied by the ancient Greeks to one particularly fertile spot in the Libyan desert (part of the Sahara). A waterhole does not have lush vegetation around it. It may be less permanent than an oasis and even dry at certain seasons. Some oases are nearly as small as an average back yard; others may cover an entire valley. A river flowing through desert may create ribbon-like oases along its banks. The Nile Valley is the largest oasis of this kind in the world.

An eland quenches its thirst while zebras wait their turn. This bulky antelope is surprisingly agile, and can leap as high as 8 feet. Waterholes such as this are a boon to the animals of the Namib Desert—a barren, practically rainless strip along the southwestern coast of Africa.

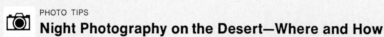

PHOTO TIPS
Night Photography on the Desert—Where and How

A waterhole offers the best opportunity for night photography in the desert. It is one of the few places animals are sure to come. Plan your shots in advance, during the daylight hours.
• Choose a place where animals have been observed drinking, or where footprints indicate animal traffic.
• You should stay as far away from the waterhole as possible, in order not to frighten the animals. Put the camera on a tripod, and use a telephoto lens or a long shutter-release attachment to keep your distance. In any case, you will have to use a flash.
• A moonlit night is often best for this kind of "hunting." Bring a flashlight to check camera settings in the dark, binoculars to see if the animals are in position, and a campstool for your personal comfort while you wait.

The photographer framed this night picture between rugged tree trunks. Two coyotes are caught as they pad to the stream to drink.

An oasis is an unforgettable sight. Few contrasts in nature are as striking. Wherever water is present, the barren desert bursts into vegetation. This is especially true where the water irrigates plantations of date palms, citrus fruits, vegetable crops, and cereal grains. Such oases sustain many animals, both domestic and wild, that are rarely found elsewhere in the desert.

Where does an oasis get its water? Since desert rains are few and brief, the source is invariably far distant—as much as 500 miles away. Sometimes an underground channel rises to the surface in the desert. On a number of deserts, the groundwater follows the gravelly deposits beneath a dry riverbed; slanted underground tunnels that were dug generations ago are still tapping these sources. In the Nile oasis, water is still brought up by means of the *shadoof,* an ancient system consisting of a bucket and rope at the end of a pivoted pole.

In rocky areas, the water may burst spontaneously through the desert floor. Such natural springs are common in the oases of both the Australian and Saharan deserts. Where the desert is sandy, the wind may help in uncovering a water supply. As it slowly piles up the sand into dunes, it occasionally exposes the water table. A spring or waterhole may then break through. For a time, plants and animals may take advantage of this natural oasis, but the waterhole is soon covered again by the wind. Eventually, another sand dune may smother the temporary oasis.

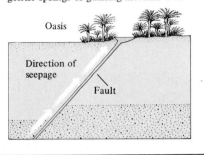

The Geology of an Oasis

The water that feeds many oases travels for great distances underground through porous layers of rock. Its path turns up where a break, or fault, in the rock creates a conduit to the surface. Such geological formations produce either gentle springs or gushing artesian wells.

Oasis

Direction of seepage

Fault

A lush island of green, the Tunisian oasis of Gabès is located on the eastern fringe of the Sahara. This fertile agricultural area, which boasts some 300,000 date palms, is watered by the Oued Gabès. (Oued is the Arabic word for a stream that dries up for part of the year.)

When the Rains Come

The desert is one place where you can stand outside during a rainstorm and not get wet. On many deserts, thunderheads churn up and rumble, lightning flashes, and it rains—but in the hot, dry desert air the rain evaporates before it hits the ground. You may even be able to see rain falling in the sky and still not get wet. Desert rainstorms are probably the most localized in the world. Rain may fall beside the road you're driving on, yet not a drop may strike your windshield. Or you may be traveling a sunlit road and suddenly run into an area where rain is pouring. The wet part of the highway begins as abruptly as if the water had been applied with a giant paintbrush.

On parts of the Sahara, no moisture at all has fallen for about 10 years, but most deserts get at least some rain annually. As a rule, the less rain a desert gets, the more unpredictable its storms will be. When they do arrive, that desert may get its entire annual rainfall in a single cloudburst. Deserts such as the Kalahari generally receive rains at certain seasons of the year.

A desert rainstorm is often spectacular. It may pour so heavily that dry stream beds suddenly become roaring torrents—the raging stream often rips out bridges and highways, and uproots trees. Soon after the storm has passed, the water soaks in and the streams return to their former placid condition.

Storm clouds over the Kalahari Desert in southwestern Africa herald the arrival of autumn (which is in March in the southern hemisphere).

Unlike many deserts, much of the Kalahari has fairly good plant cover —grasses and acacia trees, which depend on this short rainy season.

Water sometimes collects in immense playas (shallow lakes) that may temporarily cover several square miles.

An arroyo—a dry "wash" or gully that is common in deserts—is no place to be during a rainstorm. You may have come upon an arroyo when driving in the southwestern United States. It often appears to be a mere dip in the road. Arroyos are dry nearly all year long, but sometimes storms create thick, muddy rivers—mixtures of water and sediment in which boulders may be carried along. These rivers of mud can bulldoze banks and stream beds.

Campers new to dry conditions may not recognize the hazards of setting up a camp in what looks like a peaceful, sheltered area. In a matter of moments, a cloudburst far away can flood an arroyo, sweeping everything in its path. The hazard is impossible to predict— clear conditions locally are no guarantee of safety. And at night, when there may not even be the warning of clouds on the far horizon, the result can be catastrophic. Whenever you camp, backpack, or even hike, stay alert to the situation—be sure you are never in a low-lying gully that could suddenly fill up and overwhelm you.

In other areas, seeping storm water may slowly remove underground sediment, leaving a series of large channels. These channels have created fantastic natural arches and bridges that stand revealed when most of the roof has fallen away. The giant arching formations on many deserts were produced by water, not by wind.

The feel of the soil underfoot reveals one reason for desert flash floods. Unlike soil in a forest, desert soil isn't mixed and tunneled by earthworms, or covered with decaying leaves. As a result, some parts of a desert are underlaid by a layer of compacted soil and rain does not soak into the ground.

Desert storms sometimes go on for a few days, and may be accompanied by strong winds and hailstones. Within an hour, a desert floor may be carpeted with hailstones, which melt as quickly as they appeared. After a rain, the burning desert heat may be replaced by freezing cold. On some deserts, such as the Mojave, snow may fall, creating a beautiful, if somewhat incongruous, scene. This is another reason (beyond day-night temperature changes) why travelers to a desert should be prepared for cold as well as hot conditions.

Desert rainstorms are often violent. The rain does not soak into the rocky or compacted soil, but goes on a rampage down gullies that were dry a few minutes earlier. If the water is in a sandy region, as here in New Mexico, it may soak into the ground and quickly disappear.

NATURE OBSERVER
Mirages: When You Seem to See Water

Mirages are often thought of as peculiar to the desert, but strange optical effects may also occur over the ocean and in very cold regions. You have probably seen many mirages—those "wet spots" that appear on highways on sunny days, but disappear as you approach. Ocean and cold-air illusions generally appear to loom high above the horizon in an upright position. Desert images look like lakes or ponds. Occasionally, a palm tree or a caravan will appear to be elongated or upside down.

A shimmering lake seems to be in front of the trees on a dry plain in Tanzania. The "water" is a mirage. Some mirages make a distant object appear much closer than it really is.

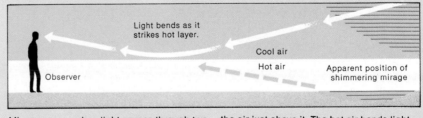

Mirages occur when light passes through two layers of air with different temperatures. The desert sun heats the sand, which in turn heats the air just above it. The hot air bends light rays. The shimmering image of the sky is thus seen below the horizon, and looks like water.

Deserts That Bloom Like Magic

After rains soak a desert, wildflowers take over the barren land. Yet if you lived on this same desert and watered the soil faithfully, very few flowers would grow. Most desert wildflowers sprout only after a certain amount of rain has fallen, within a certain length of time, and during a certain season. Even if the proper amount of water reaches the seeds by soaking through the soil, they will remain dormant; the water has to be in the form of rain. Such seeds, in effect, have a built-in rain gauge, clock, and calendar. Some of them even have a "yardstick." They must be carried a certain distance by a stream before they will sprout.

How can seeds tell what's going on around them? The seed coatings of many desert plants have a substance that inhibits sprouting and must be washed away before the seeds can germinate. If too little rain falls, or if the water reaches the seeds by soaking through the soil, the inhibiting chemical remains. Laboratory experiments have shown that some desert wildflowers can "tell" how much rain falls to within a half inch. If the rain comes in spurts, even though it might be the right quantity, the seeds will not sprout—the coatings on the seeds replace the inhibitory substances during dry spells.

The seeds of many desert plants also seem to know the season. Usually, the seeds of winter-sprouting species will not sprout after a summer rain; likewise, many summer-sprouting flowers are unaffected by winter rains. Greenhouse experiments have revealed that summer seeds require warm temperatures as well as the proper amount of rain in order to germinate, while winter seeds require cool temperatures. Amazingly, only 5 to 10 degrees Fahrenheit separate the "correct" temperatures for some species of so-called summer and winter plants.

The smoke tree, named after its smoke-like clusters of flowers, grows along the banks of stream beds that are usually dry. This desert plant has a curious distribution; frequently, the young trees are some 50 to 100 yards downstream from the parent plant. Scientists have discovered that it is the bruising action of the floodwaters in the stream bed that "triggers" germination. If the seeds are not washed far enough, their coating remains resistant and prevents germination. If they are swept downstream for too great a distance, the seeds may be so bruised that they never germinate.

Over millions of years, desert plants have become finely tuned to their environment. It is easy to see the survival value of these adaptations. If seeds germinated after a light rain, the soil would not retain enough moisture to support their growth. Similarly, a series of light rains might evaporate quickly.

Desert plants that can reproduce quickly, while moisture is sufficient, have an advantage in the desert. One of the record-holders for speed is a North African member of the four-o'clock family. It sprouts, flowers, and produces mature seeds within only about a week to 10 days. Such fast-blooming plants, called ephemerals (from the Greek for "lasting a day"), turn some desert regions into flower gardens overnight. Even if you know the reason for this amazing transformation, the sudden bloom of a desert still seems like magic.

BIRDING TIPS
When Rain Falls on the Desert, Courtship Begins

Many desert birds are opportunists—they breed whenever and wherever rain falls. Even before the rain stops, these birds respond with courting and nesting activities. Following heavy rain, there will be an increase in plant growth and numbers of insects—food for young birds.

Often the rained-on area is only a narrow strip. In neighboring dry areas, the same species of birds may not breed for several seasons. This opportunism is called adventitious breeding and occurs among many arid-country birds, ranging from ostriches to tiny zebra finches.

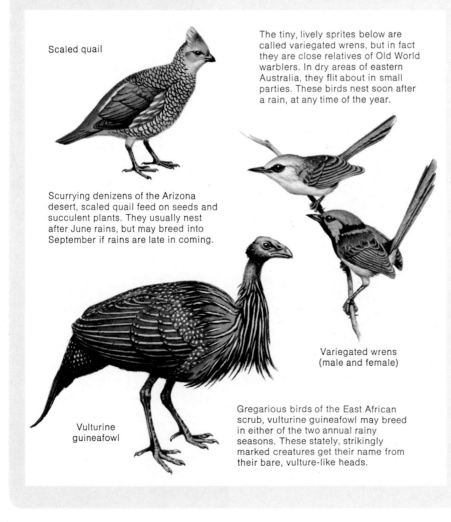

Scaled quail

The tiny, lively sprites below are called variegated wrens, but in fact they are close relatives of Old World warblers. In dry areas of eastern Australia, they flit about in small parties. These birds nest soon after a rain, at any time of the year.

Scurrying denizens of the Arizona desert, scaled quail feed on seeds and succulent plants. They usually nest after June rains, but may breed into September if rains are late in coming.

Variegated wrens (male and female)

Vulturine guineafowl

Gregarious birds of the East African scrub, vulturine guineafowl may breed in either of the two annual rainy seasons. These stately, strikingly marked creatures get their name from their bare, vulture-like heads.

Flaming cups of desert mallow (left) light up the rocky slopes of ranges near Death Valley, California. Smaller desert flowers crowd around the base of this handsome perennial.

In favorable years, trumpet-shaped flowers of purple mat brighten areas of Death Valley. In dry years, the plants may put out almost no leaves and perhaps a single blossom.

An inch of winter rain may be enough to trigger a profusion of spring flowers. At left, pale-yellow evening primroses cover the sand near Lake Mojave, Nevada.

Clumps of daisy-like flowers carpet the reddish soil outside Alice Springs, in central Australia. The scattered mulga trees were killed by prolonged drought.

221

Plants Adapted to the Desert

The cactus is a plant without leaves. In most plants, leaves are the site of photosynthesis, the "factories" where the sun's energy is used to make food. Why then do cacti and many other desert plants lack leaves?

Though leaves help a plant, they can also do it some harm. Their microscopic openings allow gases—including water vapor—to enter and escape. During a single summer day, a large tree may lose several tons of water. Usually, this is not a problem for plants, but in the desert, water loss can be deadly.

For most of the year, the ocotillo, a common North American species, is a thorny bundle of brown, wand-like branches, each about 10 to 20 feet long. Soon after the spring rains—if they come—brilliant red flowers emerge from the end of the wands (they give the plant another of its common names—candlewood). Within a few days, leaves emerge from the stems; their small size minimizes water loss. By early summer, the leaves have fallen.

Like the ocotillo, the creosote bush (its Spanish name means "little stinker") has small leaves that remain on the plant for only a short time. But the creosote bush goes the ocotillo one better—in a severe drought, it loses twigs and even branches. In addition, the creosote bush poisons neighboring plants—a substance secreted by its roots kills other seedlings, which might compete with it for water. Creosote bushes often grow evenly spaced, as if they were planted in an orderly fashion by human beings. The spacing is a living record of the climate; the heavier the rains were in preceding years, the closer together the bushes grow because the moisture washes the root poison deeper into the soil. (Liquid creosote, the familiar wood preservative, is made mainly from coal tar, not from these shrubs.)

Many plants in the crassula family

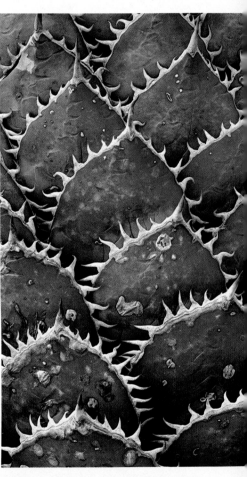

Awesome teeth that resemble cactus spines (above) border the leaves of a yucca. Native to North America deserts, yuccas belong to the lily family; Spanish bayonet is one example.

This is ocotillo at its finest, with leafy stems topped by scarlet blossoms (left). Ocotillo, smoke trees, paloverde, and a number of other desert species shed their leaves during dry periods. Since plants lose water through their leaves, this helps them to conserve moisture.

(one member, the jade plant, is a common house plant) have leaves with a night life, so to speak. At night, they take up gases from the air. During the day, the leaf openings close, thereby preventing water loss.

Cacti have spines, not leaves. Because the spines have no openings, water loss is not a problem. In addition, the spines are believed to provide some shade for the cacti and to trap an insulating layer of air. And of course, the spines also serve as a deterrent to plant-eaters.

A cactus's outer skin is a tough, waxy coating that further protects the plant from water loss, almost as if it were covered with plastic wrap. Photosynthesis takes place in the stem of the cactus, which also stores water. Cacti are included in a group of plants called succulents, which are juicy and retain water. The moisture in many succulents takes the form of a gummy sap. (The plant can nevertheless be used as a water supply for thirsty travelers, if the pulpy interior is pulverized.) The sap may dry out if the plant is wounded, creating a plastic-like "bandage" that lessens water loss. Long after a cactus is dead and gone, these cup-like formations—called desert shoes by some Indians—may remain on the desert floor.

A coating of salt gives the Australian saltbush its grayish pallor. Notice the regular spacing among the bushes, which lessens competition for water. By taking up salts from the soil, these plants make the land more useful.

Feathery white blooms are the only clue that these South African "pebbles" are actually plants. The color and pattern of these living stones may help conceal them from the eyes of hungry or thirsty animals. Living stones make interesting house plants—but be sure not to overwater them.

HOW TO
Grow a Cactus Garden

A collection of cacti is a personal thing—*you* choose the species, the container, and the arrangement of the plants.
- Many variety stores have a good selection of cacti. You can buy more unusual species from specialized mail-order firms. Or obtain cuttings from a friend's plants. In the case of cacti, cuttings are actually "breakings"; many species produce shoots at the base, which are easily broken off. Let the cuttings dry for a few days before placing them in soil. This will lessen the chance that a fungus infection will set in.
- Cacti are notorious for their ability to defend themselves with their spines. The easiest way to handle them is with a piece of newspaper folded into a "collar."
- Use a shallow clay container and sandy soil. (Buy the soil at a garden-supply store.) To "landscape" the cactus garden, include a few stones or bits of wood.
- Cacti need lots of sun but infrequent watering. In fact, one of the joys of a cactus garden is that these plants will do quite well without much care.

To give your cactus garden a natural look, choose plants of varied shape, texture, and hue. This garden includes one cactus-like species (the Haworthia) that is actually a member of the lily family.

Bunny ears
(*Opuntia microdasys*)

Old man cactus
(*Cephalocereus senilis*)

Lady finger
(*Mammillaria elongata*)

Golden barrel cactus
(*Echinocactus grusonii*)

Haworthia
(*Haworthia fasciata*)

Bishop's cap
(*Astrophytum myriostigma*)

Animals at Home in a Hot, Dry World

If a caravan is lost on the desert (perhaps in the aftermath of a blinding sandstorm), the leader may simply turn his camels loose and follow them. If there is water to be found, the camels will find it—some of these "ships of the desert" can detect water as far away as 30 miles. It is difficult to estimate how many times this capability has saved human lives over the approximately 3,000 years since desert peoples began using camels as beasts of burden.

Over the years, the camel has come to symbolize the desert. Indeed, it is completely at home there. Along with the burros of the Great American Desert, camels are the only domesticated animals that can live in such harsh conditions. Their coarse, yellowish hair—which appears mangy to the uninformed observer—is a good insulator against both the heat of the day and the chill of the night. A camel's nostrils have special valves that shut out sand and dust. Long hairs around the ears and long eyelashes—which give the animal an incongruously sophisticated expression—serve the same purpose.

The camel has soft, pliable hooves, which resemble leather-covered cushions and prevent the animal from sinking into soft sand. Thick callouses protect the camel's knees whenever it sits or kneels. The animal has a leathery mouth and tongue that let it make a meal of thorn trees and fibrous shrubs; in fact, a camel will eat these thorny desert plants even when there is plenty of grass nearby. It picks the foliage with its versatile split lip, almost the way an elephant uses its trunk. The lip also aids the animal in spitting—a feat it performs at remarkable ranges and with impressive accuracy, when anything incurs its displeasure. Visitors to zoos (where camels are a popular attraction) have sometimes learned about this the hard way.

The camel's most renowned feat is its ability to carry several hundred pounds of baggage over the burning sand, going for 4 to 5 days without water. This is not a matter of storing water in its hump, which is a common misconception. Extremely efficient kidneys help a camel to conserve water. Like other mammals such as the horse, it sweats as a means of cooling off. However, unlike a horse, a camel loses very little moisture in this way.

Even more remarkable desert mammals are the many small rodents that never drink water at all but extract or produce water from their food. This characteristic is confined to the male of the species (pack rat, gerbil, or kangaroo rat); the females need water when they are nursing their young. Appropriately, the breeding period coincides with the brief rainy period on the desert.

Surprisingly, some amphibians, such as the spadefoot toad, can also live in the desert. This smooth-skinned creature takes its name from the scale-like bump on each rear foot, used for digging into the ground. As the ground begins to dry out, the spadefoot digs into the soil and secretes a protective, gelatin-like envelope around itself. This means of waiting out a dry spell is called estivation—a sort of dry-weather hibernation, when the body processes slow down.

Like most frogs, a spadefoot's eggs must be laid in water. Thus, a rainfall is needed—and a good one—to move the spadefoot out of its protective location. After a rain has created a puddle, the spadefoot races through courtship and mating. The development of this species from eggs to tadpoles to adults is swift —it may take place in only 12 days.

A camel like this African dromedary may lose 200 pounds while crossing a desert. But as soon as it arrives at an oasis, the camel is capable of rapidly drinking some 30 gallons of water.

If you encounter a spadefoot toad, you may have a chance to watch its "disappearing act." This amphibian is an expert digger, and if frightened, can dig so rapidly that it may seem to be literally sinking into the ground.

The migration of a butterfly seems strange because the insects appear to be so fragile. Nevertheless, a number of species have elaborate life-cycles that include traveling over great distances. The European painted lady is extraordinary for its journey across the Mediterranean Sea. Both the Sahara and the British Isles have members of this species. Some individuals reach as far north as Finland. They have even been seen fluttering through the Alps at very high altitudes. The American painted lady is also a migrator.

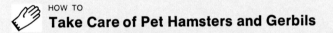

HOW TO
Take Care of Pet Hamsters and Gerbils

Gerbils and hamsters are animals native to arid regions of Africa, Asia, and Europe. Though they are both rodents (gnawing animals), they rarely bite or scratch when handled gently.

• Plastic or wire cages designed for small mammals are available from pet stores, or you can make your own. The cage should include an exercise wheel. Both species are active at night.

• Keep an inch or two of dry, clean wood shavings on the floor of the cage. Change the material twice a week.

• Put the cage on a shelf or table away from drafts and from direct sunlight.

• Gerbils and hamsters require little water, but it must be available when needed. Place a water bottle in the cage (this, too, can be purchased at a pet store). Wash the bottle and change the water as needed.

• You can feed these pets on birdseed and sunflower seeds, commercial rodent chow, unsugared breakfast cereals, or salad scraps.

• Like all rodents, hamsters and gerbils must gnaw frequently or their teeth will grow too long. Give them wood scraps and cardboard for "teething."

• Keep males and females in separate cages unless you want them to breed.

• Gerbils, which mate for life, will live compatibly with their babies. Male hamsters will attack their young, so remove the male from the cage before an impending birth.

Golden hamsters are friendly with owners, reserved with strangers. A "bribe" of sunflower seeds or a piece of carrot sometimes helps as an introduction.

Gerbils (left) retain their desert-adapted way of life —they store food wherever they can in their cages. In spite of these caches, the animals rarely overeat.

CHAPTER EIGHT

Weather and Astronomy

We tend to think of weather as a daytime phenomenon, and of astronomy as possible only at night. This is an illusion, caused mainly by the atmosphere.

W e rarely think of ourselves as "bottom-dwellers" living beneath a vast sea, but this is exactly our situation. The blanket of air above us—the mixture of gases called the atmosphere—acts like a fluid. It is often compared with water, which also exerts increasing pressure at greater depths. At sea level, the weight of the atmosphere is about 15 pounds per square inch. Of course, we are so accustomed to this weight, we seldom notice it.

But even a slight change in altitude, such as a ride in an elevator, can cause our ears to pop, as the air pressure within the ear adjusts to the pressure outside. Airplanes are pressurized because of the requirements of the human body. Like bottom-dwellers in the ocean, human beings cannot leave the atmosphere without being "fish out of water." Thus astronauts have to wear pressurized suits when they travel in outer space, where there is no atmosphere.

The atmosphere has a profound influence on what we see. Just as a straight soda straw appears bent when you see it in a glass of water, so the atmosphere also bends images. This is what allows you to see the sun for a few minutes after it has actually gone below the horizon. The twinkling of stars is another effect in the atmosphere, not a result of the behavior of the stars themselves. For centuries, the atmosphere hampered the study of astronomy. Now, from spacecraft, we have an unencumbered view of the universe.

Seen from a spacecraft, the outlines of planet earth's continents appear as reddish masses against a blue sea. The swirls of white are clouds. These veils of condensed water give some idea of just how thin the atmospheric layer actually is, relative to the globe itself. Paradoxically, it is only at night, when the rays of the sun cease to dazzle our eyes with light striking the atmosphere, that we can see to the star-strewn universe beyond.

Watching Sky Spectaculars

In the mid-1880's, people in widely scattered parts of the world began to notice that their sunsets were unnaturally red, a condition that lasted for several years. The cause was the greatest volcanic eruption in modern times—that of Krakatoa, in Indonesia, in 1883. The gigantic explosion shot a billowing column of smoke and debris 33 miles into the atmosphere. It was the dust from this explosion that colored the sunsets.

As in other spectacular displays in the atmosphere, it is not the air itself that creates the effect, but minute particles. In Krakatoa, it was volcanic dust; in other instances, it may be moisture. For example, the setting sun is much more impressive when there are clouds present. Water droplets in the clouds reflect the last rays of the sun and give them infinite nuances of color, form, and shading.

But why are sunsets red? This too is due largely to impurities in the atmosphere. Sunlight is made up of different wavelengths of light. You can see this when light shines through a prism, and the various colors (red, orange, yellow, green, blue, and violet) are separated into a spectrum. When the sun sets, impurities in the air scatter most of the light. It is mainly the red wavelengths that reach the earth.

Something similar happens at midday, when the sun is higher in the sky. At this time, all the colors except blue are scattered, and the sky appears blue. The difference between the blue sky and the red sunset (or sunrise) is caused by the thickness of the "prism" —the atmosphere—that sunlight is passing through. At noon, the sun is perpendicular to the atmospheric layers surrounding the earth. In the morning and evening, the sun shines edgewise through the blanket of air.

The scattering of light is also responsible for another beautiful phenomenon—twilight. Night would fall like a lamp being turned out, if it were not for the atmosphere and its impurities. Particles scatter light from the sky and reflect them into the earth's shadow, causing the soft, gentle rays of twilight to linger after sunset.

Water sometimes forms a natural prism, as you may know from seeing an array of colors when sunlight shines through a glass of water. Droplets in the air do the same thing, if the sun strikes them at a particular angle. The result is a rainbow. To see a rainbow, you have to have the sun at your back.

Water in the form of ice particles in a cloud will also act as a prism. This creates a halo around the sun or moon. Sometimes, the light of the sky is so bright that you can see only the more visible colors of the spectrum (usually red, orange, or yellow). The Zuni Indians of North America believed that when the sun was "in his tepee" (that is, inside a halo), rain would follow— and often this is, in fact, the case.

Perhaps the most impressive of all sky spectaculars is the northern lights, or aurora borealis. Curtains, streamers, trails, flashes, and pinpoints of colored light seem to dance across the night sky. Auroras originate on the sun. Solar winds emit vast quantities of electrically charged particles. The particles that reach the vicinity of the earth are deflected by the earth's magnetic shield. Though some enter the belts, most are sent spinning toward the poles. As the charged particles fall earthward near the poles, they bombard the gases there. Energy is given off as light.

Who is not awed when nature sets out a lavish sunset display? Vast clouds pile up, shift, change hue, then vanish. Few of us are up early enough to see the equally vivid sunrise panorama. Here, it's 5:30 a.m. in California.

📷 PHOTO TIPS
Rainbows Are the Highlights of a Rainy Day

Look for rainbows on days when rainy spells alternate with sunshine. You might even see a double bow, like this one. In a single bow, the red is always on top; the second, fainter bow reverses the order of the colors. Have your camera ready because a rainbow is often short-lived. Underexpose slightly.

228

This cold-weather cousin of the rainbow occurred when the sun went behind a screen of high-altitude, cirrocumulus clouds. Ice crystals separated the sunlight into colors, but the effect is scattered.

The aurora borealis means northern dawn; the southern hemisphere equivalent is aurora australis. These ghostly lights, which change in color, intensity, and form, are most clearly seen in polar regions.

The Amazing Properties of Water

F ire produces water. You can watch this happen at a campfire, where a film of water forms on rocks that surround the flames. Whenever a substance containing hydrogen (and carbon) burns, the hydrogen unites with oxygen from the air, forming the familiar molecule of water, H_2O. (Although it is a well-known fact that water is often a by-product of combustion, the actual quantity of water produced by this means is small.)

Water is a unique substance. H_2O does not behave like any other molecule. For example, both hydrogen and oxygen are very light gases that float in the air. Even when they are combined, one might think they would still float. Why is H_2O a liquid, and not a gas, at moderate temperatures? Not until the dawn of nuclear physics was it possible to solve water's mysteries. Physicists learned that when two hydrogen atoms combine with one atom of oxygen, the shape of the resulting molecule is like the head of a toy bear. The oxygen is its head, and the two hydrogen atoms are the ears. The hydrogen atoms have positive electrical charges, the oxygen atom has a negative charge.

Because of the relationship of the atoms (called chemical bonds), the top of the water molecule, or its "head," is positively charged and the "chin" is negatively charged. Thus the molecule H_2O is like a tiny bar magnet. Opposite charges attract, and so the positive "ears" readily hook up with the negative "chin" of another water molecule. This forms a chain of H_2O molecules. Water is not really H_2O; it is H_2O-H_2O-H_2O-H_2O—and so on. The length of this chain depends on many factors, but under typical conditions, the chain may contain about 40 H_2O molecules.

Early theories about water molecules showed the hydrogen atoms hooked up with the oxygen symmetrically, so that the "ears" were on exactly opposite sides of the "head." It was not until the position of the "ears" was understood (that is, the position of the chemical bonds) that scientists could account for water's strange behavior. For example, nearly all other substances contract when they are cooled. Water contracts only until it begins to freeze, and then it expands—which you have seen when ice cubes dome-up in the refrigerator. As water freezes, the chains of H_2O do not fit together compactly. Thus water

The film on the surface of water is one of nature's strangest habitats. Some plants and animals—such as duckweed and water striders—are supported on top of the film, the way these leaves are (above). Just beneath the surface, there is a vastly different world. Aquatic animals, such as the backswimmer (right), walk on the underside. If a small inhabitant of either world is caught on the wrong side of the film, it may perish because it does not have the power to rise (or dive) home.

is less dense as a solid (ice) than it is as a liquid—which is unlike the behavior of nearly every other substance.

Another interesting property of water is the way it forms a strong film at its surface. This is what enables some aquatic insects to walk on water or to attach themselves to it from below, as mosquito larvae do. This same characteristic also causes drops of water to take a rounded shape when hanging from a leaf or falling through the air.

Water makes things wet. Wetness is a tactile impression of an object; roughly speaking, the physical effect is one of attraction. If you look closely at a glass of water, you will see the water clinging to the inside of the glass and rising slightly at the edge. This is because hydrogen in the water is attracted to oxygen in the glass. The rising is halted when the weight of the water is in balance with the force of attraction to the glass.

The hydrogen in water is attracted to most substances. Thus just about everything will dissolve in water. And water has been the chief architect of our landscape. It is the vehicle of life for plants and animals. If it weren't for water's remarkable properties, the earth would be barren of life.

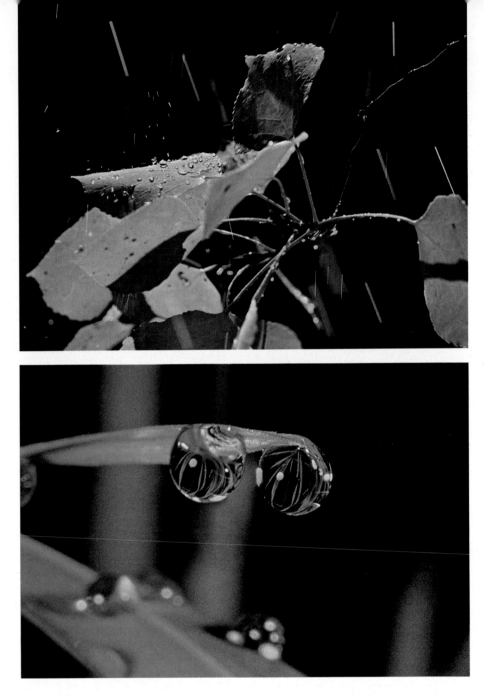

Contrary to popular opinion, water drops are not usually drop-shaped. Surface tension acts like a tight "skin," which tends to make the drop as compact as possible. Since the sphere is the most compact of forms, most drops are nearly spherical, whether falling through the air as rain (right, above) or clinging to a blade of grass after the rain has fallen.

HOW TO
Investigate the Way Water Behaves

One of water's most impressive properties is strength—it can support an object that is both heavier and denser than itself.

• Cut a small square of facial tissue and put a needle or razor blade on it. Gently float the paper and its cargo on the water in a small container. The tissue will slowly sink and leave the needle or razor blade supported by the water's surface tension, which forms a film on the water.

• The wetness of water is largely a result of surface tension. Add a drop of wetting agent, such as a dishwashing detergent, to the water. This will greatly decrease the surface tension, and the needle or razor blade will sink.

• Put a transparent soda straw in a glass of water. If you look at the straw closely, you will see that the water inside has flowed uphill slightly. This "climbing" property is called capillary action. Place a sugar cube on a teaspoon, and slowly submerge the spoon in a cup of coffee, tea, or other colored water. Hold the spoon steady as soon as the liquid touches the sugar. Note that the water rises in the sugar cube. It rises higher than in the straw because the spaces between the grains of sugar are smaller than the inside of the straw. In a tree, water can flow upward more than 300 feet because of capillary action.

• Hold two small, bare wires against a flashlight battery, one at each end. Bend the wires so they are close together but not touching. Submerge the wires in water. Water conducts electricity, which will split some of the water molecules. After a few moments bubbles of gas will begin to form on the wires—the gases are hydrogen and oxygen.

• Oil and water do not mix. You can see this whenever you make a salad dressing with olive oil and vinegar (which is mostly water). The two will quickly separate, with the oil on top. Oil is the reason why waterfowl are able to land in water without getting soaked. They have oil glands (usually near their tails) that secrete a waterproofing substance. Preening helps distribute this water-repellent.

Snow, Frost, and Hail

When you look at photographs of snowflakes, notice how faithful they are to one pattern—they are all hexagonal. Until one flake collides with another, or is jarred and damaged, or melts, it is six-sided; and each snowflake is unique in its configuration, within this hexagonal plan.

Such hexagonal patterns have a fascination for everyone who deals with snow and ice, whether in glaciers or forming on the wings of airplanes at high altitudes. It is difficult for an amateur naturalist to get a good look at an individual snowflake, for each flake is extremely small and fragile. (The array of nine snowflakes at right was photographed by a man who spent years in pursuit of the hobby.) The fine detail may disappear even as you come close, melting just from the heat of your breath. With luck and a powerful hand lens, you may nevertheless be able to see the fine details of snowflakes.

Flakes that fall like fat coins may contain as many as 100 individual snowflakes, each much altered by collisions with one another. They may make good snowballs (if they are not too soggy—which is to say, close to melting), but they will not lend themselves to the study of their origins.

An easier subject for examination is frost. One of the unusual properties of water is its ability to change directly from a gas (water vapor) into a solid (ice) without going through the familiar liquid stage. When liquid water freezes, it may develop into sleet or hail. But when water *vapor* freezes (a process called sublimation), the results are often lightweight and diaphanous —the snow that melts so quickly, and the frost that forms on windows and has the look of delicate etchings. Perhaps the easiest place to see and enjoy the effects of frost is in your own back yard. As the ground cools, usually at nightfall, moisture in the air settles on leaves and turns immediately to tiny ice crystals that look like confectioner's sugar. All around the edges of blades of grass, but mainly on the undersides of leaves and branches, there is a powdering of frost, sometimes light, sometimes heavy. Frost is more durable than snowflakes, and if you are careful not to melt the crystals with handling (or with your breath), you can get a good look at frost.

Hail is another form of frozen water. Sleet was once known as "soft hail." This precipitation, which is simply frozen drops of rain, is common in winter; but in summer, it usually melts before landing. Hailstones, on the other hand, are more complex; they may start out as sleet, but the pellets are tossed upward on wind currents, where they collect a watery coating. This subsequently freezes. Thus hailstones are built up, layer on layer, sometimes reaching the size of golf balls before their sheer weight causes them to fall. Hailstones inflict damage on crops, and a person's first experience of a hailstorm is astounding—it's like having mothballs dumped on you from the sky.

All of the forms of frozen water— snow, sleet, and hail—may be changed still further once they have reached the earth. The accumulations may melt almost at once, or refreeze over and over, or become compacted. Sometimes, powdery snows on mountain slopes are buried by later snows, eventually becoming unrecognizable—hard, ancient, and glass-like at the bottom of a glacier.

A bison in Yellowstone National Park marches across the frozen surface of a pond. The air is foggy with moisture, the trees are dusted with snow. In a snowbound world, drinking water is scarce, obtained from pools of meltwater.

A sudden drop in temperature crystallized the morning dew on a clump of wild strawberry. If you chance to see this outdoors, use a hand lens to examine the glittering fringe of ice.

When Water Freezes, Exquisite Shapes Develop

In 1880, a 15-year-old Vermont farm boy was given a microscope for Christmas—a gift that enabled him to see snowflakes in all their beautiful detail. For nearly 50 years thereafter, Wilson Alwyn Bentley photographed the many forms of snow (a few are shown above). Bentley was not a scientist, just an enthusiastic amateur. The illustrations at right show one current system used to classify shapes of ice crystals. But as you can see, the variations leave some room for discussion.

Varied Forms of Ice Crystals

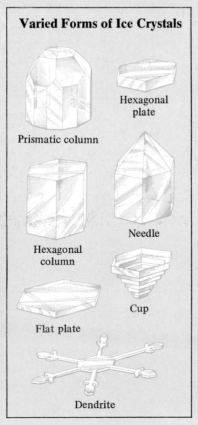

Prismatic column

Hexagonal plate

Hexagonal column

Needle

Flat plate

Cup

Dendrite

In a remarkable color photograph, a spray of ice crystals lands on a winter pond in Vermont. Seconds later, the flakes melted.

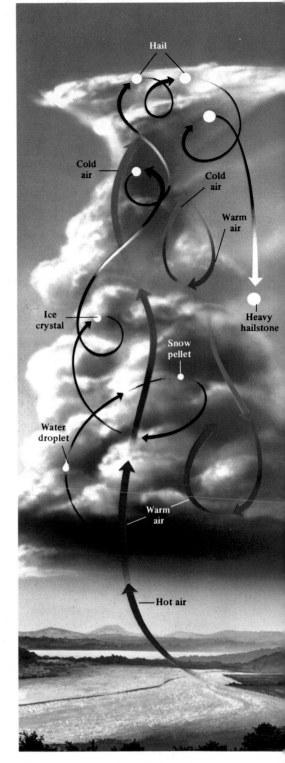

Hail

Cold air

Cold air

Warm air

Ice crystal

Heavy hailstone

Snow pellet

Water droplet

Warm air

Hot air

The Build-Up of a Hailstone

One peculiarity of hailstones is that they form mainly in summer, rather than during the winter. As the diagram above indicates, the turbulent air within a thundercloud tosses water droplets, snow pellets, and ice crystals in updrafts. When hail first forms—perhaps beginning as a frozen raindrop—it may fall to earth, or it may be thrown aloft again, and more moisture condenses around it. When it falls, the "stone" may be layered like an onion.

The Anatomy of a Hurricane

Early inhabitants of the Caribbean named hurricanes after an evil god, Hurakán, who was believed to be the source of these destructive storms. Hurricanes often wreak havoc by dropping tons of water in a short time, producing massive floods, uprooting trees, and toppling houses. Hurricanes can also cause giant waves—up to 40 feet nigh—that inundate low-lying coasts and sometimes sweep away entire communities.

Numerous photographs from satellites show that the raging storm looks like a huge doughnut. Concentric rings of puffy clouds, towering thunderheads, and heavy rains all spiral toward the center. The doughnut may be 300 to 600 miles across, even though the area swept by high winds may be only about a tenth as wide. Here, winds may reach a speed of 200 miles an hour,

dropping almost solid sheets of rain as they pass. The center (eye) of the hurricane is relatively small—only about 25 miles wide—and it is calm. Often there are no winds, clouds, or rain in these areas.

Hurricanes are born over tropical seas, and have different names in different places—the Caribbean and South Atlantic storms are called hurricanes; in parts of Asia, typhoons; and in the South Pacific, cyclones. Although the path of hurricanes may vary, they gradually veer away from the equator and pass into higher latitudes. Hurricanes usually move with the major prevailing winds. In the hurricane belt of the northern hemisphere, this is to the west.

Hurricanes are seasonal in the Atlantic. Most occur in late summer, though they may strike Mexico, the Caribbean, and the southeastern United

States any time from June through October. When the sun has warmed the surface of the sea to a temperature of 80°F. or higher, a hurricane may begin to develop. At such temperatures, millions of tons of water evaporate every day. The layers of air close to the ocean also absorb heat from the water. The warmed, moistened air begins to rise in a column. When this happens, the rotation of the earth twists the air counterclockwise in the northern hemi-

The Tremendous Force of Vast, Swirling Winds

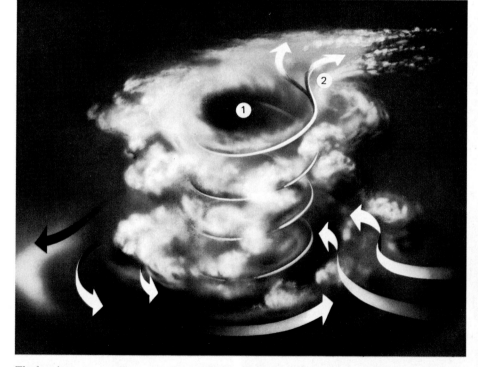

The hurricane system illustrated above has been greatly compressed to show the direction of the winds. Actual hurricanes, as seen from space, look like thin discs—even though they may be some 60,000 feet high. The calm eye of the storm (1) is the hub around which the winds (2) circulate. The storm system usually originates over water. It generally moves westward at a steady pace of 15 miles an hour; eastern coasts are usually harder hit than western shores. Recent satellite studies have provided new information about the incredible force of a hurricane's winds. Even a moderate-size hurricane can produce more energy than a nuclear explosion. In addition, hurricanes often spawn tornadoes, which may be more destructive locally because of the concentration of whirling winds.

Cross-Section of a Hurricane

1. The eye of the hurricane is often calm.
2. High-speed winds exit at the storm's top.
3. The eye-wall has the heaviest rains and winds.
4. Rainbands spiral inward toward the eye.
5. The lowest clouds are about 500 feet high.
6. The air flow pulls in more warm, moist air.

sphere, clockwise in the southern hemisphere. The rising column creates a suction force—an area of low pressure —at its center, the same way your boots cause suction when you try to pull your feet out of the mud. If this low-pressure system (the twisting warm air) grows in strength, it may develop into the eye of a hurricane.

As the air moves higher above the ocean, it cools. The moisture condenses and forms clouds around the low-pressure system, releasing heat in the process. A large hurricane may condense up to 20 billion tons of water in a single day, and the heat produced in this way is tremendous.

The heat of a hurricane increases the updraft, which in turn attracts more moist air off the surface of the sea. As long as the hurricane is over warm water, it continues to draw in moist air. The spiraling winds grow stronger and stronger, and when they reach a speed of about 75 miles an hour, the storm is considered a hurricane.

Fortunately, hurricanes are short-lived, usually lasting only about a week. Some, however, have retained their fury for more than 15 days. The storm's awesome power diminishes when it moves over land or cool water and loses its fuel of warm, moist air. This explains why inland regions, such as central Europe, are spared the devastation of these violent storms.

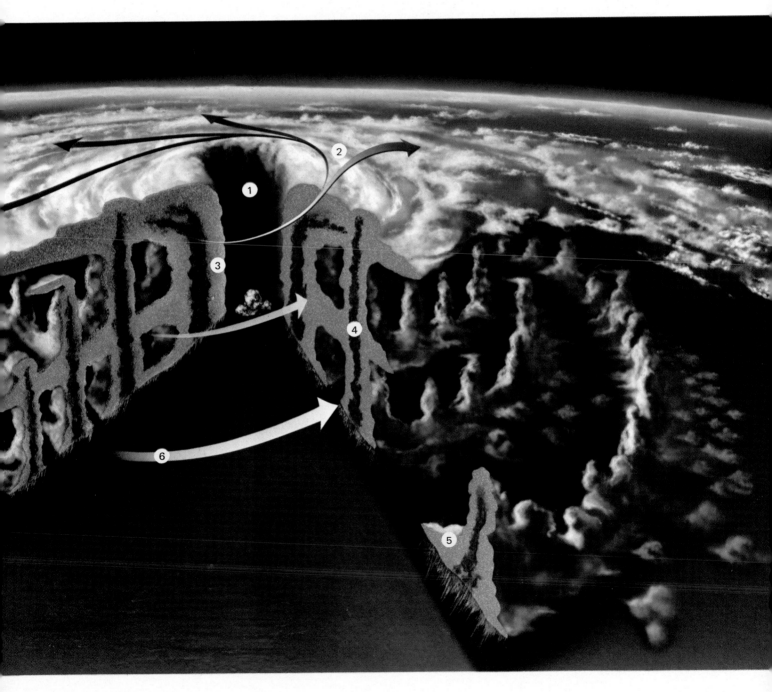

Where We Are in the Universe

Probably the simplest way to learn about astronomy is to postpone efforts to comprehend the numbers involved. They really *are* astronomical, and just thinking about the basic unit of measure—the light-year—is enough to send the mind reeling. (Light travels at 186,000 miles per second; a light-year is the distance light travels in one year, going at that speed.)

Another way to get into the subject is by reading science fiction; much of this literature is based on sound astronomy, and some of the better authors will give you a feeling for the effects of gravity, the varied distribution of the elements, and the immensity of space. Science fiction helps you to accept such incredible ideas as the fact that light reaching us from distant stars was produced long before our solar system was even formed.

The scale of early discoveries in astronomy was limited by its uses—for example, as calendars to help farmers choose the times for planting seeds—and also by the capabilities of human eyesight. In many cultures, the heavens were of great religious significance,

and the approach to astronomy was more reverent than analytical. The use of a telescope by Galileo in the early seventeenth century is often cited as the most important breakthrough in astronomy. Indeed, his drawings of the moon are remarkable. But of almost equal importance in the development of astronomy was the precision of data-collecting made possible by photography. With photographs two people could be certain they were discussing the same celestial topics; through time-lapse photography they could follow the movement of stars over long periods of time.

Over the centuries, we have learned that the earth is one of nine planets in orbit around a medium-sized star called the sun. The earth is not remarkable—not the largest planet, nor the smallest, nor the hottest, nor the coldest. We are not the only planet to have a moon revolving around it. But the earth is probably the only planet in our solar system that has conditions favorable to the development of life.

We know, further, that the solar system itself is part of a larger group of

stars, gases, and dust called a galaxy; our particular galaxy is called the Milky Way. As you can see from the illustration at right, the solar system is located in one of the arms of the Milky Way. Because of the relatively slight tilt of the earth on its axis (as it travels around the sun), some parts of the galaxy can be seen only in the northern hemisphere, and other parts only in the southern hemisphere.

Viewed from many light-years away, our galaxy may look like a single star, a bright spot against the velvet black of outer space. It is not a really large galaxy, even though it is so big that it stretches the human imagination to the point of amazement.

To observers here on earth, the Milky Way galaxy is a glowing band in the nighttime sky. But this band is simply the densest part of the galaxy (the region with the greatest population of stars), and almost all that we see, including every constellation, is in the Milky Way. If we were to view our galaxy from afar (right), it would appear as a disc with arms spiraling out from the center. The sun and its planets are in one arm (see inset).

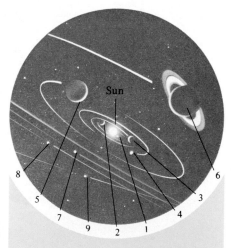

Nine planets revolve around the sun, traveling in elliptical orbits. They are numbered here in the order of their distance from the sun. Jupiter (number 5) is the largest, although from this perspective, Saturn (6) appears bigger. Pluto, known as the outermost planet, has an orbit at an angle to the others. At times, Pluto crosses Neptune's path, making Neptune the outermost planet.

1. Mercury	4. Mars	7. Uranus
2. Venus	5. Jupiter	8. Neptune
3. Earth	6. Saturn	9. Pluto

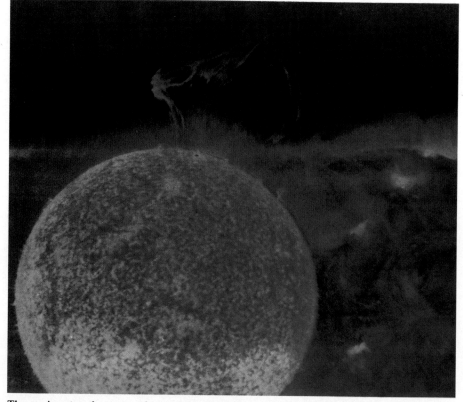

The sun is a star, the center of our solar system. The textured effect on the surface of the sun is created by the upwelling of hot gases. At the top of this photo, a solar flare blows outward.

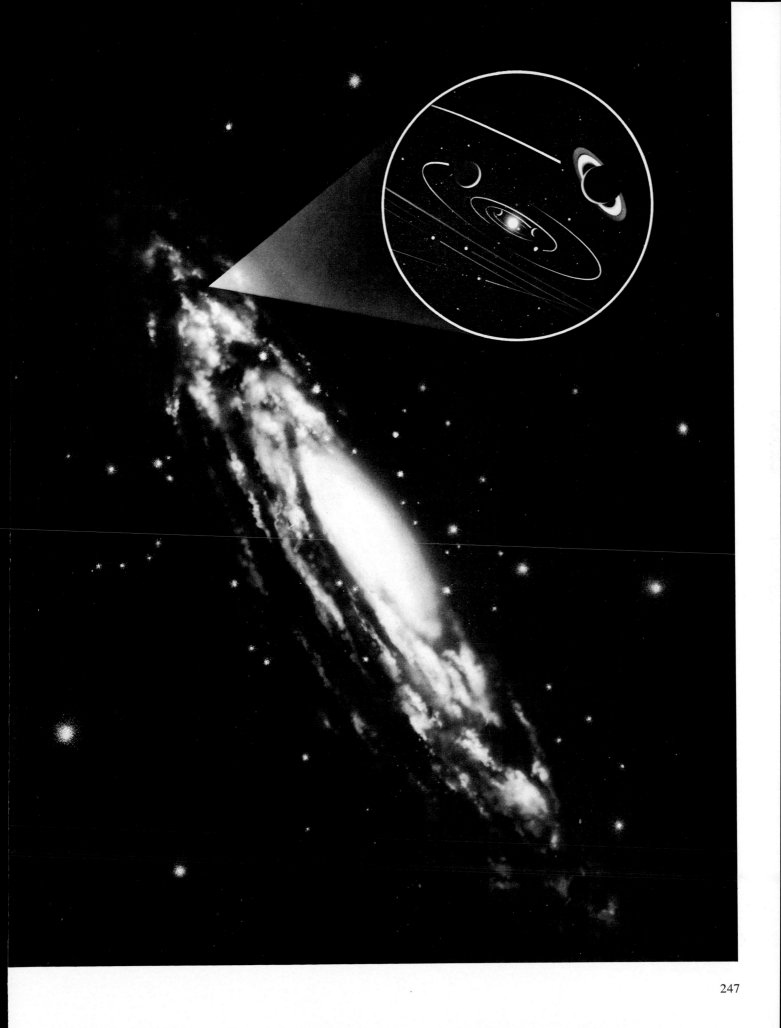

Star-Gazing in Your Own Back Yard

Familiarize yourself with a map of the heavens *before* you go out to look at the sky. Star charts are available in natural history magazines and in periodicals that specialize in astronomy. Each month, these charts are slightly different, because of the earth's movement around the sun. For star-gazing, you can also use a movable star wheel like the one shown below, which can be adjusted to the sky for any time of year and for any time of night.

Star charts simplify the sky. Instead of showing all the stars (some 2,000 may be visible on a clear night), they include only the major ones. The moon and planets are not on such charts because they move too quickly across the heavens.

Usually, some of the stars on a chart have been drawn larger than the others. Locate these first—they are the brightest stars. In most cities, star-gazing is greatly simplified—lights block out all but the brightest stars, which is why urban areas are especially good for amateur astronomers. For the same reason, beginners do best without telescopes or binoculars, which pick up the fainter stars and confuse rather than help the observer.

Fortunately for beginners, the stars are not distributed evenly in the sky. This gives you more "landmarks." To the ancients, stars seemed to form into groups, called constellations, and modern star charts still depict these groupings. Though their shapes may bear little resemblance to their names, constellations are often easier to locate than individual stars. For example, the Big Dipper is a well-known landmark in the northern sky. This constellation will help you to find Polaris, or the North Star. (The stars at the outer edge of the dipper point to Polaris.) If you follow the curving handle of the Big Dipper, you will find another bright star, called Arcturus, in the constellation Boötes (which is pronounced Boo-OH-teez).

Certain stars, such as Arcturus, are easy to locate in a particular region of the sky because of their color. The color of a star is one of its characteristics (that is, it remains the same for centuries). Scientists have discovered that color tells something about the temperature of a star—the hottest stars are blue-white (Spica is a good example), and the colder ones (such as Arcturus) tend to be reddish-orange. "Cold" in this sense is a relative term; a star with a comparatively low temperature is nevertheless extremely hot —at least 2,000°F.

The important thing to remember about star-gazing is that there is no hurry—the stars will still be visible the next clear night. Don't try to find all the constellations or prominent stars in one evening. Give yourself time to let the wonders of astronomy come to you, just as light does from the stars.

All star maps, such as the one shown at right, function in a similar way. When held above your head in the correct north-south orientation, the stars on the map match those in the sky at a particular time. (This map is for the late-evening hours in May.) The red line is the ecliptic—the sun's path in the sky. The blue line is the celestial equator.

NATURE OBSERVER
How to Get Your Bearings in the Night Sky

Star-gazing is a portable hobby—all you need to start is a sky map with the major constellations printed on it. There are two types of maps—star charts, which are often printed in natural history magazines and apply to a particular month, and star wheels, which are adjustable for any time of the year. Whatever kind of map you obtain, read it indoors, where you can see it clearly, before trying to use it outdoors.
• Some sky maps are luminous and can be read in the dark. For others, you may want to use a dim flashlight, or one with red cellophane covering the glass. This makes it easier for your eyes to adjust to the change from light to darkness.
• Choose a clear, moonless night, and a place that is free of obstructions.

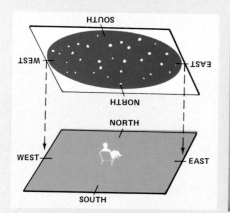

In matching a sky map to your own location, you'll have to overcome a lifelong habit of holding reading material below eye level. You and the map should be positioned as in the diagram above. This may seem awkward at first, but it will soon become automatic.

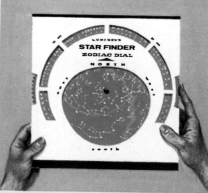

The advantage of a movable star wheel over a star map is that once you have set the wheel to the appropriate date and time, the cardboard or plastic "mask" on the wheel will block out any part of the sky that will not be visible at this particular time.

Landmarks in your own back yard can make it easier to become familiar with the direction the constellations move, hour by hour. The silhouette of house or garage will give you something against which to gauge the speed of stars and planets. Relax in a lawn chair.

As Earth Moves, Other Stars Come into View

Why Certain Stars Seem to Rise and Set

Beginning star-gazers are sometimes puzzled when a particular constellation isn't where it appears on a star chart. What has to be taken into account is the fact that the sky changes from hour to hour, because of the rotation of the earth. The easiest way to understand this change is to visualize the sky as a huge celestial dome, with the stars attached to it. (This is the method used in planetariums.) In this view, the earth appears as a flat disc, bounded by the horizon—the limit of the observer's sight.

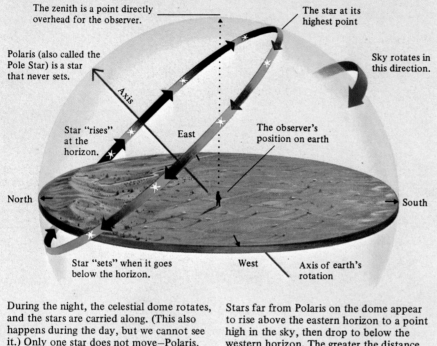

The zenith is a point directly overhead for the observer.

Polaris (also called the Pole Star) is a star that never sets.

Axis

Star "rises" at the horizon.

East

North

The star at its highest point

Sky rotates in this direction.

The observer's position on earth

South

Star "sets" when it goes below the horizon.

West

Axis of earth's rotation

During the night, the celestial dome rotates, and the stars are carried along. (This also happens during the day, but we cannot see it.) Only one star does not move—Polaris, which sits above the north pole, at the tip of the axis on which the earth rotates.

Stars far from Polaris on the dome appear to rise above the eastern horizon to a point high in the sky, then drop to below the western horizon. The greater the distance a star is from Polaris, the less time it can be seen above the horizon.

The entire universe is in motion. But the stars are so distant from the earth that their relationship to one another seems fixed. Their position in our sky *does* change; however, this is more an effect of the earth's movements than anything else.

The earth rotates around its axis in 24-hour cycles. During this time, different stars come into view. Sunrise occurs when our nearest star, the sun, rises above the horizon; sunset, when it drops below. Similarly, as the evening progresses, certain stars rise in the east and set in the west. For example, in early July, in the constellation Virgo, a bright star called Spica is visible only till midnight, when it falls below the horizon.

The stars seem to circle around a fixed point in the sky. In the northern hemisphere, this point is Polaris, the North Star. Constellations that appear near this star are visible the entire night; these include Cassiopeia, Draco (the Dragon), and the Big Dipper (which is actually part of a larger grouping called Ursa Major, or the Great Bear). Near the pole, where there is prolonged darkness during the winter, such constellations are visible for the entire 24-hour cycle. But because they appear to be circling around Polaris, they don't always look the same—witness the change in Cassiopeia, from the shape of the letter M to a W, and back again (see the diagrams below).

The other motion that affects our perception of the heavens is the earth's revolution in an elliptical orbit around

Following Two Constellations That Circle Polaris Every 24 Hours

In most regions of the northern hemisphere, certain constellations never set—in other words, they are visible as long as there is darkness. These constellations are in the part of the sky near Polaris (the North Star), and are known as the circumpolar constellations; they include Cassiopeia and the Big Dipper. As the hours pass, these constellations slowly revolve around Polaris, and take on a different appearance—the Dipper flips over (as you can see in the sequence at right). If you look at the sky once an hour for several hours, you can see some of the sequence (though you may come in on the middle of it). But to see all of it, you need a 24-hour period of darkness.

Cassiopeia

Polaris

Big Dipper

1st hour

4th hour

8th hour

the sun. The earth is tilted at a 23½-degree angle (perpendicular to its path around the sun). The seasons are a result of this tilt. To put it another way, if the earth were not tilted on its axis, there would be no seasons on earth. The slight tilt of the earth may make astronomy difficult for beginners—but it introduces a far richer panorama of sights from outer space than would otherwise be visible here on earth.

Every night, the location of the constellations—at a particular hour—is slightly different. The constellations are actually in the same position, but are seen 4 minutes earlier than the night before. (In other words, if you were to photograph the Big Dipper at 9:00 on a Friday night and at 8:56 on a Saturday night, its position would be identical in the two photographs.)

This 4-minute difference is not great, but it means that from one month to the next, there is about 2 hours' change in the skies. So as the year progresses, a different group of stars appears. These may be stars that were above the horizon only during the day earlier in the year (and thus not visible), or only in the early-morning hours. For example, the constellation Leo is an important landmark in the spring sky; Orion is prominent in the winter. Many people attribute the bright skies of winter to the cold, clear weather, but this is only partially true. The winter stars are actually the brighter ones. Then too, the portion of the sky that we see in winter is especially rich in stars.

📷 Capturing Star Trails on Film

Star trails are the brilliant curving streaks of light you can photograph as stars travel slowly across the night sky. You'll need a tripod to keep the camera steady (or place it on a solid object). The shutter setting may be "T" or "B." The "B" setting requires a locking cable release, so that the shutter can be kept open. The exposure will depend on weather, the phase of the moon (avoid a full moon), incident light from cities, and the brightness of the stars themselves. You can experiment with various f-stops and times of exposure, starting with one hour.

This photo, taken in Monument Valley, was the result of a relatively long exposure. The arching star streaks were recorded when the moon was present, but did not dominate.

12th hour | 16th hour | 20th hour | 1st hour

Of Stars, Constellations, and Planets

Human perceptions are geared to our experiences here on earth. If two objects appear to be the same size, it is natural to assume they are the same distance away. Only with the development of telescopes and radio-astronomy could scientists establish the locations of stars, relative to the earth. But even though we now know the true distances of stars, the human mind still thinks in traditional ways. For example, the stars in a constellation may seem quite close to one another, but they are usually far apart. Our eyes simply cannot perceive depth in outer space. Yet even astronomers use constellations as reference points in the sky—artificial and out-of-date though such configurations may be.

We have all observed that certain stars shine more brightly than others. Here, too, the element of distance comes into play. Some stars shine brightly in our sky because they are large and hot; others seem bright because they are relatively close to the earth. The star Betelgeuse (BE-t'l-jooz), which is located in the constellation Orion, produces much more light than does Sirius, in the constellation Canis Major (the Big Dog). But because Betelgeuse is nearly a hundred times farther from earth, it seems fainter. (See the star chart on page 249, to make your own comparison. Sirius is the brightest star in our night sky.)

Stars are nuclear furnaces, explosively giving off gases and light in huge quantities. In thinking about the behavior of stars, we are again impeded by our own earth-bound conceptions. It is difficult to comprehend the fact that nuclear reactions can continue for billions of years. Yet all the evidence indicates that this is indeed the case, at least for certain stars.

Stars are born of dust and gases that collect in outer space. Influenced by its own gravity, the mass contracts and begins to radiate heat and light. In young stars, this happens because of the chemical conversion of hydrogen gas to helium. Scientists believe that when the hydrogen is finally used up, the star cools and expands, becoming a red giant or super-giant. (Betelgeuse is one example of a star at this relatively advanced stage of development.)

Some stars "die" at the red-giant stage. But the larger ones may recycle the helium, using this gas as fuel and changing it to carbon and oxygen in the process. If the star is large enough, these elements will also be recycled. Though it sounds unbelievable, the star may eventually develop an iron core. When most of a star's materials can no longer be used as fuel, a large star will contract, becoming what scientists call a white dwarf or a neutron star. Such stars are incredibly small and dense, relative to other heavenly bodies; some can be de-

What Is the Zodiac?

Though the earth moves around the sun, it is the sun that appears to change position from month to month. You can see this for yourself by looking at the sky just after sunset, or just before sunrise. Each month, the sun sets (or rises) near a different constellation— one of the constellations in the zodiac. The zodiac was invented thousands of years ago by astronomers as a frame of reference for such movement and for the passage of the seasons. Modern astronomers no longer use the zodiac.

Zodiac means circle of animals, though not all signs depict animals. Zodiac figures (on the wheel) were designed to include all the stars of a constellation, but do not form its outline.

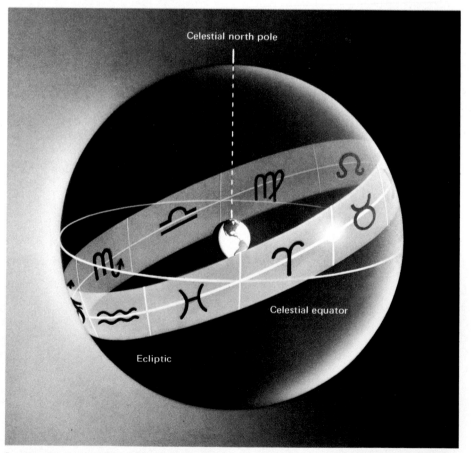

Imagine the sky as a huge globe, with the earth at its center. An extension of the earth's axis points toward the celestial north pole. Similarly, the celestial equator is the extension of the earth's equator. Constellations in the zodiac occur along a line called the ecliptic, which traces the sun's yearly path in the sky. The moon and the planets also follow this line.

tected only with special equipment. For example, if our sun were to become a neutron star (it is about the right size to do so), it would easily fit on the island of Manhattan. Fortunately for mankind, it will be billions of years before the sun reaches old age.

Stars produce their own light; and planets shine with reflected light from the sun. At least, that's the way most of us were taught to differentiate between stars and planets. It seems, however, that Jupiter is half a star, half a planet. Detailed measurements indicate that Jupiter emits more radiation than it receives from the sun, and that its internal temperature is some six times as hot as the surface of the sun. Jupiter is believed to be a star that failed—it never quite achieved the temperature required to light its nuclear furnaces. We have no direct evidence of how rare or common such "stars that never made it" may be in the universe.

The True Distances of the Seven Stars in the Big Dipper

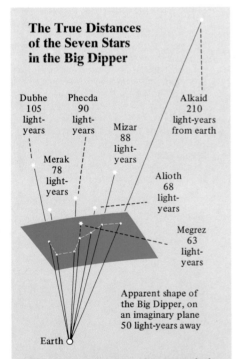

Dubhe
105
light-
years

Phecda
90
light-
years

Alkaid
210
light-years
from earth

Mizar
88
light-
years

Merak
78
light-
years

Alioth
68
light-
years

Megrez
63
light-
years

Apparent shape of the Big Dipper, on an imaginary plane 50 light-years away

Earth

Though the stars themselves are real, the constellations are an invention of man. All the stars in a constellation appear to be associated with one another—but in reality they are light-years apart (a light-year is nearly 6 trillion miles). The diagram above shows the actual distances between the earth and stars of the Big Dipper; the stars were named by Arab astronomers in ancient times.

NATURE OBSERVER
The Word Planet Means Wanderer

From one month to the next, the planets shift position relative to one another and to the constellations. The Greeks noticed this long ago, and named these roaming celestial objects after their word for wanderer. Our solar system has nine planets. Each takes a different length of time to orbit the sun, which is why they seem to shift position.

• To get to know the planets, locate them on a monthly star chart before you look for them in the sky. The number of visible planets varies from month to month; so do the times that each one rises and sets. Any planet you can see will always be near one of the constellations of the zodiac (see the page at left).

• Some planets go through phases like those of the moon, and their brightness changes drastically from month to month. Only five planets are ever visible to the naked eye. Mercury, the small planet closest to the sun, is elusive; for all but a few weeks of the year, it is hidden by the light of the sun. Venus—the brightest object in the nighttime sky (except for the moon)—is sometimes a "morning star," sometimes an "evening star"; this is the planet nearest to the earth. Mars is easy to spot because it has a reddish hue. Jupiter, the largest planet, is almost as dazzling as Venus. Saturn is the ringed planet. Uranus, Neptune, and Pluto are usually not visible except through telescopes.

The rings of Saturn are a unique feature of this planet, though without a telescope, the planet is simply a bright "star." Saturn is the outermost planet visible to the naked eye. Because of this, it appears to move more slowly than the other planets against the backdrop of the sky.

This is Jupiter, photographed from a spacecraft. Near its center, one of the planet's 12 moons casts a circular shadow; the Great Red Spot lies to the left. Jupiter is conspicuous for nearly the entire year, but to see any of its moons, you will need binoculars or a telescope.

Following the Motion of the Moon

Because we have sent astronauts to the moon, one might assume that the moon is of greater significance in this day and age than in the past. The reverse is true. In old almanacs, the monthly illumination of the moon was carefully logged; only when the moon was out could anyone hope to travel safely at night. Not only were the roads rutted and unpredictable, but there was no artificial illumination on either vehicles or highways.

The moon, of course, doesn't really appear and disappear once a month—this only seems to happen because the moon moves around the earth. Moonlight is really the reflection of sunlight bouncing off the lunar surface. When the lighted side of the moon faces the earth, we see the so-called full moon (really only half the moon). When the shaded side is toward the earth, it can

A reddish halo around the moon, faintly seen beyond the haze (called the lunar corona), is a subject for meteorologists, not astronomers. Halos are ice crystals in the atmosphere.

Changes Real and Apparent

The moon has two basic movements—it rotates, or spins, on its axis, and it revolves around the earth. Because a complete rotation and a complete revolution take exactly the same time, we always see the same face of the moon. (The red triangles in the diagrams at right illustrate this point.) We see only the sunlit portion of the moon, which, like the earth, means only half of the sphere at any one time. The phases of the moon—waxing and waning—are a result of the fact that not all of the sunlit portion of the moon can be seen throughout the lunar month.

This composite photo compares two views of the moon, one taken approximately 2 weeks after the other. The moon does not really change. Instead, because the moon has an elliptical orbit, its distance from the earth changes; when close to us, it looks larger.

Moonrise over Manhattan was "captured" by a photographer taking multiple exposures. (This view is toward the south; the moon always appears to rise in the east.) On this particular night, the earth's shadow fell upon the moon, creating a partial lunar eclipse.

254

be seen only in faintest outline (the so-called new moon). These and other lunar phases are shown below.

The waxing and waning of the moon are old and poetic terms—holdovers from the days when little was known about the movements of the moon. (Wax means grow, and this is what people believed was happening.) You can tell whether a moon is waxing or waning by looking at the crescent. If the outer edge is toward the right, the moon is waxing; if the outer edge is to the left, it is waning.

One of the surprising facts about the moon is that we always see the same side. (It wasn't until the U.S.S.R. sent a spacecraft around the moon that the other face was seen for the first time.) Like the earth, the moon rotates. But rather than rotating once a day (as does the earth), the moon turns only about once every 28 days. This is roughly the same time that the moon takes to travel around the earth. Because the two movements happen to synchronize, we have the illusion of stability.

Like the earth, which travels in an elliptical orbit around the sun, the moon has an elliptical orbit around the earth. This means that once a month the moon is especially close to the earth (a situation called perigee) and it appears larger than usual; when farthest away (at apogee), the moon looks considerably smaller. This is not to be confused with the "moon illusion," where a full moon seems to shrink as it rises during the night. One explanation for the illusion is that at the horizon the size of the moon can be compared with buildings and trees, which make it look immense.

In ancient times, the moon's predict-able phases led to its use as a calendar. However, no matter how one fiddles with the figures, there is no way to make a specific number of lunar months (each about 28 days long) add up to a solar year (the time it takes for the earth to orbit the sun, returning to the same place). Because it is the earth's relationship with the sun that determines the seasons and governs farming, mankind had to discover the means of tracking the sun. The array of pillars at Stonehenge in Britain is actually a solar observatory.

The moon's actual influence on earth is not as a timekeeper but as a force on the oceans, creating the tides. The tides reflect the relationships of the moon, earth, and sun to one another. Tides exhibit greatest variation when the three bodies are lined up, least when at right angles (see page 112).

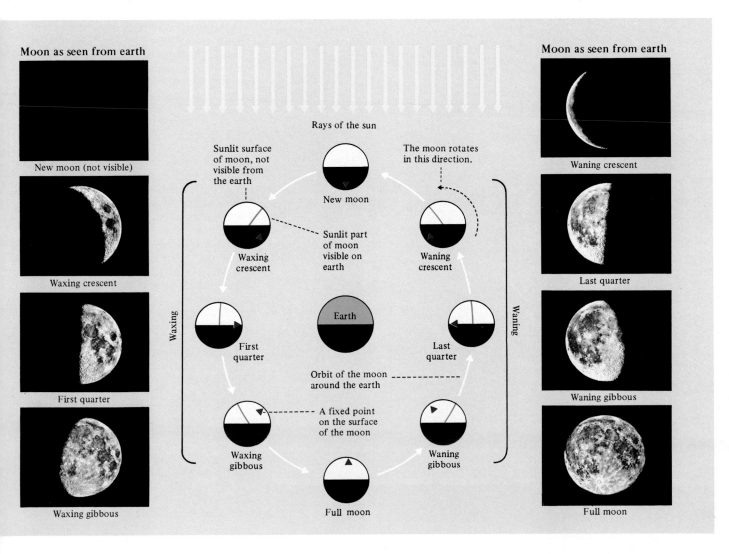

Moon as seen from earth

New moon (not visible)

Waxing crescent

First quarter

Waxing gibbous

Rays of the sun

Sunlit surface of moon, not visible from the earth

New moon

The moon rotates in this direction.

Sunlit part of moon visible on earth

Waxing crescent

Waning crescent

Waxing

First quarter

Earth

Last quarter

Waning

Orbit of the moon around the earth

A fixed point on the surface of the moon

Waxing gibbous

Waning gibbous

Full moon

Moon as seen from earth

Waning crescent

Last quarter

Waning gibbous

Full moon

Visitors and Invaders from Space

This is Comet Bennett—a particularly bright comet that visited our solar system in 1970.

Comets have always seemed mysterious. Long ago, they were regarded with terror; now that the earth has survived the close approach of numerous comets, scientists and amateur astronomers alike are delighted by the prospect of a comet coming toward us.

Part of the mystery associated with comets is their structure. According to a generally accepted theory, the head of a comet is a "dirty snowball"—a mixture of frozen gases (including water vapor) and dust. This part of a comet is relatively small, perhaps some 50 miles in diameter. In the early stages, while the comet is still at a great distance from the sun, there is only a head. The tail develops later (composed of gases or dust), and may stretch for millions of miles. Slowly it becomes increasingly radiant and visible. Then, the light of the comet is masked by the greater brilliance of the sun. As the comet continues on its way, it may reappear on the other side of the sun, or it may split in two, or it may disappear entirely.

Calculations of a comet's orbit around the sun provide data on when—if ever—a comet will come close to the earth again. Scientists may be able to determine whether a comet has been near the earth before or is a new comet. Halley's Comet, shown at the top of the facing page, is an example of a comet that returns regularly, within a relatively short period of time. Certain other comets keep returning at shorter and shorter time intervals.

Though variations in behavior of comets are of great interest to astronomers, they can be frustrating to the rest of the world. For example, in 1974, Comet Kohoutek disappointed many sky-watchers; it simply did not live up to its advance billing.

Although amateur astronomers often make discoveries, it is unlikely that a non-professional will spot a comet before the scientists, because so many comets cannot be seen by the naked eye. On the average, nine comets, including some repeats, are recorded each year. Because interest in astronomy is increasing, newspapers, news magazines, and natural history periodicals often print announcements about comets. Planetariums, too, can tell you the date and time that a particular comet is expected to be visible, and its location in the sky, relative to stars or planets. Frequently, comets are best seen at sunset, near the western horizon, or just before sunrise, near the eastern horizon.

Meteors may be the debris of comets —fragments produced during their orbit around the sun. Many scientists believe that meteor showers occur when the earth crosses the path of a comet (that is, where a comet has already passed by). Meteor showers are regular events during the year (see far right); at such times, numerous "shooting stars" streak across a particular region of the sky.

There are special terms for shooting stars. Far out in space, the debris is called a meteoroid. When it vaporizes or glows in the earth's atmosphere, it is known as a meteor (or, if it is especially bright, a fireball). If the debris lands on earth, it is called a meteorite. However, in spite of the many meteorites that land, few are large enough to produce noticeable meteor craters.

A comet sweeps through our solar system, its tail always pointed away from the sun. Unlike the planets, which stay within our solar system, some comets have orbits that take them outside.

Here, a comet is shown making a hairpin turn in its trip around the sun. This illustration depicts the solar system from beyond Saturn; the earth is the third planet from the sun.

Halley's Comet Was Last Seen in 1910, and Is Due Back in 1986

As Halley's Comet neared the sun on its most recent visit, its tail lengthened to some 150 million miles. Its closest approach to the sun occurred in mid-May; after that, the tail shrank.

In the seventeenth century, Edmund Halley, an English astronomer, first calculated the period of this comet. As comets go, this one has a short period—its next appearance will be in 1986.

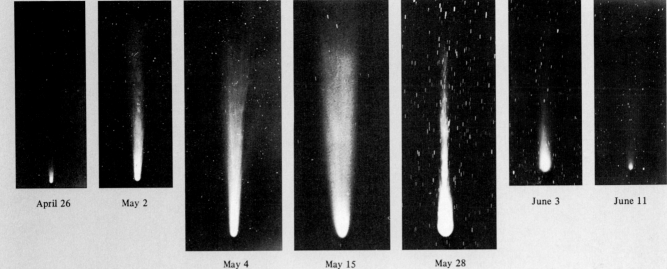

April 26   May 2   May 4   May 15   May 28   June 3   June 11

Meteorites and Meteor Craters

Fortitude and scientific curiosity brought a 34-ton meteorite from Greenland to New York City in the late 1890's. On display at the American Museum of Natural History, it is the largest meteorite in any collection. You can also see meteorites in Chicago, at the Field Museum of Natural History, and in Washington, D.C., at the U.S. National Museum.

The impact of a crashing meteorite is believed to have produced this Australian crater, which measures more than 3 miles wide; the crater's rim extends some 600 feet above the dry plain. Nearly a hundred meteor craters have been identified, including several in North America.

NATURE OBSERVER
Meteor Showers

At certain times of the year, you can see dozens of meteors in an hour.
• Meteor showers take place when the earth encounters huge clumps of debris in its orbit around the sun. Each year, the earth passes through these areas on about the same date (see the list below). The most impressive showers occur on cloudless nights when the moon is not visible. You will see the most meteors after midnight.
• Choose an observation site that is as dark as possible. Most meteors seem to originate near a particular constellation (see below). Locate the constellation in advance, and choose a site where you have an unobstructed view of that part of the sky.
• Meteor showers require no special equipment; a telescope or binoculars actually interfere with observation. A reclining lawn chair will make your evening more comfortable.
At the right time, simply lean back in your chair, looking for "stars" that shoot across the sky, then fade.
• Expect meteor showers on or about:

Date	Constellation
January 3	Hercules
April 21	Lyra
May 4	Aquarius
July 29	Aquarius
August 12	Perseus
October 22	Orion
November 3-10	Taurus
November 16	Leo
December 13	Gemini

257

and carri
wind. As
may beco
kinds of
seams, ro
—the var
seen, the
mentary
are flat, s
standing
nally laic
in the ea
of the ro
The r
so fantas
same ap
oddly sc
in so-cal
dens are
tion of
rocks ha
material
wear the
first, lea
ing out

in south
has pro

CHAPTER NINE

Geology and Earth History

Geological events that took place millions of years ago are influencing our lives today— to an extent we are just beginning to realize.

I t's fun to be in on the start of something important. Suddenly, geology has become the super-star of sciences. After decades of quietly accumulating data about the earth and its history, geologists find themselves with a whole new body of information, and the far-reaching implications of a fundamental theory: the continents have apparently shifted their positions on the globe. The result is that every established fact (from geomagnetism to pole reversal) has to be re-examined. Does our present information confirm continental drift? Or does some obscure fact—as yet unappreciated—prove that they could *not* have moved as we now believe?

Not long ago, the theory of continental drift was ridiculed. Today, it's hard to challenge. What will the outcome be? No one knows for sure. One startling fact has emerged—in places where the earth is known to have shifted, there is a greater supply of valuable ores than elsewhere. Petroleum deposits, too, are connected with continental movements.

Those who first prodded the rocky surface of the earth were dealing with evidence they were unable to evaluate. The earth is so large and its movements are usually so slow, that the connection between the two went undetected until recently. But now, with the development of sophisticated equipment, we can monitor the behavior of a whole continent, even if it moves no more than an inch. We can predict earthquakes, although not to the precise time as yet. Perhaps the "instrument" that was most important in this new world of geology was an open mind—which enabled us to contemplate such fantastic things.

A natural bridge is surprising because it looks like something built by man. Such bridges were once believed to have been cut by wind; but in actuality they were made long ago by underground rivers. This one—in what is now an arid region of Utah—is a striking example of the work of water. The play of shadow and light dramatizes the structure of the bridge.

When the Crust Erupts and Shifts

Several billion years ago, when the earth was young, every part of it (probably including the ground beneath your feet) was influenced by volcanoes. Today, volcanic activity is much more limited—it is usually confined to fairly well-defined zones around the Pacific (called the Ring of Fire); to areas along the mid-Atlantic Ridge; and to parts of the Mediterranean and Caribbean Seas.

Many present-day volcanoes are cone-shaped, but some are more dome-shaped than conical because the flow of lava is relatively slow. Some, called fissures, are simply cracks in the earth. In the 1880's, one large fissure in New Zealand produced lava from a crack more than 8 miles long.

Earthquakes sometimes accompany volcanic activity—when the "throat" of a volcano becomes blocked and pressure increases, the earth may shake for miles around. But earthquakes often occur independently of volcanoes. The strain builds up in the earth with no outward sign, until suddenly the crust breaks like a cracker. A break, called a fault, usually occurs along a line of weakness. When the earth's crust breaks, the ground may tremble, great roaring noises may be heard, and the land on either side of the break may shift.

The word earthquake conjures up an image of disaster. A quake can devastate hundreds of square miles in a few seconds; no other natural phenomenon can destroy so much so quickly. However, you may have lived through some earthquakes without even knowing it. Any shaking of the earth's crust, no matter how slight, is an earthquake.

Earthquakes are rated according to their intensity on the Richter Scale, named for an American seismologist. (Seismology is the study of earthquakes.) A quake rated as one on the scale is so minor that it is detectable only by instruments called seismographs. A quake rated 2 might cause hanging objects to swing slightly. A number-3 quake might cause rattling of objects on shelves, but would probably do little damage. The highest-rated earthquake recorded recently is the one

No spectacle on earth can match the seething fury of a volcanic eruption, such as the explosion of Volcán de Fuego (Volcano of Fire) in Guatemala. At 2:30 a.m. on October 14, 1974, the top of the mountain blew apart.

Eight hours later, when this picture was taken, clouds and volcanic ash were rising thousands of feet into the air. Such eruptions show the awesome heat and pressure below the earth's cool crust.

A bal
the s

that hit Alaska in 1964, rated at 8.9.

Most shifts in the earth's crust occur on the ocean floor. The waves created by such quakes are sometimes called tidal waves; but because they have nothing to do with tides, scientists usually give them their Japanese name, tsunamis. They are also called seismic sea waves. By any name, such waves often cause heavy damage when they reach the shore. In 1896, one of the largest waves ever—about 100 feet high—battered miles of the Japanese coast and washed away some 10,000 houses. Although seismic sea waves travel at 400 to 500 miles an hour, they are much slower than the tremors from the earthquakes that cause them. Thus, scientists can detect the location and magnitude of ocean-floor quakes and give a few hours of warning to coastal areas.

Human activity can trigger an earthquake. Seismic studies have shown that in some localities, pumping out water or petroleum from the earth (or pumping wastes in) can cause tremors. So can the construction of a dam; as a reservoir fills, the weight of the water puts stress on the rocks. In the future, geologists may be able to "defuse" a potentially disastrous quake by setting off a series of minor quakes, thus relieving the strain. Realizing the age-old dream of predicting earthquakes would be a great advantage on a planet where crustal activity is a fact of life.

Catastrophic Waves from an Underwater Earthquake

When an earthquake strikes the ocean floor, convulsions in the earth's crust may churn up giant waves, called tsunamis or seismic sea waves. The waves spread from the quake area in ever-widening circles, the way ripples do when you throw a pebble in a pond. In deep water, these waves are barely noticeable —they are only about 1 or 2 feet high and may measure 100 miles or more from crest to crest. However, when such waves approach a coastline, the friction of the shallow sea floor causes the waves to pile up, sometimes as high as 100 feet. Fortunately, a global monitoring system radios news of tsunamis and gives coastal areas hours of warning.

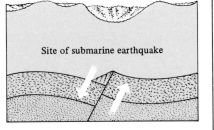

Site of submarine earthquake

A typical tsunami results from a major submarine earthquake that occurs less than 30 miles beneath the sea floor.

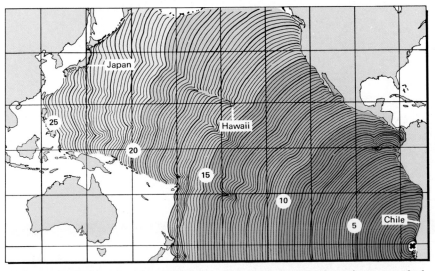

On May 24, 1960, a submarine earthquake near Chile produced a tsunami that spread over the Pacific with the speed of a jet.

Some 15 hours later the main wave crashed into Hawaii, 7,000 miles away, and in 25 hours it ravaged the eastern coast of Japan.

A minor fissure in the ground, such as the one that cracked this roadway in California, is produced by the same forces as those that cause major earthquakes. The ground may rise and fall in undulating waves, or in a more violent fashion. A giant tremor is often accompanied by a loud roar. The earth on either side of a fissure may move several yards, or it may become a gaping chasm. Such quakes can turn a tall building into a pile of rubble in a matter of minutes. In many earthquake-prone areas, the heights of buildings are regulated by law.

Hot Springs and Geysers

The biggest problem that faced the members of the first expedition to the mountain plateau that later would become Yellowstone National Park was not only of supply or transportation, but how to make their report believable. Sitting around their campfire one chilly September night in 1870, they wondered who would take them seriously when they described steam and water shooting hundreds of feet into the air, and springs that were hot and

Quiescent for the moment, a hot spring lends itself to study. Note the mouth of the spring, and its elevation above the surrounding land.

steaming even on the coldest days. Even now, when we know how these natural wonders work, they still seem unreal.

If you have ever seen a hot spring or geyser, or even a photograph of one, you know that heat is an important factor; the steam makes that obvious. This heat is geothermal—earth heat. It is evidence that the interior of the earth is much hotter than the surface. Over most of the globe, the hot zones of the mantle lie miles beneath the surface; but in some places, the overlying crust is relatively thin. Such regions are usually associated with volcanic activity, and this is where hot springs and geysers are likely to occur.

Water is the other component of a geothermal area. Groundwater collects in cracks, where it is heated. When this water bubbles to the surface, it is called a hot spring. In some places, the water does not have a chance to collect in the underground spaces, but is continually expelled as steam. These hissing openings are called fumaroles. A geyser is a hot spring with an underground structure that causes the build-up of steam; the pathway to the surface is crooked and has pockets where heat is trapped, steam collects, and pressure builds. Periodically, the boiling water will emerge explosively in a geyser. The word geyser means to rush forth.

Each geyser has its own "style" of spouting. Some erupt regularly, almost

on an hourly timetable; others spurt only at long, unpredictable intervals that may be reckoned in decades. One of the most regular of all geysers, Old Faithful in Yellowstone, erupts at intervals that range from a half-hour to an hour-and-a-half. The world's largest geysers spout water as high as several hundred feet into the air. Other geysers are mere squirts, with water pushed only a few inches above ground.

Some plants can live in hot springs. The presence of blue-green algae may indicate even the temperature. (Such algae do not grow where the temperature is greater than 170°F). The waters of hot springs and geysers carry large amounts of dissolved minerals, which also lend color to the formations. As the hot, mineral-laden water reaches the surface, the water may evaporate. This often causes the dissolved minerals to drop and form a crater-like wall; where the water flows down a slope, ornate terraces may be created. Such deposits are often colored yellow, pink, or blue, depending on the particular minerals that were in the water.

Geothermal energy is sometimes used by man to generate electricity and heat buildings. It is also used by wildlife. For example, during winter, bison can be seen grazing near thermal areas in Yellowstone; bears locate their dens nearby; and ducks swim on the warm ponds when all other waters are frozen.

Steam clouds the air and mud oozes down the side of the "crater" as water at a temperature of more than 100°F. wells up in a hot spring.

A steaming fumarole resembles an inferno. Such hot-air vents, named after the Latin for smoke, hiss and sputter when hot gases (mainly water vapor) emerge from the earth's interior. The scorching heat prevents all but certain kinds of algae from growing near fumaroles.

Hot Water Rising Under Pressure

Heat and water are two obvious requirements of geysers, hot springs, and fumaroles. But what cannot be seen are the fissures that extend downward to the hot regions of the earth's interior. It is in these natural channels that water circulates and picks up heat.

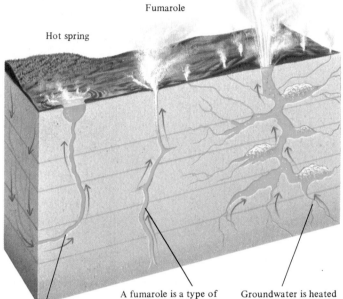

Geyser

Fumarole

Hot spring

Water seeps down and is recycled.

A fumarole is a type of hot spring that spouts steam, not water.

Groundwater is heated by molten rock, which lies about 3 miles below the earth's surface.

Old Faithful geyser in Yellowstone National Park does not erupt at exact intervals. Nevertheless, the geyser deserves its name—it has spouted about once an hour for as long as records have been kept.

The waters of a hot spring at Yellowstone's Mammoth Hot Springs run down sloping land. The heavy concentrations of minerals in the water account not just for the terraces, but for their multi-colored hues as well.

Minerals: The Building Blocks of Rocks

One of the attractions of rockhounding is the possibility that you'll find something unusual. Here, on a bed of quartz, is an extraordinary "sunburst" of white mica.

Walking on air is usually taken as a figure of speech, but in one sense it is literally true. Oxygen, the gas that makes up about 20 percent of the air, also makes up some 50 percent of the crust of the earth. It seems impossible that a substance we can neither see, taste, touch, nor smell is such an abundant substance in rock and soil. But this is indeed the case. Because oxygen combines readily with many other substances, it forms most of the earth's minerals—the building blocks of its rocky crust.

Geologists usually define a mineral as a naturally occurring, uniform solid that has never been part of any living thing. You probably ate at least one common mineral today—salt. Most gems, ores, and many industrial raw materials are minerals. But there are so many minerals and so much disagreement about exactly what they are, that no one can state precisely how many kinds exist on earth. Estimates range from 1,500 to 3,000. The possible combinations are beyond calculation.

As in the classification of plants and animals, the different kinds of minerals are known as species. The most common are the silicates—combinations of oxygen and silicon, which is a glass-like solid. Silicates alone make up about 90 percent of all material in the crust of the earth, and more than a quarter of all known species of minerals.

Learning to recognize minerals is like playing a parlor game out-of-doors. The best way to start is by eliminating everything that is *not* a mineral. According to the definition, minerals have never been alive. Although they are necessary to all forms of life, once they are incorporated into living tissue, they are no longer considered minerals. This presents some interesting paradoxes. For example, oyster shells and pearls are composed of the same substance as a mineral called aragonite, but oyster shells are produced by animals.

All man-made substances can also be discounted, because minerals must occur naturally. A diamond found in the earth is a mineral, but a man-made diamond—although it may be identical in composition—is not. This part of the definition has caused arguments among the experts. One controversy concerns a substance called larium, found in the sea off Greece. Larium was formed when sea water reacted with slag (residue from lead mines) dumped in the sea more than 2,000 years ago. So is larium a natural substance?

The structure of a mineral is one of its most distinctive characteristics. Minerals are made up of symmetrical shapes called crystals; for example, there are crystals of salt and, on the inside of a geode, crystals of quartz (see below). Though most crystals are microscopic, the crystalline structure of minerals can often be seen in large formations.

A certain purity of chemical composition is one way to identify a mineral, but there are other tests. Hardness, luster, color, and melting temperature all aid in mineral identification. Some minerals produce an electrical current when heated or put under pressure. Then, too, there are various specific tests—such as reactions to acids and to burning. Other minerals glow (fluoresce) when placed under "black" (ultra-violet) light, giving them a dramatic look when shown this way.

Geodes—The Surprise Within

Geodes, sometimes called thunder eggs, begin as bubbles in rock-forming material. In sedimentary rock (which is usually laid down as mud on the sea floor), the bubble may be a pocket of water. After the mud hardens into rock, the center fills with water-borne minerals (usually silicates). The minerals crystallize on the interior walls. Later, when the surrounding rock is worn away, the geode is left behind. If you heft a plain, round stone that weighs much less than you expected, it may be worth splitting open—perhaps it is actually a geode.

Start with Silicates—They're Easy to Identify and Often Beautiful

Because there are so many kinds of minerals (some difficult even for mineralogists to identify except with laboratory equipment), it's a good idea to start with something abundant and relatively obvious. Silicates are ideal because two of their components —oxygen and silicon—are the most abundant elements in the earth's crust. Nearly all of the rock-forming minerals are combinations of silicon, oxygen, and one or more metals. Silicates may differ widely, ranging from crystal-clear quartz to coal-black obsidian (which is volcanic glass, thrown out during an eruption). But most silicate specimens of any size are relatively hard and have a definite glass-like sheen. Sand is primarily quartz, but this is not obvious because the grains are tiny. Manufacturing processes use silicates for products as diverse as ordinary glass (which is made from sand), porcelain, filaments for sensitive electronic instruments, and roofing materials. Many silicates are considered to be gems—agate, onyx, jasper, opal, jade, and others.

White veins of glassy quartz, above, are found in many rocks, particularly granite. (The red spots are lichens.) Such veins may indicate to prospectors that valuable ores are present.

Wavy bands of jasper coat a streamside rock in the Australian Outback. Jasper is an opaque, fine-grained variety of quartz; an iron-rich mineral called hematite gives jasper its red color.

Vivid rings of agate were formed when water deposited silicates inside a rock cavity (a similar process also creates geodes).

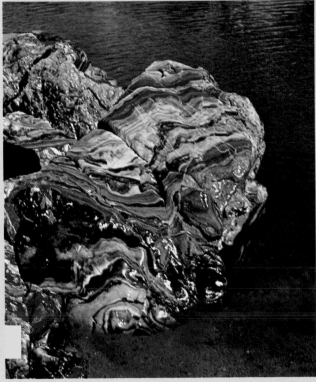

271

The Hunt for Valuable Ores

In the 1960's, an oceanographic ship cruising in the Red Sea made an amazing discovery—parts of the sea bed were "paved" with valuable metals. Deep-sea drilling brought up one sample that indicated some of the sea bed was about 30 percent iron, with lesser amounts of zinc, copper, lead, silver, and gold. Even more surprising than the original discovery of the metals was the discovery of how they got there. The metals along zones in the Red Sea and many similar areas are the result of refining—not refineries operated by humans, but by vast natural processes that operate on the crust of the earth.

The explanation for the existence of

The Many Forms of Copper

Copper is termed one of the seven metals of antiquity because it was one of the relatively few metals known and used in primitive times. The others, which were also either available in a free state or in easily melted ores, were tin, gold, silver, mercury, iron, and lead. When copper was mixed with tin (about 90 percent copper to 10 percent tin), the result was bronze. Bronze Age implements were stronger than other tools, and brought about drastic changes in civilization.

such deposits of metals goes back to the theory of continental drift. The hard outer crust of the earth is fractured into gigantic plates that shift like chunks of ice in a river. Where hot rock rises from the earth's interior into the sea (as it does in the Red Sea and certain other places), the material cools and then cracks. Sea water invades the fissures and dissolves the many kinds of metals that occur naturally in the basalt (volcanic rock). As the water becomes heated, it rises and is replaced by more cold water, and the process continues. The metals, which are present in only small amounts in basalt, become concentrated in the mud on the sea floor.

The iridescent tarnish on rock called bornite reminded miners of peacock feathers—hence bornite's common name of peacock ore. To a chemist, peacock ore is copper iron sulfide.

The brilliant color and striking bands of this African malachite make it seem quite different from other types of copper. But malachite is indeed a form of copper—copper carbonate.

Near some rifts, this refining process has even created veins of pure metal.

The growing plates on the globe are, in effect, like slow-moving conveyor belts. As new material is welded to the plates along a rift, the plates are enlarged. The metals that are concentrated at the rift are carried outward, to the opposite margin of the plate. When the outer edges of two plates collide, the heavier plate may slip beneath the lighter one. It is believed that the lower plate is pushed downward into the earth's molten interior, where it melts. As the plate descends, metals concentrated on its upper surface may be scraped off by the edge of the upper plate, thus creating an even greater concentration of metals. (Sometimes the intense pressures that occur where plates collide transform common minerals into precious stones, including emeralds and jade.) In other areas, the metals may be carried downward with the plate.

As these ideas developed, geologists began to see that continental drift might be a clue to finding valuable ores (ores are metal-bearing deposits). Traditionally, looking for ores was a hit-or-miss proposition that depended mainly on a lucky prospector's discovering an obvious outcrop. As maps were checked, the theory was strengthened; it became apparent that most existing mines are located along the borders of plates. For example, it was discovered that the Mediterranean island of Cyprus, which has been a major copper-producing area for thousands of years, was once under water. In fact, Cyprus is near a former rift that has been lifted above sea level. The great metallic wealth of western South America is a result of a plate's continually slipping under the continent for millions of years. Gold deposits, such as those in Alaska and California, are associated with plate boundaries.

The new knowledge is already beginning to bear fruit. In 1972, a copper mine began production on Bougainville, an island in the South Pacific that stands beside an active ocean rift; the mine is estimated to hold some 900 million tons of ore. The exploration of similar areas in other parts of the world is expected to yield comparable returns. Of course, many of the richest areas lie at the bottom of the ocean. However, with the progress that has been made in undersea research, miners will someday pluck these metallic riches from nature's giant "refineries."

The burnished hue of native (pure) copper makes it easy to identify. The ore came from a lava flow in Michigan, which was worked by Indians long before Europeans arrived.

Ores Are More Abundant at the Boundaries of the Plates

The edges of the earth's crustal plates are vast repositories that abound with metals, especially near chains of volcanic islands. This map shows margins of major crustal plates. As water on the ocean floor is heated, it dissolves and then deposits ores along ridges in the middle of the ocean. The slow expansion of the plates carries metals upward and outward from the ridges. Thus concentrations of metals increase. Two plates that grow outward from a common ridge are often alike in mineral content. Ores found in one plate can lead prospectors to ores in a nearby plate. Metals such as zinc, copper, and gold are deposited separately—often in a predictable sequence. In the case where one plate goes underneath another (subduction), some metals are concentrated above the surface; others are carried down.

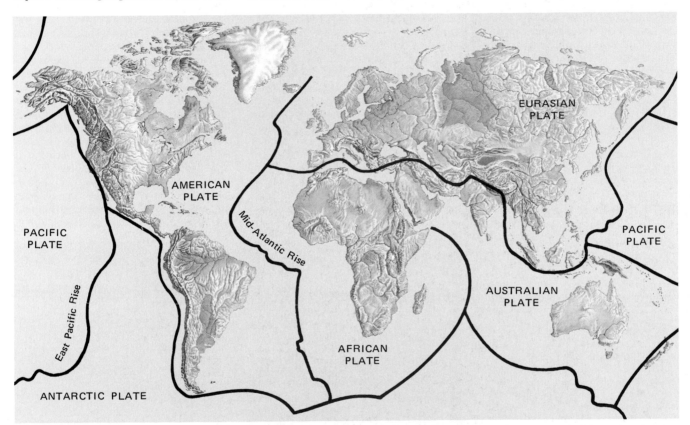

The six major plates, and two mid-ocean rises, are still being charted. In addition to the plates shown, there are many active smaller plates.

Hot, molten basaltic rock wells up from deep within the earth, at the ridges where the earth's crustal plates are formed. When the basalt reaches the sea floor, it cools and cracks. Sea water infiltrates the cracks and dissolves metals contained in the basalt. The water itself is heated and rises back up to the sea floor, where it cools again. Cold water is not as good a solvent as hot water, so most of the dissolved metals are deposited as silt on the sea floor. Much the same process takes place at the opposite edges of the plates, where they collide. One plate is usually deflected deep into the earth, carrying the metal-bearing silt and some sea water with it. When this water is heated in the earth's interior, it rises and deposits the metals once again, in a more concentrated form.

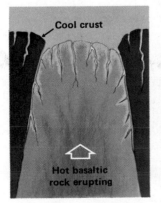

A column of hot basalt rises between two crustal plates where the sea floor spreads.

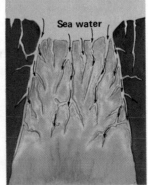

As basalt reaches the top, it cools and cracks. Invading sea water dissolves many metals.

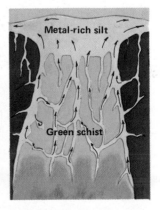

Metals are deposited in silt on the ocean floor. Here, the rock has changed into schist.

Why Some Minerals Are Called Gems

What most gems have in common is their beauty. A cut diamond will refract light into dazzling, fiery flashes; polished rubies and sapphires may show a star pattern when light strikes them; opals are famous for their rainbows of shimmering flecks and dots. Gems generally share two other characteristics—they are rare and durable.

The definition of a gem is influenced by history. Long before chemists classified minerals by features such as crystalline structure, many small bits of hard materials—often lustrous or colorful—were prized in the making of jewelry. Thus certain "gems" are not stones at all. Amber is fossilized sap, pearls are produced by oysters, and coral is the skeletal remains of marine animals.

In common usage, a gem is any mineral (except a metal, such as gold) that is used as jewelry. Fewer than 100 species of minerals are classified as gems. A particular mineral, such as the kind called *beryl*, may provide a variety of gemstones. Some specimens of beryl are green, because of the presence of minute quantities of chromic oxide. In a way, chromic oxide might be considered an imperfection, although a valuable one—emeralds are stones of green beryl. Aquamarine is beryl with small amounts of iron; morganite (another gemstone) is beryl colored pink by lithium. The hue of a gemstone also varies with the *amount* of the trace substance—or, in the case of diamonds, with the crystalline structure.

Though important in the past, the distinction between precious and semiprecious stones is not particularly significant today. The value of a gem may change with time, depending on fashion and the relative rarity of the stone. (Currently, rubies are the most highly prized.) Technological advances also influence the value of a gem. Perhaps the greatest breakthrough came in 1955, when genuine crystals of diamonds were made in the laboratory for the first time. Diamonds are a form of pure carbon. To make them, scientists heated carbon-containing substances to a temperature greater than 3,600°F. and applied a pressure of a million pounds per square inch. To date, the diamonds synthesized in the laboratory have been made for industrial purposes, such as the cutting points of drills, and not as gemstones. (The artificial diamonds sold in jewelry stores do not have the same chemical and physical properties as genuine diamonds.)

In nature, as in the laboratory, diamonds are produced by intense heat and pressure. What apparently happens in the earth's interior is that magma, or molten rock, pushes its way up through weak areas to the surface. For diamond formation, carbon and large amounts of gas have to be present. Because of the heat and pressure, some of the carbon may be crystallized into rough diamonds, somewhat the way sand can be melted to form glass. As the gas

The Cutting of a Diamond Is the Key to Its Brilliance

In their natural condition, diamonds look like dull pieces of glass (see below). The ultimate value of a diamond depends on several factors —its color and weight (measured in carats after the stone has been cut), and whether it is without serious flaws. There is considerable risk involved in the cutting of any potentially valuable stone. If it is struck correctly, its maximum size can be retained, and further cutting can enhance its brilliance. However, if struck at the wrong angle, the stone may shatter. The diamond at right is a splendid, well-cut specimen of approximately 5 carats.

Ideally, a diamond will reflect light whether it is seen from above or from the side. Many of the famous stones of royalty are surprisingly dull, by modern standards. This is because the art of diamond-cutting (or the cutting of other jewels) was not perfected until relatively recent times. So-called crown jewels may have less luster than their fame might suggest, but no one would risk changing them.

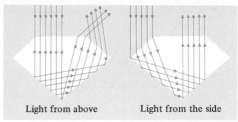

Light from above   Light from the side

erupts at the surface, the diamond crystals are propelled upward. When the core of magma cools, it forms a diamond-rich plug, or pipe, in the earth. Such pipes are made of a rock called kimberlite, first found in Africa.

Diamonds don't always stay in the kimberlite pipes awaiting discovery by man. Those near the surface may be carried great distances by streams and glaciers, and can often be traced back to their source. Near the middle of the nineteenth century, some farm children found a pretty pebble along the banks of a South African river. The pebble, which turned out to be a valuable diamond, led to the discovery of the now-famous diamond mines of South Africa. A number of diamonds have been found near the Great Lakes, in North America. It seems reasonable to suppose that these diamonds were carried to this location by glaciers (from kimberlite pipes farther north). But so far no one has found their source.

The rounded cut of this ruby brings out the brilliance of the star. This effect, which is called asterism, is caused by gas bubbles trapped inside the stone during formation.

The Burmese Star of Asia, a sapphire, differs from a star ruby not in crystal form, but in the presence of trace elements that give color.

Capturing the Essence of Mineral Structure

To create a striking photograph of a mineral, emphasize the special qualities of your subject, such as its crystalline structure, cleavage planes, and color. For example, white mica (below) has minute "terraces" that project at the edges of the crystals. Each terrace is a fracture plane that can be split open with a sharp blade. Mica is often found in "books" with large, transparent "pages."

• The best place to photograph a mineral is at home or in a studio—not out in the field. You can adjust the position of the mineral to show maximum detail of its surface. Use a steady light source, such as photofloods. The light from a flash is generally too brief to let you see all the reflections and shadows.
• Make sure the camera is steady during the exposure; a tripod is ideal.

White mica reflects light like glass, and requires careful placement of the light source. The natural, tilted structure of this mineral creates "caves" that add mystery to the photo.

Selenite crystals often form in caves. The branching form results when crystals of gypsum are free to grow in any direction.

Fibrous green crystals of pyromorphite seem to grow like moss, but the mineral is actually a type of lead ore.

How Caves Are Formed

Typical North American cave scenery surrounds this cave entrance in West Virginia—well-watered vegetation, gently rolling hillsides, and outcroppings of the underlying limestone rock.

Caves Invade the Earth as the Water Level Drops

Like most formations of stratified rock, the large beds of limestone that underlie many parts of the world are riddled with tiny cracks and seams. The fracture zones run in two directions, vertically and horizontally. (In many schematic drawings, limestone is shown like brickwork, which is close to reality.) Acidic groundwater, which dissolves limestone, infiltrates these slim channels and slowly undermines the entire limestone formation.

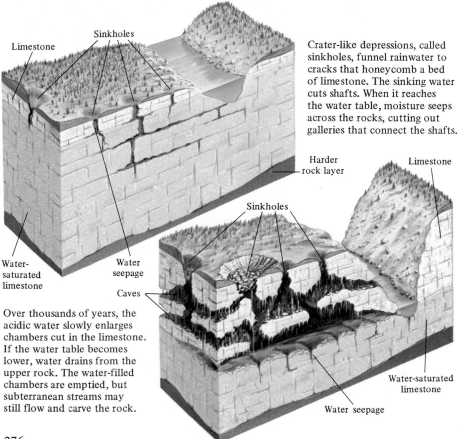

Crater-like depressions, called sinkholes, funnel rainwater to cracks that honeycomb a bed of limestone. The sinking water cuts shafts. When it reaches the water table, moisture seeps across the rocks, cutting out galleries that connect the shafts.

Over thousands of years, the acidic water slowly enlarges chambers cut in the limestone. If the water table becomes lower, water drains from the upper rock. The water-filled chambers are emptied, but subterranean streams may still flow and carve the rock.

Caves are usually formed by water, and most of them are cut in limestone. This kind of rock differs from others because it is formed from the remains of tiny marine plants and animals, and also coral and shellfish. These organisms, which were more common millions of years ago than they are today, absorbed calcium compounds from the sea and concentrated them within skeletal tissues. When the organisms died, the chalk-like materials accumulated and hardened into thick beds of limestone. (Some limestone is formed by other processes, such as evaporation.) As the crust of the earth shifted, many of these former sea beds became part of the continents. Today limestone is especially abundant in certain regions of North America (Indiana, Kentucky, and Virginia), and in France, Yugoslavia, and China.

A limestone deposit on dry land is still affected by water. As rain falls through the air and seeps into the soil, it picks up carbon dioxide and forms a mild acid. The acidic rainwater dissolves limestone, slowly enlarging its numerous cracks.

Most of this activity occurs in underground layers of rock within the water table—the zone that is saturated with groundwater. Water percolates slowly through limestone formations, carrying substances dissolved from the rock into rivers, and ultimately to the sea. Water-filled cavities are created in the limestone. Some are like huge pits or chimneys; they were formed along vertical cracks in the rock. Others are horizontal chambers, which developed as water oozed along planes of weakness between thick layers of limestone.

As the cavities increase in size, they may connect and form extensive labyrinths filled with slowly moving water. Sometimes the water table drops, because of drought or shifts in the earth's crust. This drains the chambers, leaving the caves dry. Water may still flow through parts of the cave as an underground stream, although other sections may remain completely dry.

At this stage, the flow of a stream may be swift, and a different force may begin to shape the cave. Often, water seeping into the cave is heavily laden with silt and debris, which acts as an abrasive on the underground stream bed. Thus the rate of erosion is increased.

Not all caves are cut in limestone. Some are formed from lava flows. As lava streams downhill, the surface usually cools and hardens before the lava underneath it. When the flow of lava stops, a shell may be left behind that resembles a long tunnel. Such chambers have an appropriate name—lava-tube caves. Many are small, but at least two, Ape Cave in Washington and Kazumura Cave in Hawaii, are over 2 miles long.

Some of the most spectacular caves are carved in the ice of large glaciers. One room in an ice cave on Mount Rainier (in Washington) measured about 250 feet high. Scientists believe ice caves are cut primarily by meltwater, or perhaps by warm air flowing through cracks and crevices. Such caves grow and collapse quickly—sometimes within a few years. Ice caves are hazardous to explore because so-called "flakes" of ice, weighing up to several tons, may fall from the ceiling.

The Dead Sea Scrolls, found in a Jordan cave, are religious texts believed to be 2,000 years old. Relatively cool and dry conditions in the cave had the effect of a natural time-capsule.

Do's and Don't's of Cave Exploration

Cave explorers, who are called spelunkers, say that the greatest danger underground comes not from natural hazards, but from faulty equipment and negligence on the part of the explorers themselves. The first rule of caving is: Never enter a cave alone. Join a spelunking club so that you will always have experienced companions.

• Someone on the outside should be given all the details of your planned cave expedition—the number of people in your party, where you are planning to go, and, most especially, when and where you expect to re-emerge. This assures that help will be sent if you do not show up at the appointed time and place.

• Be sure that you are in good physical condition, and recognize your limitations. Don't explore an unknown cave if you suspect it will be beyond your capabilities.

• Cave exploration bears a resemblance to mountain climbing, and calls for some of the same equipment. For example, you will need a nylon rope that will support at least a ton, wire ladders, pitons, mooring pins, and a well-stocked first-aid kit. Proper caving equipment includes more than one light source—a carbide lamp, flashlight, candles, and waterproof matches.

• Protecting your head with a helmet of the kind used by miners is a good idea. Wear fairly tight-fitting, snag-proof clothing, so as not to be encumbered when you wriggle through narrow passages. Spelunkers haul their equipment behind them in a Gurnee can—a bullet-shaped metal cylinder 10 inches in diameter and 3 to 4 feet long. Extended cave exploration will require a lightweight sleeping bag, plenty of water in canteens, dehydrated meals, and a stove on which to cook them.

• Take along a map of the cave, if one is available. If not, sketch your route as you explore. Note landmarks by looking backward; this is the way they will appear if you return the way you went in. As an extra safety measure, you might take along a packet of small aluminum squares with a piece of double-stick tape on the back. Use these squares to mark your trail. Remember to remove such tapes as you leave the cave.

• Don't make a descent if you aren't sure you will be able to climb out again.

• Never explore a cave with sinkholes (or in low-lying ground), if there is a chance of rain. There may be no escape from a cave flood. Leave a weather-watcher at the cave entrance to warn the exploring party if heavy rain does threaten.

A waterfall pours into a cave in Box Canyon, Colorado, with the force of a fire hose. Such a gallery is unusual, and changes shape rapidly.

Strange, Silent Worlds

Some of the world's most spectacular scenery lies hidden in the dark recesses of caves. In windless chambers, rivers and pools as smooth as glass reflect formations that look like waterfalls, icicles, flowers, and lily pads. Although many of the shapes suggest life and movement, they are all made of stone. Sometimes the only sound to be heard is a ceaseless dripping—the tapping note of water.

Water not only removes material from a cave, but also makes a contribution. As water drips from the ceiling, it evaporates and a load of minerals (dissolved from the limestone rock) is left behind. As each drop adds its load, an "icicle" may form. Like a soda straw, it has a hollow center—a slender channel through which the drops flow. When the straw reaches several inches in length, the hollow center usually becomes plugged; water begins to trickle down the outside. The straw becomes a solid, carrot-shaped stalactite, one of the most familiar cave formations.

Frequently, some water falls to the cave floor before it evaporates. On the floor, another type of formation—a stalagmite—builds up. Stalagmites are usually thick and rounded, because the drops of water splash over a fairly wide area. Many people confuse stalactites and stalagmites. Here's one way of remembering which is which: think of a stalac*tite* as *holding tight* because it hangs from the ceiling. A stalactite and a stalagmite may grow together, forming a column. Some columns grow to immense proportions and resemble the fluted pillars of a Greek temple. One column, in a Spanish cave, measured nearly 200 feet high.

Some cave formations represent growth that occurred over thousands, perhaps millions, of years. But the growth may be quite rapid, if the rate of evaporation is fast and the concentration of minerals in the water is high. Newly abandoned mining machinery in a British cave has stalactites that are already about 6 feet long.

Occasionally, water seeping through the ceiling trickles downward along the contour of the cave roof. In such cases, the deposits may form draperies with flowing folds and wrinkles. Slow seepage may produce small corkscrew-like shapes called helictites. If a crack is filled with deposits from evaporating water, a slight pressure apparently develops and squeezes the material from the crack. Curving, petal-like formations called cave flowers are the result.

Most of these curious forms are made up of calcium salts dissolved from the surrounding limestone. They are usually white, with sheens of other colors, almost like a wash of shellac. Occasionally, other dissolved substances, such as iron or copper, will show up. These impurities may color the cave formations beautiful tints of red or blue. (In caves where there are guided tours, any green tints you may see are probably algae—encouraged to grow by the presence of lights.)

A cave pool may contain lovely subterranean sculpture. A rocky projection above the pool sometimes develops a

Dream Lake in Luray Caverns, Virginia, is a good example of the world of silent beauty to be found in caves, many of which are open to the public. On a guided tour, hidden rivers, exquisite cave formations, gaping chasms, and vaulted domes can be inspected in safety— nearly all caves are naturally "air-conditioned."

wafer-thin collar of mineral deposits that looks like a lily pad. In especially quiet pools, small mineral rafts actually float on the surface of the water. Minerals are sometimes deposited around grains of sand at the bottom of the pool, forming exquisite shapes called cave pearls. Where the pools spill over, minerals are deposited and may form ornate sculptures that resemble waterfalls. Like the other cave formations, these waterfalls are permanently frozen into their dream-like shapes.

The Fanciful Sculptures of Water and Minerals

Stalactites never grow to great lengths— the longest one known measured less than 40 feet. Calcite, the chalky mineral that comprises most cave formations, lacks tensile strength; this means that it cannot sustain much weight. Therefore, when a stalactite reaches a certain size, it usually breaks and falls from the ceiling. If you visit a cave, you will probably notice stalactite fragments on the floor. On the other hand, stalagmites and columns often grow to truly gigantic proportions.

The mineral-bearing water that formed the dripstone above created a series of tiny dikes on the stone's surface. As water flowed around the obstructions, it produced the many ornate, drapery-like ridges.

Unusually delicate, needle-like flowers, often called helictites, grow in clumps along walls in Virginia's famous Skyline Caverns.

Three Variations on a Single Theme

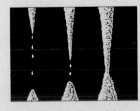

How fast the water drips and evaporates affects the shape of cave formations. Here, most of the water evaporated before it fell.

This stalagmite (on the ground) has grown faster than the stalactite above it. The two forms may eventually merge.

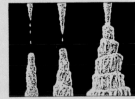

Columns that look like wedding cakes may develop if there is a great amount of dripping water. Note frozen appearance of drips.

Cave-Dwelling Creatures

Caves are nature's time capsules. Their vast underground chambers harbor many kinds of animals that have not been seen on the surface of the earth for thousands or even millions of years. Caves have become refuges because, unlike the earth's surface, caves change very little. Ice Ages come and go, forests dry up and become deserts—but underground life goes on just about as usual.

If you have ever visited a cave, you probably noticed that various parts of it differed greatly. For example, the opening of a cave is very much like the exterior—sunlight, rainfall, and temperature are virtually the same as on the outside. But as you go deeper into a cave, the light intensity lessens and the air becomes damp and cool. This is called the twilight zone—a halfway world between the outside environment and the interior. As the last rays of light fade away, you enter the unchanging world of the deep cave, where the temperature remains nearly the same throughout the year (usually around 50°F.).

The inhabitants of the cave change with the zones. Most of those that live at the mouth of the cave are also found in the outside world. Mosses, ferns, lichens, and vines cling to the walls. Swallows, phoebes, or other birds nest in the crevices near the cave's mouth. Frogs, mice, and other small animals scurry through the accumulation of dead leaves and twigs. Many of these creatures regularly venture into the shelter of the twilight zone, as do snakes, salamanders, and hosts of crickets. Perhaps the best-known of all cave residents are bats. Although bats may show a preference for using the twilight zone as shelter, these animals return regularly to the outside world to hunt for food.

The most specialized cave animals are those that never leave the inner cave. These animals, which include certain species of fish, crayfish, and flatworms, resemble their counterparts outside the cave. But many of the cave-dwelling species have a ghost-like pallor and cannot see. Some of them do not have any eyes at all. The animals are born, reproduce, and die without ever leaving the cave, unless they are accidentally carried out. They are called troglobites—cave-dwellers.

The study of cave life is one of the newest sciences. Apparently, many cave animals are "living fossils." In fact, most troglobites that live on and in cave soil (such as cave crickets) are believed to be descendants of similar species that inhabited the forest floor during the last Ice Age. As the earth's climate warmed, these creatures took refuge in caves, where conditions continued to resemble their original habitat. During countless generations, they "lost" their color and their eyes—which served no function in a lightless environment. Numerous cave-dwellers developed enlarged, sensitive feelers (such as the unusually large antennae of cave crickets), which enabled them to perceive their surroundings. Many cave animals respond instantly to the slightest vibration.

All life depends on water, and this is true of cave life as elsewhere. Dry caves not only are devoid of life, they are often like museums, where mummified animals and plants are preserved in dried form. A wet cave is sometimes called "live"—meaning that it can support an animal community. Ultimately, all caves depend on replenishment from the outside world, whether through underground streams, or food brought in by other animals.

Life-Styles Vary in the Three Different Zones

Living conditions, especially the amount of light, change dramatically from a cave's entrance to the dark interior. Though the zones are not sharply defined, and animals move about from zone to zone, different species usually prefer different zones. Near the entrance, certain creatures may use the cave only temporarily. A cave swallow seeks a site for its cup-shaped nest. A snail will find a dark, moist refuge here. Reddish salamanders favor the slippery rocks of the twilight zone, their climbing activities aided by long tails. Cave crickets and harvestmen feed on decaying material in this region. Contrast the brown crayfish with its close relative from deeper in the cave; the cave crayfish is colorless and has much longer antennae. Similarly, the blind salamander lacks pigment and functional eyes, which would be of little use in the dark interior.

1. Cave swallow
2. Cellar glass snail
3. Cave salamander
4. Cave cricket
5. Harvestman
6. Brown crayfish
7. Cave crayfish
8. Blind salamander

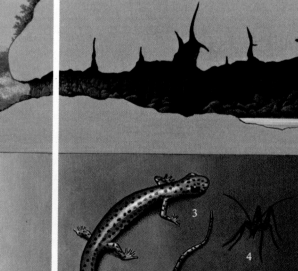

Cave Entrance

Twilight Zone

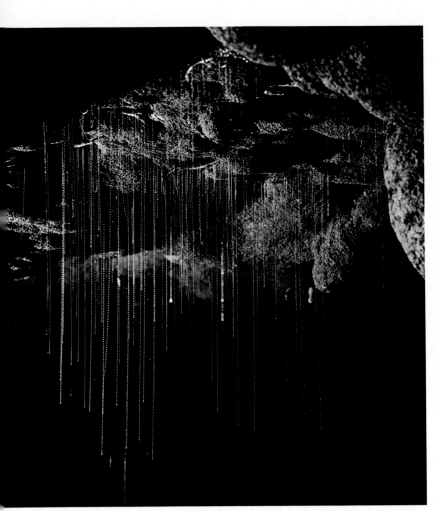

Eerie blue threads hang from the roof of the Waitomo Caves in New Zealand. The sticky, luminescent threads are lures spun by glowworms—the larvae of certain gnats. Insects that stick to the lures are reeled in.

Swooping through the dark, a European bat locates insect prey by sending out sound waves. Many kinds of bats roost in caves during the day and emerge in great numbers when night descends. In winter, certain species of bats hibernate in huge colonies inside caves.

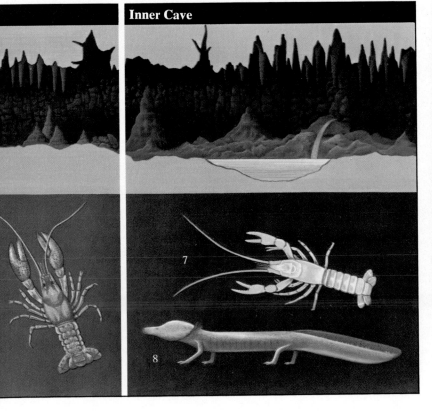

Inner Cave

6

7

8

Oilbirds nest on ledges inside caves. Like other winged residents of caves, oilbirds bring in food (fruit) from the outside. Palm nuts transported from a nearby forest have sprouted inside this Trinidad cave. The bird sees well in the dark; its clicks also act as a kind of sonar.

281

Following Ancient Clues

Clues to the mystery of the earth's past are all around us. Steep-walled valleys, glacier-scarred mountain slopes, outcroppings of rocks—all these are full of information. As in every good mystery, the challenge is in recognizing what the clues reveal.

The first great geological sleuth was an eighteenth-century British surveyor named William Smith, who became intrigued by the layers of rocks he saw while building canals in the south of England. He was the first person to notice that the layers (strata) occurred in the same sequence in various locations—as he put it, "like slices of bread and butter." Smith, nicknamed Strata by his friends, also noticed that each layer had "fossils peculiar to itself," and that these fossils could be used to identify the layers.

Such an idea seems obvious today, but before Smith's time, few people had realized that the earth had passed through many stages of development, and that each stage had its own characteristic forms of life, which were often preserved in layers of sedimentary rock. Smith did not realize the full significance of his discoveries, but later scientists did. Earlier conceptions about our planet—including estimates that the earth was only 6,000 years old—were effectively overthrown.

For about a century, fossils were used to establish the age of a particular rock stratum. But it was soon discovered that fossils alone did not explain the records in stone. Climate was part of the story. For example, a period of tropical climate resulted in the formation of great swamps that produced not only characteristic fossils, but ultimately deposits of coal as well. Periods of colder climate produced different fossils, and also other clues, such as the ice-cut valleys and low hills left by glaciers. By using the evidence from both geological and biological sources, scientists divided earth's history into the Precambrian, the earliest; the Paleozoic (old life) era; the Mesozoic (middle life) era, when dinosaurs existed; and the Cenozoic (modern life) era, which includes the present.

The earth's fossil time-clock is a relative one. It lets us know which rocks and fossils are older than others, but does not tell us absolute time—the age of the earth in number of years. This could not be detected until the twentieth century. The discovery that radioactivity in rocks (such as uranium) changes at a particular rate opened the way to more accurate dating methods. The earth is now thought to be about 4.6 billion years old. The earliest fossil record, of one-celled bacteria, is believed to be about 3.4 billion years old. Thus life has been present for most of earth's history; human beings have been around for only a relatively short period.

⊲ NATURE OBSERVER
Ice-Age Evidence

The periods of time in historical geology are so great, they seem unreal to many people. One of the few "landmarks" one can check is evidence left over from the Ice Ages. About a million years ago, late in the Cenozoic Era, ice began to pile up and travel. There were four major advances and withdrawals of massive glaciers (and any number of minor ones). They left a great deal of evidence as they moved over the land. There are grooves and gouges in rock, and huge amounts of gravel, which is called glacial till. The effect of the Ice Ages is less apparent in the southern hemisphere.

Fences made from glacial till (left) are a worldwide solution to this problem. Grazing is possible, but plowing is clearly not.

Melting glacial snows left Geiranger Fjord in Norway (above) with the characteristic steep walls of such "drowned" valleys.

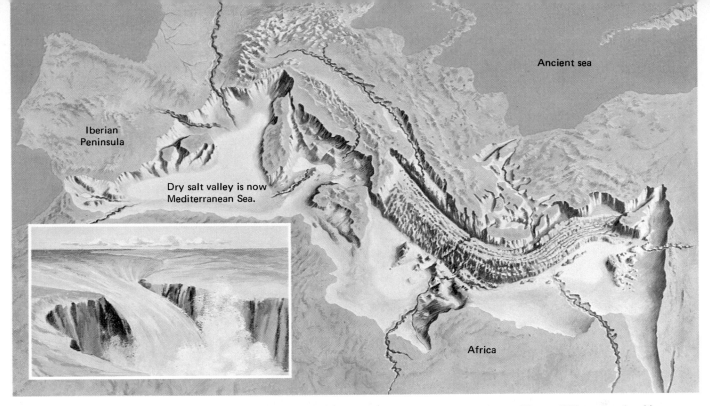

Iberian
Peninsula

Dry salt valley is now
Mediterranean Sea.

Ancient sea

Africa

About 6 million years ago, the Mediterranean probably looked as it does in the painting above—like a huge, dry "death valley" lying some 10,000 feet below sea level. Its waters had evaporated because the sea's connection with the Atlantic (at what is now the Strait of Gibraltar) had been blocked by a shifting in the earth's crust. A later shift re-opened the Gibraltar "faucet." Water thundered in over a waterfall (inset), in a flow estimated at several hundred times greater than Niagara's. But it took about a century for water to fill the basin.

Tilted Layers of Rock, Millions of Years Old, Are on View at Capitol Reef

It is obvious from the colorful formations at Capitol Reef National Park, in Utah, why the Navajo Indians called this area "the land of the sleeping rainbow." Striations of different colors in the photograph at right show some of the major strata depicted in the diagram below. (At the top of the photo is the Kayenta formation, then the Wingate, the Chinle, and the Moenkopi.) The diagram—of a region not far from where the photo was taken—is a transect. That is, the diagram takes a straight course across the land and records all the formations along the way. Because the crust shifted, the formations are like so many tipped dominoes. They range in age from the Permian Period, which began about 270 millions of years ago, to the Cretaceous, which ended 65 million years ago. More than once, ocean waves washed inland, covering the area. These seas laid down the major layers of silt. Each in turn hardened into sedimentary rock—mostly shale, sandstone, and limestone.

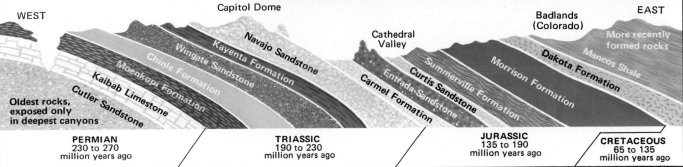

WEST

Capitol Dome

Cathedral
Valley

Badlands
(Colorado)

EAST

More recently
formed rocks

Navajo Sandstone

Kayenta Formation

Wingate Sandstone

Chinle Formation

Moenkopi Formation

Kaibab Limestone

Cutler Sandstone

Mancos Shale

Dakota Formation

Morrison Formation

Summerville Formation

Curtis Sandstone

Entrada Sandstone

Carmel Formation

Oldest rocks,
exposed only
in deepest canyons

| PERMIAN 230 to 270 million years ago | TRIASSIC 190 to 230 million years ago | JURASSIC 135 to 190 million years ago | CRETACEOUS 65 to 135 million years ago |

Where and How Fossils Were Formed

Everyone knows what a dinosaur looks like, but have you ever wondered *how* we know? After all, dinosaurs have not been around for 60 million years. We derive our knowledge of dinosaurs—and countless other animals and plants, some extinct for 3 billion years—from fossil records.

A fossil is a relic, a trace of ancient life. Usually, a relic must be at least 12,000 years old to be called a fossil. Some fossils are circumstantial evidence: that is, nothing remains of the animal itself except footprints. For example, about 180 million years ago large numbers of dinosaurs walked on huge, claw-like feet over the region now known as the Connecticut Valley. Their tracks in mud are now fossil imprints in stone.

To become a fossil, a plant or animal usually has to have been buried; this prevents it from decaying quickly or being eaten by scavengers. A few fossils exist because of freezing: the woolly mammoths and other animals frozen during the last Ice Age are the most perfectly preserved animals ever found. Unfortunately, these frozen fossils are rare and perish quickly once they have thawed. Other well-preserved fossils have been mummified by drying.

Molds and casts make up the majority of fossils. The original plant or animal was covered by sediment, which later hardened. The organism decayed and its materials shrank, leaving a cavity. This empty space became a natural mold. The mold then filled with clay, sand, or other fine material, which hardened into a cast.

The most remarkable molds are found in northern Europe, near the Baltic Sea. There, insects were entombed in the sap of now-extinct coniferous trees. The resinous sap turned into amber, a very hard substance. Though the insects themselves may have decomposed, a look at an amber mold under a microscope reveals incredibly fine details.

The process of petrifaction makes fossils that are actually stone. The soft portions of the organisms, buried in moist soil, soon decay, and water permeates the hard parts that remain. The water deposits minerals in the fine structure of bone or shell, thus reinforcing the strength of the structures. Some fossilized shells of marine animals and bones of land animals were preserved in this way.

Petrified forests are groups of fossil trees whose cellular structure was invaded and preserved by the mineral silica. This type of petrifaction is called replacement. One unusual thing about certain specimens is that some of the original wood has remained intact. The preservation has been so perfect that the cellular structure and annual growth rings of these trees are clearly visible.

Fossils reveal change, presenting a tantalizing chain of evidence of the evolution from simple to advanced forms of life. Some, called index fossils, also give the age of rock formations. The extinct trilobites—three-lobed marine animals sometimes called fossil butterflies—are index fossils. Trilobites gradually evolved longer tails and more ornate structures. Because scientists know when the different types of trilobites were common, they can tell the age of rocks containing these fossils.

Fossils lend support to the drifting-continent theory of geology, which includes the idea that all the continents were once joined in a single supercontinent. Fossils of related animals have been found oceans apart. Because these animals could not have traveled such distances, scientists assume the continents must have done the traveling.

Trilobites, which flourished in the Paleozoic Era (600 to 200 million years ago) ranged in size from a quarter of an inch to 27 inches.

Amber is fossilized sap, which often contains preserved insects. The largest amber deposits occur along the coasts of the Baltic Sea.

When this fish died, its body was gently covered with silt. In time, other minerals took the place of its bones.

The petrified stumps (below) are of ancient trees. Some of the specimens are in amazing condition; when the silica was dissolved, the actual wood was still in good shape!

Piecing Together the Evidence

In the long period of human history before evolution was understood, man was beset with puzzles. Huge, inexplicable bones kept coming to the surface, and there was no theory to account for their existence. Gradually, as prehistory came into focus (which explained, among other things, how sea-shell remains found their way to the tops of mountains), the pieces began to fall into place. A backbone, such as the one above, being extracted from its stone bed, is part of just such a detective story. More bones and other remains have been lost than have been found. More can be expected in the future. The pursuit never ends.

How can you read footprints? Animals, ancient and modern, leave distinctive markings. Spacing reveals stride, which gives a clue to height and weight.

One of the most complete fossils ever discovered was that of Tyrannosaurus, an enormous flesh-eating dinosaur. The animal, complete with musculature, has been reconstructed from its bones. From tip to tail it was about 50 feet long, and stood 20 feet tall.

Many amateur fossil-hunters have made important discoveries in the field. By following a few simple rules, anyone can join in the exciting journey back through geological time.

• First check to see if you need a permit to dig. Some sites are strictly off limits, as for example, the region in Africa where traces of early man are still turning up. In national parks such as the Petrified Forest in Arizona, collecting would damage the park and its reason for being a park.

• Fossils of animals with backbones are rarely discovered. If you find one, ask for help from a paleontologist (you can get in touch with one through any local college or university).

• But beyond this, the field is wide open and very inviting. All you need is a geologist's pick, large and small chisels for freeing the specimens, newspapers for wrapping fossils, and a knapsack to carry your finds.

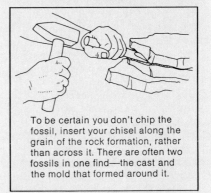

To be certain you don't chip the fossil, insert your chisel along the grain of the rock formation, rather than across it. There are often two fossils in one find—the cast and the mold that formed around it.

• Nearly all fossils are found in one general type of rock—the sedimentary layers of sandstone, shale, and limestone. These rocks were originally deposited in fine films of sediment—gently, layer on layer. Eventually, the pressure of the accumulated layers turned this relatively soft material to stone. But the layers remain, almost like pages in a book.

• A prime place for fossil-hunting is where roads are being built. Any site where layered rock is exposed, new or old, is a likely place. This includes stream beds, construction sites, and quarries. (Be careful, of course, not to get in the way of bulldozers, or set off avalanches of loose sand.)

• Keep a record of when and where a specimen was found. The identity of the fossil is usually easy to determine from guidebooks on the subject.

• This is a hobby that can be enjoyed alone, but often there is a club you can join, where you can get tips on good sites, help in identifying finds, and perhaps trade specimens.

Coal and Petroleum: A Precious Legacy

The energy stored in coal and petroleum originally came to the earth from the sun. The bulk of the present-day supplies was laid down some 200 to 600 million years ago, when tropical conditions were widespread. Lush, swampy forests produced huge trees; warm coastal seas swarmed with microscopic forms of life. When these organisms died, much of their tissue was recycled as it is today—through scavenging and decay. But a significant amount of dead plant and animal material was covered with mud, which prevented complete decomposition.

With the passage of time, as layer upon layer of fine sediment was deposited over the once-living material, the sheer weight turned the sediments to rock. Sandwiched between the layers, both coal and petroleum were produced and preserved under pressure. Coal was formed mostly of giant fern-like plants that have only small counterparts today. (Coal may still be forming here and there on earth, but conditions are not right for the production of significant quantities.)

The weight of the sedimentary rock gradually caused some changes in the coal lying beneath it—pressure produces heat, and heat accelerates chemical reactions. The coal subjected to less pressure is softer and more porous; this type is called bituminous coal. Anthracite is harder, burns more cleanly, and is generally found deeper in the earth; it may occasionally be found near the surface. But anthracite is always the product of great pressure.

Under the microscope, coal's origins are astoundingly clear. It is not uncommon to find the imprint of a perfect fern frond in a piece of coal that has split open along the seam, where the frond settled gently in the mud.

Petroleum is mainly of animal, rather than plant, origin. It has been known and used since ancient times, but more as a medicine and a curiosity than anything else. Not until the development of the internal combustion engine did petroleum assume any great importance in the lives of human beings. Today, petroleum fuels provide most of our energy needs; coal is second.

Petroleum was formed mostly of single-celled marine animals, similar to the planktonic (or floating) animals found today. These microscopic animals ate plants, such as algae, which had originally captured the energy of the sun by photosynthesis.

Unlike coal, petroleum may not be found where it was formed. Being a liquid, it readily flows through the porous rocks around it, sometimes collecting in so-called traps. These traps usually occur where layers of impervious rock cap a segment of porous rock, holding the petroleum the way you hold something in your cupped hands.

Although geologists speak of "pools" of petroleum, it is usually stored in countless, minute pores of rock such as sandstone. When these rocks are drilled, the petroleum flows, as from a sponge released from pressure. Sometimes, a gusher results, literally raining "buried sunshine."

Coal Was Formed in Swamps Millions of Years Ago

Coal varies so greatly in its composition that geologists classify it simply as a sedimentary rock—one of the few rocks that will burn. The purest coal, containing up to 95 percent carbon, may have been formed from a swampy forest such as the one in the illustration at right. Ideal conditions for the formation of coal were forests that grew continuously for many centuries, free of muddy inundations. If the plant remains were later buried at a great depth, under tremendous pressures, the result would be the finest coal (anthracite). In international trade, coal is divided into about a dozen different kinds on the basis of hardness and other physical and chemical properties. Impurities in coal, such as clay, are what produce most of the ash and cinder left behind when coal is burned. When coal has sulfur in it, smog may be the result.

Key to Ancient Coal Forest

1. Tree fern
2. Giant dragonfly
3. Scale tree (Lepidodendron)
4. Giant horsetail
5. Giant cockroach
6. Scale tree (Sigillaria)

What All Fossil Fuels Have in Common . . .

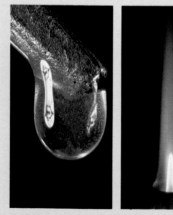

Refining can transform crude petroleum into a wide array of products—from asphalt for roads to lubricating oils to gases for fuel.

Where life is present (or has left its remains), so too will you find hydrogen and carbon—in chemical compounds that are called hydrocarbons. Materials as diverse as paraffin, benzine, naptha, and asphalt are all hydrocarbons. So are the gasolines that power automobiles and the coal that heats the furnaces of home and industry. With a skill that would make the ancient alchemists green with envy, modern chemists are able to transform hydrocarbons to the kinds of substances needed for many particular functions. The simplest hydrocarbon has one carbon atom and four hydrogen atoms. It is so light, it is a gas—methane. The heaviest hydrocarbons—such as pitch and asphalt—have immense molecules with as many as 100 carbon atoms. Some, called aromatics, give off a distinct odor.